Muslims and Modernity

Also available from Continuum:

Prophets in the Quran, Brannon Wheeler
Six World Faiths, W. Owen Cole

Muslims and Modernity

An Introduction to the Issues and Debates

Clinton Bennett

continuum
LONDON • NEW YORK

Continuum
The Tower Building   15 East 26th Street
11 York Road   New York
London SE1 7NX   NY 10010

© Clinton Bennett 2005

British Library Cataloguing-in-Publication Data
A catalogue record for this book is available from the British Library.

ISBN: HB: 0–8264–5481-X
PB: 0–8264–5482–8

Library of Congress Cataloging-in-Publication Data
Bennett, Clinton.
    Muslims and modernity : an introduction to the issues and debates / Clinton Bennett.
       p. cm.
    Includes bibliographical references and index.
    ISBN 0–8264–5481–X—ISBN 0–8264–5482–8 (pbk.)
    1. Islamic modernism. 2. Islamic renewal. 3. Islam and civil society. 4. Human rights—
Religious aspects—Islam. 5. Islam—21st century. I. Title.
    BP166.14.M63B45 2005
    297.2′7—dc22

                                                        2004063212

Typeset by YHT Ltd, London.
Printed and bound in Great Britain by MPG Books Ltd, Bodmin, Cornwall

Contents

Acknowledgements   ix

Pedagogical Preface   xii
  – In the public eye   xii
  – Aims and approach   xiii
  – A left–right analysis   xvi

Introduction: Voices and Viewpoints   1
  – Methodology: virtual insidership   1
  – Polarized viewpoints   3
  – Media and anti-Islamism   9
  – Does Islam threaten the West?   11

1. Modernity, Postmodernity and the World of Islam   17
  – The crises of modernity   17
  – What is modernism?   24
  – Postmodernity and Islam   27
  – Postmodernism and Marxist analysis   30
  – Muslim responses: Akbar Ahmed (1992) and Ziauddin
    Sardar (1998)   31

2. Muslims and Democracy   40
  – Democracy – whose version?   40
  – Double standards   42
  – Four models   44
  – Summary of the historical legacy   46
  – Mawdudi's model: theo-democracy (centre right)   49
  – Rule by an elite: the case of Saudi Arabia   53
  – The centre-left's model: Taha's Second Message of Islam 56
  – Secular Islam: the far left   57
  – Literary case study: Ahdaf Soueif's *The Map of Love* 61

3. Muslims on Human Rights   63
  – An imposition from outside?   63

– Mawdudi and the Muslim right: human rights and Islam   65
– The *hizb-ut-tahrir* and human rights   67
– The Universal Islamic Declaration of Human Rights (1981)   68
– Bassam Tibi on human rights   69
– An-Na'im on Islam and human rights   73
– Freedom of expression and the limits of dissent: *Hisbah*   76
– Literary case study: Hanif Kureishi's *The Black Album*   81

4. Muslim Voices on the Qur'an   85
– Common ground   85
– How Muslims view the Qur'an   86
– A multiplicity of voices   97
– Progressive contributions   101
– A contextual approach   104

5. Islamic Epistemology   107
– The Islamization of knowledge: supporters and critics   107
– Al-Faruqi: Islam the religion of reason, science and progress   108
– Nasr: the goal of education is to actualize all the possibilities
  of the human soul   111
– Nasr and Mawdudi: convergence and divergence   114
– Bucaillism: the Qur'an as a scientific text   115
– Sardar: a critique of al-Faruqi and Nasr   116
– Reviving the Mu'tazalite heritage   120

6. Muslim Voices on Gender in Islam   129
– Introducing the debate   129
– Mawdudi: equal but different   131
– Feminist Muslim responses   135
– Male contributions   142
– Islamic feminism: human rights and humanist critiques   144
– Literary case study: two Egyptian novels and *Alf Laylah
  Wa Laylah*   150

7. Non-Muslims in the Muslim World: Voices and Views   156
– Four positions on Islam and non-Muslims   156
– Mawdudi: theory and reality of the classical *dhimmi* model   159
– The centre left and non-Muslims in an Islamic state   164
– The radical left   168
– Literary case study: Nasrin's *Lajja*   173

8. Muslims as Minorities: Voices and Views   177
– Three strategies   177
– Muslims in non-Muslim territory: what do the founding
  discourses say?   177
– India: a case study of the three strategies   180

– The confrontational response in Diaspora Islam   184
– The separatist response   185
– The integrationist mode   188
– Literary case study: Monica Ali's *Brick Lane*   195

9. War and Peace in Islam: The Traditional View   198
– Muslim understanding of war and peace   198
– Sayyid Qutb on *jihad*   198
– Mawdudi's and Qutb's impact on contemporary Muslim life 205
– The case of Palestine   209

10. Progressive and Moderate Muslims on War and Peace   219
– Rethinking *jihad*   219
– Shaltut's treatise on 'The Koran and Fighting'   220
– Al-Qaradawi and *jihad*   223
– Muslims on 9/11   226
– The issue of suicide   227
– Progressive Musims on pacifist Islam   228
– Some non-Muslims respond to 9/11 and Islamic terrorism 236

11. Algeria: A Study in Islamic Resurgence, and Bangladesh:
Culture v. Islam   240
– Algeria's colonial legacy   240
– *Al-Jaza'ir 'Arabiyya wa al-Islam dinuha* (Algeria is Arab and
Islam is its religion)   241
– Literary case study: Camus's *L'Etranger*   242
– Post-independence   244
– The demand for autonomy   247
– Democracy as a movable feast   249
– Bangladesh: a case study   251

Bibliography   257
Index   277

To all who taught me, at school, college and at university

Acknowledgements

I am grateful to Professor Ziauddin Sardar, Dr Farid Esack, Professor Tariq Modood, Lord Ahmed of Rotherham and Dr Zaki Badawi for past face-to-face encounters and to Professor Bassam Tibi for electronic communication. All these scholars have enriched my understanding of contemporary Islamic thought and my indebtedness to their writing is self-evident. I am especially grateful to Imran Mogra, former head of RE at Birchfield Community School, Aston and currently Senior Lecturer in Religious Education at the University of Central England for loaning me his copy of Ahmed Von Denffer's *'Ulum-Al-Qur'an* and for conversations relevant to the themes of this book. Mr Mogra was kind enough to comment on draft sections of my manuscript. I wish to express appreciation to all my Muslim friends, colleagues and acquaintances for the benefit of their knowledge and insight. I am grateful to Dr Philip Lewis of Bradford University's Department of Peace Studies for inviting me to speak at the Bradford Inter-Cultural Leadership Seminar in October 2002, where it was my pleasure to meet Dr Azzam Tamimi of the Institute of Islamic Political Thought. Conversation with Dr Tamimi, at the seminar and via our subsequent email correspondence, made a material contribution towards developing the arguments and analysis contained in this book.

I am indebted to Prof Jørgen Nielsen and Dr Jabal Buaben for appointing me a Visiting Fellow of the University of Birmingham's Graduate Institute for Theology and Religion, which enabled me to make full use of the University Library. Dr Buaben, now Director of the Centre for the Study of Islam and Christian–Muslim Relations (CSIC) at Birmingham, and I were fellow doctoral students back in the 1980s. Professor Nielsen, who now directs the Graduate Institute, an expert on Islam in Europe, taught me most of what I know about the history of the Khalifate. My status as an Affiliated Lecturer of the Centre for the Study of Jewish–Christian Relations (CJCR), Cambridge, gave me reader's rights at Cambridge University Library, and I am extremely grateful to Dr Edward Kessler and to Dr Melanie Wright of CJCR for this appointment. Communication with my CJCR students has been stimulating and the source of no few ideas and bibliographical sources that have enriched this book. I am also grateful to Dr Sigvard von Sicard, who once examined my doctoral thesis, for inviting me to lead a Graduate CSIC Seminar on 21 October 2003, where I was able to test some of the ideas and material developed in Chapter Three of this book, and to Dominic Corrywright, field chair of Religious Studies at Oxford Brookes University, for inviting me to teach several units on Islam in summer term 2003. This provided me with another valuable opportunity to test some of the discussion material contained in the book. I also wish to express appreciation to my friend and master's dissertation examiner, Dr Jan Slomp, for kindly sending me copies of his 2003 chapter on Mawdudi's *Al-Jihad Fi Al-Islam* and of his 2004 chapter on six modern Muslim thinkers. Thanks are also due to Moira K. Foster-Brown, Head Teacher, and to all my colleagues at Birch-field Community School, Aston, where I am currently Operations and Marketing Support Manager, for their encouragement and support. I am indebted to the Interreligious and International Federation for World Peace (IIFWP) through whose conference programmes I met Lord Ahmed of Rotherham, Minister Michael Muhammad of the Nation of Islam (UK) and Dr Ghayasuddin Siddiqui, Leader of the Muslim Parlia-ment of Great Britain, whose speech on 10 July 2004 at a conference on 'Building a Culture of Peace: Identity, Multiculturalism and Integration in the 21st Century' I cite in this book. At two IIFWP conferences during 2003, I was also privileged to hear the former Indonesian President, Abdurrahman Wahid, who has combined scholarship with a career as a religious and a political leader. He believes that Muslims have a choice between two paths. They can either choose a more legal-political Islam, or a more universal, cosmopolitan Islam. With others cited in this book, he considers the legal-formal option to be a distortion of Islam. It elevates one version over all other possibilities and at the same time forecloses debate.

Some of the material contained in this book has been derived from lectures I gave and from Open Learning material I wrote while teaching at Westminster College, Oxford (1992–98) and at Baylor University, Texas (1998–2001). Westminster Open Learning manuals drawn on were *Islam and the West, Islam in Britain* and *Fundamentalisms.* I am grateful to these institutions for providing me with past opportunities for scholarly endeavour. Most of all, I am grateful to all my students for constantly questioning and challenging me to be a better teacher and scholar. I especially wish to express appreciation to Donald Hedworth, on whose MA thesis I have drawn in this book. I did not have the pleasure of teaching him but I did have the privilege of being an examiner of his thesis. I have also drawn on reviews I have written for various journals, which I shall refrain from listing.

Libraries used for researching this book were those of Baylor University, Texas, Birmingham University (especially the Orchard Learning Resour-ces Centre at the Selly Oak campus), the Aston, Central, Erdington and Sutton Coldfield branches of Birmingham City Council's network of public libraries, Cambridge University Library and Wolverhampton University Library. I am grateful to all these institutions for help and advice. Unfortunately, as work took me from place to place, from country to country and from library to library, one problem I encountered was not always accessing the same edition of a text. I have tried my best to standardize references but I cannot guarantee that I have always succeeded. Accents are used whenever possible, but only the apostrophe is used to indicate a diacritical mark in Arabic. Following custom in English, the singular *hadith* rather than the plural *ahadith* is used. Some texts consulted but not cited are included in the Bibliography as additional resources for readers. As ever, I am grateful to Continuum International for all their hard work, especially to Janet Joyce for accepting the project and to Philip Law and Anna Sandeman for continuing to run with it even when deadlines had come and gone. I would like to include Sarah Douglas and all members of the production team at Continuum in these acknowledgements. I am also indebted to the Trustees of the Spalding Trust, since without their financial generosity this project would have floundered long ago. Finally, a big thank you to my wife, Rekha Sarker Bennett, for emotional support and encouragement during what proved to be a longer, bigger and more complex project than I had initially expected.

This book is dedicated to all who have taught me.

Birmingham, August 2004

Pedagogical Preface

Critical pedagogy needs a language that allows for competing solidarities and political vocabularies that do not reduce the issues of power, justice, struggle and inequality to a single script, a master narrative that suppresses the contingent, historical and the everyday as a serious object of study. This suggests that curriculum knowledge not be treated as a sacred text but developed as part of an ongoing engagement with a variety of narratives and traditions that can be re-read and re-formulated in politically different terms.

Henry A. Giroux's fourth principle of critical pedagogy (1991)

In the public eye

This book discusses a selection of contemporary themes within Islamic thought. When Nielsen wrote that 'the field of Islam ... and the wider concerns of relations between the Muslim world and the west, Islam and Christendom, is one which will not go away' (1999: 138) he could hardly have anticipated the explosion of interest in Islam and its relationship with the West that followed the tragic events of 11 September 2001 (referred to in this book as 9/11). On 9/11 at 8.46 am a hijacked plane flew into the North Tower of the World Trade Center, New York. A second plane hit the South Tower at 9.05 am The Twin Towers imploded and more than 2,600 people died as a result of that attack. At 9.37 another plane 'slammed into the Western side of the Pentagon'. 125 people lost their lives. At 10.03 a fourth plane 'crashed in a field in Southern Pennsylvania', killing 256 people. It is believed that this plane was aimed at the White House or at Capitol Hill. Nineteen Arabs, 'including known al-Qaeda operatives', were responsible, hijacking the planes by using or threatening to use 'small knives, box cutters, and cans of Mace or pepper spray', although the plane that crashed had been retaken by American passengers (*The 9/11 Commission Report Executive Summary*, July 2004, pp. 1–2). Those events, and the 'war on terrorism' ('Operation Enduring Freedom', originally called 'Infinite Justice') that they provoked, have generated a great deal of debate, literature, broadcast and Internet material.

Although this project began sometime before 9/11, it proved necessary to revise much of what had already been written after that date (references in this book to the *9/11 Commission Report* are to its *Executive Summary*). Subsequently, extensive use was made of both electronic and hardcopy material produced in response to 9/11 and also to military intervention in Afghanistan and Iraq. This book's selection of themes (chosen before 9/11), including human rights, war, the nature of the Islamic state, democracy and gender, all feature in this body of material. In his 2003 book, *Islam Under Siege: Living Dangerously in a Post-Honor World*, Akbar Ahmed usefully explores many of the issues discussed in this book as he attempts to answer key questions asked about Islam, including 'Why do they hate us?' 'Is Islam compatible with democracy?' 'Does Islam subjugate women?' 'Does the Koran preach violence?' (for Ahmed, see Chapter One).

Aims and approach

In what follows, discussion of these themes is pursued in the context of Muslim response to modernity/postmodernity and of Muslim encounter with Western civilization. This book's thematic treatment of these issues will make it an attractive text for college use, which remains its main purpose. The aim is to encourage critical discussion, so questions for debate are included in the text. While specifically designed for classroom or for seminar use, general readers might also find these questions useful as a stimulus to further reflection and analysis. It is perhaps this approach to the material that gives this book a degree of originality, not that a textbook need claim any! Part of its purpose is to introduce the significance of some individual Muslim contributors, so where possible it focuses on particular Muslim thinkers and on the movements that they represent or founded.

This book is designed so that over a semester of 15 weeks or so instructors can cover a theme per week, with time in hand for detailed work on a case study, a novel or a selected text. None of the themes fit neatly into watertight boxes. All spill into each other. Almost all Muslim thought begins with the Qur'an, for example. Democracy can hardly be discussed without some reference to human and minority rights or to gender, while use of force or violence is an issue that surfaces repeatedly throughout the book. This book's strategy, however, is to discuss or to refer briefly to these issues as questions concerning them arise in the text, while reserving substantive discussion to their particular chapters. Overlap between issues means that earlier analysis also provides background for this book's treatment of subsequent themes. Discussion, for example, of Muslim approaches to the Qur'an overlaps substantially with discussion of Islamic epistemology. The role played by culture in the Islamist critique of the West, Huntington's 'threat' thesis, debate about the nature of *Shari'ah*, dispute about who should govern the Muslim community post-632 CE, tension between the local and the universal in Islam (between the nation-state and a universal Islamic entity) and the issue of whether Muslims can draw on non-Muslim thought, are all recurrent themes throughout the book. Some repetition is inevitable. However, chapters were written with the possibility in mind that readers might not read them consecutively and that they therefore need to be freestanding. Case studies are used to allow for analysis of specific issues and situations in an effort to avoid over-generalization.

If this book is used as a general introduction to Muslim thinking on these issues, it could be accompanied by representative texts of the two positions described in the Introduction, revivalist and modernist. For example, a Mawdudi or a *hizb-ut-tahrir-al-ielami* (Islamic Liberation Party) text could be used alongside Taha's *The Second Message of Islam* (1987), Bassam Tibi's *The Challenge of Fundamentalism: Political Islam and the New World Disorder* (1998; there is an extended 2002 edition but analysis in this book is based on the 1998 text), Abdolkarim Soroush's *Reason, Freedom and Democracy in Islam* (2000) or Fatima Mernissi's *Islam and Democracy: Fear of the Modern World* (1994). To help readers to access material easily, this book uses extracts from several anthologies, including Esposito (1983), Ahmad (2nd edn, 1976 [there is a 3rd, 2001 edition]) and Kurzman (1998). Ahmad and Kurzman contain so many key texts on the issues under discussion that these two anthologies could be used as readers to accompany this book. For classical material, references are usually to Peters (1994) or to Khan's 1987 English/Arabic edition of *Sahih al-Bukhari*, although Robson's 1963 translation of the *Mishkat-al-Masabih* compiled by Imam Tabrizi (or Tirmizi, d. 1104 CE) is also used (referenced as MM), while Qur'anic references are derived from the English/Arabic text of Yusuf 'Ali's *The Meaning of the Holy Qur'an* (new edn, 1989, revised by Ismail al-Faruqi). All Muslim scholars draw on classical texts, so readers of this book will want to see what these have to say on the issues and questions under discussion. Classical sources are referenced in order to give historical perspective, as in Chapter Two, and also to draw attention to how different texts support different views. This book does not offer anything like an exhaustive treatment of the classical tradition, however, since its focus is contemporary, but it is interested in how the classical sources are interpreted, or read, by modern Muslim scholars. Although it may seem dated, the 1976 edition of Ahmad is cited because multiple copies were available in libraries used while writing this book. It would not be difficult for instructors to adapt references to accommodate use of the most recent edition of this or of other texts cited in the text.

Reference is also made to television material and journal and magazine articles. Perhaps unusually for a text addressing the themes under review, novels, especially of the post-colonial genre, are also discussed in this book. Several novels are discussed in longer 'literary case studies', others are alluded to within the main text. Dating in this book uses the Western calendar (CE = Common Era) rather than the Islamic (AH = After Hijra; this starts in 622 CE). Main sources are referenced in the Bibliography;

minor sources such as Internet, broadcast and newspaper material are referenced in the body of the book. Since a primary aim of this book is to direct readers to original material, additional resources and texts are recommended in most sections.

Non-Muslim scholars are cited, too, mainly as sources of information but also because such writing influences Muslim thought, which does not take place in a vacuum unaware of what Westerners are saying and writing about Islam. Each chapter analyses primary sources in some detail, so it will not be necessary to read every text referenced in the book. In the context of a class or seminar, instructors, who may substitute their own material for some of mine, will guide their students in use of this text. However, it would probably make little sense if users were to consult none of the texts on which substantive discussion has been based. Texts by Mawdudi and by the Islamic Liberation Party, *hizb-ut-tahrir-al-Islami*, for example, are available on the worldwide web (see *www.khilafah.com* and *www.hizb-ut-tahrir.org*). Reference is made to Internet material by Muslim and by non-Muslim scholars, to such organizational websites as *hizb-ut-tahrir*, to other Islamic and to academic sites. The website of the International Forum for Islamic Dialogue (IFID), *www.islam21.net*, also has articles on Islam and modernity/postmodernity, including Sardar's 'Islamists in Postmodern Times' and Sayyid's 'Democracy and Islam' (*www.islam21.net/pages/keyissues/key3-8htm*). The IFID was founded in 1994 as a voice calling for 'a modern, moderate and enlightened understanding of Islam' and to provide a platform for Muslims to develop 'a humane, democratic Islamic thought'. Of course, who knows how permanent some of this material will be? Primary material is also available on the web, for example at *http://islam world.net*, which includes Qur'an and *hadith* search engines.

Given the almost daily rate of publication of books and articles relevant to this enquiry, no attempt has been made to include everything. What this book does try to do, however, is to reference material that, while not always the most recent, represents significant and probably durable contributions that continue to influence Muslim thought and action. Mawdudi's own writing falls into this category. He died in 1979 but remains so hugely influential that his thought still represents contemporary approaches. The selection of texts that are likely to remain significant is intended to give this book some shelf life as a textbook and discussion primer. In most cases, material has been chosen (sometimes over other equally suitable material) based on accessibility, although in some instances the significance or relevance of a source dictated its use instead of a text that would be easier for readers to locate. For example, Badawi's 1976 chapter on gender is easier to access (see *http://www.iad.org/books/S-women.html*) than the Mawdudi text, which is used in Chapter Six. Since these texts are described in detail, it is not absolutely necessary for readers to access the original. In such instances, however, tutors could recommend an alternative. *Answering-islam.org* describes Badawi as 'without doubt the best known Muslim speaker in the West for the last two decades' and has a rebuttal page (*http://answering-islam.org.uk/Responses/Badawi/*).

A left–right analysis

Throughout, this book draws on its author's own experience of encounter with Islam and with Muslims. He does his best to preclude the need for textual archaeology on this book to unearth its assumptions, as no research can be 'conducted in some autonomous realm that is insulated from the wider society and from the particular biography of the researcher' (Hammersley and Atkinson 1995: 16). Following Neuman (1994), this book aims to take 'advantage of ... personal insights, feelings and perceptions'. Its author takes 'measures to guard against the influence of prior beliefs or assumptions', therefore instead of 'hiding behind "objective" techniques', he makes his 'values explicit' in his text (p. 322). For example, my familiarity with the Islam of the Indian subcontinent and with the thought of Abu'l A'la Mawdudi has influenced the fact that I draw on his writing more substantially than Sayyid Qutb's. Slomp (2003), however, comments that when one compares the 'number, scope and impact of the writings' of the three men who have been dubbed fathers of Islamic fundamentalism, Hasan al Banna, Sayyid Qutb and Mawdudi, 'Mawdudi surpasses the two Egyptians' (p. 239). To do justice to Qutb, his text on *jihad* rather than Mawdudi's is used in Chapter Nine. Mawdudi's text (I am citing from the 1996 edition of his English tract; for his larger Urdu work, see Slomp 2003), though, is well worth reading (and is cited in this book's Introduction).

The division of Muslim approaches to the issues under review into two broad 'categories' is not intended to force square pegs into round holes or to deny the diversity of Muslim opinion. It is used rather as an aid to locating views along a spectrum of thought. Although two key texts will be used as the basis of discussion in most sections, reference is also made to other views and contributors in an effort to present a plurality of views and to avoid any suggestion that Islamic thought is bipolar or even (though some have it that it is) monolithic. All scholarship involves ordering data, identifying ideas, mapping out how ideas relate with other ideas, tracing sources and predicting impacts. Nonetheless, this book's chief pedagogical assumption is that the world of thought, including Muslim thought, is multifaceted and that any attempt to confine thought runs risks, even when intended (as in this book) solely as an analytical aid. Nor is this book's tendency to compare and contrast 'right' and 'left' views (although centrist views are not ignored, including centre left and centre right) meant to imply that either is 'better' than the other.

'Left' in Western usage usually implies socialist principles (for example, state-run welfare) while 'right' implies preference for the free market and for private enterprise. This does not necessarily follow for Muslims. Figure 1 indicates how these terms are used in this book.

Left	Right
Stresses freedom – tackling causes of crime, rehabilitation. Knowledge is to be discovered.	Stresses discipline in relation to education, penology, etc. Knowledge is given.
Feminist – upholds gender equality.	Men are 'in charge' of women.
Inclusive – fluid view of belonging. Embraces plurality of opinion within and outside Islam.	Exclusive – static view of who belongs to Islam (e.g. those who agree with the official version).

Figure 1 Derived from J. A. C. Brown's *Techniques of Persuasion* (1963: 60).

Those on the Islamic right (often called Islamists), for example, want to Islamize the world, those on the left want to humanize Islam. Those on the right see Islam as a political-religious entity, an ideology; for those on the left it is a faith, a spiritual and ethical tradition. The right look to the past for perfection, the left towards the future. Language such as 'return', 'awaken', or 'reawaken' (and renewal, *tajdid*) is typical of the Islamist movement (see al-Azmeh 1993; 22, 27; Voll 1983), while modernists and progressives speak of reconstructing (Iqbal 1930) or of rethinking Islam (Arkoun 1994). There are people who proudly describe their worldviews, their politics or their theologies as 'right', as 'left', as 'conservative' or as 'progressive'. They themselves may hold a negative view of others' positions (progressives probably regard conservatives as out-of-date, conservatives probably regard the progressives' version of Islam as dangerous) but this book does not set out to evaluate views. Readers, though, may use its analysis to form their own judgements about the views it describes. While opinions and approaches are labelled in this text, it is hoped that they are described fully enough for readers to decide for themselves how they would categorize them and whether or not they agree with this writer's categorization. Openness about my values compels me to declare that my personal sympathy lies with progressive interpretations of Islam. However, I have tried rigorously to be fair in describing and analysing all interpretations. Albeit, my likes and dislikes may very well be evident in the text. Indeed, this writer is convinced that personal bias is inevitable, though he also believes that its worst excesses, misrepresentation and false attribution, can be avoided. He cannot like the views of a Mawdudi but he can admire his clarity of thought and the sincerity of his views. This book is written from a Religious Studies perspective that draws on a range of disciplines to illuminate its subject matter. That subject, Muslim thought, is obviously religious in nature. Therefore, this book does draw on theological discourse. Yet, setting aside debate about the political nature of Islam, political systems, legal codes and cultural practices have all been derived from Islam, so anthropology and sociology also inform this text.

This book therefore takes the view that Religious Studies is a subset of
Cultural Studies. The Introduction explores methodological issues in
more detail and identifies some of the voices and viewpoints that feature
in the following chapters.

Introduction
Voices and Viewpoints

Methodology: virtual insidership

As an outsider scholar discussing Muslim thought on the themes addressed in this book, this writer's aim is to listen to insider voices. He believes that this should always be a major objective of any class or course on Islam, if our aim is to understand Muslim thought. This does not mean that 'outsider' voices lack any validity. Everyone has a right to a point of view. Non-Muslims will carry on dealing with Muslims and will continue to express their opinions about the Muslim Other. Indeed, Muslim voices are often heard in response to what non-Muslims have said about Islam: in other words, Muslim thought does not occur in isolation from Western. Much of what both sides say is in response to the other side's perceptions and misperceptions. While this text aims to give students access to Muslim voices, albeit as interpreted by this writer, it sets these voices in the context of Islam's engagement with the West and of Western perceptions of Islam. Mawdudi's tract on *jihad* shows the degree to which Muslims consciously respond to non-Muslim views. It typifies the apologetic nature of some Islamist writing. He responds to apologetics and polemic in his opening section (1996: 1–3). In reply to Western critics for whom the word *jihad* conjures up 'the vision of a marching band of religious fanatics with savage beards and fiery eyes brandishing drawn swords and attacking infidels wherever they meet them and pressing them under the edge of the sword for the recital of *Kalima*' (p. 1), some Muslims claim that Islam has known nothing of war (p. 2). So 'taken aback' were they when they saw 'this picture of ours painted by foreigners' that they 'started offering apologies in this manner – Sir, what do we know of war and slaughter. We are pacifist preachers like the mendicants and religious divines' (*ibid.*). In their effort to please Islam's critics, such apologists admit of but one crime: 'we plead guilty to one crime, though, that whenever someone else attacks us, we attacked him in self-defence' (p. 3). Mawdudi says that Muslims failed to look behind the foreigner's picture to see 'the visage of the painter' (p. 2). To restrict *jihad*, says Mawdudi, to 'waging war with tongues and pen' is tantamount to surrendering to the enemy. It concedes that 'to fire cannons and shoot with guns is the privilege of your honour's government', while 'wagging tongues and scratching with pens is our pleasure' (p. 3). 'Islam', says Mawdudi, in a much cited paragraph, 'requires the earth – not just a portion of it – not because the sovereignty over the earth should be wrestled from one or several nations and vested in one particular nation – but because the entire mankind should benefit from the ideology and welfare programme or what would be truer to say from "Islam" which is the programme of well-being for all humanity' (pp. 6–7).

This writer is convinced that engagement with the Other involves the imagination. In order to pass over into their worldview (to achieve virtual insidership), we must try to think, feel and see as they do. This is why this book uses some fiction, to assist the process by which a non-Muslim can become a 'virtual Muslim'. This writer is also convinced that more needs to be done to address the West's increasing fear of Islam, fuelled by the fact that, as Sayyid (1998) puts it, Islamists refuse to play by the West's rules (p. 160). This book also aims to examine the causes of Western anti-Muslimism. Although this book is not unique in addressing anti-Muslimism – Halliday, Sayyid and Akbar Ahmed all analyse this phenomenon – there is much evidence to suggest that a large audience still needs to be reached.

W. C. Smith (1916–2000) argued in favour of scholars writing and thinking not just for their own communities but also for the global community. We live, he said, interconnected lives in the modern world and can (indeed do) no longer write only for 'ourselves' (see 1981: 186ff). Authors ought to aim at constructing 'religious statements that will be intelligible and cogent in at least two different traditions simultaneously' (1957: vii). An outsider writing on Islam might even 'break new ground in stating the meaning of a faith in, say, modern terms more successfully than' Muslims (1959: 43). An account, says Smith, will have failed if 'intelligent and honest Muslims are not able to recognize its observations as accurate, its interpretations and analyses as meaningful and enlightening' (1957: vii). Nasr (1994) comments that the 'works and thought of those scholars of Western origin who have discovered, in an authentic fashion, aspects of the Islamic tradition' is a neglected area of enquiry. He says that, despite the errors of many Orientalists, there are some who belong to the category of those whose love and knowledge of Islam is 'genuine, if not always complete and total' (p. 253; see also p. x). He singles out for praise Louis Massignon, Henry Corbin and Titus Burckhardt, of whom only the latter embraced Islam existentially.

Discussion topics
● Bassam Tibi (2001) says that as religious knowledge is a human construct, it is equally accessible to Muslims and non-Muslims:

Cultural systems – such as Islam – require, in order to be adequately understood, a reference to their own terms. This requirement does not mean, however, that anything else is simply 'Orientalism'. I reiterate my firm position in stating that knowledge is human. To make judgments about Islam requires knowing Islam which can also be achieved by a non-Muslim. Such an assessment would similarly apply to all sociology of Islam and to all social historical investigations of it. . . . Muslims may like it or not, but religion is not off-limits to scholarly enquiry. (p. 109)

Phenomenology and W. C. Smith's approach to Religious Studies suggest that a text created by an outsider scholar, such as a non-Muslim writing about Islam, is validated when Muslims say 'amen' to its contents. Does this mean that material, perhaps offering a sociological or psychological analysis of data and perhaps contained in the same text but which does not elicit Muslim approval, is wrong or inaccurate? Does this approach unfairly privilege a 'believer's' viewpoint over-and-above alternatives, such as political or sociological or psychological interpretations of Islam? Does this not also privilege religious belief over the views of scholars who may be humanist, atheist or agnostic?

- At this stage, do you think that this book has set itself an impossible task?

- Can an outsider hope to accurately reflect 'insider' voices? Or is it best for us to study and to write about our own cultures (sometimes called 'nativism')?

- What objective criteria, if any, judges that an 'insider's' view must be right, while outsiders' views must be wrong, suspect or open to challenge?

- Could a Muslim write a book on Christianity that Christians might find 'not only admissible' but also 'illuminating', as Smith suggests (1957: viii) and could such a book represent a real contribution to Christian thought?

Polarized viewpoints

Studies of the themes discussed in this book, in the context of Islam in the modern world, tend to polarize responses, either arguing 'yes, Islam and human rights, or democracy, or gender equality are, after all, compatible', or 'no, Islam and human rights, democracy, gender equality, remain incompatible'. Ahmed (1992) writes that Islam is characteristically regarded by the West as a 'force for anarchy and disorder', yet observes that this is the very opposite of how millions of Muslims perceive it (p. 3). From the nineteenth century onwards, when Western writers became aware of Muslim modernists in Egypt and India and elsewhere, a standard response was to declare such Muslims too influenced by non-Muslim ideas to represent an authentic Muslim view, thus 'Islam reformed was Islam no longer'. Since these modernists embraced democracy, for example, it suited the colonial administrators and scholars to declare their views as 'heterodox'. The Orientalist scholars, of course, knew authentic Islam, which was totalitarian, autocratic and intolerant, when they saw it. Sir William Muir (1891) wrote:

> The Islam of today is substantially the Islam we have seen throughout history. Swathed in the bands of the Coran, the Moslem faith ... is powerless to adapt ... to varying times and place, keep pace the march of humanity, direct and purify the social life and elevate mankind. (p. 598; Muir maintained a remarkable friendship with Sir Sayyid Ahmad Khan, despite their opposite estimate of Islam's influence in the world.)

A basic assumption behind the writing of this book is that a flaw of much Western scholarship of Islam has been its depiction of Islam as monolithic and unchanging, not only the same throughout time but also wherever it is encountered. This is now more or less recognized as facile; most contemporary writers are well aware of historical as well as of contemporary diversity and of geographical differences. Few serious writers now speak about 'Islam saying this or that' but of Muslims in 'this context saying such and such', although journalists and reporters may well do so. Al-Azmeh (1993) writes that 'presumptions of Muslim cultural homogeneity and continuity do not correspond to social reality' (p. 4). Instead, he says, 'There are as many Islams as there are situations that sustain it' (p. 1). Use of the term 'Islam', says Said (1997), too often ignores 'time' and 'space': 'if you speak of Islam you more or less automatically eliminate space and time, you eliminate political complications like democracy, socialism, and secularism' (p. 42). The Runnymede Trust, in the on-line version of its 1997 report, *Islamophobia*, identifies 'some of the differences and diversity which are ignored or over-simplified in much Islamophobic discourse'. These include failure to distinguish between the Islam of the Middle East, South Asia and Nigeria, between the perception of Muslim women and men, and between different interpretations of the Qur'an and Islamic tradition.

Al-Azmeh comments that, once named, '*homo islamicus*' is endowed with 'changeless' and 'ageless characteristics' that have 'no specificity', so that 'All in all, things Islamic' are seen as 'uniform, indistinct, amorphous' (1993: 139). Tibi (2001) points out how both Western Orientalists and Islamic fundamentalists (see Chapter Two for a discussion of this controversial term) regard Islam as 'immutable ... an all embracing essential culture, valid without accommodation for all times, places and people' (p. 26). The *homo islamicus* of the Orientalists and the 'Islamist notion of "true Muslim" are strikingly similar', says Tibi (*ibid.*).

Clearly, the 'essentialist' version of Islam must be rejected. On the other hand, as writers such as W. C. Smith and W. M. Watt point out, many

Muslims do affirm that Islam is an international and unitary system and what is identifiable as a classical expression remains the norm for millions of Muslims. The central theme of Watt's 1988 book is that 'the thinking of the fundamentalist Islamic intellectuals and of the great masses of ordinary Muslims is still dominated by the standard traditional Islamic world view and the corresponding self-image of Islam' (p. 1). Earlier, Smith wrote that 'The classical version of Islam remained official, and has always remained socially conservative' (1957: 45).

Another reason for rejecting the view that there is really no such thing as Islam and that we can only speak of Islam in specific contexts is that this becomes a device to control Islam. In other words, instead of analysing, discussing and dealing with Islam as a single entity, Islam is deemed to lack any genuine unitary aspects at all. This divides and rules; Muslims can now only be dealt with as national or as ethnic groups, not as members of a unitary entity. The colonial powers conveniently recognized Muslim leaders when it suited them while on other occasions they refused to concede Muslim leaders any legitimate authority. For example, the British were happy to deal with Muhammad Jinnah and with the Aga Khan as leaders of Indian Muslims and with the Mufti of Jerusalem in Palestine. However, they denied the Ottoman Sultan's right to claim the title of Khalif, since this would give him at least spiritual authority over Muslims under the British flag, which they deemed unacceptable. While Tibi affirms both the contemporary and the historical diversity of Islam and regards the ideal of Islamic unity as a pious fiction (2001: 32), he also distances himself from the tendency to speak only of the local. This is where he parts company from Geertz (whose theory of religion as a cultural system he finds attractive; see Geertz 1973: 90, 1968: 97). Geertz, he suggests, has 'no grasp of civilization'. He is so interested in the locality of culture that he fails to see the relationship between local cultures and 'regional civilizations' that 'are increasingly becoming pivotal in post-bipolar world politics' (2001: 25). 'Related local cultures', says Tibi, 'group to form a civilization' (p. xii). 'We are dealing', he says, 'with a great variety of local cultures more or less embedded in a single great civilization' (1998: 6), which equally applies to the West. He is thus able to write of Islam as offering an 'alternative civilizational worldview' to the West's, although both 'civilizations' contain 'a great number of local cultures' (2001: 99). 'There is', he writes, 'a specific Islamic view of the world shared by all Muslims' (p. 53).

Belief that Islam represents a meta-narrative, that it is a global system, runs counter to postmodernity's rejection of 'a view of the world as a universal totality, of the expectation of final solutions and complex answers' (Ahmed 1992: 10). Since many Muslims see Islam as a 'universal totality, a final solution and a complex answer', this may pit it against current intellectual trends. Sayyid argues that Islam operates as a 'master signifier' for Muslims, which challenges those Westerners who insist that 'Islam cannot be the master signifier' (1988: 48). Certainly, many of the

Muslim writers whose ideas are discussed in this book write for Muslims everywhere; they offer their views as solutions to the challenges faced by all Muslims. Nasr (1976) criticizes the idea that Islam is some sort of 'partial view of things' that can be 'complemented by some form of modern ideology'. Islam, he says, is 'a complete system and perspective in itself . . . whose very totality excludes the possibility of its becoming a mere adjective to modify some other noun which is taken almost unconsciously as central in place of Islam' (p. 219).

This book resists the temptation to reduce everything in Muslim societies to 'Islam', overlooking cultural, political, economic and historical factors, and the opposite temptation, which is to overlook Islam altogether and to explain everything with reference to the particularity of the social-political context. Sayyid describes the 'dissolution of Islam as an analytical concept' as the 'hallmark' of what he calls the 'anti-orientalist approach' (1998: 37). Orientalism posits a single, monolithic essence, Islam, which 'occupies the core of . . . explanations of Muslim societies'. 'Anti-orientalist narratives' reverse this, so that 'Islam is decentered and dispersed' (p. 38).

Discussion topic: Contradictory tendencies?

- Are there two contradictory tendencies within Religious Studies? On the one hand, W. C. Smith did much to popularize the view that Islam, Christianity or Buddhism do not really exist as monolithic systems. In part, they are intellectual abstractions created by Western scholars. Why should Hinduism as practised in a village be less authentic than that of the Brahmanical tradition? Academic study should focus on local and particular manifestations of a tradition, not on privileged and elitist great traditions with which relatively few people actually identify. On the other hand the dominant methodology in Religious Studies over the past 20 years, phenomenology, invites us to give priority to 'insider voices'. When we listen to Muslim voices, we hear many Muslims claiming that Islam is a totalitarian, immutable, perfect system true for all people in all places at all times.

- If, as a student of religions, you want to recognize both the diversity of Muslim experience and Muslims' claim that Islam is a single reality, how might you proceed?

- Reflect on the use of the term 'the West' in many texts and articles on Islam and 'the West'. Is it as wrong to reduce the 'West' to a single, homogenous cultural, intellectual and social 'reality' as it is to see 'Islam' as a monolithic 'entity'? Does 'the West' regard itself as a single 'reality'? If so, is this the source of such notions as 'the Western mind', the 'Eastern mind', 'the Muslim mind'? These divisions assume that 'we' are 'all the same'; Others are also 'the same' but different and distinct from us.

- Al-Azmeh's title *Islams and Modernities* suggests that just as there is no single 'Islam' out there, so there is no single modernity. Often, 'modern' is used as a synonym for Western technology, philosophies and ideas. It assumes some evolutionary scheme with say Australian aborigines towards the bottom and Microsoft executives at the top! How would you critique this?

Even the West's development and aid project assumes the superiority of Western values, argues Sardar (1998):

'Humanitarian work', 'charitable work', 'development assistance' and 'disaster relief' are all smokescreens for the real motives behind the NGO presence in the South: self-aggrandisement, promotion of Western values and culture, including conversion to Christianity, inducing dependency, demonstrating the helplessness of those they are supposedly helping and promoting what has been aptly described as a 'disaster pornography'. (p. 78)

Egyptian feminist writer, Nawal el Saadawi agrees. 'Development', she writes, 'is just another word for neocolonialism ... the word "aid" can be just as deceiving' (1997: 13). As long as the economic world order is controlled by the North and operated for its benefit, the South (including the Muslim world) will remain impoverished. What is needed is 'fair trade laws between countries, not aid or charity. Charity and injustice are two faces of the same coin', she continues, but if there is 'real equality between people and between countries, there will be nothing called "charity" or "aid"' (*ibid.*). 'The result of development carried out in our countries (in line with the policies of these international institutions) are increasing poverty – both economic and cultural – a resurgence of fanatic political religious groups, and increasing oppression of women', she says (p. 136). Tibi (2001) uses the term *al-takhalluf* (backwardness) to describe how many Muslims perceive the state of the Islamic world and contends that this has been a direct result of 'European capitalist expansion' (p. 94). A major voice in this book, Tibi champions 'Euro-Islam'. Born in Syria, he is a German citizen and teaches at Göttingen. He was a member of the Harvard based 'fundamentalism project'. He remarks how he and other critical scholars risk the charge of heresy: 'Orthodox Muslim *fiqh* scholars respond in an intolerant manner against all reformers, not hesitating to invoke the weapons of *takfir* (pronouncement that the offender is a mis-believer) against culturally innovative Muslims' (p. 164). He describes himself as a 'mediator', commenting that he was honoured to be called such by Akbar Ahmed who shares this 'go-between' goal, among others cited in this book (p. 22; see Ahmed 1999).

Discussion topics

- Do you agree with this description of Western aid? Imagine yourself a publicist for World Vision, Christian Aid, Save the Children Fund or Help the Aged with the job of responding to Sardar's criticism. What arguments would you offer?

  Moghissi (1999) comments that the postmodern argument that there is 'no single standard' and that 'societies proceed' developmentally 'with "different speeds" and in "different ways"' overlooks the crucial question of why the proposed standard did not work in colonial and post-colonial countries. Can we imagine', she continues, 'that the development of each of these different worlds has been totally independent? Was one world's speedy development not directly contingent upon, or, at least, costly to, the other world? Yes, colonialism and the slave trade speeded up the West's industrial development, but what did they do to Asia and Africa?' (p. 62).

- How would you answer Moghissi's question? What implications might this view have, if accepted, for aid and development policy-making in the so-called 'first world'?

- 'If Islam's immediacy makes it seem directly available, then its divergence from our familiar reality and norms sets it against us directly, threateningly, drastically. The net result is that Islam has acquired a polymorphous status of a tangible, recognizable reality about which many statements and logical strategies – most of them anthropomorphic – become possible without restraint' (Said 1997: 42). Given that some anthropologists contend that the human mind builds language and culture by using binary opposites, might this negative polarizing of 'us' and 'Others' be the result of psychological patterns, alongside such polarities as sacred and profane, good and bad, permitted and prohibited? (see Sardar 1998: 35–8 and Al-Azmeh 1993: 20–2).

References to Islam's 'classical' tradition begs the question whether what is represented as 'classical Islam' is the best or the truest or the only possible version that might have emerged, even though it is the dominant one. Majorities are not always right. Politics, self-interest, gender and other factors had much to do with the classical version's victory over its alternatives. Nasr champions what he calls 'traditional' Islam yet in his view this is neither the Islam of the fundamentalists nor of the modernists (1990: viii). Neither is the language of reform (*islah*) peculiar to any particular group of Muslims. Most agree that revision is needed, though for some that revision represents a return to what was, for others it means the building of something new.

Media and anti-Islamism

Ahmed (1992) discusses the role of the West's media in perpetuating negative images of Islam (pp. 222–65, 'The evil demon: the media as master'). Edward Said (1935–2003) explored this extensively in *Covering Islam: How the Media and the Experts Determine How We See the Rest of the World* (rev. edn 1997). Said calls anti-Muslimism the acceptable face of racism, arguing that 'Malicious generalizations about Islam have become the last acceptable form of denigration of foreign culture' (p. xii).

In 1995, following the Oklahoma City bombing, the media immediately reported that Muslim terrorists were responsible and at least one Muslim suspect was detained. The actual perpetrator was an American white supremacist. In the introduction to her 1994 book, Rana Kabbani recounts how she completely failed to recognize anything she had said in an interview with a *Vanity Fair* reporter when she read the article, which represented a 'catalogue of horrors about Islam'. Kabbani (1989) comments that 'Western culture remains permeated with anti-Islamic reference. Today's media coverage carries echoes', she continues, 'of medieval polemic' (p. 9). Syrian-born British resident Kabbani has had to ask herself whether she could remain resident in the West without committing cultural treason (p. x). Her own inclination is to strike a balance, since there are aspects of Western culture she admires and wants to adopt just as there are 'many things about Islam' that she wants to 'cling to'. She sees herself as an unashamed 'champion of her culture' but is 'by no means a defender of the many abuses ... committed in the name of Islam'. Her PhD thesis at Cambridge, *Europe's Myths of Orient: Devise and Rule* (1986), examined Western writing on the 'Orient' and argued that scholarship was 'heavily influenced by the realities of power' and perpetuated 'misrepresentation and sheer dislike of the Muslim world', that justified the doctrine that 'Easterners were incapable of governing themselves' (1989: 56–7). Suggesting that both misogyny and racism were involved, 'it took three years and eight examiners to be awarded a doctorate' (p. 57). Bhikhu Parekh (2000) comments how media coverage of the Rushdie affair (see Chapter Three) actually made Muslims more extreme. By 'creating the overwhelming impression that the *entire* Muslim community was seething with a bloodthirsty spirit of vengeance', the media 'unintentionally created a new orthodoxy' among Muslims that 'made support for the *fatwa* a badge of Muslim identity and solidarity'. Thus, many who 'disapproved of killing Rushdie' failed to 'dissociate themselves from, let alone condemn, the *fatwa*' (p. 300).

In her novel *The Map of Love* (1999), described as 'a must for anyone trying to understand the complexities of the ongoing transition in Middle Eastern culture' (back cover), Ahdaf Soueif (interviewed by Kabbani in her *Letter to America*) describes one of her character's reactions as follows when she heard that an American woman reporter wanted to meet her:

Amal could not pretend that she was not wary. Wary and weary in advance: an
American woman – a journalist ... she braced herself: the fundamentalists, the veil,
the cold peace, polygamy, women's status in Islam, female genital mutilation – which
would it be? (p. 6)

Halliday (1996) argues that anti-Muslimism is not only a relic of Europe's
past animosity towards the Muslim world, as a traditional enemy as well as
a religious and cultural 'other', but expresses 'new racist and anti-
immigration policies' as well (p. 186). As early as Renan's classic rejection
of Ibn Rushd as an authentically Muslim philosopher, and his assertion
that Ibn Rushd's death (1198 CE) assured the triumph of Qur'an over free
thought in Islam, racism may also have played a part in Europe's evaluation of Islam (see Renan 1866 and al-Azmeh 1993: 51–2).

From two novels by Muslim writers

In Naguib Mahfouz's novel, *The Palace Walk*, al-Sayyid Ahmad, forced to
help fill a hole in a Cairo street by the occupying British soldiers, reflected
'The Prophet Muhammad, God's peace and blessings on him, fought a
Battle of the Trench and worked alongside the other men, digging the dirt
with his own hands. His enemies were pagans back then. Why are the
pagans winning today? It's a corrupt age ...' (1990: 450).

In a somewhat different vein, African Muslim novelist Cheikh Hamidou
Kane writes in *Ambiguous Adventure* (English translation 1972) of how the
colonizers not only 'knew how to kill with effectiveness, they also knew
how to cure' (p. 49). 'They destroyed and then constructed', raising the
question why had Europeans 'conquered without being in the right?' (p.
152). 'For man's welfare', says one of Kane's characters, 'and happiness,
we must have the presence and the guarantee of God', yet the West had
abolished God (p. 102). Kane's principal character, Samba Diallo, is sent
to the French school, then to university in Paris, to discover the foreigners'
secret. Exposure to modernity results in Samba's inability to pray. He finds
himself losing interest in the affairs of his cousin, the Chief. Yet he feels
equally alienated from the godless, materialistic society he experiences in
France. This novel usefully explores some of the issues discussed in this
chapter.

In Kane's novel, Samba Diallo struggles to overcome his doubt that any
other 'reality' from the Western 'exists', although 'the ever living example
of his country was there, finally to prove to him, in his moment of doubt,
the reality of a non-Western universe' (pp. 156–7). Adèle, 'the exile on the
Seine', on the other hand, born in France of African parents, had no such
luxury; 'He at least was a "half-breed" only by his culture ... Adèle did not
have her country. When she happened to discern in herself a feeling or a
thought which seemed to her to cut in a certain fashion into the backdrop
of the Occident, her reaction for a long time had been to run away from it'
(p. 157).

Discussion topic

- How useful are novels or films as aids to academic exploration of other worldviews, or of encounter between religions and cultures?

Does Islam threaten the West?

Ahmed (1992: 3) and Sardar (1998: 83) both draw attention to a popular Western conception that, post-communism, Islam is the greatest threat. Tibi (1998) says that 'the decline of communism in the East and the crises of meaning plaguing the West have together paved the way for non-Western civilization – above all Islam – to pose their competing challenges to Western modernity and Western hegemony' (p. 15). He comments that while 'Islam as a religion is definitely not a threat' (p. 41), political Islam (which he finds obnoxious) may very well threaten the West, since it creates disorder (p. 19; see Chapter One of this book). Esposito (1999) comments that 'it seems that the West's attitude towards communism is being transferred to or replicated in the elevation of a new threat, "Islamic fundamentalism"' (p. 218). The green menace has replaced the red menace. Jansen (1980) was one of the earliest books to depict 'militant Islam' as a possible threat to the West.

Samuel P. Huntington (1996) famously predicted that the next 'conflict' would be between the West and Islamic nations (possibly in alliance with what he calls 'neo-Confucian' states). 'Islam', he says, 'has bloody borders' (p. 34). He wrote:

> The Muslim propensity toward violent conflict is also suggested by the degree to which Muslim society is militarized. (p. 258)

> Some Westerners ... have argued that the West does not have problems with Islam but only with violent [Muslim] extremists. Fourteen hundred years of history demonstrate otherwise. (p. 209)

Conflict will occur because, in his view, the Western-led process of globalization and Islamic values (civilization) are on a collision course. Huntington also (often overlooked by his critics) reprimands the West for assuming that the rest of the world either needs or wants its 'culture', 'values, institutions and practices' (p. 78). 'Non Western societies', he says, 'can modernize without abandoning their own cultures' (p. 78). Huntington's book (and earlier article) was a response to talk of a 'new world order' by President George Bush, Senior (US President 1989–93) and others following the end of the 'bi-polar' divide between the West (Capitalist) and East (Communist) blocks in 1990. 9/11 and the subsequent attribution of blame to Osama bin Laden's al-Qaeda network, followed by punitive action in Afghanistan, then by the war to depose Iraq's Saddam Hussein, for some commentators proved Huntington right.

The 'war on terrorism' ('Operation Enduring Freedom'), declared by President George W. Bush and supported by (among others) British Prime Minister Tony Blair (7 October 2001) represents exactly what Huntington had predicted, a war on Islam. Bush's early use of the word 'crusade' to describe his war on terrorism, too, rang alarm bells for many Muslims who feared a modern version of the medieval 'crusades'. In their turn, some Muslims spoke of the need for a *jihad* in response (see further discussion in Chapter Five of this book). Nor did Muslims find the description 'Infinite Justice' much better, since, as Mostyn (2003) points out, it translated into Arabic as *'adala ghayr mutanahiya*, which implies 'divine retribution being arrogated to itself by an earthly power', which is exactly what many people think President Bush has done (p. 192).

Discussion topic

Said (1997) describes Huntington's book as a 'diatribe' (p. xxxiv). The 'millennial thesis that militant Islam is a danger to the West' is, he says, 'at the core of Samuel Huntington's books'.

- Do you agree with this evaluation of Huntington, from what you have read of or about his theory?

Tibi refers to 'deplorable shortcomings' in Huntington's thesis but commends him for 'bringing culture into the social-scientific debate' (1998: 16; 2001: 190, 213). 'Culture' and 'civilization' have been 'mostly ignored by scholars of international studies preoccupied with "the state"' (1998: 16).

Widely reported comments by the Italian Prime Minister, Silvio Berlus-coni, that Islam was incompatible with Western civilization helped to fuel the view that the 'war' was indeed 'against Muslims' and that it was along civilizational and cultural lines. It also followed for some that if the war is against Islam, then this includes Muslims who live in the West (see Chapter Eight of this book). Certainly, post-9/11 sales of Huntington's book increased considerably. This implies, too, that British or American Muslims cannot be loyal citizens, but are a 'fifth column' (see further discussion in Chapter Eight). In Britain, Blair found it necessary to meet with Muslim leaders in order to assure them that the war was not against Islam but against those who had planned 9/11. Muslims, he said, are peace-loving and shared the 'same spiritual heritage as Christians' (Press Statement, 27 September 2001).

Blair declared that the term 'Islamic terrorist' ought not to be used, since Islam was a religion of peace and the events of 9/11 contravened all the tenets of Islam. *The 9/11 Commission Report* in the USA also affirmed that 'The enemy is not Islam, the great world faith, but a perversion of Islam' (p. 16). Oxford professor Richard Dawkins, however, disagrees. For him, religion lurks behind not only the 9/11 atrocity (which could not have occurred without 'belief in an afterlife') but also the Israeli–Palestinian and Northern Irish conflicts, not to mention numerous other trouble spots around the world. Linguistic gymnastics that avoid using the word 'religion' are misguided and dangerous, since it is religion that presents the real threat (Dawkins 2001). Dawkins, who is professor of the public understanding of science at Oxford, considers religious faith to be 'a type of mental illness' (1989: 330) since it is capable of justifying anything, such as that a person 'should die – on the cross, at the stake, skewered on a Crusader's sword, shot in a Beirut street, or blown up in a bar in Belfast' (p. 198). In a widely circulated and cited article, Rushdie (2001) also argues that 9/11 and its aftermath is 'about Islam', seeing bin Laden's popularity throughout the Muslim world as proof of the link between violent acts and Islam.

Discussion topic: What is culture?

The terms 'Western Culture' and 'Muslim Culture' have been used in this book. However, does either really correspond to any reality? Arkoun (1998a) argues that these serve as 'mutually exclusive imaginary worlds ... constructed out of the postulates of hegemonic reason'. This juxtaposes a 'dynamic, modern, secular West open to all innovations because it comprises agents who are more free' with a 'static, dogmatic, essentialist, transcendentalized religious world' that demands 'to be respected'. Both, he says, are as mythical as is the depiction of the West as immoral and of the East as spiritual (p. 177).

- If you think that these terms carry genuine meaning, how would you define them? If European culture embraces the whole of Europe, how would you distinguish French (secular) from Norwegian (Lutheran) or Greek (Orthodox) from Spanish (Roman Catholic) culture? Are they subsets of 'Western culture'? Similarly, would you distinguish Indonesian culture from Arab culture or Syrian from Saudi within Muslim culture?

In the West, scholars also distinguish between popular and 'high' (classical) culture and between the cultures of different groups in society, such as 'gay culture' and 'youth culture'.

- Is it more appropriate to speak of Western civilization and of Muslim civilization as broad categories to describe sets of shared values that cross national (and, in the case of Europe, religious) boundaries and to reserve the term 'culture' for more localized realities?

> Muslims, too, live in the West and make their own cultural con-
> tributions (see Chapter Four).
>
> ● Is it therefore sustainable to juxtapose Western and Muslim
>   culture? Are they not intertwined to some degree?

'Related local cultures', says Tibi, 'group to form a civilization' (2001: xii).
'We are dealing', he says, 'with a great variety of local cultures more or less
embedded in a single great civilization' (1998: 6), which equally applies to
the West. He is thus able to write of Islam as offering an 'alternative
civilizational worldview' to the West's, although both 'civilizations' contain
'a great number of local cultures' (2001: 99). 'There is', he writes, 'a
specific Islamic view of the world shared by all Muslims' (p. 53). His own
concept of Euro-Islam was dismissed by one scholar: ' "No, there is only
one Islam; take it or leave it. Islam is not a buffet from which you select
what you want!" With these harsh words he dismissed my concept of Euro-
Islam', says Tibi (p. 26).

Some Muslims view the action against terrorism as indeed a war against
Islam. In its *Communiqué* of 9 October 2001 the *hizb-ut-tahrir* declared, 'On
Sunday 7/10/2001, America, the head of *Kufr* and her ally Britain
declared a brutal war against the Muslims'. Furthermore, to aid America
or her allies represents 'a great crime' against Islam (statement issued 18
September 2001). In their view, the real aim of 'Operation Enduring
Freedom' is the imposition of American dominance (the so-called 'new
world order') on the world. Thus:

> They are waging it under the banner of what they call fighting terrorism, through
> deliberate lies and deception, to strike Islam and the Muslims, and to protect their
> treacherous agents – the rulers of the Muslims who are colluding with them in this
> war – those rulers who have opened up the airports and territories of the Muslims to
> their military operations throughout the length and breadth of the Islamic world.

Earlier *hizb-ut-tahrir* warned of an American and Western campaign to
suppress Islam. Following the demise of Communism's challenge to the
imperial aspirations of Western capitalism, now only Islam stands in the
way of Western dominance, they said (1996: 10; see Hader 1992). Islam's
rejection of interest, of the uninhibited right to own property and of
unlimited freedom of expression, all challenge Capitalism's imperial
ambitions. Indeed, 'America's campaign to make Capitalism solely dominate the world is not met by real resistance except in the Islamic world',
thus America's desire to 'suppress' Islam (1996: 8). The *hizb-ut-tahrir*'s
Khilafah.com's magazine editorial for 21 March 2003 (the day after hostilities started) announced that 'the Muslims of Iraq' were 'the latest target
in the West's continuing crusade against Islam' (p. 1). According *to hizb-ut-
tahrir*, only Islam stands in the way of America's goal of world domination,
which is why the USA has launched its campaign to 'suppress Islam'.

Osama bin Laden's own agenda, according to Peter L. Bergen, is thoroughly political. His *fatwa* of 23 February 1998, in which he urges Muslims to 'kill Americans and their allies', identifies American foreign policy as the cause of Muslim discontent:

> First, for over seven years the United States has been occupying the lands of Islam in the holiest of places, the Arabian Peninsula, plundering its riches, dictating to its rulers, humiliating its people, terrorizing its neighbors, and turning its bases in the Peninsula into a spearhead through which to fight the neighboring Muslim peoples.

Bergen (2001) suggests that 9/11 and its aftermath do not prove Huntington right, because this cannot be understood as a 'clash of cultures'. The central issues, he says, are political, especially America's foreign policy, not cultural. He writes:

> In all the tens of thousands of words that bin Laden has uttered on the public record there are some significant omissions: he does not rail against the pernicious effects of Hollywood movies, or against Madonna's midriff, or against the pornography protected by the United States Constitution ... Judging by his silence, bin Laden cares little about such cultural issues. What he condemns the United States for is simple: its policies in the Middle East ... its military presence in Arabia; US support for Israel ... its support for regimes such as Egypt and Saudi Arabia that he regards as apostates from Islam. (p. 242)

Discussion topics

Bergen writes: 'bin Laden had reasons for hating the United States, and if we understand those reasons, we will have a glimpse into what provoked the terrible events of 11 Sept' (2001: 242).

- Do you think that those who perpetrated the events of 9/11 had any legitimate grievance against the USA?

- Is it possible to accept that the perpetrators had legitimate grievances, that is, genuine grounds for 'hating the USA' while in no way endorsing the method they used to express this?

- In April 2003, after the Iraq war, the USA announced the withdrawal of troops from their bases on Saudi Arabia. Has bin Laden achieved one of his goals?

Pipes (2002) sees the battle as one within Islam, pointing out that Muslim extremists oppose moderate Muslims as well as non-Muslims. He writes: 'A battle is now taking place for the soul of Islam. On one side stand the moderates, those Muslims eager to accept Western ways, confident to learn from outsiders, oriented towards democracy, and ready to integrate in the world. On the other stand the Islamists – fearful, seeking strong rule, hoping to push the outside world away' (p. 27).

Rana Kabbani, in her 'From Our Correspondent' broadcast on BBC2's *Letter to America* (9 December 2001), also stressed the political cause of

Muslim anti-Western sentiment. Visiting the United Arab Emirates, she commented that everyone with whom she spoke disapproved of US policy in the Middle East. What people object to, Kabbani heard, was America's hypocrisy and double standards, for example, Palestinian action is terrorism while Israeli aggression escapes censure:

> America doen't seem to believe in history. I'll give you three examples ... When Bush was elected he did not know who the President of Pakistan was. Then he called Musharraf a dictator. And then, Musharraf is now America's sweetheart. (Dr Mohajerani, on Kabbani 2001)

Kabbani is one of the female voices used in this book, to ensure that male voices are not privileged. An important female voice is Fatima Mernissi, the main feminist whose work is analysed in Chapter Six but whose contribution is by no means limited to gender issues. Her 1994 *Islam and Democracy*, written after the first Gulf War, is equally critical of the West for its double standards and of the Muslim world for fearing democracy, which threatens the interests and dominance of the elite. Mernissi, whom Kurzman describes as a 'public figure' in her native Morocco, taught Sociology for many years at the Mohammed V University in Ravat (Kurzman 1998: 112). She gained her PhD from the USA. Her website is *www.mernissi.net*. Following the publication of *Islam and Democracy*, she has concentrated on 'civil society' rather than women's issues in her research. She no longer accepts speaking assignments on gender but her work is used in this book because it represents a hugely significant contribution to Qur'an and *hadith* scholarship. Unfortunately, this book cannot include everything and Leila Ahmed's contribution therefore misses the attention it merits. See Ahmed 1978, 1992 and 2000 and her website *http://www. religionandpluralism.org/LeilaAhmed.htm*. 'The silent majority of Muslims want to find a voice and not leave the voice of Islam only to the conservative, so-called observant Muslims', she says. Chapter One examines Muslim response to modernity and to postmodernity, featuring the contributions of Akbar Ahmed and Ziauddin Sardar (also a major voice on epistemology).

1 Modernity, Postmodernity and the World of Islam

'Postmodernity' [is] a fictitious sense of novelty and of radical diversity primed to become automatically operational as a means of ideological and representational uniformization whenever collective representations of global and local social and political conflict are called forth. It is a shibboleth which reduces realities to Reality, expressed in bytes, and therefore amenable to manipulation; in other words, a recent form of the ideological production which had previously been termed 'the end of ideology'.

(Aziz al-Azmeh 1993: 5–6)

The crises of modernity

The themes discussed in this book have attracted scholarly attention from at least W. C. Smith's *Islam in Modern History* (1957) in which he analysed 'the conditions and the dynamic of Islam in the modern world' (p. 47). His thesis was that Islam faced a fundamental challenge as it entered the modern world. To many Muslims, the Islamic project seemed to have been somehow derailed. Thus, 'the fundamental malaise of modern Islam is a sense that something has gone wrong with Islamic history. The fundamental problem of modern Muslims is how to rehabilitate that history: to set it going in full vigour, so that Islamic society may once again flourish as a divinely guided society should and must' (p. 47). The reality of colonial domination represented what for Muslims was a 'trauma' (Ahmad 1983: 224). Ahmad makes good background reading for the first half of this chapter. A protégé of Mawdudi who holds high office in the *Jamaati-i-Islam*, he has also been Minister of Planning and a Senator in Pakistan. As a result of colonial domination, Muslims asked 'Why has this happened – this situation of political dominance as well as the decay of our past heritage?' (*ibid.*: 219). Mernissi (1994) uses the term *'azma* (crisis) to describe the 'rampant malaise that now besets the colonized nations' (p. 46). Dissonance follows for Muslims because their religious convictions and the world no longer correspond: 'It is hard', writes Tibi, 'to reconcile ... the religious proclamation, "You are the best community (*umma*) created by God on earth" (Q3: 110) with the reality in which members of this very *umma* rank with the underdogs in the present global system dominated by the West' (2001: 54). Former Sudanese Prime Minister Al-Sadiq al-Mahdi (1983) says that colonization and neo-colonization left Muslims paralysed 'and ... in a state of spiritual, intellectual, and social decay' (p. 239). While this book uses two broad categories to describe Muslim response to this trauma, four strategies can also be identified, described in Figure 1.1 below.

Traditionalists (e.g. the Deobandis, see Chapter Eight): Withdrawing from Western influence, they make little use of Western technology. Their aim is to restore Islamic institutions. They advocate Islamic government but tend not to involve themselves in political action to achieve this. In practice they support autocratic rulers provided that they accept the authority of the Qur'an and *Sunnah* (traditions ascribed to Muhammad), since in this view God, not the *Malik* (king), is sovereign. Muhammad ibn Abd al-Wahhab (1703–92), whose followers founded the modern Saudi state, pioneered traditionalist Islam. He wanted to restore the pure Islam of the desert, free of all later additions and innovations, among which Sufism loomed large. The revival of *ijtihad* could achieve this (see below). The Wahhabis, Deobandis and such groups as the *Ahle-e-Hadith* regard Sufi Islam as corrupt, partly responsible for Islam's decline. Tibi comments that ever since al-Wahhab, Muslims have had to choose between Wahhabism and its offshoot political Islam, and 'reform Islam' (2001: 42), that is, between the Muslim right and the Muslim left. Similarly, Benazir Bhutto (1998) comments that she 'would describe Islam in two main categories, reactionary Islam and progressive Islam' (p. 107). The claim that all the resources modern Muslims need to restore Islamic ascendancy is in her past means that any idea (however novel) has to be located in that legacy (*Turath*) if it is to enjoy authenticity. Kurzman (1999) identifies the question of authenticity as a key issue and suggests that the quest for an authentic Islam and the claim by some to represent authentic Islam over-and-against 'liberal Islam' is part of a global trend to try to define cultures as discrete entities, separate from others (p. 9). He cites one convert to Islam, Gai Eaton, who calls liberal Muslims 'Uncle Toms' (a term used by African-Americans to describe a black person who is 'grotesquely servile to whites') (see Eaton 1985: 12).

Neo-traditionalists (e.g. Mawdudi's *Jamaati-i-Islam*): They criticize the West but engage with Western thought. Use modern technology to propagate their ideas, saying ' "yes" to modernization but "no" to blind westernization' (Ahmad 1983: 224). In Ahmad's view, these Muslims (among whom he counts himself) bridge 'the new and the old, the westernizing and the traditional'. They advocate reinterpreting the texts for today, for *ijtihad*, although within conservative and traditionalist parameters. For example, no Qur'anic rule can be altered, such as amputation for theft (Q5: 38). They campaign through political activism, within constitutional means, to achieve their version of the Islamic State. Sivan (1985) comments that while rejecting the progressive ideas of the modernists, the 'traditionalists' borrowed from them their apologetic approach to the West and 'a grudging acceptance of *ijtihad*' (p. 80). *Ijtihad* is 'literally, the intellectual effort of trained Islamic scholars to arrive at legal rulings not covered in the sacred sources' (Kurzman 2002: 377). While the traditionalists are content with autocratic governments that abide by the *Shari'ah* (as they understand this), almost all neo-traditionalists advocate a constitutional form of government that includes popular consultation (non-Muslims are generally excluded from any consultative or electoral process and political pluralism is usually ruled out; see Chapter Two). Like the modernists, the neo-traditionalists call for a contemporary *ijtihad*, often citing ibn Taymiyya (d. 1328 CE) in support.

Many leading neo-traditionalists have had a Western education and are highly qualified as engineers, social scientists or lawyers. Few have had formal training as Islamic scholars, in contrast to Muhammad 'Abduh and al-Raziq, for example, who were both educated as traditional *ulama* (Muslim religious scholars). 'Abduh served as chief *mufti* of Egypt. Al-Raziq was a *Shari'ah* court judge. It was, however, such modernists as Sayyid Ahmed Khan and Muhammad Iqbal who first started the trend of claiming the right to speak on matters Islamic without having undergone traditional theological training. Modernists with Western degrees were usually humanity graduates, while Sayyid Ahmed Khan was a member of the judicial service in British India (reaching the highest rank then open to Indians). For some, it was when they visited the West that they began to dislike it. Sayyid Qutb (1906–66), one of the most influential neo-traditionalists (see Chapter Nine), joined the Muslim Brotherhood (*Ikhwan-ul-Muslimin*) after studying in the USA. He saw the West as immoral, preoccupied with sex, and believed that the whole Western project had to be dismantled (see Lewis 2003: 67). An-Banna wrote:

> They [Europeans] imported their half-naked women into [our] regions, together with their liquors, their theatres, their dance halls, their amusements, their stories, their newspapers, their novels, their whims, their silly games, and their vices. Here they countenanced crimes they did not tolerate in their own countries, and decked out this frivolous strident world, reeking with sin and redolent with vice, to the eyes of the deluded, unsophisticated Muslims of wealth and prestige, and to those of rank and authority. (1979: 27–80)

Radical revisionists (e.g. Islamic Jihad): They claim that the West is engaged in a media, economic and cultural war against Islam and regard Westerners and Western interests as legitimate targets. They also regard many existing Muslim governments as illegitimate against which *jihad* as military struggle is justified. They use extra-constitutional methods to pursue their agenda (see Ahmed 1992: 33–7 on 'Islamic Resurgence'). Some revisionists see themselves as heirs of the ancient Kharijites, who had waged war against those Muslim rulers whom they saw as 'sinners'. In contrast, the Murjites held that, since Muslim unity was sacrosanct, rebellion against a Muslim ruler who sinned but paid 'lip service' to Islam was unjustified. There is some overlap here with 'neo-traditionalists' on the right of that group who also endorse violent methods. Political pluralism is completely ruled out. Individuals sometimes move from one extreme to the other: Rashid Rida (1865–1935) started off as a disciple of Muhammad 'Abduh but ended as what Esposito (1991) calls 'an Islamic fundamentalist ideologue' (p. 66). The above three categories may be described as 'fundamentalist' (see Chapter Two) and are on the 'right'. Communism was rejected as 'purely a product of man's fantasy', just as bankrupt as the West (Qutb 1976: 126).

Modernists (who are on the left): They argue that what is eternal and unchangeable about Islam are principles contained within its core texts, not historical applications manifested in systems or polity (see Iqbal 1930: 160; Sardar 1985: 119). Even the Islam of Muhammad's day was a particular but time-limited interpretation that need not, indeed should not, be replicated today. Instead, more appropriate, perhaps even better, Islamic systems can be created. Modernists do look to Islam's past for inspiration and want to recover Islam's original ethical, spiritual and esoteric principles. However, unlike traditionalists, they do not want to reconstruct the exoteric aspects of the past, such as political institutions and legal frameworks. Once discovered, original principles are to be applied to today's problems (see Figures 6.2, 7.2 and 10.1 for examples of this approach contrasted with the traditional approach). Therefore, the modernists' orientation was futuristic. Qur'anic *hudud* (punishments), derived from the word for 'limit', are exactly that, limits. The Qur'anic principle that serious crime merits harsh punishment is to be preserved but different penalties – for example a prison sentence instead of amputation – can be imposed. In India, Sayyid Ahmed Khan (1817–98) pursued a policy that differed radically from the Deobandis'. He saw much of value in Western culture and co-operated with the British in establishing the Anglo-Oriental Mohammedan College, of which Sir William Muir (cited in this chapter, and elsewhere in this book), then Lt. Gov. of the North Western Provinces, was official Visitor. Sir Sayyid's visit to Oxford and Cambridge inspired this initiative. Knighted by the British, he was one of only a few prominent Muslims who supported the British through the events of 1857 (the first Indian War of independence, usually referred to by the British as the 'Indian Mutiny'). The British administration in India largely agreed with Sir William Wilson Hunter's view, in his report of 1871, that enthusiastic loyalty from Muslims could not be expected.

Writing after a Muslim had assassinated a Chief Justice, Hunter argued that while Islam's texts could support loyalty to the Queen, they could also justify sedition. Sir Sayyid advocated a secular system within which Islam would provide moral and religious guidance. He is regarded as one of the earliest Muslim modernists (see his 'Lecture on Islam', pp. 291–303 in Kurzman 2002; see also Majeed 1998). This secular brand of Islam has been described as Westernized, which some Muslims reject as an illegitimate and innovative version (al-Mahdi 1983: 231). Innovation, or *bi'da*, is the opposite of imitation (*taqlid*) – that is, of past and legitimate Islamic models. For the modernists, '*taqlid* was not' a 'religious duty' but a device designed to 'suppress challenging views' (Kurzman 2002: 10). Dislike of innovation, which is equated with heresy, emerged in the ninth century when the four Sunni schools of jurisprudence developed and the idea that the 'gates of *ijtihad*' (of rational extension of the law) had closed. Iqbal regarded the closing of the gates of *ijtihad* as a convenient 'fiction suggested by the crystallization of legal thought in Islam and partly by intellectual laziness' (1998: 268). Sardar (1987) comments that 'it is not quite clear why the gates of *ijtihad* closed'. However, he says that the gates were probably closed to prevent unqualified people from misusing this tool. 'Fearing a massive misuse', the powerful 'declared that the exercise of independent reasoning was prohibited' (p. 54). The four schools (*madhahib*) are those named after the four Imams, Shafi'i (d. 819), Hanbal (d. 855), Malik (d. 796) and Hanifa (d. 767). The so-called closing of the gate of *ijtihad*, says Iqbal, turned such 'great thinkers into idols' (1998: 268). Writing in the fifteenth century, Ibn Khaldun (d. 1403) commented that hereafter 'all that remained ... was to hand down the respective school traditions and, for each individual adherent, to act in accordance with the traditions of his school' (Peters 1994: 243; see 'The Classical Schools' pp. 240–2 and 'The End of the Age of the Fathers', pp. 242–3).

Sir Sayyid saw himself as an heir of the Mu'tazalites (rationalists) (see Chapter Five), who had stressed human ability to 'know' the good life unaided by divine revelation. Some modernist and progressive Muslims also advocate an Islamic state (see Chapter Two), which could mean that on this issue they tend towards a centrist position. Others on the 'left' support the separation of *din* (religion) from *dunya* (the world), claiming that Islam is a 'faith' not a 'political system' or an ideology (see al-Raziq 1998: 29–36 and Tibi 1998: 161). 'Abduh also stressed the role of reason, contending that 'though there may be in religion that which transcends the understanding, there is nothing which reason finds impossible' (2002: 55). Muslims, he believed, could adopt European science (which itself owed, in his view, a great debt to Islam) without compromising Islam, although it has been suggested that he was rather vague about 'which commands of Islam' Muslims should live by and which European ideals were acceptable (Hopwood 1998: 6). Ahmad (1983) sees Muslim modernism as an agent of the West: 'Muslim modernism', he writes, 'has been the secularizing spearhead of westernization in Muslim lands'. It 'tried to super-impose the values of western liberalism on Muslim society' (p. 227). Similarly, Yusuf al-Qaradawi dismisses modernist interpretations of Islam (such as Iqbal's) as 'imported *solutions*' (*al-hullul-al-mustawralul*) as opposed to the legitimate, home grown Islamic solution (*al-hull-al-Islami*). This rejection of 'imported' solutions is reflected in the slogan of the Muslim Brotherhood, 'Islam is the Answer'. Sivan (1985) comments that *affar mustawrada* (imported ideas) 'is the ultimate term of opprobrium, an oft-repeated code word, in the language of fundamentalists of all hues' (p. 138). The Algeria case study (Chapter Eleven) was chosen as typical of an Islamic struggle with the colonial legacy.

The pioneer neo-traditionalists, such as Mawdudi and Hassan al-Banna (1906–49), founded movements. Mawdudi founded *Jamaati-i-Islam* (1941); al-Banna founded the *Ikhwan-ul-Muslimin*, the Muslim Brotherhood (1928). They therefore reached a popular audience. The modernists tended to concentrate on education. Muhammad 'Abduh (1849–1905) attempted to reform al-Azhar University, Cairo; Ahmad Khan founded a university. Thus in the main they communicated to an intellectual elite (see Shehabuddin 2000). Muhammad Iqbal (1877–1938) formulated one of the most important modernist interpretations of Islam. He was convinced that Islam had to reform and renew itself, or Muslims would never wake up from their slumber. He advocated 'progress' or 'movement', arguing that 'The teaching of the Qur'an that life is a process of progressive creation necessitates that each generation, guided but unhampered by the work of its predecessors, should be permitted to solve its own problems' (Iqbal 1930: 160, 1998: 264). It was Iqbal who first proposed the creation of a separate state for India's Muslims, at the All India Muslim League's meeting in 1930. Educated in Europe and knighted by the British, he was accused of borrowing too much from Western philosophy. Yet he was by no means uncritical of the West. He denounced its petty nationalisms and saw its materialistic worldview as bankrupt of any remedy: 'believe me, Europe today is the greatest hindrance in the way of man's ethical advancement' (Iqbal 1998: 269). Unlike Sir Sayyid, Iqbal was no secularist and his reformed *Shari'ah* would be at the centre of his ideal state. He also looked beyond the creation of a single Muslim state to 'a reunion of Independent Muslim States' (Kurzman 1998: 260). This goal is shared by neo-traditionalists: Mawdudi, Qutb, the *hizb-ut-tahrir-al-Islami* (founded in 1952 by Taqiuddin an-Nabhana, 1909–77) all aim to go beyond the local to the global.

The pioneers Afghani, 'Abduh and Iqbal are usually called 'modernists' while more recent writers, such as Sardar, Taha and Arkoun are often called 'progressive' or 'liberal', since these terms are their own preferred description. Kurzman (2002) dates modernism from 1840 until 1940. Farid Esack (1997) uses the term 'progressive Islamist' (p. 259) while Bassam Tibi (1998) describes himself as a 'liberal Muslim' (p. xv). In Safi (2003), Esack says that the term 'progressive' was popularized by Suroush Irfan's *Revolutionary Islam in Iran: Popular Liberation or Religious Dictatorship* (1983). For Esack, progressive Islam is an Islam that seeks to transform unjust societies into just ones, and people as objects of exploitation into 'subjects of history' (p. 80). See Kurzman (1999) on the term 'Liberal Islam'. This article (available online) is a précis of his 1998 anthology.

Left → ← Right

Progressive	Neo-traditionalist	Traditionalist	Radical revisionist
Some argue for the separation of Islam from the state but accept that a state whose majority is Muslim will want Islamic values to inform its laws and systems.	Conservative view of Islamic Law but open to reinterpretation in some areas when not directly contrary to the Qur'an or *Hadith* (sayings of the Prophet). Use the vocabulary of reform.	Want to rebuild the lost, ideal Islam of the past obscured by colonial rule as well as by Muslims who have deviated from the ideal.	Share much the same view as their partners on the right on such issues as *Shari'ah*, status of women, minorities. Tend to agree with the traditionalists that an elite should govern, although in their view this would consist of jurists and others qualified to apply the *Shari'ah*.
This can have constitutional status.	Advocate unity of religion and politics and campaign for the creation of an Islamic State but using constitutional methods such as standing for election, propaganda and education. Engage in dialogue with the West but reject Western solutions as non-Islamic. Call for recognition of Islamic autonomy and freedom to develop its own standards. The West is not the arbiter of human rights and political legitimacy. Ultimate aim a world Islamic order.	Share with the neo-traditionalists a conservative understanding of Islamic Law. Tend to support elitist forms of government rather than constitutional systems, perceiving monarchy or rule by an elite as closer to what they see in Islam's past – the first Khalifs were all members of Muhammad's inner circle. Later Khalifs were from a royal dynasty.	Radically oppose the West as Islam's enemy and denounce many Muslim regimes as infidel. Call for *jihad* (armed struggle) against them. Engage in what they call military action against their enemies, usually called terrorism by the West and by those whose regimes they oppose.
Some want an Islamic State, even a global Islamic entity. However, they want to reinterpret Islam's sources, distinguishing eternal values or principles from time-specific applications. Thus, even Qur'an need not be applied today without reinterpretation. The ideal Islam lies in the future, not the past.		The West is not the source of all wisdom but pragmatically many traditionalists are its military and commercial allies. May be compared with the Murjites.	Often compared with the Kharijites of early Islam.
Some identify with the Mu'tazalites (see Chapter Five).			

Figure 1.1 A left-right categorization of modern Islamic movements (Derived from categories used by Esposito (1991), *Islam: The Straight Path*, Chapter 6, 'Islam and Change: Issues of Authority and Interpretation', pp. 192–218. See Chapter Two for further discussion of how these different groupings understand the Islamic State. It should be noted that while the 'left' diverges from the 'right' in such areas as separation of religion from politics, the appropriateness of penalties, the status of women and free expression, they do stand on common ground in some areas. For example, both may advocate a redistributive economic system and hold that ownership is not an absolute right. Both uphold that the moral norm is a male–female relationship, believe in marital faithfulness and in divorce as a last resort. Sometimes, a thinker normally identified with the left may be aligned with the right in a specific area, and vice versa, which could be represented as a centrist tendency. See Figures 6.2, 7.2 and 10.1 for different interpretations of the Qur'an.

Discussion topics

- Can you suggest a better scheme to categorize Muslim movements? Is the 'left–right' scheme, developed in Western political discourse, appropriate for the Islamic context?

- Does such a 'left–right' categorization not imply that some Muslims (the progressives) are 'good Muslims' with whom secularists, liberals and even humanists can co-operate while others (conservatives) are so mired in the past that they are at odds with modern society and contemporary values?

- How might a scholar be both able to order or discipline his or her data and avoid the 'square peg in a round hole' problem?

Tibi (2001) broadly utilizes the categories described above but comments that 'taken as a whole, all these religio-intellectual tendencies in modern Islam ... are largely the preoccupation of the educated classes, who form only a tiny minority of the Muslims living today, albeit representing the "leaders of opinion" ' (p. 44). Similarly, Arkoun (1998b) comments that the Islam of the masses is what he calls 'Silent Islam', which, largely ignored by 'social scientists', attaches 'more importance to the religious relationship with the absolute of God than to the vehement demonstration of political movements' (p. 203).

Tibi also points out that a 'left–right' struggle is 'nowhere mentioned in Islamic sources, as classical Islam is not familiar with these European concepts' (2001: 125–6).

What is modernism?

It is difficult to pinpoint the beginning of modernity, especially as every age considers itself 'modern', even those labelled 'dark' by later generations. Some date modernism from Baruch Spinoza (1632–77), an excommunicated Jew. He taught a type of pantheism in which God and nature fuse but which had no room for either a 'personal god' or for an immortal soul. Spinoza's system of ethics was purely rationalist. Previously, within European thought, the existence of a personal and creator God, who would judge each human soul at the end of time, who authored fixed moral truths revealed through the scriptures, who controlled the Universe, was accepted as fact. Confidence in God's omnipotence was threatened by the discovery of laws of physics, which did not seem to need a supervising divine agent. After Spinoza, the work of Charles Darwin (1809–82) in the field of evolution also seemed to remove the need for God. Instead, science would unlock the mysteries of the universe.

Facts would be empirically verified, not found already 'given' in scriptures. Morality, too, might be contingent on social values, which could change. Among the philosophers of modernity, thinkers such as John Stuart Mill (1806–73) rejected the idea that belief in God was needed to 'underpin morality' (Spinner-Halev 2000: 13). Christianity, with its static view of morality and of God, hindered the liberal, modernist project that aimed to cultivate 'autonomous and progressive beings' (*ibid.*: 14). People should be free to 'try out different ideas, both in discussion and practice' and whatever does not inflict harm on others falls into the category of acceptable conduct. Mill thought that a world free of religion's promise of eternal reward would be more moral, since people would 'act on bene- volent motives not because of a promise for a heavenly reward, but because of the approval of the people we respect and admire' (*ibid.*: 15).

John Dewey (1859–1952) thought faith placed in intelligence rather than in a supervising god more beneficial for humanity (see Dewey 1934). Intelligence, he believed, exercised corporately, would enable each gen- eration to 'face and solve the problems of the day through experimental empiricism' (*ibid.*: 16). Religion would be man- not God-centred. Dewey called for 'faith in the possibilities of human experience and human relationships' that would 'create a vital sense of the solidarity of human interests and inspire action to make that a sense of reality' (Dewey, cited in Rockefeller 1991: 449). This is very different from the premodern notion that problems were to be solved by applying rules and morals lifted from the text of revealed scriptures, which by definition requires no experi- mentation. He did not think that certainty was possible in a 'dynamic and changing world', which perhaps anticipates postmodernity (Spinner-Halev 2000: 17). Generally, modernity believed that 'truth' or 'knowledge' could be 'discovered', at least provisionally, until and unless the consensus of experts changed. Reality could be described; it existed behind and inde- pendently of its representations or descriptions.

Morality was taken to be the majority-held view, worked out by rational people. Even though this consensus might change, the modern worldview believed that mega-theories, or meta-narratives, could explain the world – evolution, Marxism, capitalism all offered universal views that deciphered history, economics and social structures. Such meta-narratives have been called 'totalizing explanations' – of history, of science, of culture and of course, of religion, which they tend to see as a relic of human infancy rather than as a mark of human maturity. An overriding meta- or master narrative was that science and technological advance guaranteed progress. Thus, the future holds out yet unrealized and unknown potential. This contrasts with the theological view that the Bible already contains the sum of all possible knowledge. For many, 'Western civilization and culture' carries an 'absolute truth and value', and represents the 'Universal model of progress and development' (Saif 1995: 16). Everything else, other models, are devalued or ignored.

Such an understanding of knowledge lent itself to the possibility of the encyclopedia, of the compendium of all wisdom in a given area. Modernity recognized expertise and granted 'authorities', in medicine, science, education, the arts, literature, the right to determine standards and norms. Martin Irvine's useful list of the characteristics of modernity includes 'Art as unique object and finished work authenticated by artist and validated by agreed standards' and 'imposed consensus that high or official culture is normative and authoritative' (1998: 4). He also includes 'mass culture, mass consumption, mass marketing' and 'faith and personal investment in big politics – Nation, State, Party' as well as a 'sense of unified, centred self, "individualism", unified identity'. Religious belief, for modernity, is to be tolerated as a matter of private choice as long as it does not try to occupy the public square.

Saif claims that 'Western style secularization is an inevitable condition of modernization', and that it was not until 'Europe had replaced the theocratic state by the secular one' that 'the conditions for modernity were created' (1995: 16). 'Secularism', says Ben-Yunusa, 'attempted to construct a platform for human development based on a kind of moral independence from religious doctrines and worship' (1995: 82). The banishment of God from the public arena, the assumption that the unaided human intellect can construct 'truth', that revelation is redundant, all conflict with classical Islam. Thus:

> From the Islamic point of view ... separating out the secular [from the rest of Islam] is tantamount to accepting the message in part, which is in effect rejecting the whole. The secular cannot have a separate existence in an essentially Islamic civilization. Therefore, secularism in its Western connotation and current technical usage may be referred to in Islamic context as de-Islamization. (*ibid.*: 84)

In this view, Muslims who adopt a secular ideology are mere puppets of the West and their version of Islam, as noted above, is an illegitimate, Westernized version. 'In secularism', says Khurshid Ahmad, 'divine guidance becomes irrelevant and man's roots in the divine scheme of creation and his destiny in the life beyond physical existence is denied' (1983: 218). However, quite a few Muslim modernists embrace secularism, which as Soroush (2000) points out, does not have to be accompanied by the profanation of society:

> ... secularism has been understood as a deliberate effort to exclude religion from society. But the truth is that secular government is not opposed to religion; they accept it but not as a basis for their legitimacy or as a foundation for their actions. (pp. 56–7. Mernissi 1994 agrees, p. 65)

Other Muslims for whom secularism and Islam are compatible will be cited later in this book; like Ahmed Khan, they tend to see Islam as *din*, religion.

Discussion topics

- From what you know so far of Muslims' reaction to modernity, list the main points of disagreement between 'modernity' and 'Islam'.

- Many Muslims perceive 'modernity' as a Western, anti-religious project. However, in the USA, for example, the vast majority of people believe in God and that there is a connection between morals and theistic belief. This suggests that 'modernity' does not inevitably result in the demise of religion. Why, then, do many Muslims think that the ideals of modernity clash with those of Islam?

- When some Muslims look at the West, what do they dislike?

- When some Westerners look at the Muslim world, what do they see that they dislike?

- Why do you think some of the pioneers of modernity believed that religion would become redundant, at least religion that involved belief in God, even though this has not happened?

- How would you critique Dewey's prediction that a religion of humanity will evolve, in which we all stand in solidarity and 'act to make that sense a reality'? Over time, says Spinner-Halev, 'liberals thought that people would lose their attachment to revealed religion and would embrace a religion that centered around humanity, not God' (2000: 17).

- Some liberal or modernist thinkers disapprove of religion. They want to nurture citizens who make their own choices in life and see religions as denying autonomy, since they dictate what you should believe and how you should behave. Does this represent an irreconcilable conflict between modernist/liberal and religious values?

Postmodernity and Islam

Spinoza, who cut our strings, who allowed God to retire from the post of divine marionettist and believed that revelation was an event not above human history but inside it ... (Rushdie 2001: 17)

Clay, of which God, who didn't exist, made man, who did. Such was the paradox of human life: its creator was fictional, but life itself was a fact ... (Rushdie 2001: 95)

In this text, 'modernism'/'modernity' and 'postmodernism'/'postmodernity' are conflated, following Sardar's argument, which is discussed below. However, the term 'postmodern' is commonly used to describe a worldview that subverts, resists or even opposes the assumptions of modernism (see Irvine: 1). Yet postmodernity is also described as an extension of modernity, modernity in a concentrated form. Irvine (1998) lists his characteristics of modernity opposite those of postmodernity in order to emphasize contrast and discontinuity between the two. For example:

Modernity	Postmodernity
Master narrative and meta-narratives of history and national identity; myths of cultural and ethnic origin.	Suspicion of and rejection of master narratives; local histories, ironic deconstruction of master narratives; counter-myths of origin.
Faith in 'Grand Theory' (totalizing explanations in history and culture) to represent knowledge and explain everything.	Rejection of totalizing theory; pursuit of localizing and contingent theories.
Faith in the 'real' beyond media and representations; authenticity of 'originals'.	Hyper-reality, image saturation, simulacra more powerful than the 'real'; image and texts with no prior original.
The book as sufficient bearer of the word; library as the system for printed knowledge.	Hypermedia as transcendence of physical limits of print media, the Web or Net as information system.

Source: Martine Irvine (1998) 'The Po-Mo Page' on Georgetown University website, *http://www.georgetown.edu/irvinemj/technoculture/pomo.html*

Discussion topic

●   Compile a list of what you think may be points of conflict between the characteristics of postmodernity and the convictions of many Muslims. How does this debate differ from that between modernity and Islam, as perceived by some Muslims?

Many writers on postmodernity stress that while modernity was supremely confident about national identity and cultural origins and valued sameness, postmodernity rejoices in hybridity, eclecticism and pluralism. In other words, for modernity there was a single story that all English or all Germans told about their cultural roots. For postmodernity, there is no single, shared narrative. Salman Rushdie, whose novels are usually classed as postmodern, asking 'how does newness enter the world?' replies, '*Mélange*, hotchpotch, a bit of this and a bit of that is *how newness enters the world*' (1991: 394, his italics). His book, *The Satanic Verses* (1988) celebrated:

> hybridity, impurity, intermingling, the transformation that comes from new and unexpected combinations of human beings, cultures, ideas, politics, movies, songs. (1991: 394)

Rushdie asks:

How does newness enter the world? How is it born?

Of what fusions, translations, conjoinings is it made?

How does it survive, extreme and dangerous as it is? What compromises, what deals, what betrayals of its secret nature must it make to stave off the wrecking crew, the exterminating angel, guillotine? (1988: 8)

'Postmodernism', say Best and Kellner, 'is fundamentally the eclectic mixture of any tradition with that of the immediate past; it is both the continuation of Modernism and its transcendence' (1991: 11). Rejection of normative standards and of authoritative knowledge would seem to open up endless possibilities, lifestyles and life-choices, since people are free to name reality as they see it. What were previously accepted as how things are or as what really happened are rejected as versions created by elites according to their point of view. In other words, cultural or ideological interests shaped the writing of history or the determination of acceptable conduct. Mernissi argues that Islamic orthodoxy was fashioned by elite men, for elite men and at women's cost. 'Postmodernism, as the label suggests', says Sardar, 'is *post*-modernity: it transcends modernity, which in turn surpasses tradition. Thus the first principle of postmodernism is that all that is valid in modernity is totally invalid and obsolete' (1998: 8).

Discussion topic

- Discuss the relationship between 'modernity' and 'postmodernity' and the issue of continuity and discontinuity.

Postmodern epistemology owes much to the work of Michel Foucault (1926–84), in such books as *Madness and Civilization* (1961), *The Archaeology of Knowledge* (1972) and *Discipline and Punishment* (1979). According to Foucault, those who occupied the centres of power created knowledge, in each area of discipline. All knowledge is really discourse; there is no objective reality behind this discourse, only what people construed for their own purposes of power and control. Discourses function, said Foucault, to impose discipline on the general population, who were told who they were in terms of their origins and what type of conduct was acceptable. Thus:

All the authorities exercising individual control function according to a double mode (mad/sane, dangerous/harmless, normal/abnormal) and that of coercive assignment, of differential distribution: how he is to be recognized; how surveillance is to be exercised over them (1979: 199).

Of any text that claims authority we need to ask, 'who has written this, from what point of view, who were they writing for, what voices have been silenced?' Minority voices, female voices, younger voices, for example, may be absent from the text.

Postmodernism and Marxist analysis

Following the collapse of the Eastern bloc, Marxist analysis is usually depicted as past its sell-by date. In Kureishi's 1995 novel, the Marxist lecturer, Dr Brownlow, whose wife Deedee Osgood is a postmodern thinker, develops more and more of a stammer as each former Communist state falls. As the states inspired by Marx adopt capitalist economies, his distress increases. However, it can be argued that aspects of Marxist philosophy live on in postmodern thought: Marxism and postmodernity both argue that history is written by an elite, that culture is created by the powerful and that the voices of the majority of ordinary people are silenced by the privileged few.

Another postmodern concept is that meaning does not already exist, as an 'object', within the text, waiting to be extracted but is created by the reader. Meaning is as much a product of the reader's mind as of the text's author. It derives from what readers bring to the text and may bear little or no relationship with what the author intended to say, or hoped people would take away from the text. Esack (see Chapter Four) echoes this argument.

Discussion topics

This text has noted the conviction of many Muslims that Islam represents a total, revealed, immutable system governing every aspect of human life. However, according to Foucault, that 'system' (in as much as it exists) is the invention of particular interests, perhaps of powerful, male interests. Relate this to your discussion of the two contrasting tendencies in Religious Studies.

- Could any scholar influenced by Foucault's understanding of history hope to elicit Muslim approval for their writing on Islam?

- Is W. C. Smith's project of listening to Muslim voices undermined by Foucault's critique? Whose voices should we listen to? If voices offer different views of Islam, do we reflect this in our account and therefore alienate those Muslims for whom only one version is correct? Is the claim that there is a single, true version of Islam at all defensible?

Muslim responses: Akbar Ahmed (1992) and Ziauddin Sardar (1998)

Modernity's confidence in human ability to achieve the good life, unaided by a divine reality, offends many Muslims. Postmodernity's rejection of the meta-narrative, for its part, seems to pull the rug from under the claim that Islam is just that, a master signifier, a universally valid code for the correct ordering of human life, infallible and in need of no revision. Interestingly, among Muslims who have written in this field, two contrasting responses emerge, represented by Ahmed (1992) and Sardar (1998). The former is positive, the latter negative vis-à-vis postmodernism. Moghissi (1999) also favours the latter response (see Chapter Six).

Akbar Ahmed's Postmodernism and Islam: Predicament and Promise *(1992)*

Ahmed, a graduate of Punjab, London, Cambridge and Birmingham Universities, and an anthropologist (his PhD in anthropology is from London, awarded in 1978), was the first Pakistani to serve on the Council of the Royal Anthropological Institute. Ahmed has held visiting professorships at several leading North American schools (Harvard and Princeton) and taught at the Quaid-i-Azam University, Pakistan. Between 1966 and 2000, when he resigned, he was also a member of the Pakistani Civil Service, serving as Political Agent in the North West Frontier Province (1978–80) in 'some of the most remote corners' of the country (1992: 123) and as Commissioner of three districts in Baluchistan (1982–88). He was also founder Director of the National Centre for Rural Development, Islamabad. In 1988 he became Allama Iqbal Fellow at Selwyn College, Cambridge where in 1993 he was appointed the first Muslim Fellow. In 1999–2000 he was Pakistani High Commissioner to the UK but was recalled to Islamabad after only eight months. Ahmed believes this was because he had 'talked too much of [the] compassionate and tolerant Islam ideology of the democratic and forward-looking founder of Pakistan, Muhammad Ali Jinnah' (Yaqub 2001). He had just completed his 'Jinnah Project' – a film, a documentary and a novel. Currently Ibn Khaldun Professor of Islamic Studies in the School of International Relations, American University, Washington DC, Ahmed has tried, in his writing and broadcasting, to effect communication between the Western and the Muslim worlds. He himself moves comfortably within both. He writes that English translations of Islamic classics helped him to 'discover the riches' of his 'own Islamic cultural legacy' and that this exposure to the West has enabled him to 'appreciate critically the beneficial impact of the West' (1992: 123). Accused of toadying to the West and of being a Zionist conspirator, he says that 'dialogue, harmony, communication and debate' are key issues in the engagement between Islam and the West (Hawkey 1995: 16; and see Ahmed 2004).

He challenges Westerners to confront their stereotypical images of Muslims so that a genuine discourse can be created between Western and

Muslim ideas on such vital matters as population control, environmental health, famine, housing and refugees (see Ahmed 1988: 216). He says that when he writes about Islam he cannot remain a 'neutral spectator or observer', since he is also a 'participant, an actor in the drama' (*ibid.*: 2). When he sees 'Kill a Muslim for Christmas' written in a London underground station, he cannot but conclude that not only have non-Muslims failed to understand Muslims but that Muslims have failed to explain themselves (*ibid.*: 1).

Ahmed's books ask what are the keys to understanding 'Muslim societies – those which will allow us to make sense of how Muslims behave, what motivates them, what are their concepts of right and wrong?' He continues, 'How are we to explain the turbulence in contemporary Muslim society which has helped to create the negative images of Islam' prevalent in the West? (*ibid.*: 2). Ahmed says that Islam will not 'come to terms with itself' unless it can also 'come to terms with' the 'twentieth century' (*ibid.*: 8). Neither the modern nor the postmodern worlds will 'go away'; his own daughter 'will live in the postmodern world which is just beginning to shape our lives'. Is it possible, he asks, for a Muslim to find within Islam the resources he or she will need to live as a 'good, caring and decent human being in the postmodern world?' (1992: x).

In his 1988 book and in his 1992 television series (and book, 1993), Ahmed begins by establishing Islamic ideals or models (following Max Weber), then shows how Muslims have tried, in various circumstances and at different times, to live up to these ideals. Sometimes Muslims have succeeded; sometimes they have failed to approximate these: 'In the face of powerful rival forces or weak leadership Muslims have slipped from the ideal. Tension, change and challenge are created as people living in an imperfect world strive for it' (1988: 3). Throughout his writing, Ahmed is aware of the diversity of Muslim life; 'In certain ways', he writes, 'Muslims are the same everywhere, and yet their societies are different everywhere' (1988: 4), although he rejects Edward Mortimer's conclusion that there is 'not one Islam but many Islams'. In contrast, al-Azmeh appears to endorse the idea that there are many Islams, stressing its 'multi-vocality' (1993: 14). While Ahmed's 1988 and 1993 books do discuss relations between Islam and the West and Islam's response to modernity, this is the main focus of his 1992 book, which he offered as 'an attempt to understand our times' (p. vii). This text engages with the phenomenon of 'postmodernity' and asks how Islam will respond to this new 'challenge', realizing from the outset that any attempt to borrow a concept 'from one culture to apply to another' is deeply problematic (1992: 6).

Akbar on the issue of definition

Is postmodernity an 'historical period', he asks, or 'an up-to-date -style'? Is it a 'literary conceit, a philosophical concept or an architectural notion'? (1992: 6) While he goes on to include all these in his list of 'characteristics', he clearly finds the task of definition elusive and suggests that 'ambiguity' lies at the centre of the postmodern phenomenon (p. 10).

Discussion topic

- From your reading on the meaning of postmodernism/post-modernity, how would you answer the question 'is it an historical period or an up-to-date -style?' If the former, when did modernity end and postmodernity begin? Can you identify when the term 'postmodernity' was first used? (see Ahmed 1992: 8; Sardar 1998: 15–16).

Eight features of postmodernism

Akbar describes eight characteristics, or features, of 'postmodernism', in order to bring them into discourse with Muslim thought. Here is a summary of his eight 'descriptions':

1) Postmodernity assumes a 'questioning, or a loss of faith in, the project of modernity'. It embraces pluralism, rejects previously accepted orthodoxies, 'a view of the world as a universal totality' and the possibility of 'final solutions and complete answers' (1992: 10). In this view, Islam, like any other ideology, is but one option available among many alternatives.

2) There is an intricate connection between postmodernity and the role of the media as the 'central dynamic' of the present age (p. 11). The media shapes how we see the world, how we perceive events; 'pictures on television can be as devastating to a country as a fleet of gunships blockading it or a shower of missiles falling on it' (p. 12).

3) 'Ethno-religious revivalism or fundamentalism' feeds on postmodernity, says Ahmed, since 'Where nothing is sacred, every belief becomes revisable' thus 'fundamentalism is an attempt to resolve how to live in a world of radical doubt' (p. 13).

4) Postmodernity, 'however apocalyptic the claims', has not cut its umbilical cord with the past (p. 16).

5) The metropolis is central to postmodernity. Many cities experience chaos and anarchy: 'overcrowding, lack of civic amenities, collapse of law and order, endemic corruption and ethnic and sectarian violence create a deep sense of despair' (p. 22).

6) The postmodern project is driven by those who have access to the media and to means of communication, usually 'the architects, dramatists, social scientists, writers' – an educated elite. However, if it is the middle classes who lead, it is the 'masses which help to define' postmodernism 'through the process of democratization' (p. 23).

7) Postmodernism celebrates and encourages hybridity, the mixing and mingling of styles and ideas.

8) While postmodernity sees itself as 'accessible', its language is often paradoxical and enigmatic.

On the one hand, Ahmed admits outright that the potential for conflict between Islam and postmodernity is vast; Muslims, he says, 'recognise the threat it poses them with its cynicism and irony' (p. 6). On the other hand, Ahmed's thesis is that postmodernism's openness to 'exploration', its tolerance of diversity and its invitation for us to 'know and understand one another', may actually connect positively with Islam (see pp. x, 6, 27). What Ahmed sets out to do in the main body of his book is to analyse those areas where conflict is likely or already evident while also suggesting strategies for a rapprochement between Islam and the postmodern project. Below, two of these areas are described. First, the role of the media; second, the Muslim world's struggle for self-determination, which the West often perceives as a threat to its own stability, values and ideals.

'The evil demon: the media as master'

Ahmed argues that the media today shapes and informs our worldview not neutrally or objectively but by 'subverting reality', often by oversimplifying issues, or by 'creating a caricature of the image that is described' (p. 224). Sometimes, the media creates the news it reports. Sound bites replace in-depth analysis. News is presented in digestible units. Popular 'heroes' get their images and messages broadcast worldwide yet, says Ahmed, few if any of these heroes have any 'moral or spiritual substance in their lives' (p. 227). Nor do any Muslims feature 'on this list' (p. 228). The media promotes rampant individualism and materialism, 'I want it all and I want it now' (p. 245), at the expense of family and of community.

Sex has been 'elevated into the single most important human activity – the tabloids work their stories around boobs, bums and bonking' (p. 246). When Islam does get covered, the images shown tend to perpetuate age-old stereotypes of Asian societies 'as irrational and volatile'. On the one hand, the media offers a dazzling variety of lifestyles, fashion, images and art yet on the other hand it has a pronounced Western bias. Thus, 'the life of one white person – whether a murderer or a drug addict – legally held in an Asian prison is news. A thousand Asian deaths in Bangladesh or China is no news' (p. 229). The Muslim response has tended to be one of retreat 'back into the vastness of their deserts and mountains' (p. 257). Muslims, confronted with modernity, tried to 'revert to the past as if the present did not exist'. However, this is no longer an option, since technology, the satellite dish or the laser-guided missile can penetrate the remotest retreat or refuge (p. 258). Rather than retreating from the demon, Muslims must face it (p. 260). This includes Muslims participating in the media, especially those who stress Islam's central commitment to *adl*, *ahsan*, *'ilm* and *sabr* (justice/balance, compassion, knowledge and patience), which tells us a lot about Ahmed's version of Islam (see pp. 48

and 264). Ahmed wants Muslims to contribute to 'global civilization', not to hide from it.

'Confrontation and clash'

Ahmed traces the history of antipathy between Islam and the West and shows how this legacy continues to inform an attitude of suspicion and hostility on both sides. The West views the Muslim world as volatile, totalitarian, archaic; Islam sees the West as materialistic, ungodly, decadent, profligate, consumed with sexual desire and self-gratification. The West, says Ahmed, has much to offer ('democracy, human rights, literacy', p. 98) but lacks a 'heart' at its centre: 'The problem with this civilization is the hole where the heart should be, the vacuum inside' (p. 109). Nor does the dominant, almost global, Western civilization have all the answers for all the problems of the world:

> Indeed, in its arsenal of nuclear weapons, its greedy destruction of the environment, its insatiable devouring of the world's resources, its philosophy of consumerism at all costs, it is set to terminate life on earth in the near future unless it can change its ways fundamentally. (p. 109)

Ahmed does not assert that Islamic thought holds the solutions either but he does call for a genuine dialogue between non-Muslims and Muslims to solve those problems that affect us all. Postmodernism's rejection of global narratives, he says, invites such a dialogue since no one can claim that their way of construing reality or of seeing the world is the only way. Islam's 'way' may be one of many on the table, yet it has as much right to be on the table as does any other. Recognition that there are different ways of seeing the world invites their exploration. It also demands the toleration of diversity and of difference.

What must be emphasized is postmodernity's 'positive sides', its tolerance and diversity that offer us 'the possibility of bringing diverse people and cultures closer together than ever before' (p. 28). Muslims will remain alienated by postmodernity's cynicism and materialism and rejection of faith but ought to find ways of working with, instead of confronting, the West (pp. 264–5). For its part, the West needs to relinquish its old imperialistic assumptions that its ways are still the best, and extend its 'notions of justice, equality, freedom and liberty ... to include all humanity' (p. 265). This will involve the West ceasing to be duplicitous: on the one hand, it advocates human rights and democracy, on the other it props up dictators in Muslim countries out of its own economic greed:

> There is a need to push unwilling rulers, who subsist on Western arms and aid, towards conceding democracy and a fairer distribution of wealth, of ensuring the rights and dignity of women and children, the less privileged and those in the minority. These problems are interwoven, binding Muslims and non-Muslims together. There can be no just and viable world order – let alone a New World Order – if these wrongs are not addressed. (p. 265)

Ziauddin Sardar (1998) Postmodernism and the Other: The New Imperialism of Western Culture

See also Sardar's earlier writing on postmodernity, 'The Postmodern Age', pp. 54–88 in Sardar *et al.* 1991, and 'Post-modern Blues', pp. 1–7 in Sardar and Davies 1990. Sardar's post-9/11 writing includes *Why Do People Hate America?* (2003, with Davies) in which he argues that people hate the USA not because of who Americans are but because of what they do, which is to intervene in other countries solely for their own benefit. The USA is perceived to apply one standard at home and another overseas. The USA's alliance with the WTO and IMF, and its rejection of the Kyoto Treaty (on environmental protection), harms instead of helps the economy of the developing world. Inayatullah and Boxwell (2003) describe Sardar's project as both to 'contemporarise Islam as a living, dynamic, thriving civilization' and to 'critique the West through the "discriminatory eye of a Muslim"' (p. 3). Speaking on Roger Hardy's BBC programme, *Waiting for the Dawn: Muslims in the Modern World* (2002), Sardar described the challenge of engaging with modernity while retaining Muslim values as the 'mega-task' that Muslims faced. Muslims 'need to appreciate the contemporary world, use contemporary technologies, establish centres of science and learning, critique modernity and see how Muslim societies can be modern yet transform modernity from within', he said.

Like Ahmed, Sardar was born in Pakistan (1951) but has made the West his home. Also like Ahmed, he has added journalism and broadcasting to impressive academic credentials. He has been a reporter for London Weekend Television and in 1994 hosted *Islamic Conversations* for BBC2, a six-part television series that provided insight into the views of influential Muslim thinkers on violence and holy war, democracy, the rights of women, multiculturalism, Christianity, and the Islamic state and religious authority. He moved to London with his family when a child. He took a degree in physics and information science at London's City University (see his autobiographical 2004 book). He taught at universities in the USA, where he established the Center for Future Studies at the East-West University, Chicago, as well as within the Muslim world, where he worked at the Hajj Research Centre at King Abdul Aziz University, Jeddah, developing a simulation model for the performance of the pilgrimage and evaluating the environmental impact of the *hajj*. He is currently Visiting Professor of Post-Colonial Studies at London's City University. With his clean-shaven face and long hair, Sardar breaks the visual mould of the 'long-bearded-arch-backed' Muslim scholar (Inayatullah and Boxwell 2003: 1). There is overlap between Ahmed and Sardar on postmodernity but Sardar does not share Ahmed's positive assessment of the postmodern project as promising 'hope, understanding and toleration' (Ahmed 1992: x). However, compare Sardar's definition of postmodernity (1998: 15–40) with Ahmed's, summarized above. Like Ahmed, he identifies hybridity, pluralism, eclecticism, the role of the media and rejection of meta-narratives as essential characteristics. More so than Ahmed, Sardar stresses continuity between the modern and the postmodern, seeing the latter as in reality an extension of the first:

> Postmodernism continues the exponential expansion of colonialism and modernity. It is a worldview based on that pathological condition of the West, which has always defined reality and truth as its reality and truth, but now that this position can not be sustained it seeks to maintain the status quo and continue unchecked in its trajectory of consumption of the Other by undermining all criteria of reality and truth. (p. 40; note Ahmed's fourth 'description')

Sardar sees postmodernism's elevation of the 'individual' as a peculiarly Western preoccupation, since 'an autonomous, isolated individual does not exist in non-western cultures' (p. 70). Sardar does not agree that Others, Muslims included, will get a hearing at the postmodern table. Superficially and rhetorically, postmodernism embraces cultural pluralism and even what has been called 'cultural relativism'; that is, that as values are created by those who hold them, no single set can claim universal validity, so practices thought moral in one culture may be thought immoral in others (see p. 67; see also Moghissi 1999: 53). Postmodernism also borrows ideas and images from across the world. However, it then appropriates these for its own eclectic purposes, divorcing them from their contexts, histories and belief systems in order to create the type of hotchpotch of which Rushdie speaks. While in 'Other cultures history and tradition are the prime source of meaning and identity' (p. 130), postmodernism denies that this history is anything other than an imaginative construct:

> Postmodernism is concerned solely with the present, the immediate and, in rejecting Enlightenment metanarratives, abandons all sense of historical continuity and memory. (p. 130; see also p. 38)

Since all histories are 'constructs', and 'all interpretation is misrepresentation, there is no hope of rescuing the truth of non-western culture from the constructed images of the west' (p. 38). Sardar also argues that the postmodern project secularizes all narratives, 'it neutralizes the identity of the Other by subsuming all non-Western identities and histories in the grand western narrative of secularism' (p. 131). Sardar says that while the Other fascinates the postmodern project, it really views Others as being, 'out there' for its own 'consumption'. It turns Others into commodities (p. 126). For example, the exotic Eastern woman is out there to 'fulfil the sexual desires of the West' (p. 178). In effect, all this perpetuates Western imperialism. For its own purposes of exploitation and control, the West still defines Others (see p. 198). Sardar is arguing that the West's appropriation of Others' cultural ideas and forms is shallow and self-serving. It uses these as trophies to decorate its own 'stage'. Perhaps Madonna's use of Indian rhythm and words (*shanti, shanti*) in her album *Ray of Light* (1998), which has been described as 'ethno-techno-mysticism', illustrates this. The 'material girl' has also delved into Jewish mysticism (Kabbalah). Is this shallow and self-serving, or a genuine fusion and synthesis of different artistic and cultural traditions? In 'the land of the melting pot', says Sardar, 'postmodern ideology through its representation of the Other ... enables America to claim itself as the literal embodiment of everywhere', so that it 'becomes the only place' that actually gets 'represented' (p. 114).

Discussion topic: Is postmodernism a shibboleth?

- Does al-Azmeh's definition of postmodernism as a shibboleth totally remove it from discourse as a useful concept or analytical tool? Do you agree with this definition or would you want to rescue 'postmodernity' from the analytical trashcan? In your view, does Sardar also view 'postmodernity' as a shibboleth (an outworn or empty catchword)?

Liberalism alive at the core

Postmodernity, says Sardar, may reject meta-narratives yet liberalism is alive and well at its core. This is why, when it comes to human rights and 'democracy', it overlooks its own arch principle (p. 67). Instead of taking non-Western models of government or of 'rights' seriously, it arrogantly occupies the moral high ground and dictates to the whole world on 'how to be human' (p. 67; see pp. 60–1 and 65–6 on notions of democracy in non-Western cultures). However, the real aim is to promote 'the pathological expansion of the modern and postmodern liberalism and what accompanies it: free trade and market capitalism' (p. 75). As long as Others accept their treatment as passive objects waiting for the West's 'overwriting in order to become human' (p. 278), the West will continue to dominate the non-Western world at the expense of Other traditions, values and self-identities.

Many, including Muslims, will want to resist postmodernism's 'globalising and secularising tendencies' that turn 'all cultures into ahistorical, liberal, free markets' (p. 279). However, merely to elevate old 'traditions' over everything else ignores the fact that change and progress are inevitable (p. 280). Sardar is fully aware that what gets elevated, perhaps an 'ossified traditionalism', may empower some at the expense of others. What Sardar wants is for non-Westerners to assert 'viable alternatives to the West' by finding resources, sometimes for change, within their own cultures and traditions (p. 283). In Islam, this involves 'the dynamic principle of *ijtihad* – sustained and reasoned struggle for innovation and adjusting to change – neglected for centuries'. Thus:

A strategy for desirable futures for Islamic cultures would articulate methods for the rediscovery of this principle – a rediscovery which would lead to the reformulation of Islamic tradition into contemporary configurations. (p. 281)

Sardar explored this progressive view of Islam at length in one of his earlier books, *The Future of Muslim Civilization* (1979), a very influential text. 'Islam' says Sardar, 'is perforce a future-oriented world-view' (1985: ix).

For specific references to Islam in *Postmodernism and the Other*, see especially pp. 83–4, 235–6 and 258–9 on Islam as a 'threat to the West', pp. 61 and 72–3 for individualism in Islam, pp. 70 and 72–3 for Islam and human rights, pp. 121–2 for a description of how Islamic history has been represented on *a History of the World* CD-Rom and pp. 48 and 25–7 on the Gulf War.

Discussion topic

An absolutely blank vision?

- Compare and contrast Ahmed and Sardar on postmodernity. Is Ahmed too optimistic, Sadar too pessimistic? Identify both convergence and divergence in their views.

'In its most oppressive and totalitarian phase as postmodernism, western civilization wants to drown the globe in the absolute blankness of its vision. Postmodernism continues the exponential expansion of colonialism and modernity. It is a worldview based on that pathological condition of the West, which has always defined reality and truth as its reality and truth, but now that this position can not be sustained it seeks to maintain the status quo and continue unchecked in its trajectory of consumption of the Other by undermining all criteria of reality and truth' (Sardar 1998: 40).

- This clashes with the view of proponents of postmodernism, who suggest that, by drawing on multiple insights, it can offer exciting new possibilities for construing 'meaning'. Is the postmodern vision as 'blank' as Sardar, or as full of promise as Ahmed, suggests?

Additional Muslim voices on modernity: see Ramadan (2001) and *Rethinking Islam and Modernity* (2001), edited by El-Affendi.

2 Muslims and Democracy

There are two types of governments [in the Muslim world]: those that reject democracy as contrary to their identity, and those that embrace it. However, all of them use the automobile and the telephone and waste public funds on frivolous items that have no relation to the country's vital needs, like the arms that make us goggle-eyed when we hear the price and the obsolescent surveillance networks they buy to keep an eye on us.
(Mernissi 1994: 55)

Democracy – whose version?

Early modernists Rifa'a al-Tahtawi (1801–73), 'Abduh and Chiragh 'Ali (1844–95) pioneered the argument that democracy and Islam are compatible (see Bibliography). Many on the left of the spectrum used in this book contend that Islam's foundation documents do not provide a prescriptive blueprint for governing Muslim society. Those on the right advocate the opposite, believing that all that is needed to order social and political life can be derived from Islam's source documents, or by replicating Islam's past systems and practices. Within debate about what form an authentically Islamic government should take, democracy is a contested notion. Some on the right reject democracy, arguing that since divine law, not people, govern Islamic society, it should be the religious knowledge and authority of the interpreters of the law, however many or few in number, that makes their judgment acceptable, not how or by whom they are appointed (Sivan 1985: 74). Sayyid Qutb believed that Islamic legitimacy would automatically follow from the implementation of *Shari'ah* (see below). Muslims could learn nothing from Western democracy. In his view, the real rulers of the West are elites, not those who vote; 'Who will dare to claim', he challenged, 'that they [the poor] are the source of authority in the nation, based on democratic election?' (cited in Tamadonfar 1989: 42). Similarly, the *hizb-ut-tahrir*, for whom 'Abduh is a 'writer of intellectual defilement' (Kassem 2003: p 4), denounce Western democracy as a shibboleth; the 'claims of democracy have no actual reality, the claim that people rule themselves by themselves is a major fallacy' (1996: 17).

Mernissi (1994) argues that many Muslims reject democracy because they see it as 'foreign'. She argues, though, that it is 'not simply the foreign origin of democracy that makes it the centre of controversy and conflict on the Muslim political chessboard'. 'Apparently', she continues, 'unlike the automobile and the telephone, democracy is not perceived by all Muslims as being in their interest' (1994: 52). Others argue that while Western-style democracy is incompatible with Islam, a democratic system predicated on Islamic principles is not. The issue is not whether Muslims should or should not support democracy but which version merits their support. Hamdi (1996) criticizes Western scholars for operating with a somewhat imperialistic notion of democracy, failing to value other models or systems. He suggests that 'Western intellectuals should take more seriously than they do the possibility that there are limitations to their brand of democracy'. 'Money, he says, is so important in US politics that it may in fact have more influence than the people' (pp. 81–2).

He also contends that some Muslim politicians use democratic language as a ploy to attract Western support. Al-Ghannouchi, leader of the Tunisian Islamic movement, *al-Nahda*, has publicly committed himself to the principle of 'alternation of power through the ballot box', but this has not prevented critics from expressing suspicion that his espousal of democracy is merely a strategy, a means to gain power, and one that attracts Western sympathy (Wright 1996: 74). Al-Ghannouchi considers secularism 'incompatible with Islamic values' but says that 'Muslims require "modernity" no less than anyone else'. 'Genuine modernity', he says, 'entails human emancipation ... a democratic system and ... the sovereignty of the people' (2000: 106). Given a choice between 'a democratic secular government' and 'a despotic system that claims to be Islamic', the former is the lesser evil for Muslims, he says (*ibid.*: 123). Hamdi (1996) responding to Wright (1996) claims that al-Ghannouchi on the one hand holds up 'a comforting mirror to the West', and on the other has 'failed to be coherent in his views on many important issues, including his stance toward the West, the way in which to change the Tunisian regime, the status of women, and democracy itself'. This 'raises a huge question about the validity and sincerity of the "liberal" views that Robin Wright extols', he says (pp. 83–4). Tamimi, for whom al-Ghannouchi is a 'Democrat within Islamism' (see Tamimi 2002) points out that while the West warms to al-Ghannouchi, he does not advocate Western-style democracy. A former colleague of al-Ghannouchi, Hamdi parted company from him on the issue of the relationship between religion and politics. Hamdi, says Tamimi, 'assumes that Islam as a religion is non-political' (2002: 209). Pipes (2002) is outspokenly critical of Western scholars who praise al-Ghannouchi, roundly condemning Esposito's *Oxford Encyclopaedia of the Modern Islamic World* (1995) which lauds al-Ghannouchi's 'masterly understanding of Western and Islamic philosophy and ... genuine concern for reconciling' Islam's basic tenets 'with modernity and progress' while making no mention of 'his murderous plans' (p. 107). Calling Esposito 'perhaps the most important academic advisor' (that is, of the US government), he criticizes him for wrongly encouraging the Clinton administration to court 'moderate Islamists' when in Pipes' view there are none (pp. 45–6). Tibi (1998) also criticizes Esposito for contending that Islamism and democracy are compatible. Islam and democracy are, he says, but 'I fail to see that his contention of the compatibility of Islamism and democracy is supported by evidence in any of the actions or pronouncements of Islamic fundamentalists' (p. 186). Tamimi comments that Muslim critics of al-Ghannouchi are uneasy with his 'overconfidence in democracy' not because they view democracy as 'incompatible with Islam, but out of their conviction that a sound system of government would have to emerge out of local, and within the specific historical, context'.

In their view, al-Ghannouchi's ideas seem to imply that 'democratic procedures and tools can be borrowed' from the West without also importing into Islam 'unwanted components of philosophy or ideology' (2002: 213). It is, they say, 'impossible to disengage procedures from their philosophical origins' (p. 214). Ruthven (2002) argues that there is a 'severe democratic deficit' in the Muslim world, compared with 'the rest of the developing world' (p. 281), while Lewis (1996) had it that 'of the 53 OIC states, only Turkey can pass Huntington's test of democracy [at least two peaceful transitions of power]' (p. 54). The OIC (= Organization of the Islamic Conference, *Munazamat Al-Mutamir Al-Islami*), an intergovernmental body, was established in August 1969. While Lybia, Sudan, Iran, Syria and Iraq have all been accused of sponsoring anti-Western terrorism, Bangladesh (see Chapter Eleven), Indonesia and Malaysia (to which Lewis does not refer) may also pass Huntington's test. Tibi (1998) comments that he 'greatly admires' the tolerant, pluralist and open-minded Islam of South East Asia and asks whether it might become a 'model for the civilization of Islam?' Unfortunately, he adds, it is still the 'Islam of the heartland', that is, of the Middle East, that dominates the world of Islam (1998: 48, 49 and 184). The Hanafi School, which Khadduri (1955) describes as 'relatively liberal' (p. 271), predominates in South Asia.

Double standards

For many on the right the nation-state is a colonial imposition on the Muslim world and the ideal is a single, global Muslim order. Sudanese Islamist leader, Hassan al-Turabi (1983), rejects the term 'Islamic state', arguing that 'The phrase "Islamic State" ... is a misnomer', since 'Islam does not stop at any frontier' (p. 242). His ultimate aim is for 'the eventual unity of the *ummah* and beyond'. 'Islam is open to humanity', he says (p. 242). The Arabic term used for a nation is problematic. *Ummah* (the Qur'an's description of Muslims; Q2: 143, 3: 110) has a religious connotation lacking in the English term 'nation'. Thus, 'Arabs coined the neo-Arabic term *qawmiyya* for secular nationalism' which fundamentalists regards as a 'heretical notion ... a kind of neo-tribalism and an affront to the achievements of Islam' (Tibi 1988: 97; *qawm* = tribe).

The nation-state can be seen as a comparatively recent innovation in Europe, resulting from the 1648 Treaty of Westphalia that marked the end of the supremacy of the Holy Roman Empire and the emergence of France as a dominant power. It recognized the sovereignty of the German states, Switzerland and the Netherlands. Lutherans, Calvinists and Roman Catholics were given equal rights. The Treaty marks the beginning of International Law. It established that all states are equal regardless of size, that nations should not intervene in the internal affairs of other nations and that diplomacy and co-operation between states, not supranational force, is the route for resolving disputes. Western double standards also attract censure, as much from the left as from the right. Tibi says that 'Westerners need to learn that it works counterproductively when they try to teach non-Westerners about democracy and human rights' (2001: 224). Mernissi asks, 'Will the West cling to the idea of universal worth while selfishly consuming Arab oil and wealth?' (1994: 168). The West, she says, must choose between two options: either, having emerged triumphant from the Gulf War of 1991 (to update, we might substitute the action in Afghanistan, post-9/11 and the more recent Gulf conflict of 2003), she might 'jump at the opportunity to push for the democratisation of the Arab world?' Or, Western states might decide to 'only use their influence to maintain the status quo and prop up the legitimacy of the regimes that called on them for help' (p. 167).

The *hizb-ut-tahrir* is suspicious of Westerners who ally themselves with moderate Muslims. They reject 'interfaith dialogue' and 'globalization' as Western strategies aimed at the ultimate destruction of true Islam. Separation of religion from life (politics) is, it says, central to the dialogue agenda. Thus, participants in dialogue, as well as Western academics who study and claim an expertise in Islam, want to impose a 'new religion' on Muslims (see 1996: 19). Several academic institutions are named as complicit in this process, including the Oxford Centre for Islamic Studies and the Centre for Middle Eastern Studies at Durham. Western support for liberal and modernist Islam is part of a divide and rule strategy. Mailer (2003) argues that the USA is wrong to think that it can impose democracy in places such as Iraq unless and until the foundations of civil society have developed. Tibi comments that most Middle East states are 'only nominally nation states' lacking 'basic institutions required for establishing a democratically designed political community'. Their 'neo-patriarchal political cultures' create 'obstacles to democratization', he says (1998: 192). Trying to impose democracy (and human rights) is no solution. Cultures, he says, must learn to speak the language of democracy '*in their own tongues*' (p. 180, his italics).

Four models

Some on the right advocate what can be characterized as nomocracy (see Khadduri 1955: 17). Others call this rule by an elite (Tamadonfar 1989: 104). Others argue for constitutional, elected government and are happy with the term 'Islamic democracy'. Mawdudi represents this position but reference is also made to the *hizb-ut-tahrir* model constitution and to other proposed models. The elitist position is represented by the Wahhabi regime in Saudi Arabia. Common to both these models is the central role of traditional *Shari'ah* and an understanding of citizenship that privileges Muslims over non-Muslims. On the left, two positions emerge. One is a democratic Islamic system that has features in common with Mawdudi's but advocates a progressive or reformed *Shari'ah* and an inclusive, or pluralist, understanding of citizenship. Taha (1987, 1998) represents this position. The second is a secular democracy, in which Islamic values inform public discussion and the legislative process but Islam has no legal privileges. Mernissi (1994), Tibi (1998, 2001), Soroush (2000) and Zakaria (1988) represent this position. Turkey is explored as a case study. In contrast to the other three models, this one rejects the claim that the Qur'an mandates unity of religion and politics. Almost all Muslims who advocate a model or system of government, whether it is a democracy, a monarchy, a religious or a secular system, draw on the Qur'an, on the life of Muhammad and on Islamic history to justify or to support their proposals. Therefore, analysis below begins with a summary of how leadership was exercised in Islam after Muhammad's death. One novel is reviewed. The four models are summarized in Figure 2.1.

Discussion topics

- Define democracy.

- Leading member of Bush's administration Defence Secretary Donald Rumsfeld has rejected out-of-hand what he terms an 'Iranian-type government with a few clerics running everything' in Iraq; Iraq is to have democracy not theocracy, he says (interview with Associated Press, 24 April 2003). Is he denying Iraqi's right to self-determination?

- In the USA, George W. Bush was confirmed as the winner of the 2000 Presidential election after intervention by the Supreme Court (largely appointed by his father) regarding the recounting of contested ballots in the State of Florida, where Bush's brother was Governor. Subsequently, at least one popular media political analyst, CNA's Bill Press, persisted in referring to Bush as the 'selected President'. How democratic is the West?

Secular Muslims	Progressives	Revivalists	Fundamentalists
Separation of religion/state. Islam can inform the values and public ethics of the state. Any global political goals would be for a stronger United Nations based on a secular humanism that 'is an attack not on God' but puts 'a brake on the state's manipulation of religion' (Mernissi 1994: 45, 65).	Islamic state. Elected executive. Liberal view of Islamic Law on gender, minorities. Alternative punishments for theft. Tolerant of pluralism – i.e. a multi-party state. Constitutional methods to promote their policies. Tend to be Western educated, though some are also trained in traditional Islamic learning.	Islamic state with elected executive but different rights for non-Muslims and for women. Traditional view of Islamic Law on gender, punishment, e.g. amputation for theft. Limited pluralism, i.e. a one-party state. Most revivalists use constitutional methods. Critical of traditional *ulama*. Bin Laden, for example, though not trained as a religious scholar, issues *fatwas* and considers the *ulama* discredited.	Non-elected executive, e.g. a king or a jurist. Traditional view of Islamic Law. Some advocate the violent overthrow of existing regimes and military engagement with Islam's enemy, the West (by which is meant the USA and Israel). Rulers in alliance with traditional *ulama*.

Figure 2.1 Muslims on 'Religion and Politics': a left–right spectrum

- Which system is best – first past the post, single transferable vote, proportional representation?
- Do low polls illegitimate Western governments?

Summary of the historical legacy

Muhammad began his prophetic ministry in Makkah (610 CE). Early opposition to his message of social justice and condemnation of idolatry resulted in persecution. In 622 (the start of the Muslim calendar) he migrated with his followers to the friendly town of Madinah (Yathrib), where he emerged as leader of all citizens, Muslim and non-Muslim, as set down in the document known as the Constitution of Madinah (see Peters 1994: 74–5; Kurdi 1984: 131–7). A series of military campaigns, initially defensive, followed. By 630 his influence and power was such that he was able to peacefully enter, and take, Makkah, cleansing its ancient shrine, the Ka'bah, for Islam by ridding it of idols. Muslims were commanded to 'obey God and obey the Prophet and those who are in power among you' and to refer any dispute 'to God and to the Prophet' (Q4: 59).

Muhammad was judge, ruler and spiritual leader. However, Muslims stress that he did consult colleagues, based on Q42: 38 which refers to Muslims as 'those who conduct their affairs by mutual consultation', *wa amruhum shura baynahum*, and on Q3: 159, *wa shawirhum fi al-am* (see Tibi 1998: 176). Osman (1986) argues that 'public participation in reaching important decisions is a basic principle of Muslim society and state' (p. 76). Later, Muhammad's *Sunnah* (acts and word) as set down in *ahadith* (plural; *hadith* singular) or traditions acquired an authority second only to the Qur'an, which it interprets and complements. Q33: 21 refers to Muhammad's 'noble (*hasan*) example (*sunnah*)'. This was collected into official canons and, with some later additions, evolved into the *Shari'ah* (literally a path leading to a watering hole), believed by many to be a comprehensive, eternally applicable and immutable legal code. Qur'anic verses that speak of the scripture as 'complete' and as 'perfect' (see Q2: 41, 2:2) support the view, already encountered in this text, that Islam is a comprehensive scheme.

The doctrine of *tawhid* (unity), described by Ahmad as 'the bedrock' and as 'the starting point of Islam' (1976: 29, 31), is central to Islam's message, requiring the balancing of the temporal and the spiritual. For Qutb, 'Islam as a complete whole ... revolved around *tawhid*' (1976: 117). After Muhammad's death (632) the majority (Sunni) decided that, as God's message was complete, prophecy had ended. No one could rule the community. However, a leader would administer its affairs by interpreting and applying God's law. Abu Bakr became the first Khalif (deputy; see Bukhari, Vol. 5, Bk 57, *hadith* 19).

Some have it that Muhammad had actually appointed Abu Bakr (see Peters 1994: 123), others that this was a decision of the community (*ummah*) which 'would not agree in error', said Muhammad. Consensus, or '*ijmah* (MM, Vol. 1, pp. 45–6) became the main tool (*usul*) for deciding any issue for which explicit guidance could not be found in the source documents. Later, *qiyas* (analogy) and *maslaha* (public interest) and *ijtihad* (mental striving by a scholar) were also used, although different law schools disputed what was and was not admissible. Only those gathered on the day of appointment were involved in the selection process. These people became known as the *ahl al-hall wa al-'aqd* (those who are eligible to bind and dissolve, that is, to make decisions). Classically, '*ijmah* may have been limited to this elite, as was *shura* (Osman 1986: 78). Abu Bakr designated his successor, 'Umar, who appointed a committee to select his, 'Uthman. The fourth, 'Ali, was appointed by those assembled on the day. See Peters (1994) on the structure of the early Muslim community after Muhammad's death (pp. 117–27). Tradition has it that the 'best' or most suitable were chosen. Three dynastic Khalifates followed, the 'Umayyads (661–750 though they continued in Spain) who usurped 'Ali's rule, the 'Abbasids (750–1258, the fall of Baghdad to the Mongols) who revolted against the 'Umayyads, and the Ottomans. The Ottomans claim to have been ceded the title by the last 'Abbasid in 1517 but did not use the designation until 1774 when they asserted spiritual authority over Muslims in Russia.

Muslim scholars have debated how many people are required for the task of nomination. Since Abu Bakr nominated 'Umar and Mu'awiyyah, the first 'Umayyad, nominated the second, Yazid, some argue that only one influential, power-breaking nominator is needed. Others argue that Abu Bakr's nomination was only binding after it had received wider support but al-Mawardi (974–1058) points out 'that the *bai'at* of 'Umar was settled by Abu Bakr irrespective of its subsequent approval or disapproval by others' (Osman 1986: 67–8). Al-Mawardi 'believes that the people have to follow the *bai'at* (oath of allegiance)' of the binders-and-looseners 'as soon as it is offered to them' (*ibid.*: 68). Some *hadith* restrict the khalifate to the Quraishi (Bukhari, Vol. 9, Bk 89, *hadith* 254, Khan 1987: 191). Ibn Khaldun (d. 1406) thought that whoever enjoyed the support (*asabiyyah*) of the community could be *khalif*, regardless of their pedigree.

For most of Sunni history, the ruling khalif nominated a *wilayat al-ahd* (heir apparent) then sought *bai'at* for him from the 'community or a selected few' (Osman 1986: 66). Mernissi (1993) shows how in practice ability to trace descent from Muhammad's family was significant, which today helps to validate the Kings of Morocco and Jordan (pp. 15–16). The Shi'a believed from the start that a member of Muhammad's family should rule. Their Imams, who were sinless, possessed special authority. Technically, Sunnis believe in equality of all and that no one has a privileged right to declare what is and is not authentically Islamic. Shi'a recognize only 'Ali, Muhammad's cousin and son-in-law, among the Khalifs, then a succession of infallible Imams. Some, the Ismailis, still follow a living Imam, the Aga Khan, although the majority of Shi'a (Iran and the majority in

Iraq) believe that their 12th Imam is now 'hidden' and guides them through the senior *ulama* (*mujtahidun*). What Khomeini established in Iran in 1979 was rule by the jurist, *Vilayat-i-faqih*.

In classical Sunni theory the *Shari'ah*, not the Khalif, governed. In practice, however, he acted to 'all intents and purposes' as Head of State (Khadduri 1955: 152) and even when the actual power of the Khalif was 'challenged or usurped by local governors', his authority remained in theory 'indivisible' (p. 142). Some Khalifs used the title deputy of God, omitting 'of God's messenger' (see Crone and Hinds 1986: 56). Emphasis on unity made any difference of opinion, whether legal, political or theological tantamount to treason. Muslims were expected to subscribe to the rulers' version. To depart from this was *fitnah* (disorder), a word associated with the notion of 'violence' (see Mernissi 1994: 89). In the Qur'an, it represents opposition to Islam. In contrast, the term *ikhtilaf* describes divergence of legal opinion between the recognized schools of law.

The classical view is that the schools agree on major points but differ on detail (*furu*'). Some *hadith* suggest that Muhammad regarded 'disagreement' as 'healthy', while others predicted that Islam would split into numerous factions. By the end of the 'Abbasid dynasty, effective power had passed to regional Sultans although they still took the oath of loyalty. Something of a contest ensued between rulers and *ulama* (the religious scholars), since it was they who claimed to possess the knowledge needed to interpret *Shari'ah*. The Sultans therefore found ways of bypassing or sidelining *Shari'ah*, arguing that in order to protect Islam, which was their paramount duty, certain regulatory measures were necessary. The convention was that laws could be enforced, provided these did not contravene divine revelation or represent an abuse of discretion (*al-ta'assuf fi masa'il al-khiyar*).

Gradually courts (*mazalim*), originally set up so that citizens could voice their complaints, started to deal with most civil and criminal matters, limiting the jurisdiction of *Shari'ah* courts to religious and personal matters (marriage, divorce, inheritance). Classically, more was written on the qualities of the Khalif than on how he was to be appointed, or indeed removed. He must be of the tribe of Quraysh (see below), sound in body, possess all faculties, be courageous, administratively competent, knowledgeable in legal matters, and just (derived from Mawardi's 'Juridical Portrait of the Sunni Caliph', Peters 1994: 142–4). Most Muslims decided that obedience to a bad ruler was better than rebellion, so that civil strife could be avoided (Murjites). Some *hadith* support rebellion (Bukhari, Vol. 9, Bk 89, Ch 4, *hadith* 258, Khan 1987: 193), some prohibit it (*hadith* 257). The Kharijites took the former view and assassinated those they thought infidel, or compromised (including 'Ali). Later, the Shi'a Assassins took the same view (see Lewis, 1966, 2001). However, they were a disruptive element and the majority view was that even a usurper could be tolerated for the sake of unity. Ibn Taymiyya (d. 1328 CE) (who popularized Hanbali) diverged from this and issued a legal opinion (*fatwa*) to the effect that it was Muslims' duty to wage *jihad* against those who innovated or deviated (see Esposito 2002: 46). An opponent of the Sufis, he has been very influential in fundamentalist circles. Only the *salaf al-salihoon*, the most pious of the early Muslims, should be imitated, which more recently Rida (1865–1935) championed. Taymiyya was imprisoned several times. Sivan (1985) says that he was unclear on exactly when rebellion became justified (p. 100).

Mawdudi's model: theo-democracy (centre right)

Mawdudi was born in India. Mainly self-educated, he became a successful journalist and Muslim activist. He was an early supporter of the Khilafate movement that aimed to restore the central (and in theory at least, supreme) political institution of the Muslim world after Revolutionary Turkey abolished the Khalifate (1924). By 1938 when Iqbal invited him to move to the Punjab, he was committed to the idea of a separate state for India's Muslims. In 1941, he established the *Jamaati-i-Islam*, with himself as *amir*. His 'Political Theory of Islam', first presented as a paper to students at Punjab University (1939), is reproduced in Ahmad (1976; 3rd edn 2001). Mawdudi (1955) developed more detailed constitutional proposals, translated by Ahmad while Mawdudi was in prison, but the 1976 article is a useful summary of his views. In his '1955 Introduction' (pp. 1–10), Ahmad refers to the contention of 'the Westernized group' that no unanimity exists in Islam on constitutional matters and that therefore it is 'utopian to talk about the establishment of an Islamic State'. To dispute this, a convention met in Karachi in January 1951 and 'formulated unanimously the "Principles of the Islamic State" in the form of 22 Articles' (p. 5). Mawdudi's model expands these 22 Articles. He describes his model of an Islamic state as a 'theo-democracy', 'because under it the Muslims have been given a limited popular sovereignty under the suzerainty of God' (1976a: 160). He considered this similar to the notion of the 'kingdom of God' but different from the Western notion of 'theocracy', which for him implied rule by a priestly class 'marked off from the rest of the population enforcing laws of its own making in the name of God' (p. 160). In his view, all the fundamentals needed for an Islamic Constitution are available in the *Shari'ah* and in the administrative precedents established by the Prophet (1955: 32).

Western politicians, he says (as did Qutb), do not really represent their so-called electorates but the people who bankroll their campaigns. 'They often make laws not in the best interest of the people ... but to further their own sectional and class interests' (*ibid.*) A fundamental weakness of the Western system is its assumption that people, unaided by the divine, could act in their own best interest. The problem, he said, is that people rarely do so. 'Man', said Mawdudi, 'is not competent to become an absolute legislator' (p. 162). Famously, he cites as an example of what is wrong with Western democracy the US Prohibition Law, passed by 'the majority vote' (p. 162). In Mawdudi's opinion, the law was based on sound scientific and rational thinking, since 'drinking is injurious to health, produces deleterious effects on the mental and intellectual faculties and leads to disorder in human society' (p. 162). However, the people were morally unprepared for prohibition, so the law was in practice a miserable failure. Mawdudi refers to Qur'anic verses denouncing the Pharoahs of Egypt as tyrants intoxicated with their own power who thought themselves equal with God (p. 148). He considers such arrogance to be a natural result of rule of 'man by man'. This 'attempt to play the role of divinity', he says, results in 'misery and conflict' (p. 155). Such is the lot of the Western world, where people are allowed to make laws in their own names. His first principle of an Islamic State would prohibit lawmaking (p. 158) since 'God alone is the real law giver' in whom the 'authority of absolute legislation' is vested (p. 159).

The remedy is Islam, whose divine law, accepted and embraced by the people, establishes clear moral limits (*hudut-Allah*) to regulate human life. Within these limits, people are free to decide their 'own affairs and frame subsidiary laws and regulations' for their conduct (p. 163). Mawdudi believed that there should be a popular element within the Islamic system, since any 'Muslim who is capable and qualified to give a sound opinion on matters of Islamic law' is entitled to do so (p. 161). On the other hand, Mawdudi does not mean that everyone can give an opinion, since those whose views are considered unsound are obviously disqualified. Nonetheless, Mawdudi believed no one individual has special authority to determine what is or is not the Islamic position (unlike in Shi'a, where the Imam fills this role), therefore *shura* must be built into the Islamic system. For Mawdudi the Khalifate was vested in the 'whole community of believers', not in a single person. The first Khalif was Adam, not Abu Bakr (p. 168). 'There is', he wrote, 'no reservation in favour of any family, class or race'. There is, though, distinction based on merit, thus 'the ... criterion of superiority in this social order is personal ability and character' (p. 169). Several Qur'anic verses refer to 'some' having been 'raised in rank' (*daraja*) above others, including 'those who have knowledge' (Q6: 165, 12: 76, 43: 32, 58: 11). The people, however, who are all Khalifs under God, can nominate an individual to exercise authority on their behalf, 'all Muslims (or, technically speaking, all caliphs of God) delegate their caliphate to him for administrative purposes'. The Khalif, then, is answerable 'to God on the one hand and on the other to his fellow "caliphs" who have delegated their authority to him' (Mawdudi 1976a: 170).

Mawdudi's ideal system is one in which the most suitable person is entrusted with the position of *khalif*, or *amir*, 'the basic qualification for the election of an Amir is that he should command the confidence of the largest number of people in respect of his knowledge and grasp of Islam' (1986: 34). This is based on Q4: 58, which commands Muslims to only entrust their affairs to the most competent people, hence the desire of the early community to select the 'best among them'. Mawdudi, says Tama-donfar, actually 'preferred the rule of the intellectual elites to that of the majority' (1989: 104). The khalif must be Muslim, male, an adult, sane and a citizen of the Islamic state (Mawdudi calls these the 'four standards', 1955: 140–1). People would not self-nominate, as this does not ensure the best candidates. Similarly, al-Turabi argues that in an Islamic State 'there would be certain rules regarding the qualifications of candidates' who would not be allowed to conduct their own campaigns, since 'the presentation of candidates would be entrusted to a neutral institution' (1983: 248). *Hadith* (Bukhari, Vol. 9, Bk 89, *hadith* 261, Khan 1987: 195) support this. Kurdi entrusts professional associations with the job of nominating prominent members for election (1984: 82).

Mawdudi allowed for an elected consultative assembly (*majlis-i-shura*) that would assist the *Amir* in interpreting the *Shari'ah*, framing regulations consistent with its provisions, and 'legislation on questions not covered by any specific injunctions of the *Shari'ah*' (Mawdudi 1986: 35). A sub-committee 'comprising men learned in Islamic law' would scrutinize all proposals to ensure their conformity with the *Shari'ah* (1986: 35). Only those fully committed to Islam have a right to 'join the community that runs the Islamic state' (1976a: 168). In contrast to Western states, where citizenship is linked with birth and with geography (e.g. if you are born in the USA, you qualify for citizenship), the Islamic state, which is fundamentally 'an ideological state', recognizes no 'geographical, linguistic or colour bar' in respect of citizenship, thus any Muslim 'no matter to what race, nation or country he may belong', has the right to citizenship of any Islamic state (*ibid.*). Non-Muslims must accept that they have no right 'to influence the basic policy of this ideological state' (p. 167). The *hizb-ut-tahrir*'s draft Constitution for an Islamic State also allows non-Muslims membership of the Assembly but confines their role to the voicing of complaints, restricting *shura* to Muslims (1962, articles 101, 105). Taqiuddin an-Nabhana (1909–77), who founded the party in 1952, drafted this document to facilitate its application for legal registration in Lebanon. The *hizb-ut-tahrir*'s aim is to restore the universal Khalifate. For Tibi, a charitable description of Mawdudi's political system would be as a 'divine pattern of totalitarianism' (1998: 158). When Mawdudi died, the King of Saudi stated that his 'demise was a tragedy for the whole Muslim world'. Ahmad, his interpreter and translator, calls him one of the 'greatest thinkers and social reformers of the world of Islam' (cited in Slomp 1991: 32). Smith described him as 'the most ominous representative of the trend back to religious conservatism' (Smith 1945: 11). Slomp sees him as a *mujaddid* – a reviver of Islamic faith, such as those that Muhammad predicted would appear at the start of each new century (1991: 33; see Voll 1983: 33).

Centrality of the law

The *Shari'ah*, according to Mawdudi, is 'a complete way of life', 'an all-embracing social order', an 'organic whole' which must be implemented as a total scheme or not at all (1986: 19–20). It defines what is *haram* (prohibited), *makruh* (disliked), *fard* (mandatory), *matlab* (recommended) and *mubah* (permitted) (pp.18–19). When Westerners and Islamic modernists call such punishments as amputation and flogging 'barbarous' what they are really expressing is their own moral perversion (1955: 41). Those who would change Islamic Law are outside 'the pale of Islam' and 'ought to have the courage to say that they reject Islam outright' (*ibid.*). Indeed, who would 'advise them to believe in a God whose law of punishment they consider as barbarous' (1955: 42). Similarly, Doi (1984) wrote: 'If a ruler does not apply the Islamic penalty for theft, slander or adultery, preferring the judgements of man-made law, such a ruler would be considered definitely an unbeliever' (p. 39).

Mawdudi (like Qutb) was convinced that a genuinely Islamic state is 'bound to be just' (1955: 91). He believed that distribution of *zakat* to the poor and other socially equalizing measures would create 'conditions under which none is compelled by force of circumstances to steal' (1955: 29–30). Sexual crimes, too, such as 'adultery and fornication' would be rare if present at all in a society 'in which every trace of suggestiveness has been destroyed' and 'where mixed gatherings of men and women have been prohibited', unlike in 'filthy' Western society where 'sexual excitement is rampant' (1955: 30). Mawdudi and Qutb both used the term *jahilia* (the pre-Islamic period of ignorance) to describe not only the West but also modern Muslim societies, which Qutb said were more ignorant than pre-Islamic society had been (1988: 32). Mawdudi believed that 'Islam possesses a perfect moral system' (1986: 26) of 'unchangeable norms for all moral actions' (p. 24). It is 'permanent and universal and holds good in every age and under all circumstances' (p. 25). It covers every 'aspect of man's private and social life – his domestic associations, his civic conduct, and his activities in the political, economic, legal, educational and social fields'. 'No sphere of life', says Mawdudi, 'is exempt from the universal and comprehensive application of the moral principles of Islam' (p. 27).

Mawdudi's campaign for what he saw as genuine Islamic government in Pakistan angered the authorities. Between 1948 and 1964 he spent a total of five years behind bars. In 1953, a military court sentenced him to death – later commuted to life imprisonment. This followed his virulent opposition to the Ahmadiyyas, a group whom he considered 'innovators' and who were eventually declared non-Muslim in Pakistan. With several other Islamic organizations, the *Jamaati* opposed Zulfikar Ali Bhutto's presidency (1971–7). Under the regime of Zia ul-Haq (1924–88; in power from 1977, when he led a bloodless coup against Bhutto), Mawdudi became increasingly influential. *Jamaati* members occupied significant posts.

However, Mawdudi's co-operation with the military dictator was driven by pragmatism, not ideology; the regime could be supported if it carried out its promises of establishing an Islamic state. Ul-Haq entrusted his Islamic Ideology Council with the task of bringing Pakistan's laws into conformity with Islam. This was widely associated with the application of *Shari'ah*, or Islamic Law. Later, the *Jamaati* criticized military rule as non-Islamic, for placing its regulations above the law, calling for 'the restoration of democracy' (Esposito 1991: 172).

Al-Azmeh (1993) claims that 'Islamist political discourse is loathe to specify the political system that an Islamic state would create and invigilate', and that 'this lack of specification appears odd in the light of the detailed regulation attributed to Islamic Law' (p. 28). However, such model constitutions as the *hizb-ut-tahrir*'s and Kurdi's cannot be faulted for detail. Sardar, whose 1985 book reproduces a model constitution (pp. 327–45), agrees that there is no consensus on the exact nature of the Islamic state, or on how it might be established, but argues that 'Muslim scholars and intellectuals agree on the general outlines'. They also agree that 'the Islamic State is based on the consent and cooperation of the people' (1985: 127; see also Ahmad 1986: 4). Javid Iqbal thinks that even though the majority principle 'was not followed during the historical experiment of the rightly guided caliphs [the first four], its adaptation has been neither specifically forbidden nor disapproved of in the Qur'an and *Sunnah*', which ultimately leaves the method of selecting leaders 'to the good sense of the community' (1986: 47, 1983: 257). Some revivalists allow, some disallow, different political parties. Kurdi (1984) argues that political parties have no place in the Islamic state, since 'all Muslims embrace one doctrine and acknowledge one ideological system' (p. 73; see Q58: 22). Al-Banna did not believe in 'political parties' within the Islamic state (Esposito 1991: 180). The *hizb-ut-tahrir* permits political parties, provided that they are 'based on the creed of Islam' (1962, article 21).

Rule by an elite: the case of Saudi Arabia

Saudi regards itself as an Islamic State. Its constitution is the Qur'an. This understanding of Islamic government accepts any territory where *Shari'ah* is upheld as authentically Islamic, regardless of how the leader has been appointed. The Saudi regime also draws on other traditions, such as *shura* and *ba'aih*, to support its claim of Islamic legitimacy (see below). The Saudi regime and those of the Gulf States, Jordan and Morocco are usually described as 'monarchies' (sometimes as absolute monarchies) although there is no automatic succession. Wahhabism, after its founder, Muhammad Ibn Abd al-Wahhab (1703–92) is, says Tibi, 'certainly not fundamentalist' (1998: 31). He describes it as 'traditional'.

Wahhabism pioneered the idea that Islam's salvation lies in replicating her past and began as a revivalist and reformist movement. Al-Wahhab believed that Muslims had deviated from pure Islam and that only a return to its origins would safeguard them from domination and exploitation. Forging an alliance with a local prince, Muhammad ibn Saud (d. 1765), he advocated a conservative version of Islam that became the official creed of the Kingdom of Saudi, established in 1923. It was less a response to European than to Ottoman imperialism, a reassertion of 'Arab' over Turkish Islam, a 'defensive culture against the alien – in Arabia' (Tibi 2001: 120). Control of the Sacred Cities (Makkah and Madinah) was crucial to their desire to exert religious and moral leadership within the Muslim world. Sufi Islam (Islam's mystical strand) was targeted as corrupt, too concerned with the inner life, too little with external obedience, although political considerations were also involved. The Wahhabis' desire to assert control of the *hajj* at Makkah meant that rival pilgrimages could not be tolerated. Lindholm's research, too, suggests that Sufi orders, with their charismatic Sheikhs (with their special powers and blessings, or *barrakah*), effectively functioned as micro-economic-social alternatives to the Khalifate, which may have regarded them as undermining centralized, autocratic authority (see 1996: 189–90). Many Sufi authorities ascribed the Qutb (the 'world pivot') of the day with a legal standing that equalled that of the *khalif*; thus, there 'might no longer be a Caliph with power in the ordinary political sense [but] there remained a true spiritual Caliph' who was for Sufis God's 'immediate representative' (1996: 189). In contrast to the Wahhabis, many progressives admire Sufi Islam; Mernissi remarks that 'the Sufis' freedom, abolishing the barrier between man and God, threatened the caliphs. In deifying man', she says, 'the Sufis gave him back his rights' (1994: 92). Tibi thinks that Sufi Islam 'increases the human room for manoeuvre in the relationship between God and man, since man can take the initiative', commenting that this is considered '*kufr*, heresy', by orthodox Muslims (2001: 46). Rahman and Iqbal, though, disapproved of Sufism (see Denny 1991: 101; Iqbal 1998: 257). See Hamzeh and Dekmejian (1996) on contemporary Sufi engagement in politics.

Wahhabism recognizes only one Sunni legal school, Hanbali. Reluctant to rule on any matter not explicitly covered by Qur'an and *Sunnah*, Hanbal (d. 855 CE) left what is not covered to the interpretation of the jurist (mainly in fiscal and administrative areas) and to *'urf*, or local custom. Muhammad permitted *'urf* if it was not contrary to Islam. In many areas, Saudi has been innovative. The King is 'informally elected by a council of Saudi princes' (Esposito 1991: 105), representing the *ahl al-hall wa al-'aqd*. Once elected, he remains subject to the *Shari'ah*, which in the main is interpreted by the *ulama*, among whom the descendants of Wahhab remain influential. The *ulama* are consulted on most issues. In 1975, they endorsed the transfer of power from King Saud to his brother, Faisal. During the Gulf War, they issued decrees justifying the presence of foreign troops in the Holy Cities, as did Egyptian *ulama*. This may suggest a mutually beneficial relationship between the rulers and their expert Muslim advisers.

The *hizb-ut-tahrir* regard the Saudi monarchy as 'American agents', especially when American troops were stationed there (Kassem 2003: 4).

For Osama Bin Laden this was a defilement of 'Islam in the holiest of places, the Arabian Peninsula' (1998). In 1993, King Fahd established a *shura* council. Tibi comments 'this is not binding' and in the decree all reference 'to democracy is carefully avoided' (1998: 30). As noted, some Muslims support the view that *shura*, though obligatory, is not binding. Nor does a *shura* council have to be elected. Zia ul-Haq appointed a *shura* assembly that had no binding authority (Esposito 1991: 172). Iqbal (1983) refers to 'some schools of law' that hold that the *shura* 'is merely a body of advisors or experts which must be appointed by the caliph ... through selection and nomination and not election' (p. 257). Osman concludes that the leader's 'legitimacy does not necessarily depend on instituting a separate arrangement for public approval' (1986: 68). Tamadonfar (1989) comments that 'It is not clear whether the Qur'an intended to make it obligatory on the part of the caliph to follow the advice of the community' (p. 81).

Some Qur'anic verses seem to question the 'majority principle' (see Q12: 21, 12: 103, 6: 116 and 5: 100). Tibi (1998) says that 'only those Muslims with an intimate knowledge of Islamic sources', in effect the *ulama*, were regarded as 'the appropriate class for interpreting the will of God, the one and only legislator' (p. 176). Tibi, discussing *shura* as an alternative to democracy, complains about the circular argument of Muslim fundamentalists, for whom the answer to both the question 'what is Islamic government?' and 'how do you institute it?' is the same. 'Islam knows only one system of government, which is *shura*. If we want to know how to implement the *shura*, then we have to refer to the *shura* itself', says Abu-Ziad-Fahmi (cited in Tibi 1998: 175). He suggests that '*shura* thinking virtually reflects the tribal tradition of pre-islamic history' in which the 'king and his tribal family are the only source of power' (p. 30).

A similar relationship exists between the *ulama* and the King of Morocco, whose regime they legitimize. During Ottoman times, too, the *sheikh-al-Islam* (chief mufti) could veto any imperial decrees deemed un-Islamic and even depose the Khalif for violating Islamic law, thus Ibrahim (1648), Mehmed IV (1687), Ahmed III (1730) and Selim III (1807) were all removed from office (see Esposito and Voll 1996: 48). Lewis (2003) says that Saudi's oil wealth results in its ability to wield an extraordinarily significant influence throughout the Muslim world (p. 109). Wahhabi Islam dominates 'organized Muslim life' in both the USA and Europe (p. 111). Saudi's oil wealth and that of other Gulf States impedes democratization, he claims, since 'Governments with oil wealth have no need for popular assemblies to impose and collect taxes' (p. 112). Ruthven (2002) accuses the Saudi regime of supporting terrorism throughout the Muslim world. 'Petrodollars from Saudi and the Gulf' have contributed to 'religious extremism and to the appeal of fundamentalist leaders' by 'promoting versions of Islam that verge on neo-Kharijitism', he says (p. 270). Wahhabi and Saudi 'sponsorship of anti-Christian and anti-Jewish religious polemics' contributes to Western Islamophobia (p. 174). Ahmad Deedat received the 1986 King Faisal Award for Services to Islam for his anti-Christian preaching (p. 173). Depending for their legitimacy on the *ulama*, the rulers allow the former a free hand in 'propagating religious extremism abroad' (p. 173). *The 9/11 Commission Report* describes Saudi as 'a problematic ally in combating Islamic extremism' (p. 11).

The centre-left's model: Taha's Second Message of Islam

Mahmoud Mohamed Taha (1909–85), leader of the Republican Brothers (founded 1945), faced with the imposition of traditional, unreformed *Shari'ah* in the Sudan (which resulted in the ongoing civil war) and appalled at the consequences for women and non-Muslims, advocated a rethinking of Islam. He believed that the Madinan experience (the ideal for traditionalists) was actually an historical concession to the needs of the time, a 'descent' from Islam's real message and meaning. Almost all the legal material (dealing with crime, marriage, divorce, gender) is from this period. This represents the stage of *'aqida* (dogma), while the earlier, Makkan period represents *haqiqa* (truth). Qur'anic material from this period is of a more general ethical nature, less specific. Muslims have mistaken the period of descent for real Islam. What is now needed is an ascent into Islam's second, higher phase, not a return to the past. Thus, the

> Second Message calls for a return from the subsidiary verses to the original verses, which were temporarily abrogated because of circumstances and material and human limitations. We must now elevate legislation by evolving and basing it on original Qur'anic verses. In this way, we shall welcome the age of socialism and democracy and open the way to absolute individual freedom through worship and humane dealing with other people. (1998: 283, 1987: 161)

Taha aimed to extrapolate rules that, while Islamic, could be equally embraced by non-Muslims, because they are also humane. To do so, he revived and revised the traditional doctrine of *naksh* (abrogation, see Chapter Four) but reversed its usual direction, abrogating later with earlier texts. Taha also frequently refers to the Sufi doctrine that verses have outer (*zahir*) or literal and inner (*batin*) or spiritual meanings. An-Na'im says that 'Explicit and definite texts ... that were the basis of discrimination against women and non-Muslims under historical *Shari'ah* are set aside as having served their transitory purpose' (1987: 23). Neither slavery, nor polygamy, nor divorce, nor the veil, nor *jihad* were 'original precepts in Islam', says Taha (1987: 137–43, 1998: 276–7; see Peters 1994: 249–51, 'Divorce in Islamic Law'). He identified Islam's perfection not with completeness today but with potentiality to evolve towards completion. Taha advocated *tatwir-al-tashri'* (evolution of the law) (1987: 167). Islam's real message was freedom and no nation had yet 'deserved the name *muslimin*' (1987: 151; see 1998: 272). Taha, like Iqbal, rejected the secular option. Taha's state would be Islamic but with laws in harmony with international standards of human rights, so non-Muslim Sudanese would still gain all the benefits of secularism, despite the state's 'strongly religious orientation' (1987: 27). Taha negatively contrasts the Islam of the subsidiary verses as 'community law' with the Islam of the original verses as *Shari'a fardiyah*, individual law, since 'The ultimate Islam is the level of individualities' (1987: 152). Imprisoned with other members of the Republican Brotherhood in 1984, Taha was tried as an apostate (the original charge was treason) and executed in January 1985. 'Re-thinking Islam', says Tibi, 'can lead to one's being listed among those apostates to be executed' (1998: 156).

Secular Islam: the far left

Tibi points out that although 'there have been movements towards a secularisation of Islam' for more than a century, it 'arouses great agitation if a Muslim mentions secularisation in public' (2001: 44). He describes himself as one of a few Muslims who write in Arabic in favour of a 'disentanglement of religion from politics' (1998: 106). Secular nationalism is seen as a neo-colonial ploy, part of the West's conspiracy to destroy Islam through Westernized agents who promote a political ideology that stresses common cultural, linguistic or regional rather than Islamic identity (Tibi 1998: 100; Tamimi 2000: 26). Even the pan-Arab movement was problematic for some, at 'odds with the notion of Islamic *umma* because, on the one hand, it excluded all non-Arab Muslims (for example, those in Indonesia, the largest Islamic nation) from this entity and, on the other it included Arab Christians (for example, those living in Lebanon and Egypt) as citizens and no longer as *dhimmis*/protected peoples, that is, minorities' (Tibi 1998: 144; see also p. 53 and 2001: 122).

Tibi criticizes the pioneer Muslim secularists for trying to impose secularism from the top and for 'wanting to put Islam aside'. It is no surprise that they failed (1998: 97, 207, 2001: 14, 80). Muslim writers too often confuse a social process (*'almanana*) with an ideology (*'ilmaniyya*) (see 1998: 97–8, 196, 2001: 111). In contrast fundamentalists increasingly translate secularism as *ladiniyya*, or anti-religious attitude (1998: 207). Tibi, Mernissi, Soroush and Zakaria (former Deputy Leader of the Indian Congress Party) challenge the assumption that 'the secular character of modernity' is 'anti-religious' (Tibi 1998: 75). The secular does not have to be profane (Tibi 2001: 113, 114; Soroush 2000: xvii; Mernissi 1994: 65; see Arkoun 1998a: 217–18 and al-Ghannouchi 2000: 111). Mernissi (1994) says that Islam would not only survive but 'thrive in a secular state' (p. 65). In a religious society, says Soroush, a 'purely secular government would be undemocratic' (2000: 126). Indeed, 'If a society is religious, its government too will take a religious hue' (p. 61). He is convinced that a state 'becomes more religious as it grows more free' (p. 145). For these Muslims, Muhammad did not personally appoint a successor or establish a mechanism for appointing a leader because 'he never intended to found a political state' (al-Raziq 1998: 36; see Zakaria 1988: 281; Tibi 1998: 150–1, 166, 2001: 164). Tibi (1998) says that 'historical circumstances imposed on the Prophet the need to act politically' but that unity of religion and politics is not 'a constitutive part of Islamic beliefs' (p. 166). According to Tibi (1998) the *din wa dawla* (unity of religion and state), 'a cardinal principle of fundamentalist (or political) Islam,' is a fiction (p. 163). He points out that neither formula *Din wa dawla* or *nizam Islami* (or *nizam siyasi*/political system) exists in the Qur'an, or in the *Sunnah* (1998: 61). He has no objection to a constitution based on Islamic principles, provided it is recognized as a fallible, human construct (1998: 176, 188).

The idea that there is a single, ideal and 'true Islamic political form' that can be imposed on society is a myth. Al-Azmeh and Tibi argue that by offering its view of Madinah under Muhammad as the ideal, fundamentalists seek to 'eliminate history', regarding it 'as, at best, an illegitimate accretion onto the pristine beginning' (al-Azmeh 1993: 96; see 139–40; see Tibi 1998: 14). Calls for the implementation of *Shari'ah* and for *shura*, supposedly the 'underpinning for the call for an Islamic State' leave us none the clearer about its 'concrete political' details (Tibi 1998: 177). Tibi thinks it puerile that two Qur'anic texts are used as the basis for a 'putative Islamic system of government' (p. 209). Kurdi (1984) takes the opposite view, arguing that the Qur'an did not establish a definitive blueprint because, although the 'instructions might have been perfect for the time the Islamic message was revealed, they would probably not have been suitable for the future' (p. 70). In this view, lack of a blueprint is providential, not an oversight or defect.

Progressive writers object to the fundamentalists' contention that the *Shari'ah* is a perfect, immutable code. Al-Azmeh describes it 'as the nominal umbrella of a variety of different things' and as 'by no means univocal'. Moreover, the 'majority of its rulings do not have the finality attributed to them by modern studies' (1993: 94). It exists as 'a body of narratives' that offer 'paradigmatic' advice (p. 94, p. 25) which has never been codified. It simply cannot be 'applied'! Sardar agrees. In his view, the classical Imams had never intended their rulings to be binding on future generations, indeed 'without exception' they had 'emphasized that their rulings were their own opinions ... and should not be accepted uncritically' (1985: 109). The *Shari'ah*'s 'principles and values are not a static or indeed a priori given, but are dynamically derived within changing contexts', he says (2004: 248). Tibi (1998) says that most of those calling for the implementation of *Shari'ah* 'know little about it'. They are unaware that 'should they seize power, they will not find a coherent legal system at hand that they can apply to situations, conditions and events overnight – as events will demand' (p. 168). The 'traditional understanding of Islamic law', he says, 'rested not with the state ... but rather with religious societal communities, the so-called *madhahib* (the four legal schools in Sunni Islam)' (1998: 214; see also p. 189).

The case of Turkey

Brooks (1994) cites a Turkish Muslim:

> *There are two types of Islam – American Islam, and Muhammad's Islam – and in Turkey we have American Islam. In American Islam, religion is separated from politics, because it suits the superpower interests. Our government is very much afraid of Islamic revolution, because it wants to grovel to the West.*
> (p. 19)

Esposito (1981) describes Turkey under Atatürk as the 'only Muslim country to choose a completely secular path' (p. 169). In the dying days of the Ottoman Empire, regarded as corrupt from within and from without, Mustafa Kemal Atatürk (1881–1938) set out to transform Turkey into a Western-style secular nation-state. A graduate of the Military Academy and a hero of the First World War, during which he repulsed the Allied landing at Gallipoli (1915), he led a revolt against the occupying Allied powers, whose plan for Turkey would have stripped it of most of its territory. By August 1922, he had forced an Allied withdrawal. He declared Turkey a republic. Elected President in 1923, he remained in office for the rest of his life. In 1924, he abolished the Ottoman Khalifate, already exiled. The Turkish state, he said, would belong to the people, not to the Sultan. He looked to Europe as the only civilization. To sell his Europeanized secular state in Muslim Turkey, all things Islamic had to be neutralized, all education secularized. Islamic law was replaced by a concoction derived from various European systems, the Turkish alphabet was latinized, the 'fez was outlawed and replaced by European hats' (Ahmed 1988: 69). Religious endowments (*waqf*) were nationalized and seminaries were closed. In fact, far from separating Islam from the state, Atatürk placed Islam firmly under state control.

However, proving the point made by Zakaria, Mernissi, Soroush and Tibi, that secularization does not necessarily result in a decline of religion, Islam has continued to be the personal faith of 99 per cent of Turks. Its continued popularity has resulted in the reopening of seminaries as well as in the formation of Islamic parties within the political arena. The Islamic Virtue (Welfare) Party emerged as the largest party in parliament with 102 deputies and led the coalition government for a year. In June 2001 the Turkish constitutional court 'banned' the party 'because it had become a focus for anti-secular activity' (BBC News, 22 June 2001). However, in November 2002 the Justice and Development Party, which has Islamic roots, won an overall majority in the elections, the first party to do so for 15 years. Its leader, Recep Tayyib Erdogan, responding to fears that the new government would preside over an Islamic revolution, stated that Turkey's secular constitution would be respected and that Islam would not be imposed on anyone. The party, he said, was European Conservative (BBC News, 5 November 2002). Turkey is actively seeking membership of the European Union. It joined NATO (the North Atlantic Treaty Organization) in 1952.

The term 'fundamentalist'

Tibi argues that 'a closer look at the political concepts of Islamic fundamentalists, seen as an expression of the repoliticization of Islam for non-
religious ends, shows that we are dealing with a modern phenomenon
dressed up in traditional symbols' (1998: 33). Sayyid (1998) prefers the
term 'Islamism'. The term 'fundamentalist', he says, is too demonized to
be useful (p. 17). Esack (1997) writes that 'Islamic fundamentalism, as
popularized by the Western media, represents a stereotype with pejorative
and disparaging connotations', too 'sweeping in its generalization and
insensitive to the many nuances in the world of contemporary Islam' (p.
xi). A common argument against using the term is that its origin in conservative Christian discourse, where it was used as a self-description, creates problems when applied to Islam, as Moghissi comments: 'How the two
fundamentalisms can be equated is not obvious' (1999: 65). Christian
fundamentalism, for example, is largely a doctrinal not a political movement. When its dogmas are transferred to Islam, they represent what
almost all Muslims believe – such as the infallibility of scripture and the
virgin birth of Jesus. However, she thinks that none of the alternatives,
such as revivalist or Islamist, adequately 'define the new radical Islamic
movements'. Although they do not themselves use 'the term as a mark of
their identity', they share, she says, certain core characteristics that are best
described as 'fundamentalist'. She sums these up as 'anti-modernity, anti-
democracy and anti-feminism' (p. 70).

   Like Moghissi, Tibi rejects that it is 'politically incorrect to speak and
write in blunt terms about fundamentalism'. He identifies Islamic fundamentalism as 'simply one variety of a new global phenomenon in world
politics' (1998: 2). Various 'fundamentalisms' represent, he suggests,
responses to 'the problems of globalization and fragmentation' (p. 5). He
thinks the term appropriate, though, since in his view Muslims do apply the
label to themselves. In the 1980s, he says, they coined the neo-Arabic word
usiliyya, from *usul*, principles/fundamentals, and *iyya* (ism) 'to make clear
that their goal is to make Islamic fundamentals the bottom line of Muslim
public life'. Thus, use of the term 'fundamentalists' does not 'constitute
imposing' the term 'on them, nor does it arise from Eurocentric bias'
(1998: 53). What characterizes Islamic fundamentalism, according to Tibi,
is its '*mobilization of religion for political ends*' (1998: 37; Tibi's italics). The
'prototype of an Islamic fundamentalist', he says, is 'a *homo politicus*', not a
'*homo religiosus*' (2001: 3). He conflates the terms 'political Islam', which he
often uses, and 'Islamic fundamentalism' (see 1998: 12). Tibi maintains a
'strict distinction between *Islam as a religious belief*', to which he himself
adheres, and '*Islamic fundamentalism as a political ideology*' based on a
'selective and arbitrary politicization of religion' (1998: 13; Tibi's italics).
However, he is critical of Western writers for whom Islamic fundamentalism
equals terrorism, which he says is a side aspect of fundamentalism, and not
an 'expression of Islamic fundamentalism *per se*' (2001: 212).

Resources

The Institute for the Secularization of Islamic Society (ISIS) was 'formed to promote the ideas of rationalism, secularism, democracy and human rights within Islamic society'. Its website is: *www.secularislam.org.*

The Centre for the Study of Islam and Democracy: *http://www.islam-democracy.org.* See articles by CSID board member Muqtebar Khan, 2001a and 2001b.

Literary case study

Ahdaf Soueif's The Map of Love, *a novel on Egypt's struggle for freedom, identity and independence in the colonial and post-colonial world*

The plot of this novel oscillates between the beginning and the end of the last century. In scenes set in the early period, the backdrop is colonial Egypt and the emerging independence movement. Characters include Lord Cromer, 'Abduh and Rida. Even W. H. T. Gairdner, the C.M.S. missionary whose writing on Islam earned him a considerable scholarly reputation, appears in the pages of this well-researched novel. Lord Cromer (1841–1917) was for 25 years Consul-General of Egypt and was regarded as an authority on Islam and on how best to govern Muslims. His book, *Modern Egyptians* (1908), says Said, was regarded throughout Britain's Empire as a handbook on the governance of Muslim subjects, since knowledge gained in one part of the Muslim world, transferred elsewhere, would be equally applicable and valid. *Homo islamicus* was the same everywhere, regardless of place or time. Tibi points out how this view of Islam as 'immutable ... an all-embracing essential culture, valid' without further 'accommodation for all times, places and people' is 'in a bizarre way' one shared by Orientalists and Muslim fundamentalists alike (2001: 26).

In a scene early in the novel, older British colonial hands debate with some younger gentlemen 'the question whether savage nations had a right to exist' (p. 13). The older set thought that they did not. In other words, it was the duty of advanced nations like Britain to act as imperial guardians. Cromer, says one character, was most certainly a 'patriot and ... serves his country well. We understand that', she continued; 'Only he should not pretend that he is serving Egypt' (p. 248). Cromer believed that only he stood between Egypt and chaos. Moreover, he knew Egypt's needs better than anyone else. Thus, he tells Anna (who is involved in plans, supported by 'Abduh, to open a women's college) that 'if [she] knew Egypt better [she] would know that the religious leaders would never agree to women being encouraged out of their lowly status' (p. 248). Islam, Cromer asserted, could never reform. Muslims who attempted reform were branded by the colonialists and by fellow Muslims as heretics, as well as by the latter as 'in the pay of the British'. Attacks on 'Abduh took 'the form of publishing scandalous (and counterfeit) pictures of him drinking and consorting with foreign women' (p. 394). Cromer would not countenance an elected assembly.

The complexity of nationalist and of independence aspirations is skil-fully presented throughout the book. 'All are united in their desire to get rid of the British' but differ on how to proceed. Some wanted to strengthen links with the Ottoman Sultan, asserting a united pan-Islamic identity over-and-against Europe. Others thought the Ottoman Empire too weak to be a viable alternative to Western power and looked to establish a new Khalifate in Arabia. Those that looked to Arabia hoped that the Sherif of Makkah (a descendant of Muhammad) might establish a new caliphate, reviving Arab-Muslim leadership of the Muslim world lost since the demise of the 'Abbasids. In collusion with the British (and opposing French ambitions in the region) the Arab Revolt took place during World War I, led by the Sherif's sons, Faisal and Abdullah with T. E. Lawrence (1888–1935; Lawrence of Arabia) as military adviser. Zakaria (1988) records that the Sherif and his sons had actually spent 15 years as the Ottoman Sultan's guests in Istanbul. The Ottomans were trying to counter growing anti-Turkish sentiment among the Arabs (p. 170). The Arab–British alliance defeated the Ottomans at Aqaba and took Damascus. They felt betrayed when the British assumed control of Palestine (as they did when the State of Israel was established), which they had hoped would become the jewel in the crown of a new Arab state. Set up by the British as the rulers of Iraq and Jordan respectively (Faisal had briefly ruled Syria, 1918–20), the brothers were regarded by many as agents of British inter-ests but saw themselves as spearheading what would become a united Arab kingdom, forging the former Ottoman provinces into a single entity. Others thought that Egypt should stand alone, drawing on her own history and identity, one that included its non-Muslims as equal citizens of what would emerge as a modern, secular state.

In a remarkable passage, one of Soueif's characters echoes what many Muslims cited in this book argue, that the West seems to reserve democ-racy for itself. She has US President Roosevelt (1901–09) tell a packed auditorium of Cairo's elite that 'it would take generations before they learned to govern themselves' (p. 456). The novel continues: 'All in all it is very sad – not so much in itself, but as a new disappointment to the Egyptians and further proof that the Nations of the West hold one system of values dear to themselves while denying it to their fellows in the East' (p. 457). The Egyptians felt especially let down, since Roosevelt's 'Nation [stood] for Democracy and Liberty and [had] not (yet, in any case) sullied its hand in a Colonial endeavour' (p. 456).

Scenes in the more recent period have as their backdrop conflict between the Arab world and Israel.

3 Muslims on Human Rights

Given the central position accorded to human rights in the Islamic scheme of social and political relations, both the current lack of interest in this issue on the part of modern Muslim political theorists and the dismal record of most Muslim countries with regard to these rights becomes especially unfortunate.

(Mumtaz Ahmad 1986: 22)

An imposition from outside?

Many of the contributions to the debate on Islam and human rights, from inside and from outside Islam, replicate discussion and positions regarding Islam and democracy. For example, the origin of 'human rights' discourse in post-Enlightenment Europe is problematic when it claims to be a universal standard of human conduct equally applicable in the Muslim and non-Muslims worlds. Some Muslims ask, 'Why should a discourse that arose in the West attract Muslim support? Is its imposition not an extension of the colonial project?' 'Human rights' are taken as those set out in the Universal Declaration (UDHR), drawn up by members of the United Nations in 1945. Many believe that there is a fundamental clash between the Charter and Islamic practice and that the record of 'human rights' in the Muslim world suggests an inherent conflict between Islam and 'human rights'. When the UN General Assembly voted in 1948 to ratify the Declaration, Saudi Arabia abstained (together with South Africa and eight Communist states) on the grounds that it did not acknowledge that rights are God's gift and it contravened the Qur'an by asserting a right to change one's religion. Pakistan ratified the Declaration, arguing that the Qur'an permits people to believe or to disbelieve. No nation voted against the UDHR.

Mumtaz Ahmad admits the abysmal human rights record of many Muslim countries. However, like other Muslims, he does not blame Islam for this, but corrupt and unjust rule. An-Na'im says that if they implement historical *Shari'ah*, Muslims 'can not exercise their right to self-determination without violating the rights of others' (1998: 221). Others defend Islamic practices that clash with human rights as defensible on the grounds that different cultures have different values. Postmodern affirmation of difference may allow the condemnation 'here' of what is declared culturally appropriate 'there' (Tibi 1998: 213). He is aware that 'double standards' are an issue here. It is, he says, 'significant that Western politicians never address the human rights violations in Saudi Arabia' (1998: 195; see also p. 41). He therefore recognizes the difficulty of persuading Muslims that a discourse that originated in the West does not somehow also favour the West (1998: 206). However, he is somewhat scathing of those fundamentalists who on the one hand hold Western cultural relativity in contempt yet use 'multicultural tolerance to establish legitimacy for themselves' (2001: 133; see also p. 137; 1998: 106). Cultural relativity, he says, 'virtually prohibits a critique on non-Western culture' (2001: 132; see 1998: 183). An-Na'im upholds the universal validity of 'human rights' since they are 'appreciated by a wide variety of cultural traditions' (1998: 224). 'Human rights may emanate from a Western tradition', he says, '*but do not belong to the West*' (p. 205, his italics). Mernissi (1994) on 'The United Nations Charter' (pp. 60–74) also represents an important contribution, and is well worth reading.

Discussion topics

In Kureishi's novel *The Black Album*, Dr Brownlow, the Marxist lecturer, suggests to Riaz, the fundamentalist Muslim student group's leader, that people must decide good and evil for themselves. Riaz replies, 'Man is the last person I shall trust to such a task' (1995: 81).

- How are humanitarian and ethical norms or values or rights, such as those enshrined in the UDHR, imbued with value?

- Is the source of their value and authority dependent on society's ability to police them?

- Does their value derive from society or is it inherent, implicit within the values themselves?

- Do you think that human rights favour the West? Do you think that a practice regarded as immoral or even criminal by one culture can be tolerated in others?

- Tibi recognizes that the prevailing international system, including international law, reflects Western norms and values (2001: 196). In your opinion, are the international conventions simply another Western device to extend its neo-colonial project?

Below, the contributions of Mawdudi, the *hizb-ut-tahrir* and the Universal Islamic Declaration of Human Rights, representing the 'right' (with some reference to Sayyid Qutb) of Muslim opinion, and of Tibi and An-Na'im representing the 'left' are examined in some detail. Excellent background material and analysis is available in Bielefeldt (1995). This chapter also presents two case studies – of the Abu Zayd (or Zaid) and Salman Rushdie affairs, both of which involve the issues of the limit of dissent and of free expression in Islam. For an-Na'im, the Rushdie affair serves to illustrate 'the drastic incompatibility between *shari'a* and modern standards of human rights' (1998: 236). A literary case study on Kureishi's 1995 novel concludes this chapter.

Mawdudi and the Muslim right: human rights and Islam

Mawdudi's 1976 tract (1976b) won the King Faisal prize for 'outstanding services to Islam'. Available on the Internet, it remains one of the most influential Muslim texts in this field. In Chapter One, he compares and contrasts the 'Western' and the 'Islamic Approach' to human rights. He is especially critical of the West's arrogant claim, as he sees it, that everything good emanates from the West, that it 'invented' human rights while the rest of the world 'was steeped in ignorance' (p. 13). However, his fundamental criticism of the Western concept of human rights is that it expresses a humanist, secular understanding of 'man'. In contrast, Islam's understanding of 'human rights', says Mawdudi, is rooted in divine disclosure and is always mindful of God's rights as well as men's/women's. God's rights (*haq Allah*) are above human rights (*haq adami*). However, Mawdudi calls 'human rights a part and parcel of Islamic faith', whereas the 'West had no concept of human rights before the seventeenth century'. Since Islam's 'Charter of Human Rights' was 'conferred by God', it cannot be amended or rescinded by human authorities, unlike the rights drawn up by the UN which 'have no sanctions behind them, no force, physical or moral to enforce them'. In the remainder of the book (Chapters Two, Three and Four) Mawdudi turns to the Qur'an and to Islamic law to show how, as he interprets the material, all necessary rights are guaranteed by the system. He divides his treatment into what he calls 'Basic Human Rights' (Chapter One), 'Rights of Citizens in an Islamic State' (Chapter Two) and 'Rights of Enemies At War' (Chapter Four). Since his intent is to demonstrate the self-sufficiency of Islam with reference to human rights, he does not create any real dialogue between the Islamic and 'Western' approaches or discuss 'possible tensions and conflicts between the two'. Indeed, given his belief that Islam is a perfect system, it is difficult to see how Mawdudi could concede the need to justify an Islamic perspective against a standard from outside Islam, such as the UDHR. This would appear to suggest the possibility that Islam needs to put its house in order or that is has lessons to learn from the 'house of unbelief'.

Turning to the Islamic tradition, however, Mawdudi is able to offer a list of basic rights that Islam clearly and unambiguously affirms, such as the right to life, security, justice and freedom. In Q5: 32 murder is equated with the slaughter of all humanity, for example, while justice is a theme that pervades the Qur'an. He cites Q5: 8 and 4: 135, among other verses. Indeed, Sayyid Qutb passionately believed that if a true Islamic State were to be established, justice would be guaranteed. For Qutb, justice was intricately linked with *tawhid* and as integral to Muslim society as a free market is to Capitalism, a 'branch of that great principle on which all Islamic teachings are based' (1976: 118). Islamic social justice, said Qutb, 'is comprehensive . . . embracing all sides and basic factors of life' (p. 125). Like Mawdudi, he argues that while the Western tradition (which in this article he calls 'Christianity' but he is really referring to Capitalism) elevates the individual above community, Islam perfectly balances individual and societal rights (p. 127). Marxism, for its part, is wrong to depict life as a 'continual strife and struggle between classes'; life in Islam 'is a matter of co-operation and mutual responsibility, not a constant warfare' (*ibid.*).

Bielefeldt (1995) suggests that Mawdudi's choice of 'rights' reflects his *a priori* assumption that Islam needs no supplement or correction. He emphatically denounces, and has no difficulty calling on the Islamic tradition to do so, all forms of discrimination or inequality based on 'colour, race, language or nationality' (Mawdudi 1976b: 23). However, Mawdudi does not 'mention gender in this context', thus 'he seems to ignore the fact that' human rights as 'enshrined in international standards implies the universal recognition of equal liberty' (Bielefeldt 1995: 603). His discussion of gender issues (Chapter 2, Section 3) is entitled 'Respect for the Chastity of Women'. Mawdudi's view of women is that they are equal but different from men and that it is therefore inappropriate to assume that women's 'rights' are identical to men's (see further discussion in Chapter Seven). Thus, men's rights in marriage (up to four partners) and in divorce are different from those of women. Nor can women exercise political authority over men, since men are the guardians of women (see Mawdudi 1976a: 163, 1986: 40). On religious freedom, Mawdudi points out how minorities are allowed, under the *dhimmi* arrangement, to practise their faiths without any hindrance or interference and that 'no force will be applied in order to compel [non-Muslims] to accept Islam', since Q2: 256 prohibits 'compulsion in religion' (1976b: 32). Bielefeldt points out here, however, that Mawdudi 'fails to . . . address . . . the ban on conversion from Islam to another religion and the restrictions on inter-religious marriage' (p. 604) which violate Article 16 and Article 18 of the UDHR respectively. Article 18 specifically refers to the right to change one's religion (see also Mernissi 1994: 87). Saudi Arabia abstained from Article 18 (the right to convert) when the United Nations voted on the UDHR in 1948. In traditional *Shari'ah*, the penalty for apostasy (*ridda*) is death (this is not a Qur'anic penalty but is based on *hadith*), hence the *fatwa* on Salman Rushdie, and the widespread demand for his death and for that of those considered 'apostates' (*murtad*) throughout the Muslim world (see an-Na'im 1998: 236; Tibi 1998: 157).

The *hizb-ut-tahrir* and human rights

The *hizb-ut-tahrir*'s approach to the issue of 'human rights' is more robust and aggressive than Mawdudi's approach. Mawdudi did not dismiss 'human rights' out of hand but was anxious to show that, in his view, Islam had no case to answer in this area. The *hizb-ut-tahrir*, in contrast, dismiss 'human rights' as another 'weapon' invented by the West and used by the West in its campaign against Islam. *The American Campaign to Suppress Islam*, which has a chapter on 'human rights' (Chapter Five) and also chapters on 'freedom of belief', 'freedom of expression' and 'personal freedom' (Chapters Six, Seven and Nine), is a book of just 41 pages available electronically on the Internet as well as in hardcopy format. The *hizb-ut-tahrir* regards its literary project as a form of Islamic *da'wa* (call, mission), thus its intended audience is Muslim rather than non-Muslim. The aim of this publication is to warn Muslims that the West is engaged in an ideological struggle against Islam in order to suppress Islam and exert its own dominance. Marxism lost its place in the global struggle for ideological supremacy not because Communist regimes collapsed following the events of 1989 (when the Berlin wall was demolished) but because people renounced Marxism and adopted Capitalism instead. Muslims have not abandoned their ideology, even though the historical Khilafah state was destroyed. As Tibi says, according to fundamentalism, dominance (*ghallab*) and superiority (*al-taghallub*) are hallmarks of Islam (1998: 57, 92), thus the *hizb-ut-tahrir* posits a struggle for global dominance between Islam and Capitalism; 'in terms of universality', the demise of Communism leaves only 'two ideologies' (p. 6) as credible rivals for world dominance.

America is therefore engaged in a 'campaign against the Islamic world'. This takes different forms and 'depends on a number of pillars'. These are summarized in Chapter Two: one, America forces Muslim states to adopt Capitalism, making them compliant to her own agendas; two, America recruits other states to aid her campaign, many of which also view 'Islam as a threat'; three, international law and UN Charters are tools of the USA designed to camouflage its plans under the guise of this so-called law; four, the USA controls the media, which 'distorts the image of Islam' and incites 'the world against those who adhere to it'; five, the USA is aided by apostate Muslims who, attracted by 'Kaafir culture', are 'in reality nothing more than secularists' (p. 12). Unfortunately, some Capitalist ideas 'have achieved widespread circulation throughout the world and ... acceptance by some Muslims' that do not realize that these ideas are actually 'slogans of the American Campaign in its ferocious attack on Muslims and Islam' (p. 14). It is 'prohibited for Muslims' to adopt these ideas, which are 'democracy, pluralism, human rights and free market policies'. Detailed but brief chapters then refute each slogan, calling on Muslims to reject them as contrary to the teaching of Islam.

The *hizb-ut-tahrir* is not interested in defending Islam's human rights record but in warning Muslims that what the West is trying to do is to subvert and corrupt them with ideas that are alien and anathema to Islam. Its rejection of democracy and human rights is predicated on the view that these concepts substitute human sovereignty for God's (p. 15) and that 'any evil that is committed by man is a result of restricting his will' (p. 20). The issue of religious freedom is not ignored. Rather, 'freedom of belief does not exist for Muslims because' Islam forbids Muslims 'to embrace any other creed', therefore the Islamic State cannot tolerate freedom of religion (p. 25). The *hadith*, 'whoever changes his *deen* [religion], kill him', is cited. Similarly, the type of 'pluralism' promoted by the West is intolerable, since it would allow the existence of political parties opposed to Islam's fundamentals, such as unity of religion and politics (p. 18). Nor can free speech be permitted, although Muslims who live in 'suppressive police states,' whose rulers 'prevent any person from expressing' an opinion contrary to their own, find this attractive. However, Islam 'restricts [Muslims] only to opinions derived from the Islamic creed or those built upon it' (p. 27). It does not allow unrestricted free expression since this would enable Islam's enemies and hypocrites to 'openly call against Islam' (p. 27). The *hizb-ut-tahrir*'s draft constitution for the Islamic State's Article 190 forbids belonging to 'any organization which is based on something other than Islam' or which applies non-Islamic rules. This includes international organizations like the United Nations, the International Court of Justice, the International Monetary Fund and the World Bank, and regional organizations like the Arab League.

The Universal Islamic Declaration of Human Rights (1981)

In 1981, the Islamic Council for Europe drew up and published its Universal Declaration (UIDHR). The Council is a non-governmental organization, so the Declaration does not have legal standing. The 'Cairo Document', published in 1990 by the Organization of the Islamic Conference, in contrast, does carry some political if not legal authority. These two documents are not dissimilar, however, and express a similar approach. The UIDHR has proved popular and is easily available on the world wide web. In its *Foreword*, it states that 'human rights are an integral part of the overall Islamic order'. Thus, as for Mawdudi, for the drafters of the UIDHR, human rights are endemic to Islam and do not need to be introduced from outside. This also precludes the need to reform or rethink Islam in the light of an external standard, since it is itself the perfect standard. Again following Mawdudi, the UIDHR declares that since these rights are of 'divine origin, no ruler, government, assembly or authority can curtail or violate them'. The UIDHR elevates 'duties' (*fara'id*) over 'rights', thus 'our duties and obligations have priorities over our rights', which implies a criticism of the UDHR's exclusive focus on 'rights' (see Tibi 1998: 62–3). The UIDHR defines 23 'rights' that it believes are 'inviolable and inalienable', including 'Right to Freedom', 'Right to Justice', 'Right to Fair Trial', 'Rights of Minorities', 'Right to

Freedom of Belief, Thought and Speech' and 'Right to Freedom of Religion'.

Under the 'Right to Justice' (article IV), *hisbah* is included. Under 'Right to Freedom of Belief, Thought and Speech' (article XII), the right to free expression is upheld but within 'limits prescribed by the law'. These limits include libel, slander and national security but also the holding in 'contempt of ... the religious beliefs of others' and the incitement of 'public hostility against them'. Under this provision, Salman Rushdie's novel *The Satanic Verses* would almost certainly attract censure. Article XIII, on religious freedom, reads, 'Every person has the right to freedom of conscience and worship in accordance with his religious beliefs' but no reference is made to the issue of conversion, whether a Muslim is free to change his or her religion. The right of women to work is affirmed (Article III). The same article states that 'All persons are equal before the law and are entitled to equal opportunities', which may seem to contradict Q2: 282 that requires two women witnesses (2 women = 1 man). There are a total of 124 references to Qur'an and *Sunnah* to support the rights contained in the Declaration.

Discussion topic

- Compare and contrast the UDHR and the UIDHR. In what respects are they similar? How do they differ? What philosophical assumptions inform these documents? How do you understand the word 'Universal' as used in each document?

Bassam Tibi on human rights

The Islamic definition of an international law lays claim to the imposition of Islam on the entire world and is therefore in blatant contradiction to the ideal of worldwide cultural pluralism (2001: 158).

Tibi regards 'democracy' and 'human rights' as 'standards of civilization' and as necessary for the establishment of peace and justice within the international order, which is his own ultimate concern. As a scholar of international relations, he wants to promote 'an inter-civilizational morality covering human rights and democracy' (2001: 189; see 1998: 182). Without this, he suggests, a clash between Western globalization and Islamic neo-absolutism is inevitable, since both want to impose their own political structures and/or economic institutions on the other (2001: 152, 158). In order to create the right conditions for the type of cross-cultural discussion of morality that Tibi wants, the West needs to abandon its programme of imposing its values and systems on the rest of the world. Also, the 'North–South gap' must be addressed (2001: 91, 96). Tibi fully recognizes that the prevailing international system has been constructed 'along Western norms and values' (2001: 196), that current international law is 'basically European law' and 'does not correspond with a universal legal awareness' (p. 149). However, it would be equally impossible to develop an international morality under 'the dominance of an Islamic notion of law' (*ibid.*: 152), therefore his agenda is to bring Muslims and Westerners and those of other cultures to the dialogue table to work out a moral consensus based on 'commonalities' and 'shared values' (*ibid.*: 200). 'Replacing Western dominance by an Islamic dominance/*ghallab* cannot bring world peace', he says. The solution is to first establish a genuinely pluralist 'secular international morality' (1998: 28). Tibi does think that the UDHR, widely accepted across existing cultural and national borders, provides a basis for discussion in as much as 'its principles are ... in a certain regard postulative' (*ibid.*: 152).

In Tibi's view, however, political (fundamentalist) Islam is incapable of entering this dialogue because it cannot recognize the Other as having anything to contribute. It sees the Other as inferior, which blatantly 'contradicts the call for equality and for cultural pluralism within the international system' (*ibid.*: 185). As noted earlier, Tibi contends that democracies are by nature pluralist. He therefore believes that only an Islam that embraces pluralism, or is at least open to dialogue with the Other, can take its place at the negotiating table. To do this, Islam must abandon its division of the world into *dar-al-Islam* and *dar-al-harb* (2001: 91, 152) and its project of imposing political Islam on the whole world. Instead, it must find ways to embrace pluralism. Tibi sees hope here if the Enlightenment project could be resurrected in Islam, dormant since the time of the rationalists and Hellenized philosophers, whose more open and tolerant attitude towards 'truth' outside the revealed tradition resulted in a period (especially in Moorish Spain) when Muslims had encountered Europeans 'on the grounds of this spirit of *'aql* (reason)' (2001: 204; see 1998: xv, 182, 202). Tibi is well aware, though, that the rationalist project floundered because it failed to gain Islamic respectability, and was dubbed 'foreign' (2001: 172; see also 1998: 29, 70–2). This tradition, he says, 'does not enjoy the respect of political Islam' (2001: 141).

Nonetheless, he thinks that a revitalization of rational Islam is more promising than its politicization (2001: xiv). Islam does have resources within its history that enables 'cultural borrowings' (1998: 202). 'In principle', he says, 'Muslims have been able to draw on their own civilization for a historical record of learning from other civilizations' (*ibid.*: 184). Cultural borrowing is 'one of the great sources for enriching mankind' and, says Tibi, 'this is also true for Islam' (2001: 139). Cultural pluralism is central to Tibi's approach. By this, he does not mean 'multiculturalism', which in his view is dangerous, since it 'ends up in an endorsement of ghettoes in which civil personal identity has no space and secularity is objected to' where, in the name of multicultural tolerance, the intolerable is tolerated (2001: 2002). There are 'limits to accepting difference':

I am not willing to discuss rejections of any individual human rights (for example, gender equality) or secularity, let alone the claims to absolutism in terms of acknowledging the 'difference' in the name of tolerance. (2001: 93)

He is scathing of 'cultural relativists' who deny the 'universality of standards and values' and of those who fail to defend their own values, thus 'If Europeans do not respect themselves, they cannot expect others to have respect for them ... values ... such as democracy and human rights need to be defended in the dialogue against any form of neo-absolutism' (2001: 229). He finds it amusing that some fundamentalists 'cite postmodernist and cultural-relativist approaches posited in the West to sustain their neo-absolutist program' when these same Muslims detest cultural-relativists and hold views that 'have nothing in common with postmodernism' (1998: 106). Indeed, their neo-absolutism is the antithesis of postmodernism.

In his 1998 chapter on human rights, Tibi is critical of the UIDHR and of writers such as Mawdudi for, in his view, denying that Muslims are also human. By claiming that there are specifically Islamic human rights they 'unwittingly' divorce Muslims from humanity (p. 212; see also p. 148 on '*homo islamicus*'). There cannot be, he says, different 'human rights' for Muslims, Hindus and others. 'Are Muslims and non-Muslims not equally human beings?' (p. 203). The claim that human rights are the 'property' of Muslims, he says, that they have always existed in the Qur'an, represents a 'proprietary attitude' that is inconsistent with his concept of an international morality; 'the self-congratulatory claims that "We Muslims had everything, including a human rights tradition, before the Europeans did" does not help', he says (1998: 209). In Tibi's view, 'human rights' are a recent addition to moral discourse, a 'product of modernity' and therefore 'prior to modern times these rights did not exist as a cultural understanding in any religion or civilization' (p. 208). However, for those Muslims for whom 'truth' can only be revealed truth, no value from outside Islam, such as human rights or democracy, can have any moral authority. Soroush and Tibi disagree, in the main, because they believe that Islam is primarily a religious and ethical discourse, while 'human rights' are 'a secular concept that need not be seen as impinging on religious faith' (Tibi 1998: 207). Mawdudi and the drafters of the UIDHR occupy purely Islamic grounds in their discussion of human rights. Therefore, they do not really defend Islam from possible censure based on the UDHR. Tibi moves the debate (see further discussion in Chapter Five) from Islamic to humanist or secular ground: 'embracing of secular human rights', he says, 'would facilitate placing Muslims in their proper place: humanity' (1998: 206). Soroush (whose own books in Iran are published with a censsor's caution) writes:

contemporary advocates of human rights can claim no monopoly on truth and justice; nonetheless, religious societies, precisely because of their religious nature, need to seriously engage in discussion of the issues they pose ... extrareligious debates of our day, which happen to concern human rights, must be viewed as worthy and useful exchanges of opinion in Islamic societies. (2000: 129)

Discussion topic

- Comment on Tibi's statement that 'The need to establish human rights as the substance of international morality is not consistent with any culturally exclusive or proprietary attitudes' (1998: 209).

Tibi (see Chapter Five) wants a rethinking of Islam that embraces 'rationalism within Islamic thought' (1998: 207) and regards the Qur'an as containing 'general principles that allow for varying interpretation'. God had never intended apparently prescriptive legal verses to be read as rigid laws (2001: 162). This opens up a new understanding of Islam as an ethical and religious, not political, worldview. Muslims can have a universal outlook but must abandon universal political ambitions. Tibi is not arguing for the imposition of human rights (or of democracy) onto the Muslim world by the West but for a rethinking of Islam within the Muslim world that will prepare the ground for these concepts to take root, to develop their own indigenous institutions, and to flourish. He is anxious to draw a line between 'broadly tolerant Islam and single-mindedly intolerant fundamentalism' (1998: 206–7). 'Human rights', he says, 'need to be made compatible with Islamic ethics, and compatibility here cannot be made a code word for imposition'.

Tibi wants Muslim countries to learn how to 'speak the language of secular human rights' in their 'own tongues' (1998: 207). 'Human rights and democracy', he says, are the 'primary guarantors of human dignity' (1998: 200). 'True Islamic ethics' will 'always have their place in an international morality based on a cross-cultural foundation' (p. 214). However, even if the secular origin of human rights continues to be denied by Muslims, this is 'tolerable if the *substance* of human rights is honoured' (1998: 213, his italics). Fully aware of 'double standards' in Western discourse (see above), he nowhere suggests that the West can simply teach the non-Western world what to do: 'Westerners need to learn that it works counterproductively when they try to teach non-Westerners about democracy and human rights. The response' to this, he says, 'is mostly defensive ... and self-asserting' (2001: 224). Tibi offers his 'international morality' as an alternative to both 'Westernization and the challenge of fundamentalism' (1998: 28, 81). 'In the pursuit of a united humanity sharing an international morality, it is essential that a basic program of human rights and democracy be asserted and honoured by all of the world's civilizations', he says (1998: 183). Without such an ethical convergence, there will be no 'peace between civilizations'.

Discussion topic

- Compare Tibi's approach to human rights with those of Maw-dudi, the *hizb-ut-tahrir* and the UIDHR. What is the principal difference between his and other approaches?

First Iranian to win Nobel Peace Prize

Iranian human rights activist, Shirin Ebadi, was awarded the 2003 Nobel Peace Prize. The Nobel committee 'lauded her for arguing for a new interpretation of Islamic law which is in harmony with vital human rights such as democracy and equality before the law' for women and men. According to the committee, Ebadi's 'principal arena is the struggle for basic human rights' and 'in an era of violence, she has consistently supported non-violence'. After receiving the prize, Ebadi said, 'I'm a Muslim, so you can be a Muslim and support democracy' (*Guardian Unlimited*, 10 October 2003, 'Iranian activist wins Nobel peace prize').

An-Na'im on Islam and human rights

An-Na'im is a law graduate of the Universities of Khartoum, Sudan, Cambridge, England and of Edinburgh, Scotland. He gained his doctorate from Edinburgh. He is a leading campaigner for human rights in the Muslim world. When he wrote *Towards An Islamic Reformation: Civil Liberties, Human Rights and International Law* (1990), he was aware that his book was 'likely to be banned in some Muslim countries' (p. 238; references are to the 1998 extract). He is a champion of M. M. Taha's approach to the reformulation of Islamic law. Like Tibi, his starting assumption is that traditional *Shari'ah* and human rights are incompatible (p. 222), therefore Islamic law needs to be reformed. He does believe that Islamic law has positive features, however, so the agenda he set himself was to 'identify areas of conflict ... and seek a reconciliation and positive relationship between the two systems' (1998: 222). He accepts that there is debate about the 'genuine universality' of the UDHR but says that 'this does not mean that there are no universal and binding standards' or that 'enforcement should be abandoned' (p. 223). He suggests that a 'normative principle' that runs through all cultures, that calls on others to treat us as we wish to be treated, opens up the possibility of establishing and sustaining 'universal standards of human rights' (*ibid.*). This is what Tibi means by a cross-cultural, international morality (Tibi refers to an-Na'im as an 'intellectually significant Muslim' who hopes 'to apply reason to Islamic reform', 1998: 31; on p. 203 he calls an-Na'im 'my reformist Muslim colleague'). Like Tibi, an-Na'im contends that the type of rights that qualify as universal are those to which 'people are entitled by virtue of being human' (p. 224), therefore they cannot belong exclusively to a specific culture or religion.

An-Na'im parts company from Mawdudi and from the UIDHR, arguing that when the *Shari'ah* was formulated 'there was no conception of universal human rights' (p. 227). Thus, slavery was tolerated. The Qur'an does not specifically ban slavery, although it does regulate it. Similarly, the equality of men and women did not exist as a concept. At the time, the 'most that *shari'ah* could do was to modify and lighten the harsh consequences of slavery and discrimination on grounds of religion or gender' (p. 227). Islam did improve 'on the pre-existing situation' but this does not mean that its provisions remain acceptable today. Also, just as it took account of what was considered to be humane and just at the time, so 'modern Islamic law cannot disregard the present conception of human rights'. An-Na'im comments that much of what Muslims write on human rights is 'not helpful because they overlook the problem of slavery and discrimination against Muslims and non-Muslims' (p. 228). In fact, the UIDHR declares that Islam 'abhors slavery'; while Mawdudi claims that the problem of slavery was quickly solved in Islam because the Qur'an encourages the 'freeing of slaves' (see, for example, Q90: 11–13). An-Na'im, however, argues that Muslims continued to practise slavery – for example, prisoners captured during military conquest were enslaved – and now need to recognize that even though tenth century *Shari'ah* tolerated slavery, 'subject to certain limitations and safeguards', they should now 'prohibit slavery for ever' (p. 230).

Drawing on Taha's concept of the evolution of Islamic Law and on the abrogation of the Madinan verses, an-Na'im proceeds to discuss the position of minorities and women in Islam with detailed analysis and discussion of Qur'anic material. He lists verses that are 'discriminatory', including the right of men to marry up to four wives while women can only have one husband, the right of men to marry a Jewish or Christian woman while women can only marry Muslims, the right of men to unilateral divorce, while women must have their husband's consent or a juridical decree, and the difference in inheritance rights (women receive less). He notes that in ratifying the 1979 International Convention on the Elimination of all Forms of Discrimination against Women, Egypt registered reservations about Articles 9, 16 and 29. Article 16 calls for full gender equality 'in all matters relating to marriage and family relations' (p. 233). In order to reconcile Islamic Law with 'human rights standards', says an-Na'im, all discriminatory laws must be repealed and replaced with laws guaranteeing complete equality. This can be achieved by recognizing that the relevant Qur'anic rules have fulfilled their 'transitional purpose' and can be set aside in favour of new ones. In this view, Q4: 34 'which establishes the male guardianship over women' would be displaced by a verse such as Q33: 35, which affirms the spiritual equality of the sexes. Spiritual equality should be translated into legal equality, in conformity with the original intent of the Qur'an's ethical message.

An-Na'im also discusses the Rushdie affair. He repudiates the validity of Khomeini's *fatwa* that called on Muslims to kill Rushdie, since '*shari'ah* requires that a person be charged with an offence and allowed a chance to defend himself' and because '*shari'ah* does not give the ruler of an Islamic state the power to punish a citizen of a non-Muslim state' (p. 236). Following through his concept of the evolution of the law, an-Na'im argues that the death sentence for apostasy can have no place in 'the law of Islam today' (p. 236). He thinks that 'toleration of unorthodoxy and of dissent is vital for the spiritual and intellectual benefit of Islam today' and that the law of apostasy endangers this. By applying evolution of the law, the death sentence can be replaced by a 'discretionary punishment (*ta'zir*) short of death'.

The same argument can be advanced with respect of the *hudud* penalties (amputation for theft; see Peters 1994: 248–9. 'Crimes and Their Penalties in the Qur'an'). Since *hudud* are meant to deter crime by establishing an extreme limit, an alternative punishment that also deters (such as a harsh prison sentence) would fulfil the Qur'an's ethical intent. Sardar (1985) argues that such penalties represent not the norm of the *Shari'ah*, which is 'mercy and forgiveness,' but the 'maximum retribution anyone can expect' (p. 120). There are Muslims, though, who defend the *hudud* on the grounds that Islamic Law has surrounded their application with so many caveats concerning the value of the stolen property, the number of offences committed by the accused, and what other conditions must be met (for example, a man is not guilty if he steals to feed his family and has received no support from the community or help in finding a job, in which case guilt lies with the whole community) that (it is alleged) they have rarely been implemented throughout Islamic history. Others point out that the Qur'an always encourages victims to forgive and not to punish perpetrators. Others argue that in an Islamic society where the rich care for the poor and resources are redistributed via *zakat* (money distributed to the poor; 2/2.5% of a Muslim's disposable income), no one would need to steal.

Discussion topics

On History
Mernissi (1994) says that in order to present their authoritarian version of Islam as the only authentic version, Muslim regimes manipulate history, lest Muslims look into 'that distant gloomy past when the cry for individuality and dignity was stifled in blood' and find that they are 'less alienated by the West and its democracy' because of that history (p. 20) in which individuals did exercise personal judgement and Islam was subject to different understandings. Tibi says that fundamentalism's belief in Islam's essential timelessness 'leaves no room for the study of history' (1998: 102).

- What role does history play in different contemporary under-standings of Islam?

- Can the study of history challenge those who exercise power? How? If the powerful and the 'winners' write history, how can the voices of the silenced or of minorities or of those who did not win the debates (but whose ideas were perhaps of value but not in the interests of the elite) actually be heard?

On Duplicity

- Can you think of examples of Western states being duplicitous in respect of United Nations resolutions or conventions?

- Can you identify any inconsistencies between the conduct of Western states and the UDHR? For example, the USA refused to treat combatants captured in Afghanistan either as civilians or as prisoners of war on the grounds that they were 'illegal comba-tants' not soldiers. Arguably, however, the Taliban were the legal government of Afghanistan, even if only recognized by neigh-bouring Pakistan, and the USA was engaged in a war against that regime. Detainees in Camp X-Ray, Guantanamo Bay, Cuba, were denied legal advice and kept in custody without being charged with any offence, or given a court hearing. Iraqi prisoners in the US-run Abu Ghraib jail, Baghdad, have been abused, humiliated and tortured. Some allege that responsibility went 'right to the top' and that the soldiers who carried out the maltreatment were obeying orders. In your opinion, does this honour inter-nationally recognized Conventions (such as the Geneva conventions)?

- Can you identify any contraventions of human rights in a Muslim country? What is the source of your information? Is it biased, in your opinion? If you think it an objective, neutral source, how is this objectivity established or verified?

Freedom of expression and the limits of dissent: *Hisbah*

The case of Abu Zayd (or Zaid): accused of spreading cultural AIDS

Hisbah is the traditional institution for 'enjoining the good (*maruf*) and prohibiting wrong' (*munkar*). It provides for public vigilance (exercised by religious police) and for private redress, even if whoever makes an accu-sation has no direct involvement. The Universal Islamic Declaration of Human Rights upholds *hisbah* (article 4c; see also the Muslim Council of Europe's Model Constitution, Sardar 1985: 336). In 1995, *hisbah* was used to dissolve the marriage of the Egyptian scholar, Nasr Hamid Abu Zayd on the grounds that his view of Qur'anic interpretation made him an

apostate, and a 'Muslim woman cannot be married to an "apostate"'
(Tibi 1998: x). Egypt passed a new *hisbah* law in January 1996. An attempt
has also been made to use *hisbah* to prosecute Nawal El Saadawi.

After being found guilty of apostasy and divorced (by the court) from
his wife, Abu Zayd left Egypt for Europe, where he has been teaching at
Leiden University in Holland. A late entrant to the academy, he worked
for twelve years in the telecommunications industry but from an early age
had wanted to follow the footsteps of the Egyptian modernist scholar,
Taha Husayn (1889–1973). Husayn was Professor of Arabic Literature at
the university and a renowned novelist as well as a critical scholar. His
thesis that pre-Islamic poetry had been a later forgery courted controversy.
Zayd joined the Department of Arabic at Cairo University after graduation
in 1972 and was directed by the Faculty to major in Islamic Studies for his
research degrees. He was not keen on this because of the fate of an earlier
PhD thesis that had applied literary criticism to the Qur'an, which the
examiners had failed. After that, the Chair in Islamic Studies had
remained vacant. In his Master's research, Zayd explored the metapho-
rical approach to the Qur'an pioneered by the Mu'tazalites (see Chapter
Four). His PhD thesis then examined the work of Ibn Arabi (d. 1279), the
great Sufi thinker, for whom Islam was an open-ended religion of love. Ibn
Arabi also believed that the same fundamental truth informed all the great
religions and wanted to bring about harmony both within Islam among its
different schools and outside Islam, with other religions. His work on Ibn
Arabi convinced Abu Zayd that hermeneutics is always conditioned by the
context in which the interpreter lives and that throughout Muslim history,
the Qur'an has been used as a political tool by different groups, who all
use it to defend their views against their opponents. The advocates of
contemporary political Islam were manipulating the text to further their
agendas, just as others had done before them. Too often, Muslims have
subjected the Qur'an to 'political and pragmatic manipulation' (1998:
200).

His work began to attract opposition and when he applied for promotion, he had to wait six months while the university committee evaluated
his work and reached a decision based on three written reports. The vote
was seven against and six in favour of his appointment as full professor.
Two of the reports were positive. One, by Dr Abd el-Sabour Shahin, was
highly critical. Abu Zayd had questioned the *bona fides* of various Islamic
banks that claimed to offer an authentic alternative to the Western interest-
based system, which religious authorities, including Shahin, endorsed.
Abu Zayd said they swindled innocent Muslims out of their savings. In his
view, they were simply the modern creation of political Islam.

Two weeks after the decision not to promote Abu Zayd, Dr Shahin
denounced the scholar from the pulpit of the Amr Ibn al-Aas mosque as
an apostate (2 April 1993). The following Friday, *ulama* from all over Egypt
repeated the allegation; one Imam accused him of spreading 'cultural
AIDS' and of having 'enthusiastically championed *The Satanic Verses*'

(Mostyn 2002: 154). A court case ensued, in which Abu Zayd's accusers petitioned for the annulment of his marriage on the grounds of apostasy under the law of *hisbah*, while newspapers pointed out how his continued tenure at the university endangered his students' faith. The lower court rejected the petition. The court of appeal overturned this decision, annulled Abu Zayd's marriage and declared him to be an apostate. At the same time, Muslim Brotherhood member Sheikh Mohammed al-Ghazali (1917–96), former government official and Professor of Islamic Law, defending Farag Fouda's assassin, stated at the trial that if the state failed to fulfil its duty, all Muslims should do so instead; 'the killing of apostates', said the Sheikh, 'cannot be prosecuted under Islamic Law because' it is 'just' (see Tibi 1998: 155). Fouda, a Professor of Agricultural Economics at Ein Shams University, Cairo and a newspaper columnist, was assassinated for 'publicly' proposing 'the adoption of secularist philosophy in Islam' (Bielefeldt 1995: 615).

See *Index on Censorship* Vol. 25, No. 4 1996, pp. 30–9, 'The Case of Abu Zaid' and 'When Words and Ideas Lead to Exile', *Middle East Times* 16 June 2000 (*metimes.com/2k/issue2000-24/eg/when_words_and.htm*); and Abu Zayd with Esther R. Nelson (2004).

Discussion topic

● Is the *hisbah* law a violation of the right of free expression, or necessary for the preservation of religious values in a religiously based society?

The Salman Rushdie affair

Why is the imagination so terrifying that we have to censor it? What can we think that is, so to speak, unimaginable? (Kureishi, 'Something Given', essay on his website *http://www.hanifkureishi.com/something_given.html*)

Tibi (1998) calls the 'slaying of Muslim intellectuals who disagree with the visions and solutions presented by the fundamentalists – in, for example, Algeria, Egypt, and Turkey ... the foremost violation of human rights in contemporary Islamic societies' (pp. 199–200). Earlier, Muir had it that

> Every rising doubt must be smothered, every question vanish. If doubts did arise, the sword was unsheathed to dispel and silence them ... to the combination ... of the spiritual and political elements in ... the Mahometan government must be attributed the absence of candid and free investigation into the origin and early incidents of Islam ... The faculty of criticism was annihilated by the sword. (1894: xxxviii–xxxix)

In Rushdie's case, a novelist writing in Britain provoked the anger of many Muslims, who called for his execution following a *fatwa* (14 February 1989) by the then leader of the Iranian Islamic Revolution, Khomeini, declaring that good Muslims should kill Rushdie and all involved in producing and distributing his book, *The Satanic Verses*. As a result of the controversy, the somewhat technical term *fatwa* (legal opinion or ruling on a point of law), previously known only to specialists and to Muslims in the non-Muslim world, entered the popular vocabulary with the meaning of 'sentence' or, as Bernard Lewis comments, of 'putting out a contract' (2003: 109). Hence the phrase 'a *fatwa* against', which ignores the fact that a *fatwa* (the Islamic equivalent of the Roman *responsa prudentium*) can grant permission for Muslims to, say, be organ donors. Al-Azim (1994) argued that Khomeini's *fatwa* was not a *fatwa*, but the type of 'judgement' or 'death sentences' that an 'imam', a 'grand mufti' or a '*faqih*' might issue in 'moments of grave danger to Islam and for the defence of the integrity of the faith' when normal due process may be bypassed (p. 22). For Pipes (2002) the *fatwa* was a political device by Khomeini to claim moral leadership of Islam. He failed to eliminate Rushdie but he did stir 'something in the soul of many Muslims, reviving a sense of confidence about Islam'. For Pipes, this had a negative impact, 'inspiring Islamists around the world to go on the offensive against anyone perceived as defaming their Prophet, their faith or even themselves' (p. 172). Some point to incidents in Muhammad's life when he appears to have ordered or to have condoned the summary execution of enemies, including poets, as evidence of Islam's intolerance towards the creative imagination. On one occasion, Muhammad asked 'who would rid him of Marwan's daughter?', the poetess Asma bint Marwana, and 'Umayr 'went to her house that very night and killed her', to be later told by Muhammad that he had 'helped God and his apostle' (Guillaume 1955: 675–6). More recently, Nobel Prize- winning Egyptian novelist Naguib Mahfouz attracted censure for his novel *Awlad Al Haratna* (*Children of Gebelawi* (1959)), which '*ulama* accused of causing offence to the prophets of Islam from Abraham onwards' (Mostyn 2002: 147). In 1994, a young man, who considered Mahfouz an infidel, stabbed him in the neck as he walked to his weekly literacy circle. Before his execution, the condemned attacker admitted that he had not read any of Mahfouz's books but said that his sheikh had condemned the novel.

For Muslims critical of Rushdie, see Kabbani (1989), Akhtar (1989) and Sardar and Davies (1990). Kabbani argues that Rushdie committed cultural treason. She contends that those whose insider knowledge give their voices authority and credibility have a responsibility to tell the truth. Failing to accept accountability, Rushdie's writing is 'self-indulgent and politically irresponsible' (p. 67). Akhtar takes the view that the book was a 'calculated attempt to vilify and slander Muhammad' (p. 6). He rejects Rushdie's defence that it is a work of literature exploring the phenomena of revelation, since in his opinion Rushdie 'leaves too many clues to show that unprincipled abuse rather than disciplined critique was his dominant intention', which is why 'one cannot take his book seriously as a powerful work of art' (p. 35). Sardar argues that those who defend Rushdie's book in the name of free speech set one man's 'distorted imagination' over the 'experience and knowledge of the overwhelming majority ... of Muslims'

(p. 242). 'The vast majority of Muslims', says Sardar, 'wish Salman Rushdie no physical harm; but equally, they are not able to forgive him' (p. 7). Sardar argues that writers, even of fiction, have a duty and a responsibility to consider the effect of what they write on 'real people in society' (p. 265), which Rushdie failed to do. Muslims who write in defence of Rushdie, including Arkoun and al-Azmeh (1994) do not especially like the book but believe that it raises important issues, as al-Azmeh says, 'that the pure, unitary Islam of Rushdie's opponents which they say he has libelled and misrepresented is as much a fiction as his Islam'. It is 'wholly imaginary', the 'very fantasy exploded in the book'. The Rushdie affair represents a battle between the 'modern, enlightened critical spirit' of which he is 'such a brilliant representative' and 'religious reaction', the 'notion of a single authentic culture' (pp. 26–7).

What caused offence?

The novel is primarily about the search for identity and, as Rushdie says, explores the 'experience of uprooting, disjuncture and metamorphosis (slow or rapid, painful or pleasurable) that is the migrant condition' as a 'metaphor for all humanity' (1991: 394). Rushdie describes himself as a 'secular, pluralist, eclectic man' (p. 405), although he has also spoken about supporting the 'concept of the secular Muslim' and says that Islam does not have to mean 'blind faith'; it can also mean, as it did for him, 'a culture, a civilization' and an open-minded disputatious philosophy (p. 435). However, the 'granite, heartless certainties of Actually Existing Islam' convinced him that his 'fantasy of joining the fight for the modernization of Muslim thought, for freedom from the shackles of the Thought Police, was stillborn' (p. 436). Charged with apostasy, Rushdie felt that he had 'been concealed behind a false self' (p. 405).

In the book, one of Rushdie's characters dreams about the founding of a new religion, propagated by the Prophet Mahound (a medieval Western demonization of 'Muhammad'; see Rushdie 1991: 402), a womanizing scoundrel, who has 'no time for scruples, no qualms for ends and means' (1988: 363). This echoes medieval fantasy about Muhammad's sexuality and about Islam as catering to male debauchery. In one scene in the book, Mahound mistakes for God's words those that are actually from Satan (pp. 118–25). In another, he takes words that are those of his scribe, based on the Allah ibn Abi Sarh incident (p. 367). Here, Rushdie draws on his knowledge of Islamic sources, some of which record an incident when Muhammad appears to have temporarily conceded the efficacy of prayers to three of the goddesses of Makkah, an incident that Muir also recounts at length (1858–60, Vol. 2, pp. 150–62; see also Guillaume 1955: 146–8). This suggested the possibility of a rapprochement between Muhammad and the Qureishi and precipitated the return of some of the refugees from Abyssinia, who arrived in Makkah to find that the putative verse of the Qur'an had since been abrogated by Q53: 19–22.

In the novel, Mahound's arch opponent offers him money in return for the concession. Mahound himself is confused by the words he had uttered. After reflecting on this, he issued a retraction. Muslims argue that Satan had in fact spoken the original concession. According to Q22: 52–3 Satan always attempts to substitute his words for the divine word, 'but Allah will cancel anything that Satan throws in'. In Rushdie's version, however, his character Gibreel admits that he was the source of both the 'statement' and its 'repudiation' (1988: 123). Gibreel tells Mahound that he had really brought him the Devil (p. 125). As an atheist, Rushdie believes no more in Satan than in God, so what he was really suggesting was a human origin for Islam. One of the areas he set out to explore in the book was how the 'mystic's conscious personality informs and interacts with the mystic event ... to try to understand the human event of revelation' (1991: 408).

Discussion topic

Esack (2003) suggests the 'Satanic Verses affair' might 'provide a glimpse into how the Prophet may have subconsciously willed revelation' (p. 44). Rushdie writes in order to question and to challenge '*everything in every possible way*' (1991: 429, his italics). As one of his characters in *The Satanic Verses* says:

> A poet's work is to name the unnameable, to point at frauds, to take sides, start arguments, shape the world and stop it from going to sleep ... and if rivers of blood flow from the cuts his verses inflict, then they will nourish him (1988: 97).

- Rushdie describes his book's exploration of the human event of revelation as a legitimate 'secular man's reckoning with the religious spirit' (1991: 396). Do you think that his exercise was legitimate?

Literary case study: Hanif Kureishi's *The Black Album*

Hanif Kureishi's novel, *The Black Album* (1995), is set in East London in 1989. The Berlin wall had collapsed, communism and the Soviet empire were no longer 'the enemy' and Islam was starting to fill that role. One character has it that Muslim migrants are a 'fifth column', 'they are entering France through Marseilles and Italy by the South. Soon they will be seeping through ... into the heart of civilized Europe. Soon books and bacon will be banned' (p. 159). For the speaker, Muslim migrants and terrorists are synonymous and 'surely ... [they] must be eradicated from society'.

A long time friend of Rushdie, Kureishi deliberately set out while researching the novel to find out both why fundamentalists hated Rushdie and 'why they disapproved of sexuality, of books, of the creative imagination'. Kureishi described Khomeini's *fatwa* as an act of 'extra-ordinary intellectual terror'. However, the 'attack on Rushdie' also stimulated thought about 'the point and place of literature, about what stories were for, and about their relation to dissent' (1997: vii, 2002: 215). In *The Black Album* and also in *My Son the Fanatic* (1997) he set out to explore why it was that young British Asians were attracted to fundamentalist Islam.

Both stories also explore the immigrant condition. The book's central character is a young British Asian, Shahid, who chooses to read English at a rather down-at-heel London college because he admires one of the postmodernist teachers, Deedee Osgood. His own travel business-owning and financially quite affluent family are very nominally Muslim. Osgood encouraged her 'students to study anything that took their interest, from Madonna's hair to a history of the leather jacket' (p. 22). Shahin and Deedee become lovers. However, Shahin also becomes a member of a group of Muslim students who regard themselves as activists and who assert the primacy of their Muslim, not Asian or British Asian, identities. Shahin wants to discover his identity and is attracted to this group because he hopes that through them he might find out more about his own people (p. 76). Shahin is fully integrated into British society (his father props up the local bar and talks endlessly about his war experiences fighting for the Brits) but the group argue against assimilation: 'We must not assimilate, that way we lose our souls ... It's not we who must change, but the world' so the group's aim is to bring about the world's Islamization (p. 67).

Riaz, the group's leader, declares that the Muslims will not be 'ghettoized' when it seems that the aubergine that had started to display Allah's confirmation that Rushdie was a blasphemer is to be displayed somewhere other than the town hall. It had to be the town hall, where 'there is already a picture of Nelson Mandela' and an 'African mask' (p. 149). Riaz keeps his disciples spellbound with his street-wise talks, entitled 'Rave to the Brave?', 'Adam and Eve, not Adam and Steve', 'Islam: A Blast from the Past or a Force for the Future?', and 'Democracy is a Hypocrisy'. It is the Ayatollah's *fatwa* that galvanizes the group into action – as one member puts it, *The Satanic Verses* has 'been around too long without action'. Rushdie has 'insulted us all, the prophet, the prophet's wives, his whole family. It's sacrilege and blasphemy' and the 'punishment is death' (p. 140). The *fatwa* is fully endorsed and the group rejoices 'in the Ayatollah's action' (p. 141). Riaz, however, is sympathetically portrayed in the book as a sincere, devout young man fully committed to his faith. *The Black Album*'s title is from an album by Prince, whose music Shahin and Deedee both admire. In the book, Prince represents postmodern culture: 'He's half black and half white, half man and half woman, half size, feminine but macho too. His work contains and extends the history of black American music' (p. 21).

Shahin finds the group's attitude towards the book disturbing. As a known defender of Rushdie, Deedee is also subject to denunciation. Now her lover, Shahin is naturally equally disturbed by their description of his teacher; according to the group, she was a sexual predator, a 'pornographic priestess' who encouraged 'the brothers of colour to take drugs' and whose 'screams' could be heard 'half-way across London' when 'she is screwed' (pp. 190–1). Shahin persuades the group to at least discuss the book and their response to it and finds that he is its only defender. It was fiction, a work of the imagination; 'a free imagination . . . ranges over many natures. A free imagination, looking into itself, illuminates others', he says. If Rushdie has insulted them, could they not just forget it? But Riaz pronounces that the 'free and unbridled imagination' of 'corrupt men' such as Rushdie 'must be caged as if they were dangerous carnivores' (p. 153). 'Fiction', says Riaz, is 'by its very nature' a form of 'lying – a perversion of the truth'.   Shahin rebels against the group's certainty, against 'their lack of doubt' that 'hell fire [was] for disbelievers . . . and heaven for the rest' (p. 67). He also feels suffocated by the way the group try to control his whole life: 'Chad [Riaz's henchman] assumed that Shahin was their possession; they wanted to own him entirely; not a part of him could elude them' (p. 106). When he is with his friends, their story compels him but when he leaves them, he starts to doubt; 'he found the world to be more subtle and inexplicable'. Stories, too, 'were made by men and women', so 'could not be true or false, for they were exercises in that most magnificent but unreliable capacity, the imagination, which William Blake called "the divine body in every man"' (p. 110). But imagination is anathema to the group, who will admit not a splinter into their beliefs, 'for that would poison all, rendering their convictions human' and therefore 'fallible' (p. 111). It is when the group burn the book in the college grounds that he finally parts from them, choosing doubt instead of their certainty: 'the alliance terminated the moment' that the book was 'soaked in petrol. He had been taught much about what he did not like; now he would embrace uncertainty. Maybe wisdom would come from what he did not know, rather than from confidence' (p. 190). 'How', reflects Shahin, 'could anyone confine themselves to one system or creed? Why should they feel they had to?' There was 'no fixed self'. 'Surely our serial selves melted and mutated daily? There had to be . . . innumerable ways of being in the world', so 'he would spread himself out' (p. 228).

Discussion topic

- In a pluralist, democratic society, should there be a legal mechanism for a member of a religious faith to petition for the banning, withdrawal or censure of published or broadcast material that they believe misrepresents or ridicules their beliefs? If so, what form might this mechanism take? What issues would be raised in any discussion of proposals for such a legal mechanism?

Resources

See the US Constitutional Rights Foundation website for additional discussion material: *www.crf-usa.org/terror/rushdie.htm*, 'Blasphemy, Salman Rushdie and Freedom of Expression'.

Material on the Rushdie affair, on Rushdie's writing, literary criticism and discussion of related political and cultural issues may be accessed on the postcolonial website: *http://www.postcolonialweb.org/pakistan/literature/ rushdie/rushdieov.html*

Atheism.com has a useful chronology of the Rushdie affair: *atheism.com/ library/misc/blrushdie.htm*

4   Muslim Voices on the Qur'an

Tafsir (exegesis) of the Qur'an is the most important science for Muslims. All matters concerning the Islamic way of life are connected with it in one sense or another since the right application of Islam is based on proper understanding of the guidance from Allah.
   (Denffer 1983: 123)

Common ground

While the statement 'all Muslims believe that …' may be risky, given Islam's diversity, a conservative Muslim such as Ahmad von Denffer and a progressive Muslim such as Farid Esack writing on the Qur'an agree on many fundamental aspects of its study. Esack remarks that his own book on the Qur'an 'follows the broad contours of critical Muslim scholarship in most of its assumptions about early prophetic history', although as a 'critical and progressive Muslim' Esack does, though, present some 'other opinions for consideration' (2002: 10). Yet there are, says Esack, 'notions about the Qur'an that are stabilized and accepted by the vast majority of scholars in the last millennium or longer' and while terms such as 'mainstream' or 'majoritarian' Islam are 'not entirely accurate', it is possible to speak of 'majority opinion', if only for 'lack of an alternative' (*ibid.*).

Where contemporary Muslims differ and diverge is less about the nature and status of the Qur'an than on how it is to be interpreted and applied. Divergence in the political and legal arenas has been a constant theme of previous chapters of this book. For example, those on the political left who believe that the Qur'an does not mandate the unity of religion and politics are free to look elsewhere, outside Islam, for help in constructing legal and governmental systems. For Muslims on the right for whom the Qur'an mandates the unity of religion and politics, all legal and governmental systems must be rooted in Qur'anic concepts, if they are not specifically described in its text. It is not surprising, then, that 'conservative' Muslims (traditionalists, neo-traditionalists) adopt an approach to Qur'anic interpretation that can be broadly characterized as on the theological 'right', while liberal Muslims (modernists, progressives) adopt an approach that is broadly on the theological left, as their theologies inform, mould and shape their politics.

Denffer describes his popular *'Ulum al-Qur'an as* 'a descriptive account of the traditional subject of *'ulum-al-qur'an*' (p. 8), while Esack (2002) also describes his book as 'essentially a descriptive work' (p. 10). The Islamic Foundation, Leicester, a study and research centre that has close links with *Jamaati-i-Islam* (Khurshid Ahmad is a former Director of the Foundation) published Denffer's book, which is also available on the internet (*http:// www.islamworld.net/UUQ/*). Denffer is a German Muslim. The book's approach to the Qur'an is orthodox, although Muslims on the left are unlikely to disagree with much of its contents (with the possible exception of the section on abrogation). Esack adopts what he himself describes as a 'progressive' approach to the text of the Qur'an that includes listening to what 'critical outsiders have to say'. Esack graduated from two conservative seminaries in Pakistan, took his PhD in Birmingham (his 1997 book is derived from the thesis) and also studied Bible in Germany. He suggests that his book, which is intended for outsiders as well as for insiders, is 'arguably the first introductory book on the Qur'an by a Muslim that reflects that attempt to listen' (p. 11). Denffer comments that 'his volume' is, 'to the best of my knowledge, the first of its kind in a European language' (p. 9). He writes for insiders, whom he hopes will be better able, as a result of the book, to 'grasp fully the message of the Qur'an and to apply it' in their lives (pp. 9–10). Writing post-9/11 and for non-Muslims as well as for Muslims, Esack is anxious to show how the Qur'an informs a commitment to peace, rather than to violence. The fact that the earlier Denffer text does not stress the Qur'an's concern for justice and peace reflects its pre-9/11 date, rather than the author's disinterest in these issues. This, and other differences between the two texts, may raise the question whether it is legitimate to compare them. While the analysis below does identify similarities and differences between the two texts, its main aim is to present in some detail two approaches to the Qur'an to illustrate how these two scholars deal with the same text. What follows is perhaps more of a contrast, given the writers' different perspectives. It focuses on areas of divergence between progressive and traditional approaches, drawing on additional material from Arkoun, Rahman and Zayd, who have influenced Esack, and from Mawdudi and Brohi whose views support Denffer's.

How Muslims view the Qur'an

Much of what Muslims believe about the Qur'an derives from what the Qur'an says about itself. This is supplemented by *hadith* material and by what became recognized as orthodox theological beliefs within Islamic thought, following some early controversies and debates about the nature of the Qur'an. Most Muslims consider that both the Qur'an and the *hadith* are 'from Allah' but with the clear distinction that the former consists of God's direct speech communicated to Muhammad by the Angel Gabriel, while the latter consists of accounts of 'the Prophet's own words and actions' (Denffer 1983: 19). Also, *hadith* are 'not necessarily reported in their precise wording as the Qur'an is' (*ibid.*: 20). The term '*wahi*' (usually rendered 'revelation') is applied to both Qur'an and *hadith*. However, the Qur'an's text consists of 'recited revelation' (*wahi matlu*') while the *hadith* is 'unrecited' or 'unrehearsed' (*wahi ghayr matlu*') (Esack 2002: 100). The Qur'an itself uses the term *wahi* in several ways. In some texts the word carries the meaning of 'inspiration', for example Q28: 7, 'we sent this *wahi* to the mother of Moses', and Q16: 68, 'your Lord sent *wahi* to the bee to build its hives' (Esack 2002: 42; Denffer 1983: 22–3). Esack says that the assumption here is that women or birds cannot 'become messengers of God in the same way that men do' (p. 42). When applied to men, the term *wahi* usually carries the meaning not of 'inspiration' but of 'revelation', although this 'revelation' is always communicated via some sort of inter-mediate medium, such as a dream, or via a messenger such as an angel. When used in this sense, says Esack, 'prophethood' (see below) is 'implied for the recipient of such revelation'. Both Esack and Denffer cite Q42: 51:

> It is not fitting for a man that God should speak to him except by inspiration, or from behind a veil, or by sending of a messenger to reveal with God's permission what God wills.

Esack and Denffer both explain the meaning of the word 'Qur'an' (derived from *qara'a*) as 'recitation', pointing out that the original usage of the word was not 'restricted to the written form of a book' (Denffer 1983: 17; Esack 2002: 30). Esack, though, develops this into a lengthy discussion about the nature of the Qur'anic revelation, while Denffer does not. Esack stresses that as first 'revealed' and 'recited', the Qur'an was 'oral' and not 'written speech' and an 'active and ongoing reality' not a closed one (p. 20, citing Graham 1984).

Denffer is confident that the Qur'an, which Muslims cherish today as their most authoritative text, indeed as literally God's word, contains the very words (and those very words alone) that God communicated to Muhammad between 610 and 632 CE. Denffer writes, 'Prophet Muham-mad ... received the revelation of the Qur'an through a special messenger sent by God ... the Angel Gabriel, who recited to him God's words exactly' (p. 24). Esack agrees that 'The universal Muslim consensus today is that, in terms of content, the current version of the Qur'an is the authentic one which was read during the time of the Prophet and was left with the community at the time of his departure from the world' (p. 78).

Denffer points out that just as there have been numerous prophets, so there have been 'numerous written records of their messages', some of which are referred to in the Qur'an as *suhuf* (sheets or leaves) or as *kitab* (a book). Specific references include the *taurat* of Moses (see Q5: 44) and the *injil* of Jesus (see Q48: 29). Denffer sums up traditional Muslim belief about these pre-Qur'anic scriptures as follows:

> Besides carrying the same basic message about Allah, the Master of the worlds, and man His creation [they] also brought specific instructions addressed directly to particular communities ... at given points in history and in particular circumstances. (p. 16)

Being 'situation-oriented', these scriptures were 'not completely universal' in nature or in application, so 'with changing circumstances ... new guidance from Allah was required'. Hence, new scriptures were revealed. Finally, when the time was right God chose the prophet Muhammad as recipient of God's complete, final, definitive and comprehensive revelation, intended not only for a limited period of history or for a specific, particular context but for all time and for all contexts (Denffer 1983: 16–17). Or, as Esack puts it, 'The Qur'an is God speaking, not merely to Muhammad in seventh century Arabia, but from all eternity to all humankind' (p. 31). The Qur'an describes itself as completing and confirming the contents of previous scriptures (see Q3: 3), while Christians and Jews are accused of having somehow 'corrupted' their scriptures (see Q5: 13 and discussion in Chapter Seven of this book). Consequently, while arguably the Qur'an recognizes the pre-Qur'anic scriptures, in practice 'Muslim scholars, because of this "distortion", believe that the previous scriptures have no contemporary validity ... in effect they hold that the only valid scripture is the Qur'an' (Esack 2002: 49). Muhammad, for Muslims, as the bringer of the complete and final revelation, is the last prophet (described as the seal, *khatm*, of the prophets, Q33: 40). There is no longer any role for prophethood.

For Muslims, as the Qur'an originates within the Godness of God, it is not really possible to speak about 'the history of the Qur'an' any more than it is about the 'history of God', says Esack (p. 31). There is a deeply rooted conviction among Muslims that the Qur'an is an 'extension of the divine into the human' (p. 31). For Esack, the doctrine of the inimitability (*'ijaz*) of the Qur'an, that it is wholly unique, effectively removes it from the arena of human critical discourse, making it impossible to deal with the 'text' of the Qur'an in the same way that other texts are analysed, discussed and critiqued. Use of the term 'text' is therefore problematic for some Muslims, implying that it can be compared with and dealt with in the same way as other texts. For many Muslims, the Qur'an 'cannot be subjected to any linguistic principles' since its 'language' is 'viewed as ... timeless and independent of any "non-divine" elements' (p. 69).

How did Muhammad receive the Qur'an?

The most commonly used term in the Qur'an to describe its 'revelation' is the term *tanzil* (to send or come down, Esack 2002: 42). Thus Muslims speak about the Qur'an's 'descent' (see Denffer 1983: 24). Both writers describe the 'descent' of the Qur'an as having taken place in stages (see Esack 2002: 31–3; Denffer 1983: 28–9; this is also referred to as 'progressive revelation', or see Esack 1997: 54). Both describe orthodox Muslim conviction, based on their interpretations of various Qur'anic verses, that the Qur'an first descended from God to the 'protected tablet' (al-lawh al-mahfuz) above the seventh heaven (see Q85: 21–2), then from this 'protected tablet' to the lowest heaven's abode of honour (bayt al-'izzah) (see Q97: 1–5), and finally from this lowest heaven to 'the earth in stages to the Prophet Muhammad' (Esack 2002: 32–3).

This refers to the belief that the contents of the Qur'an as 'we have it before us today' contain those verses that were 'revealed' to Muhammad 'throughout the twenty-three years of Muhammad's prophethood, first in the laila-al-qadr [night of power] of Ramadan, through the Angel Gabriel' (Denffer 1983: 24; see Q17 and 25 and 59: 21). Muslim consensus is that the Qur'an was 'revealed in stages ... and not as a complete book in a single act of revelation' (Denffer 1983: 28). The 'preserved tablet' is believed to have been a 'metaphysical substance', hence debate (see below) about whether the Qur'an pre-existed its sending down as an eternal attribute of God, the uncreated divine word (Esack 2002: 32). Denffer explains that this gradual process was required because revelation was a very difficult experience for the prophet, in order to gradually implement God's laws, and to aid the understanding, application and memorization of the revelation itself (p. 29). Q25: 32 says that God 'revealed' the Qur'an 'in pieces ... to strengthen' its hearers' hearts (see Esack 1997: 55; Denffer 1983: 29; see also Q17: 106).

Denffer narrates the traditional account without commenting, for example about the nature of the 'preserved tablet'. Esack refers to some alternative traditions and describes the whole process as the 'Qur'an's putative descent'. Among alternative traditions, says Esack, is one that regards the 'mother of the book' as 'the source of all revelation', so that the Qur'an is part of, but not the whole of, this 'more encompassing "mother of the book"' (p. 32; the Qur'an uses this term at Q43: 2–4). Denffer accepts without question the traditional view that the Qur'an contains nothing at all that can be said to have had its origin within the mind of Muhammad. Esack offers substantial discussion about the relationship between the Qur'an and its recipient. He refers to this as a 'grey area' that Muslim scholarship has traditionally avoided (p. 101).

Esack's and Denffer's respective accounts of the way in which the Qur'an was revealed to Muhammad could similarly be characterized as factual and consequently brief on the one hand (Denffer, pp. 24–9) and as discursive and consequently lengthy (Esack, pp. 39–55) on the other. Both indicate that there is discussion in classical sources about the order in which the verses were revealed to Muhammad, and about the identity of the first and last verses of revelation (see Denffer, pp. 26–8, Esack, pp. 41, 52) but Esack is much more concerned than Denffer with the prophet's experience of revelation, that is, with the nature of the phenomena of receiving the 'word of God'. It is in the context of this discussion that he refers to the 'Satanic Verses' affair (p. 44) and later to the incident involving Allah ibn Abi Sarh (p. 82), both of which informed the writing of Rushdie's novel (see chapter on human rights). Denffer makes no reference to either. Esack has a detailed account of Muhammad's life. Denffer does not give any biographical information about Muhammad, nor does he describe early Muslim history.

According to the traditional account, Muhammad was 40 years old when he first experienced the receipt of revelation (the traditional chronology is challenged by such writers as Patricia Crone and Michael Cook, 1977). The *hadith* and *sirah* (biographical accounts of Muhammad's life) describe this in detail not found in the Qur'an itself. Peters (1994) reproduces Ibn Ishaq's account (pp. 50–53; Ibn Ishaq, d. 767, wrote an early biography of Muhammad), Esack and Denffer both reproduce Bukhari's account (pp. 39–40, p. 25). Muhammad often retreated to a cave on a mountain, Hira, outside Makkah, especially during the month of Ramadan to meditate; tradition says that he was alienated from the social ethic and religion of his time. It was there, in 610 CE, that he 'underwent a traumatic experience, the first of a series of revelations, the beginning of the Qur'an as we know it' (Esack 2002; 39). Bukhari's account (Vol. 1, Khan 1987: 2–4) says that while Muhammad was in deep meditation, possibly in an altered state of consciousness, he became aware of the presence of the Angel Gabriel who commanded him to 'recite' (*iqra*), to which Muhammad replied, 'I do not know how to read'. Gabriel then, said Muhammad, 'pressed me so hard that I could not bear it any more ... He then released me and again asked me to read and I replied, "I do not know how to read". Thereupon he caught me again and pressed me a second time till I could not bear it any more. He then released me and again asked me to read but again I replied, "I do not know how to read (or what shall I read)?" Thereupon he caught me for the third time and pressed me, and then released me and said, "Read in the name of your Lord, who has created (all that exists), has created man from a clot. Read! And your Lord is the Most Generous"' (Q96: 1–3). Trembling and with beating heart, Muhammad rushed home to Khadijah, asking her to cover him with a cloak because he feared for himself. Khadijah's immediate response was that God would never humiliate or disgrace him since he kept good relations with all his family, helped the poor and was generous to guests. Khadijah then took Muhammad to see her Christian cousin, Waraqah, whose response, on hearing about Muhammad's experience, was to say it was Gabriel, the 'Angel of Revelation', 'the same one that Allah had sent to Moses', who had appeared to Muhammad.

The words cited above 'Read, in the Name of your Lord, who created you from a clot' form the opening of Surah (chapter) 96 of the Qur'an. Initially, Muhammad 'doubted the genuineness' of what he had experienced, especially as nothing similar occurred for some time (Esack 2002: 40). This period of silence, or revelatory gap, is known as the *fitra* (pause) and there is some debate about its length. Most scholars agree that the second revelation was what is now Q74: 1–5, when Gabriel appeared to Muhammad saying, 'O covered one! Arise and warn ...' (Esack 2002: 41; Denffer 1983: 26–7), although as already noted there was discussion about the order of the early revelations. According to tradition, Muhammad first received the words of the 'message' from God via the Angel Gabriel, then 'recited' these words in public, or sometimes to those who became his *sahaba*, or companions. Both Muhammad and those who became his companions would memorize the revelations. Later, scribes also recorded the words (see Denffer 1983: 37–43).

Muhammad tells us that at times the ringing of a bell warned him that revelation was about to start (Bukhari, Vol. 1, Khan 1987: 2). At other times the words seemed to be burnt into his heart. Western scholars and writers have been preoccupied for centuries with the nature and cause of Muhammad's experience. Early explanations, all of which excluded the possibility that Muhammad genuinely received divine communication, included fakery, epilepsy, insanity and self-delusion. It follows from all these explanations that the author of the Qur'an was Muhammad, not God. Denffer does not discuss any of this but for Esack this is a major issue. He cites W. M. Watt's suggestion that the Qur'an can be understood as 'the product of some part of Muhammad's personality other than his conscious mind' (Watt 1953: 53; Esack 2002: 43), and psychology influenced Rodinson that 'Muhammad really did experience sensory phenomena ... that he interpreted as messages from the Supreme Being' and consequently 'developed a habit of receiving these revelations in a particular way' (Rodinson 1980: 77).

The orthodox conviction that Muhammad could not read or write, based on his description in the Qur'an as *al-nabiyy-al-ummiy* (Q7: 157, 62: 2) as well as on the account of the first revelation, supports the view that he could not have written the Qur'an. Doubt has been expressed on the question of Muhammad's illiteracy, however, as Denffer remarks 'it is not clear whether the Prophet Muhammad knew how to write'. Denffer concludes that there is 'unanimous agreement among scholars that Muhammad himself did not write down the revelation' (p. 37). He also comments that some scholars suggest that the term *ummiy* means that Muhammad belonged to an uneducated people, that he was 'not a scholar and not a historian, neither was he a philosopher' or 'a priest' (p. 152). What Denffer implies here is that Muhammad could not possibly have composed the Qur'an, given that its contents include historical material, beautiful descriptions of God's attributes and wisdom about the meaning of human existence that, in Muslim conviction, places human authorship beyond question. Referring to the inimitability, or to the miracle of the Qur'an, Denffer states that 'no one apart from Allah' could have produced such a masterpiece.

Similarly, Esack comments that 'Muslims maintain that the prophet was illiterate and therefore incapable of producing any literary work', least of all such 'exquisite literary perfection' as the Qur'an (see below on the language of the Qur'an). Esack says that some critical scholars regard the 'Prophet's supposed illiteracy' as 'a later Muslim invention to lend polemical support to the concept of the Qur'an's uniqueness' (2002: 102). In this context, Nasr compares the process by which the word of God, in Islamic understanding, became 'a book' with how Christians understand the 'word' becoming 'flesh'. In both cases, he suggests, it is a theological necessity that the 'recipient' be considered a virgin. In the case of Jesus's incarnation, the virginity involved is that of Mary, who according to Christian orthodoxy had had no sexual relations with Joseph or with any other man. In the case of Muhammad, says Nasr, it is necessary to uphold his 'unletteredness' (1994: 44).

As the concept of an infallible, unchangeable, complete legal code emerged, Muhammad's *Sunnah* (*hadith*) was afforded 'divine' status alongside the Qur'an (see critical comments below). Muslims turn to the *hadith* for guidance in all aspects of life – how they should dress, wash, greet people, as well as for guidance in complex legal cases. Esack comments that for many Muslims, Muhammad shares something of the ontological Otherness of the Qur'an. As not only the 'transmitter of guidance' but as the 'personification of following that guidance', many see him as 'a perfect human being' (2002: 115).

The traditional account of the Qur'an's recension

Denffer's account (1983: 31–56) is matter-of-fact while Esack's (2002: 78–99) engages with what he perceives as critical issues involved in the process. Denffer stresses that the Qur'an was memorized and recorded in Muhammad's lifetime and that some very early *masahif* existed. Some of these may have accidentally included utterances known as '*qunut*, supplications the Prophet sometimes used in ... prayer' (p. 48). There were some minor differences in spelling and in the order of the verses. In his view, some of these *masahif* may have predated the completion of the revelatory process, explaining why fewer than 114 *Surahs* (chapters) were included. Difference in 'order', he says, may be due to the personal use for which these texts were written: 'As long as the *sahaba* wrote their own copies for personal use, there was nothing wrong if they did not strictly adhere to the order of the *surahs* which was the order of the Qur'an' (p. 52).

However, as more of the original *hafiz* (those who had memorized the Qur'an during Muhammad's life, whose recitations, according to tradition, were checked by him for accuracy) died (p. 44), and as it became apparent that 'there were some differences in reading the Qur'an' (p. 52), 'Uthman decided to produce an official version. Denffer is careful not to say that different versions existed but that the difference arose from how the words were read, or recited. Zaid (or Zayd) bin Thabit, one of Muhammad's chief scribes, had already compiled a 'single copy of the complete revelation' for Abu Bakr, as early as the first/second year after Muhammad's death (p. 55). Now, he and three other *sahaba* were commissioned to make fresh copies of this *mushaf* for distribution throughout the Khalifate. See Bukhari, Vol. 6, Bk 61, Ch 2, *hadith* 510, Khan 1987: 478–9, for the traditional account of the Qur'an's recension.

All surviving *sahaba* agreed that this *mushaf* 'contained what Muhammad had brought as revelation from Allah' (p. 56). 'Uthman then ordered that 'all the other Qur'anic materials, whether written in fragmentary manuscripts or whole copies, be burnt' (p. 53). Denffer points out that a preoccupation of Orientalist scholars has been establishing the 'original order of the Qur'an' (1983: 158), since in their view the order of Zayd's *mushaf* was not that of the original, or 'correct version', which was tampered with if not by many hands then 'at least by 'Uthman and/or Abu Bakr' (p. 161). Esack adds that Zayd and his colleagues 'insisted on a number of conditions before accepting any text as suitable for inclusion', such as that 'at least two witnesses' testified that they had heard the prophet recite it (pp. 86–7). Denffer's account describes Zayd as more or less copying from an already existing, single text. Mawdudi also regards Zayd's and his colleagues' role at this stage as that of copyists: 'The Qur'an, which is in use all over the world, is the exact copy of the Qur'an which was compiled by the order of Hadrat Abu Bakr and copies of which were officially sent by Hadrat 'Uthman to different places' (1967–79, Vol, 1, p. 25). Zayd, though, would not copy anything unless all three of his sources 'tallied ... Thus was compiled one correct, authenticated and true copy' (p. 23). In Mawdudi's opinion, the act of burning all other copies was one of great prudence, making the 'Qur'an safe and secure against any possible alteration in the future' (*ibid.*). The Shi'a account has Ali producing a version of the Qur'an that differed at least in arrangement from 'Uthman's. Shi'a tradition says that a 'true copy' has been transmitted to each Imam that will be finally brought to light when the Hidden Imam returns (Esack 2002: 89; Denffer does not refer to the Shi'a account).

In Esack's opinion, a 'loose collection' may have been completed under Abu Bakr, but 'the arrangement and editing seems to have taken place much later' (p. 88). Esack says that the main reason why 'Uthman commissioned Zayd to produce an official version was that he was disturbed by quarrels among his soldiers, presumably about what was and was not correct behaviour. Esack also doubts that 'Uthman's orders would have been clinically or systematically carried out, given the conflict-ridden circumstances of his Khalifate. He refers to debate about the authenticity of some *Surahs*, for example 'the rejection by some of the Kharijites of the twelfth *Surah* (Joseph) as a silly love story' and the accusation that two *Surahs* sympathetic to Ali's claims had been omitted by 'Uthman (p. 91). The doctrine of *naksh* may be relevant here. As developed by the scholars, *naksh* (or abrogation) became an interpretive tool by which earlier verses of the Qur'an could be 'cancelled' by later verses. Verses justifying only defensive war were in this view abrogated by those that are understood to permit offensive war. As used in the Qur'an, *naksh* appears to refer to certain verses that were revealed to Muhammad but later 'abrogated' and therefore 'blotted out of existence', in other words, they do not appear in the text of the Qur'an (Esack 2002: 126). This is based on Q2: 106, 'Any message which we annul or consign to oblivion we replace with a better or similar one. Do you not know that God has the power to will anything' (Esack 2002: 83). Q87: 6–7 says that God will only allow Muhammad to forget what God god's-self wills him to forget.

Esack is suggesting that *naksh* may have allowed the compilers to omit what they did not like (see below), since in his view the process by which what had been an oral and continuous revelatory tradition became a closed book was not a neutral one. In other words, the compilers had their own agendas and 'both the Qur'an and the *Sunnah*' were 'contested territory in the various struggles for authority and legitimacy' (p. 113). Esack observes that for every Qur'anic text that one scholar considers abrogated, another disagrees, raising questions about the status of some Qur'anic penalties or prohibitions (1997: 58).

Some Muslim scholars reject *naksh*. For example, al-Faruqi (see Chapter Five) argued that 'instead of viewing previous Qur'anic revelation as being abrogated by subsequent ones, it is more appropriate to continue regarding them as valid to be implemented in conditions similar to those in which they were revealed' (Esack 2002: 127). Esack also argues that before the compilation of the official version, the distinction between rehearsed and unrehearsed revelation, that is, between Qur'an and *hadith*, was blurred. It would have been difficult, he says, for Muhammad to distinguish between these two types of revelation, especially when 40 *hadith*, known as *hadith qudsi* (holy tradition), are prefixed with 'God says', as are many Qur'anic verses (p. 116). Muhammad was a human being and was even 'on occasions admonished in the Qur'an' (see Q80: 1–4) and it is said that the Qur'an entered 'upon his heart'. If so, 'does one assume that the heart – located in his unique person which, in turn, was located in sixth-century Arabia – did not impact upon what entered it and later emerged from his tongue as uttered revelation?' (p. 116). This is the very issue that Rushdie explored in *The Satanic Verses* (1988). Esack is similarly interested in the interface between the Qur'an as divine word, and the human, historical context into which the Qur'an was revealed, becoming (to cite W. Cantwell Smith) 'whatever else it is ... also an historical phenomenon' (1980: 489; Esack 2002: 111).

In company with some sceptical non-Muslim scholars, Esack argues that until al-Shafi' (d. 810), *Sunnah* was understood much more broadly as 'a pattern of just dealings that was characteristic of the period when the Prophet lived in Medina' and included the 'precedents set by any of the first four Caliphs' (p. 112). Schacht (1964) argued that it was Shafi' who was first to identify *Sunnah* exclusively with 'the contents of formal traditions from the Prophet' (p. 47) rather than with 'the policy and administration of the Caliph' (p. 17).

Shafi' was a 'traditionalist' who supported the emerging orthodox party in their struggle against the rationalist Mu'tazalites, whom Schacht calls 'extreme opponents of the Traditionalists' and who tried to use 'systematic reasoning ... to discredit the traditions' (1964: 64). For Shafi', *hadith* was co-equal with the Qur'an since Muhammad spoke with God's authority. It followed for many Muslims, especially for the *ulama* who emerged as the guardians of the definitive, fixed and immutable 'tradition' that 'the Qur'an was actually in need of the *Sunnah* to verify it ... not vice versa – and that the *Sunnah* can, in fact, abrogate the Qur'an' (p. 118). 'Various disputants' produced *hadith* 'to justify their claims and to strip their opponents of legitimacy' (p. 113). *Hadith,* possibly themselves apocryphal, warn against the falsification of traditions: 'Whoever intentionally ascribes to me what I have not said, let him occupy his seat in Hellfire' (Bukhari, Vol. 1, Bk 3, Ch 39, *hadith* 109, Khan 1987: 84). Esack accepts that fabrication and forgery was rampant (2002: 113, N. 15) but points out that while questioning the authenticity of the Qur'an has been unthinkable in Islam, 'debate on the authority of the *hadith* has been a free-for-all, even in Muslim circles' (p. 120). Esack's argument is that, over time, the *Sunnah* achieved a status almost as authoritative and divine as the Qur'an, supported by such *hadith* as 'I was given the Book, and something akin to it (*wa mitlahu ma'ahu*), which 'meant that all of the Prophet's actions deemed to flow from his prophetic mission acquired an obligatory character' (p. 118).

Esack is also close to such non-Muslim scholars as Muir when he argues that in assessing the authenticity of *hadith*, establishing an *isnad,* that is a chain of trustworthy transmitters traced back to a companion of Muhammad (or to a member of his family), took priority over *matn*, or content criticism (see Muir 1858, Vol. 1, p. cxiii). Esack says that investigation of 'the backgrounds of each transmitter' occupied scholars 'at the expense of examining the inner coherence of a *hadith* and its compatibility with the Qur'an' (p. 114). For Esack, 'intersection', between prophetic word and divine word, especially 'the fluid nature of their relationship ... before Muslim crystallization in the period when theology was written in books and its dogma fixed' is a 'relatively unexplored' area that invites investigation (p. 115).

An eternal, uncreated or a created Qur'an?

Debate about whether, as God's word, the Qur'an is created or uncreated was a major issue in classical Islamic thought. Central to this debate was the place of reason in Islamic thought and the scope of human involvement in both the legal and political spheres. In other words, were people to administer without alteration a pre-existent, complete code (which really calls for no executive leadership at all) or were they to use their gift of reason to deduce the right action in any given circumstance? The *Muhaddithun* (Traditionalists) represented the first opinion while the

Mu'tazalites (described by Esack as the 'initiators of *Kalam*', or dialectic theology in Islam, p. 106) represented the second. These two parties fought a fierce ideological battle. The Mu'tazalites were influenced by Greek thought, a result of exposure to the Greek philosophical legacy preserved within the former Byzantine territories over which the Muslims now ruled. The first Mu'tazalite was Wasil ibn Ata (d. 699).

The Mu'tazalites (from the word for separatist) were champions of reason, and their critics accused them of elevating reason above the authority of the Qur'an, although they saw themselves as defenders of God's unity and justice (Esack 2002: 107). Sardar (1989) says that they accepted 'all the basic assumptions of Greek philosophy' while being 'highly critical of Islamic sources' (p. 15). Zealous of God's 'utter beyondness', they argued that not even revelation could share any of God's characteristics. Against the emerging view that God's essence contained such divine attributes as justice, power, knowledge and will (see Peters 1994: 360), they posited an attribute-less God. In their view, if each of God's attributes shared God's ineffable nature yet were also somehow distinct from each other (God's power and God's mercy are clearly different), what you ended up with was a plurality of deities, compromising *Tawhid*. In this view, the Qur'an is *qadim*, that is, co-eternal with God (Esack 2002: 109). The emerging view that God predetermines all human actions, in their opinion, made God arbitrary and unjust. Predetermination would seem to follow from an eternal Qur'an, as Esack explains: 'If the Qur'an were eternal, they reasoned, it followed that all the events narrated therein were preordained; the players in all those events would thus all have had their fates sealed, even before birth' (p. 107). The Mu'tazalites may have developed their ideas initially as a 'tool to fight injustice' but the 'Abbasids were quick to see the political advantages of a reason-over-revelation theology, and supported the Mu'tazalites (Sardar 1989: 16). The verse 'We have made it an Arabic Qur'an' (Q43: 3), they said, clearly indicates that God made or created the Qur'an. Platonic ideas about philosopher kings appealed to the Khalifs, who realized that a created Qur'an, which could have been 'other than it is', left more scope for a human ruler to deduce God's will, as Abu Zaid comments:

> If the Qur'an is not eternal, it is then created in a certain context, and the message it contains has to be understood in that context. This ... leaves room for re-interpretation of religious law, because God's word has to be understood according to the spirit, not ... the letter. ... If, on the other hand, God's word is eternal, uncreated and immutable, the idea of re-interpretaion within new situations becomes anathema. (1998 p. 198)

Between 833 and 848, the 'Abbasids made Mu'tazalitism 'the official doctrine of the state' (Sardar 1989: 16) and all 'leading officials and other prominent personalities were forced to publicly profess the createdness of the Qur'an' (Esack 2002: 107). Among those sent to prison for refusing was Ibn Hanbal, founder of the Hanbali legal school that placed much weight on the authority of *hadith*. This period is known as the *Mihnah*, 'a kind of inquisition' (Esack 2002: 106).

A multiplicity of voices

Drawing on analogy of the love of a Lover for his Beloved, Esack describes six contemporary approaches to the text of the Qur'an (see Figure 4.1; see also Figures 6.2, 7.2 and 10.1 for different interpretations of the Qur'an). Commenting on the female identity of the Body in the analogy, he notes that in the world of Qur'anic scholarship, it has been in the main men 'who are ... the only significant players'. While the Body of the Beloved is 'passive', it 'also does something to the one who approaches it' (p. 1). Of the approaches described by Esack, three are outsiders' and three 'insiders''. He identifies his own approach as that of a 'critical and progressive Muslim'. Denffer can be regarded as a Scholarly Lover. Esack is as likely to cite from a non-Muslim writer (especially from a Critical Lover) even when describing such a key event as the first revelation (when he cites Kenneth Cragg, p. 39). He also engages in serious dialogue with the 'Voyeurs' (for example, he follows Wansborough's position on the flexible nature of early Islamic tradition, when the distinction between unrehearsed and rehearsed revelation was fluid; see p. 119; see Wansborough 1977). Denffer's use of non-Muslim scholarship is limited to English translations of Arabic primary texts and to his section on 'The Qur'an and the Orientalists' (1983: 158–64). Esack broadly accepts non-Muslim opinion about the political shaping of Islam's second most authoritative source, the *hadith*, of which Denffer makes no mention.

The conservative or traditional position

Mawdudi writes that the Qur'an possessed by Muslims today is 'completely preserved, free from interpolation and precisely in the same wording in which it was revealed to the Holy Prophet' (1980). Brohi (1976) recognizes that those of faith approach the Qur'an with a prior conviction of its veracity and refers to what he calls 'intrinsic tests' as 'valid within the framework of religious beliefs ... and ... therefore only available to the faithful' (p. 81). 'Indications ... within the Divine Book itself' will 'enable a discerning and perceptive student to appreciate the truth of its universal significance' (*ibid.*). He also claims that an examination of human history provides 'unimpeachable ... evidence' that the Qur'an 'is a Book of Guidance for the whole of mankind and that its teaching is relevant for all time to come' (p. 82). Esack does not disagree that the Qur'an addresses all people, nor that it is God's word, but he also wants to understand how the Qur'an as God's word entered the human story.

All writers stress the Arabic nature of the Qur'an. Denffer states the traditional view that the Arabic of the Qur'an is incapable of imitation and 'excels all other Arabic language' (1983: 151), hence when Muhammad's opponents were challenged to produce a book 'which is a better guide' (Q28: 49) or even a 'single *surah* like it' (Q2: 23–4) no one could (p. 150). The Qur'an was Muhammad's answer to those who challenged him to perform a miracle, thus it is a 'miraculous Qur'an' (p. 149). Esack notes that subsequent attempts to rival the Qur'an have been 'suppressed by orthodoxy' (2002: 103). The Qur'an describes itself as 'pure and clear' Arabic and as 'an Arabic Qur'an' (Q16: 103, 12: 2). In order to offer clear guidance that could be 'understood by its audience', who were Arabs, 'the message had to be in a language' that they could understand, says Denffer (1983: 71). Both Denffer and Esack describe the literary style of the Qur'an as *saj'* (rhymed prose) (Denffer 1983: 74; Esack 2002: 70). Denffer comments that the claim that the Qur'an is poetry was made 'not only by Orientalists' but by Muhammad's opponents who accused 'him of being a poet or a soothsayer' (Q69: 40–3). Poetry was held in high esteem among the Arabs (see Esack 2002: 35) but some poets, known as *Kahini*, were regarded as shamans and magicians and Muhammad emphatically rejected any comparison between himself and them (Q 26: 221–7 says that all poets are inspired by Satan).

Untranslatability

When rendered into other languages, Muslims believe that the Qur'an is not a 'translation' but an interpretation. Nonetheless, says Denffer, translations are vital in order to perform *da'wa* (the duty of proclaiming Islam to non-Muslims) and because many Muslims themselves 'have no opportunity to become acquainted with the meaning of the Qur'an unless it is rendered into their mother tongue' (1983: 146). However, the literary style of the Qur'an, which does sound poetic when recited in Arabic, is difficult to retain in translation, making the text sound strange and unattractive to non-Arabic speakers, as Kabbani (1989) comments:

> Hours spent studying the Qur'an taught me a love of language, but the verses I learned as a child were unrecognisable when I read them in an English translation many years later. I could not share their beauty with anyone I knew in the West, for the Qur'an becomes prosaic and even incomprehensible in any tongue but its own: indeed, it says of itself that it was handed from God as an 'Arabic Qur'an', as though conscious of its own indivisibility from the language in which it was communicated. I firmly believe that the work cannot be translated. A Muslim reading the Qur'an in Arabic and a non-Muslim reading it in translation are simply not reading the same book. (p. 33)

Esack (2002) points out that recently many non-Muslims have bought copies of translations of the Qur'an, eager to discover therein what may have motivated the perpetrators of 9/11, only to give up reading after a 'few pages, for the Qur'an is a difficult book for "strangers", and indeed for many Muslims who just want to read it, to negotiate' (p. 191). What outsiders also find difficult is the fact that the Qur'an, as Mawdudi (1967–

79) says, 'does not contain information, ideas and arguments about specific themes arranged in a literary order', which is 'why a stranger to the Qur'an, on his first approach to it, is baffled when he does not find the enunciation of its theme or its divisions into chapters and sections' (Vol. 1, p. 7). Rather, the Qur'an's 'literary style is quite different from that of all other books' (p. 9). Esack observes that the 'arrangement of the Qur'an is neither chronological nor thematic' so that 'to those accustomed to reading in a linear or sequential fashion' it proves 'tedious and frustrating' (2002: 64). Arguably, the Qur'an was never intended to be read sequentially; rather, Muslims read those verses and chapters that speak to particular situations, such as a wedding, a birth, a funeral, a gathering for prayer or to shed light on a specific issue, such as what God teaches about justice (Esack 2002: 177), humility (p. 170), economic conduct (p. 175), social equality (p. 176).

Anti-Muslim polemicists have ridiculed the Qur'an's muddled order as proof of its human origins. For example, the ninth-century writer al-Kindy called it a 'confused heap, with neither system nor order. The sense', he continued 'moreover is not consistent with itself, but throughout one passage is contradicted by another' (1882: 78–9). Al-Kindy says that the Qur'an's jumbled arrangement suggests that it had multiple authors, 'adding or cutting out whatever they liked or disliked'. 'Are such', asked the polemicist, 'the conditions of a revelation sent down from heaven?' (see Muir's 1882 translation, available at *http://answering-islam.org/Books/Al-Kindi/*). Muir had it that Muhammad had freely brought down 'messages from heaven' to justify a series of moral lapses as well as his political conduct:

> Battles were fought, wholesale executions inflicted, and territories annexed, under the pretext of the Almighty's sanctions. Nay, even baser actions were not only excused, but encouraged, by the pretended divine approval or command. (Vol. IV, 1858, p. 318).

Discussion topics

Rana Kabbani comments that a non-Arabic-speaking Muslim who has learnt to recite the Qur'an by memory 'without being able to understand it' is at a disadvantage because they can 'apprehend this linguistic triumph only through the screen of imperfect translation'. Non-Muslims who do not know Arabic are unable to comprehend its message; for them it remains a 'silent text'. Attempts to 'analyse it can hardly amount to anything' (1989: 34).

- If you are a Muslim, do you agree with Kabbani's comment?

- If you are a non-Muslim and a non-Arabic speaker, do you think it impossible to speak with any authority or understanding about the meaning and message of the Qur'an? Does this mean that an in-depth understanding of Islam is also impossible? If so, is there any real hope of rapprochement between the West and the Muslim world? Are we doomed to misunderstand each other?

Esack comments that, with the exception of just a few scholars, Muslims have not attempted to explain the 'disjointedness' of the Qur'an (2002: 64). Zarkashi has pointed to similarity of end sounds in adjoining *Surah*, and of rhyme patterns in 'entire chapters clustered together' (Zarkashi 1958). Esack says that apart from the Joseph story, 'narratives' appear in 'different accounts and various bits of the same account' are interspersed throughout the Qur'an. However, he comments that Muslims regard such repetition as God's 'reminders', while 'legal texts in the middle of a narrative' are seen as 'God's drawing ... attention to what has to be learnt from the texts'. 'Breaks in a narrative', says Esack, 'reflect God's freedom from human literary patterns' (2002: 68).

Non-Arab vocabulary

An issue dealt with by classical scholars was the apparent presence of some non-Arabic words in the Qur'an (see Denffer 1983: 73; Esack 2002: 68–9; al-Kindy 1882: 79–83). Denffer summarizes the traditional view that any such words were 'integrated into the Arabic language'. As belief in the Qur'an's eternal nature developed, its 'language came to be viewed as equally timeless and independent of any "non-divine" elements' (Esack 2002: 69). Esack, following Arkoun, argues that all language is of human origin and that the view that any language could be 'absolutely free from expressions or words used in another language' is untenable (p. 69). We can only access the Word as written text (*mushaf*) and we read this text 'in concrete, changing, social, political and cultural situations'. The Qur'an is constantly 'reproduced, rewritten, re-read, and re-expressed', says Arkoun (1998b: 220). There is no other way of accessing 'the absolute' other than via what has become incarnate within 'the phenomenal world of our terrestrial, historical existence' (p. 211). By treating the Qur'an as somehow 'outside history' Muslims deny its relevance to their own contexts. Certain thoughts become 'unthinkable' because 'any discussion of the readings of the received orthodox *mushaf*' was closed (p. 214). The Mu'tazalites had made 'thinkable the decisive question of God's created speech' but by imposing his famous *'Aqida* (creed) 'the Caliph al-Qadir (947–1031) made this question unthinkable' again (*ibid.*). Muslims need to recognize that the Qur'an can speak afresh to different contexts and is to be 'read and interpreted by the historical communities' that cherish it 'in concrete, changing, social, political, and cultural situations' (p. 216). For Arkoun (as for Tibi, Soroush and others) this also firmly locates discussion about the Qur'an within the wider context of the human quest for meaning, within the wider context of human philosophical and ethical discourse (1998:

221). Born in Algeria and educated at the University of Algeria and at the Sorbonne, Paris, where he is now a Professor Emiritus, Arkoun has held Visiting Professorships at prestigious universities in the USA, and is a leading proponent of re-thinking Islam.

Progressive contributions

Esack draws on Arkoun but criticizes him for not rooting his interpretation, his call to 're-read' the Qur'an, in 'a changing social-historical space' (Arkoun 1998: 220), in any actually existing space (Esack 2002: 71). While Arkoun wants to rethink Islam and to free the Qur'an from the grasp of its traditional interpreters, he appears to assume that something like an ideology-free hermeneutic can be achieved (Esack 2002: 72). Esack argues that this implies the existence of a 'class of "super-readers", expert historians or linguists who will be able to access the true meaning of a text' (p. 73). This resembles what Esack elsewhere describes as the basic assumption of 'traditional Islamic scholarship' that 'meaning is located within the text and can be retrieved by pure minds' (p. 74). Esack points out that Arkoun himself distances his 'modern perspective of radical thought' from 'islahi (reformist) thinking' (p. 69), unlike Abu Zayd and other writers who want to contribute towards reforming Islam.

Esack also acknowledges the influence of Fazlur Rahman (1919–88) whom he calls 'one of this century's most profound modernist Islamic scholars' (1997: 11; see pp. 64–8). Rahman affirmed the divine origin of the Qur'an, which 'broke through the consciousness of the Prophet from an agency whose source was God', but in doing so it also became 'part of Muhammad's speech'. It was, says Esack 'this area of overlap' (Esack's grey area) 'that earned Rahman the wrath of traditional Muslim scholars'. Rahman was forced to migrate from his native Pakistan to the USA, where he was for many years a Distinguished Professor at Chicago. He argued in favour of a unified approach to the message of the Qur'an derived from a rigorous study of its text, rather than, as has too often happened in Islamic thought, imposing ideas on the text from outside (Esack 1997: 65). Many Muslim thinkers have 'not treated' the Qur'an 'as a whole' (Rahman 1998: 311).

For Rahman, the Qur'an was a 'document that grew within a background, from the flesh and blood of actual history', thus 'any attempt to treat it with a literalist, partialist superficiality and lifeless rigidity' is misguided (ibid.). The medieval scholars had wrongly turned Qur'an and hadith into 'rigid and inflexible guides'. In Pakistan, Rahman was known as the 'destroyer of hadith' because of 'his insistence on judging the weight of hadith reports in light of the overall spirit of the Qur'an'. He insisted that the Qur'an, though not the word of Muhammad, was nonetheless, as a written text, the product of an historical context and that it must first be 'understood in relation to the times it originally addressed' before Muslims could then start to 'apply it to changing times' (Denny 1991: 104). By rediscovering 'the original thrust ... of the Qur'an', it becomes possible to judge the 'conformities and deformities of historical Islam'. This involves 'studying the Qur'an's social pronouncements and legal enactments' both in relation to 'its stated objectives' and 'against the background of their historical social-milieu' (Rahman 1998: 310). Rahman wanted to penetrate to the spirit of the Qur'an in order to identify what are its prescriptive principles, which are binding for all time, from what he described as merely descriptive (similar to Iqbal's and Sardar's approaches).

A divine and a human word

Abu Zayd, self-consciously drawing on the Mu'tazalite concept of a created Qur'an, argues that it exists as both a 'divine' and as a 'human' word. 'The Mu'tazilites' theory of the relation between man, language and holy text', he argues,

> was the most rationalistic one; it concentrates on man as the addressee of the text and the one to whom its teachings were directed. Language is a human invention simply because it reflects social convention to the relationship between the sound and the meaning. Language, on the other hand, does not refer directly to reality, but reality is conceived, conceptualized, and then symbolized through a system of sounds. (1998: 194)

As a human *mushaf*, the Qur'an is subject to linguistic-historical criticism while its divine nature is 'beyond the realm of scientific enquiry'. The written text is a 'product of culture' (*muntaj thaqafi*) to be studied in relation to 'the verifiable/observable reality of the culture and community addressed by the text'. As an historical text, although 'originally divine', the Qur'an's 'interpretation is absolutely human' (1998: 201). In Abu Zayd's view, this approach will 'yield progressive results for a number of social questions' (Esack 2002: 143–4). According to Abu Zayd, by denying the textuality of the Qur'an and 'freezing its message', Muslims had also politicized Qur'anic exegesis. In practice, an 'authority' emerged and claimed the 'prime role' in the Qur'an's 'maintenance and guardianship'. Any alternative voice becomes a dissident voice (1998 p. 198). For Zayd, the careful interpreter, who examines both the original context of the Qur'an and their own context, can identify those messages that have significance across both contexts from 'the historical and temporal, which carry no significance in the present context' (p. 200). The meaning of a text is 'fixed because of its historicity', but its 'significance', while 'firmly related and rationally connected to the meaning', is 'changeable' and trans-historical.

Muslims have been reluctant to 'explore the question of' the Qur'an's 'temporal causality' because this is seen as compromising its 'Otherness', thus 'the reasoning seems to be that if this worldly-events caused revelation then somehow revelation is not entirely "other-worldly"', says Esack (1997: 53; see 2002: 125). His own approach is contextual. The Qur'an, he says, was revealed gradually as God's word to concrete historical situations (see 1997: 54). Knowledge of these situations is necessary in order to understand the original intent of Qur'anic revelation.

Traditionally, although Esack says that this has suffered neglect as a branch of *tafsir* (exegesis), Muslims did study the 'occasions of revelation' (*asbab al-nuzul*) (2002: 124–5). Denffer also discusses *asbab al-nuzul* (1983: 92) and comments that it helps to understand 'the immediate meaning and implication' of a verse, 'the imminent reason underlying a legal ruling' and whether its meaning 'is specific or of general application' (p. 92). This admits that human reasoning is involved in determining whether a specific verse was intended to legislate for eternity or for a particular, concrete historical situation. Whether a verse is understood to have a universal or a particular application can result in radically different interpretations of what is the correct Islamic position vis-à-vis gender, punishment or the status of minorities, as shall be seen in subsequent discussion. The best *tafsir*, says Denffer, is when the Qur'an explains the Qur'an, followed by a *hadith* of the Prophet explaining the Qur'an, followed by a Companion doing it (1983: 126; see Esack 2002: 131–2).

Traditionally, verses are classed as either 'clear' (*muhkamat*), those whose meanings are unambiguous, and as 'doubtful', those whose meanings are open to various plausible interpretations (*mutashabihat*). The latter require 'further explanation' (Denffer 1983: 80). According to Denffer, verses dealing with punishment and law are all *muhkamat* while the subject matter of *mutashabihat* verses includes 'the attributes of Allah' and 'the true nature of the resurrection' (p. 81). Esack translates *mutashabihat* as 'allegorical', citing Q3: 7, which refers to some verses' meaning as known to 'none save God'. However, the verse continues, 'and those whose hearts are deeply rooted in faith'. Debate about where the first sentence ends (see Esack 2002: 58–9) makes two interpretations possible; either that only God knows the meaning and that dabbling is dangerous, or that those 'deeply rooted in knowledge' also know the meaning. For classical texts on inner–outer meanings and on allegory, see Peters 1994 (pp. 198–201 on al-Ghazzali on 'Outer and Inner Meanings', pp. 203–05 on Ibn Rushd on 'Allegorical Interpretations'). Esack comments that initially *tafsir* was a type of *hadith*, only emerging as a distinct and separate discipline with the work of Ibn Majah (d. 886) (2002: 130). Some Muslims claim that Muhammad gave their exegesis of a Qur'anic text to them in a dream; *hadith* attribute good dreams to God and bad dreams to Satan (see Bukhari, Vol. 9, Bk 87, Ch 3, *hadith* 113, Khan 1987: 95), which might preclude debate about the status of such *tafsir*. *Mutashabihat* verses include the 'mysterious letters' ('letters of the alphabet' verses with which 29 chapters begin (see Denffer 1983: 83–4).

A contextual approach

Esack rejects the idea that there is a single correct meaning contained in the text that pure minds can retrieve (1997: 63). This merely encourages conflict between rival claims to be the 'purest' mind, whose interpretation is beyond challenge; 'one person's saint is another's charlatan – and consequently conflicting monopolies over absolute truth' leave little or no 'space in any discourse on pluralism' (pp. 74–5). Rather, the text is itself a dynamic 'divine word' that, revealed within history, continues to speak to specific historical circumstances. The Qur'an answers the questions that are posed of it, he says. We all approach the text as people whose need to understand the text is driven 'by who we are and what our interests are in retaining or shedding our gender, race, class, clan or ethnic positions' (2002: 192). There is no such thing as an objective interpreter (1997: 75). 'For whom and in whose interest?' is a valid question to ask of any interpretation (p. 79). 'All interpretive activity and "meanings" are thus, of necessity also tentative', he concludes, 'and no *tafsir* ... is value free', and 'any reading of the Qur'an is eisegetical before it is exegetical' (2002: 145). Nor is there any reason why 'any particular generation should be the intellectual hostages of another' (Iqbal had argued this). The very existence of *tafsir* 'in Islam is itself proof of the creativity of commentators' who continue to assimilate, be inspired by 'and, yes, even reject the work of their predecessors' (p. 137).

This means that the Qur'an becomes a 'contested scripture' and various groups 'compete' over it 'for the right to own, access and interpret' the text (2002: 22; see 1997: 39). Esack's own approach to Qur'anic interpretation was developed in response to the situation in apartheid South Africa, where he and other Muslims looked to the Qur'an for inspiration and for resources to support their struggle for justice, equality and freedom. For Esack and his fellow progressive Muslims, the struggle was on behalf of all the oppressed, not just on behalf of Muslims. He therefore found in the Qur'an 'keys that' enabled him 'to read the text in such a way as to advance the liberation of all people' (1997: 78). Esack contends that the Qur'an especially addresses those who are oppressed and marginalized, the *mustad'afun* (see Q28: 5; Esack 1997: 98–106).

Esack realizes that others see some very different ideals in the Qur'an and that it could be argued that Muslims will find whatever they want there, depending on the questions they ask and the stances they have adopted, including use of violence. He maintains, however, that the weight of Qur'anic verses support a 'profound commitment to life and the creation of a peaceful society based on justice and compassion'. He is not 'blind to what many of' his 'co-religionists have found' but says that he is nonetheless 'certain about the overall Qur'anic picture' (2002: 192). Yet he does not want to claim absolute certainty, lest he commit the error of those who, like the Taliban, call themselves 'seekers' but approach the text

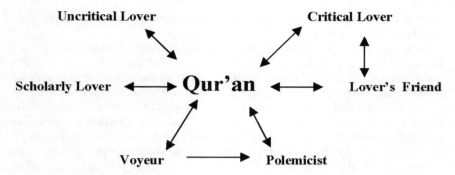

Uncritical Lover: ordinary Muslims, transported by being in the Qur'an's presence to 'another plane'; to be 'with her is to be in the presence of the divine'. The uncritical lover wants to enjoy his or her relationship with the 'beloved', not to ask questions about 'the nature of the beloved', about her body. She is a 'cure for all [the aches] that may be in [believers'] hearts' (Q10: 57) (Esack, p. 2).

Critical Lover (e.g. Abu Zayd, Mohammed Arkoun, Farid Esack): Muslims whose love of the Beloved compels them to ask questions about 'her nature and origins, her language, or if her hair has been dyed', to penetrate behind mere infatuation with her outer beauty. They regard the Qur'an as God's word but want to understand how God's word entered human experience and they approach the book as a 'text within the world' (p. 5). Such Muslim scholarship has little in common with that of Scholarly Lovers but overlaps with that of the Lover's friend. Scholarly Lovers may condemn their work.

Lover's Friend (e.g. Kenneth Cragg 1971, 1973; Wilfred Cantwell Smith 1993): approaches the Qur'an critically but as a scholar who regards him/herself as a friend of Muslims, so is sensitive towards Muslim belief. Lover's Friends accept the broad outlines of Muslim history. They may accept that the Qur'an is God's word although they do not share Muslim understanding of the nature of the Qur'an's revelation, usually arguing that God inspired Muhammad. Using participant observation, they may see their work as compensating for 'scholarly injuries' of the past. They may not be full citizens of the world of the Qur'an, but neither are they invaders or foreigners (Fazlur Rahman on Cragg). Contrary to the view that only Muslims can interepret the Qur'an, says Esack, some Lover's Friends have 'produced significant, even pioneering studies into several aspects of the meaning of the Qur'an' (p. 167).

Polemicist (e.g. www.answering-islam.org; Ibn Warraq 2002): shares the voyeurs' view of the human (non-divine) origin of the Qur'an but not their neutrality. Polemicists either reject any claim to be a divine revelation or restrict revelation to their own tradition (usually Christian). They draw on the work of the 'voyeurs' without serious discussion of their methods, or reference to the conjectural nature of their arguments (p. 10).

Voyeur (e.g. Patricia Crone and Michael Cook 1977, John Wansborough 1977, 1978): claims to be a 'value-free' scholar uninterested in what the Qur'an means to Muslims, or to anyone else. Pursues historical-literary criticism of Qur'an's origins. Sees the text as a human construct and as 'essentially a product of a Judeo-Christian milieu' (p. 9). However, they regard their conclusions as provisional.

Scholarly Lover (e.g. Mawdudi, von Denffer): wants to explain why his (or her) Beloved is a gift from God. Scholarly Lovers 'weep at others' inability to recognize the utter beyondness of the beloved's beauty'. They approach the Qur'an convinced that it is self-evidently God's word and that this cannot be subject to serious questioning or to doubt. They find the scholarship of the Lover's Friend irritating, denounce Critical Lovers as apostates and debate with the Voyeurs and Polemicists.

Figure 4.1 Six approaches to the Qur'an (adapted from Esack 2002: 2–10)

confident that they already possess all the answers. Esack remarks that absolute certainty belongs to God alone (*ibid.*).

In South Africa, Muslims who claimed the right to interpret the Qur'an for themselves faced the wrath of the *ulama*, who saw this as their privileged arena (*ibid.*: 25). These Muslims, such as members of the Call of Islam (established in 1984; Esack was a co-founder), identified themselves with Christian liberation theology (see Esack 2002: 28 and 1997: 86). Esack's contextual approach to the Qur'an, like Christian liberation theology, claims the right of particular communities to interpret scripture for themselves. At the root of his approach lie the concepts of *taqwa* (an awareness of the presence of God), *al-nas* (the people) and *jihad* (understood as liberation praxis). The Qur'an, he says, 'emphasizes the need for a community and individuals deeply imbued with *taqwa* who will carry on the prophets' task of transformation and liberation' (1997: 87). Fazlur Rahman had stressed the vitality of *taqwa* and of a commitment to 'social justice', in contrast, says Esack, to 'Arkoun's idea that the ideal search for knowledge is motivated by seemingly neutral reason' (1997: 68). For Esack, there is an essential link between exegesis and action. He advocates a cycle of reflection, action, reflection, action in what is always an ongoing process: 'there is no end to' God's 'promise to disclose' (1997: 111). 'Liberation theology', says Esack, 'is the process of praxis for comprehensive justice, the theological reflection that emerges from it and the reshaping of praxis based on that reflection' (1997: 8). Far from 'subverting the universality of the Qur'an', the 'contextualization of its message is', in fact, its basis, for it locates universality 'in the willingness of the faithful to hear the Qur'an speaking to them in terms of their deepest and most painful reality at all times' (1997: 255).

Discussion topic

- Given that, according to Esack (and also to postmodern critical theory) people find in their sacred texts what they want to find, is it fair to blame 'Islam' for what some people do in its name?

5 Islamic Epistemology

It is embarrassing, but factually correct, to point out a commonality between early Islamic modernists and current fundamentalists: both cite the Koranic notion of ilm (knowledge) to articulate the conviction that the Koran is the foremost source of all knowledge including modern science.
(Tibi 2001: 142)

The Islamization of knowledge: supporters and critics

Muslims from the 'left' and from the 'right', as well as those who occupy a centrist position, comment that the Western world is currently more developed technologically than the Muslim world, although this was not historically the case. In the ninth and tenth centuries, for example, the Muslim world was more advanced than Europe. All suggest how Muslims can reverse the trend, and regain a dominant position. Those on the right call for the Islamization of knowledge, while those on the left advocate the humanization of Islam. Yet categorization is not easy. Sardar and Nasr are both proponents of the Islamization of knowledge yet Sardar famously depicts Nasr as a 'nowhere man'. In his 1998 book, Sardar draws on the 1967 cult television series *The Prisoner*, produced by its star, Patrick McGoohan (Everyman Films). Here, he uses the 1965 Lennon and McCartney song 'Nowhere Man': 'He's a real nowhere man, sitting in his nowhere land; Making all his nowhere plans for nobody'. Tibi is categorical in his rejection of the Islamization project but at points his ideas converge with both Nasr and Sardar. This analysis begins with the contribution of Ismail al-Faruqi. Then it examines Nasr, with reference also to Mawdudi (1980). Next, it summarizes the popular contribution of Maurice Bucaille (1987) before discussing Sardar's contribution, including his critique of al-Faruqi and Nasr. Finally, it compares and contrasts the above with the humanist approach of Tibi, Arkoun, Mernissi, Rahman and Soroush.

Al-Faruqi: Islam the religion of reason, science and progress

Ismail Ragi al-Faruqi (1921–86) was a Palestinian refugee who had served as Governor of Galilee before fleeing to Lebanon in 1948. He graduated from the American University of Beirut in 1941 and later from Indiana and Harvard, earning his doctorate from Indiana in Western philosophy in 1952. Between 1954 and 1958 he studied at Al Azhar University, Cairo, adding training in Islamics to his portfolio. Next, as a Visiting Professor at McGill in Canada, he studied Judaism and Christianity. Following two years' teaching at Karachi, Pakistan he was again a Visiting Professor in the USA, this time at Chicago, before taking up his first full-time permanent post at Syracuse (1964). In 1968 he moved to Temple University, Philadelphia where he stayed until his tragic murder in 1986 (with his wife; possibly in a bungled burglary though some suspected a racial motive), although he also served as Visiting Professor at a total of 23 universities throughout the world.

Al-Faruqi's early writing stressed the centrality of what he called 'Arabism' (*urubah*); the Qur'an was to be read through Arab eyes (see al-Faruqi 1962). The Qur'an had been revealed to Arabs because they were an elite and ethical people to whom 'you are the best community' was addressed. The Qur'an is an Arabic message and Arabic Qur'an contains the ethical values to which all Muslims subscribe. Arabism included non-Muslim Arabs such as Christians since, while they have adopted a different identity, they share the values that are enshrined in the Qur'an and Arab Christians are closer to the original Christianity than are their non-Arab co-religionists. Non-Arab Muslims need to cultivate the spirit and the values of Arabism, which is the essence of the *ummah* itself.

For al-Faruqi, the essentially Arab nature of Islam and the need for non-Arab Muslims to imbibe the values and the spirit of Arabism was a strength, but others are more negative on the primacy of Arab culture. For example, V. S. Naipaul (1998) points out how the tendency of Indian Muslims to invent Arab ancestry fuelled their feeling 'of not belonging to the land' but 'to the religion' (p. 329). Islam, he says, could not tolerate sacred places other than those of Arabia, allowing only to one people 'the Arabs ... a past, sacred places, pilgrimages and earth reverence' (p. 72). Of non-Arab Muslims, 'nothing is required but the purest faith', which means they must 'strip themselves of their past'. They were to be 'empty vessels for the faith' (p. 311) which, says Naipaul, turned their lands into 'cultural deserts ... with glory of every kind elsewhere' (p. 381). Rajmohan Gandhi, the Mahatma's grandson, comments that in India Muslims have charged that Hindu 'devotion to India amounted to a worship of earth and clay'. For their part, Muslims may lose their heart to India but they can never worship her, which for some Hindus means that they fall short of complete loyalty to her soil (1986: 14).

Anthropological studies, however, show how Islam has adapted itself culturally to very different contexts and that it manifests itself in a variety of ways. Arguably, for example, Asian Islam is more flexible and pluralist than Arab Islam – see Clifford Geertz's comparison of Indonesian and Moroccan Islam: he describes the former as 'adaptive, absorbent, pragmatic Islam', the latter as stressing unity and uniformity and the *Shari'ah* as a unifying legal code, a purist Islam (1968: 16). Tibi (2001) contends that there is no such thing as an immutable Islamic identity; rather, Islam has always adjusted to 'varying conditions', which the Islamists and Orientalists both dispute (p. 202). Non-Arabs have adapted Islam to their pre-existing 'symbolic systems' and the resulting 'religio-cultural synthesis is different in each case, which totally contradicts the ... concept of the timeless cultural entity of one Islam' (2001: 45).

However, moving into the 1970s al-Faruqi's thinking underwent a radical change that substituted 'Islam' for 'Arabism', making Islam itself the key referent with 'unity' (*tawhid*) as the central, uniting principle. Everything Islamic revolves around the *shahada*, 'There is no God but God'. Islam could brook no separation of politics from religion. In his writing, Islam emerged as a comprehensive, all-embracing system. In *Al-Tawhid: Its Implications for Thought and Life*, he wrote '*Al-Tawhid* is what gives Islamic civilization its identity, which binds all its constituents together and thus makes of them an integrated, organic body which we call civilization' (1992: 17). Asking himself who he was – a philosopher, a liberal humanist – he answered 'a Muslim', and from then on it was Islam that needed to be dominant in every field (Esposito 2001: 27).

Implicit in this understanding of Islam was the conviction that Islam contains within itself all 'knowledge', thus, whether we are talking about ethics, or protection of the environment, or science, the 'answers' will be found within Islam. A fundamental concern was for what from 1982 he called the Islamization of Knowledge. In company with many other Muslim academics and reformers, al-Faruqi wanted to reverse the downwards trend of Islamic civilization which he attributed both to the Western colonial legacy, which is the legacy of a spiritually bankrupt civilization, and to the unfaithfulness of Muslim regimes. The importation of nationalism alongside secular ideology into the Muslim world represented a reversal to pre-Islamic tribalism (*shubiyyah*) that the Islamic *ummah* had, in theory, replaced. In his earlier period, he had cited the modernists, especially Iqbal and 'Abduh, but he now also had much in common with the traditionalists, such as the Wahhabis, sharing their dislike of Sufism and their emphasis on *tawhid*. Yet he was also critical of the Muslim Brotherhood, suggesting that they failed to 'delineate in sufficient detail their Islamic blueprint for society' (Esposito 2001: 28). He called for the integration of thought and action. Instead of merely denouncing what they 'were against', Muslims had to say what they were for.

Al-Faruqi became a scholar-activist in the mould of a Mawdudi, combining his professorial duties with liaising and consulting with Islamic movements throughout the world, encouraging the placing of Islamic identity at the centre of every agenda – ranging from the study of history, through international relations to the campaign for the liberation of Jerusalem. Muslim societies would be strong when they were authentically Islamic, weak when they weren't. Western systems and Western epistemology needed to be replaced by Islamic systems, by the injection of Islamic epistemology back into the educational curricula of the Muslim world, else its civilizational and developmental malaise (what he called 'the malaise of the *ummah*') would continue. His project was to recast the whole legacy of human knowledge from an Islamic perspective, in which 'truth' and 'knowledge' are synonymous and singular (since God is One, knowledge and truth must also be 'one'). Thus, knowledge needed to be sacrilized; Western epistemology presupposes that knowledge is neutral, separate from values and essentially 'secular'. His proposed method was to adopt the best that Western science and technology offered, then to imbue these with Islamic principles and to inform further development with Islamic values. He also called for a systematic response to the main problems of the Muslim world. He passionately believed that Islam was pre-eminently a religion of reason.

His ideas saw expression in the American Islamic College, Chicago and the International Institute for Islamic Thought (IIIT), Virginia (both founded in 1981) and, after his death, in the curriculum of the International Islamic University, Islamabad. The IIIT's aim is to 'enable the *ummah* to deal effectively with present challenges', to 'regain its intellectual and cultural identity and re-affirm its presence as a dynamic civilization' (*www.iiit.org*). His view of Islam as the primary referent, as Arkoun comments, implies the existence of a 'transcendant, authentic, and universal' Islamic framework 'in which all human activities and initiatives ought to be controlled and correctly integrated', and suggests that Muslims need always to 'look back to the time when the Truth was formulated' (1998b: 210). This sounds very much like the Wahhabis' and the fundamentalists' call to return to the ideal Islam of the classical age. However, al-Faruqi certainly did not share all their ideas. Unlike them, he was an active and life-long participant in Muslim–Christian and Muslim–Jewish dialogue, believing that common spiritual and ethical principles inform all three Abrahmic faiths and that these can become the basis for common action. Debate about the nature of God was of secondary importance; justice, moral conduct, duty and responsibility came first. He wrote, 'Let God be whom He may; is it not possible – nay, necessary – that all men agree to establish divine will first' (1974: 33). He believed, though, that Christians had betrayed Jesus's true teaching and that Christians writing on Islam inevitably viewed Islam through their own biases and therefore produced a distorted picture, though as Esposito comments the same can be said in reverse: 'Faruqi's analysis and critique of Christianity ... often' reflects 'judgements informed by his Muslim faith' (2001: 34).

Nasr: the goal of education is to actualize all the possibilities of the human soul

A Shi'a Muslim with a Harvard doctorate who also studied in seminaries and private homes of traditional Muslim scholars in Iran, Nasr has taught in the USA since 1979, when he left his native Iran following the Islamic revolution. As a Professor at Teheran University, he enjoyed royal patronage. He describes himself as a 'traditionalist' but roundly condemns those who reject out of hand everything thought to be 'non-traditional'; the 'non-traditional' is not always the enemy of the 'traditional' (see Smith 1991: 82). Yet he also criticizes the fundamentalists for thinking that simply by labelling something 'Islamic' they have restored an Islamic alternative (1994: 20).

Nasr's 1968 book on Islamic science identifies him as an early apologist for Islam's scientific legacy over-and-against the view that Islam and modern science are incompatible, since the former is based on a fixed, transcendent 'divine truth' while the latter is experiemental, exploratory and human. Nasr set out to demonstrate that Islam did contribute to scientific and mathematical knowledge in the past and that, by redis-covering its epistemological principle, it can do so again. In Islam, he says, 'the quest for knowledge' was from the beginning 'dominated by its sacred quality and nature' (1994: 123). Unlike in the West after the Enlight-enment, Muslim scholars never separated 'knowledge . . . from the sacred'. Instead, knowledge 'possessed a profoundly religious character, not only because the object of every type of knowledge is created by God, but . . . because the intelligence by which man knows is itself a divine gift' (*ibid.*).

In sharp contrast, the Western educational system that was imported into the Muslim world by the colonial powers assumes that men and women are answerable only to themselves (p. 104). For Nasr, the ultimate aim of knowledge is to be able to 'perfect and actualize all the possibilities of the human soul'; that leads to 'that supreme knowledge of the Divinity which is the goal of human life' (p. 150). Thus, in 'traditional Islam' the teacher was not only 'a transmitter of knowledge (*ta'lim*) but also a *mur-abbi*, a trainer of souls' (p. 123). The aim of Islamic philosophy was to 'provide keys for the understanding of the manifest in relation to the One' (p. 133). Nasr says that reason has always played a ciritical role in Islamic thought but 'this reason was always attached to and derived sustenance from revelation on the one hand, and intellectual intuition on the other' (p. 102). In contrast, the post-Enlightenment West has cut reason adrift from revelation. Thus, the challenge that modernity poses Islamic thought includes 'evolutionism, rationalism, existentialism, agnosticism and the like' (p. 109). Nasr regarded evolutionary theory as dangerous and false (1976: 228–9; see also 1990: 106; see Bukhari, Vol. 9, Khan 1987: 149: 151; Vol. 1, p. 68 for *hadith* predicting a decline in religious knowledge).

Nasr on the reform of the madrassa

Nasr argues that the most ancient centres of learning in the Muslim world, the early madrassas, while primarily concerned with 'religious sciences' (*al-usul al fiqh*), were places where theology (*kalam*), philosophy, logic, mathematics and science were also studied (1990: 126). Muslim thought was open to knowledge from outside; 'the living organism which is Islamic civilization digested various types of knowledge from many different sources, ranging from China to Alexandria and Athens; but whatever survived within this organism' was always integrated within its worldview, thus remaining 'profoundly Islamic' (p. 130). For Nasr, the Qur'an contains 'the roots of all knowledge but not . . . its details', so he parts company from those contemporary apologists who would 'make the Sacred Book a textbook of science in the modern sense of the word' (p. 122). On the one hand, Nasr states that in the traditional madrassas the intellectual sciences of logic, maths and science ('*aqli*) 'ceased to be taught after the 8th/14th century' (p. 126), while on the other he strongly rejects the claim, made by many Western writers and incidentally repeated by Rushdie (see 1991: 437), that Islamic thought decayed 'at the end of the 'Abbasid period' (1990: 207). He attributes this theory to Orientalists, who could view Islamic civilization as a 'phase in the development of their own' but not as possessing any worth of its own. Instead, they posited a 'false notion of decadence'.

The Orientalists' essentialist *homo islamicus* was incapable of change. Muir had it that Islam was 'powerless to adapt to varying time and place . . . [to] keep pace the march of humanity' (1891: 598). Muir attributed this to Islam's confusion of the spiritual and the secular, which Nasr and Sardar among many other Muslims regard as Islam's great strength. Sir Hamilton Gibb (1895–1971) had it that Islam elevated 'law' above all other discourses in place of the 'discarded sciences' (1978: 7), and that this law was inflexible (p. 72). According to Gibb, 'The rejection of rationalist modes of thought' by Muslims had 'its roots in the atomism and discreetness of the Arab imagination' (cited in Said 1978: 106). Gibb, like many Orientalists, held that all Muslims did was to copy and to preserve what they had received from Greece. Islam itself was incapable of innovation or of invention. Many Orientalists were as dismissive of Muslim modernism as conservative Muslims were – their version of Islam could not be authentic as it pretended that Islam could 'adapt to varying time and place'. Writers who discussed the modernists were told that they were wasting their time. 'Islam reformed was Islam no longer' and modernism was irrelevant to any understanding of real Islam.

Throughout his writing, Nasr wants to restore and to revitalize traditional Islam. For him this process includes the revitalization of the *madrassas*, which he does not want to see replaced by Western-style institutions. Like Sardar and Tibi (see below), he is concerned to address what he calls 'the present dichotomy' – the tension between modern technological knowledge that has been imported from the West but which has not been integrated into an Islamic framework, and Islamic religious thought. One option is to replace the already existing Islamic educational institutions with new ones, another is to preserve but to revitalize these existing institutions. Nasr contends that the modern university owes its origin to Islam's ancient centres of learning but that this has been downplayed in the West; thus 'the "Chair" in English and "licence" in French are direct translations of Arabic terms (*al-kursi* and *ijazah*, respectively)' (1990: 141; see Naipaul 2001: 59 for the suggestion that the traditional academic gown 'was probably copied from Islamic seminaries'). Tibi rejects this, seeing the university as solely a product of the West. The claim, he says, that the university descended from the madrassas is 'plainly incorrect' (2001: 169). Rather, 'without the bias of Eurocentrism' we have to 'recognize that the university as a seat for free and unrestrained enquiry based on reason is a European innovation'. Sardar agrees with Nasr that universities started in the Muslim world; he calls al-Azhar (founded 800 CE) 'the first University in the World' (1989: 12).

Like Tibi, Nasr criticizes modernists as well as fundamentalists for what they both regard as an act of repossession. The argument here is that Western science and technology depend on knowledge that was originally acquired, mainly via Spain, from the Muslim world, so that when Muslims utilize Western technology 'from computer to telephone' they repossess what was originally theirs (1990: 19). However, Nasr argues that they do so 'without any thought for the consequence of these inventions upon the minds and souls of Muslims'. The nature and character of modern science and of Islamic science, he says, are diametrically opposed to each other. Western science forgets 'the One and denies the relevance of the Trans-cendent' (p. 139). Yet, as identified in Chapter One, Nasr does not reject everything Western, since for him what makes an idea Islamic is not its origin but incorporation into Islam's worldview and while he believes that law is of central importance, it will rather be a new kind of scholar who will lead Muslims into the future, scholars who know both traditional Islam and 'the Western world in depth' (p. 307). Iqbal also held that *Shari'ah* was inseparable from Islam, as 'The Qur'an considers it necessary to unite religion and state, ethics and politics in a single revelation' (1998: 263), but thought that the *ulama* had an essential role in the reformulation of *Shari'ah*, 'helping and guiding free discussion on' legal issues. Legal education, though, would need reforming to include modern jur-isprudence if his evolutionary outlook was to be pursued (p. 267).

The simple equation of 'modern forms of knowledge with *al-'ilm*' (knowledge), says Nasr, bypasses the question 'what kind of knowledge it was that' Muhammad 'instructed his followers to seek from cradle to the grave'. Here, Nasr is referring to the notion that as *'ilm* (knowledge) is a divine quality or attribute, all knowledge is linked with the divine and Muhammad had instructed his followers to seek for knowledge, even as far as China. Thus, one meaning of the term '*um-al-kitab*' is that 'all authentic knowledge contained in all books is ultimately born from its bosom' (1990: 122). The Qur'an, says Nasr, 'has always been the alpha and omega of all Islamic education and science'. It is 'their source and goal, their inspiration and guide' (p. 123). Modernists and fundamentalists alike forget that 'the nature and character of Islamic science are entirely different from those of modern science', yet they depict the former as 'the necessary background for Western science' (p. 19). He also points out that fundamentalists condemn the 'philosophers who formulated the world-view upon which this much praised Islamic science is based', usually dismissing them as heretics (and as agents of the West; p. 148).

Nasr and Mawdudi: convergence and divergence

Nasr is close to Mawdudi when he argues that the highest form of knowledge is sacred knowledge, which is linked to human destiny. 'To know for Nasr', says Aslan, 'is to be saved' (1998: 93). In his 'The Essentiality of Knowledge for Being a Muslim', Mawdudi reflects traditional Islamic understanding that the purpose of the quest for knowledge is salvation; thus 'al-Islam is firstly the name of knowledge and then the name of putting that knowledge into practice' and 'At least that much knowledge should be acquired by every Muslim youth, adult and old person as may enable him to understand the essence of the teaching of Qur'an and the purpose for which it was revealed'. Neither Nasr not Mawdudi can contemplate an education system that divorces 'the sacred' from 'the secular'.

However, where Nasr and Mawdudi differ is that for the former, such knowledge is not really acquired but gifted by God to God's chosen (see Aslan 1998: 94), while for Mawdudi such knowledge is open to all: 'whoever accepts Islam can join the community' which recognizes no 'geographical, linguistic or colour bars' (1976a: 163). Mawdudi was pathologically opposed to Sufi Islam; Nasr is a champion of Islam's esoteric tradition and criticizes modernists and fundamentalists for 'their complete espousal of modern science and technology, indifference to Islamic sacred art, hatred of traditional wisdom and the peace and contemplation associated with the inner life, and many other aspects of traditional Islam' (1990: 160). Yet Nasr does not confine knowledge to Islam. As a proponent of perennial philosophy, knowledge for Nasr 'is not the result of inventing or discovering or knowing something unknown' but the 'rediscovery of that which has always been known' (Aslan 1998: 94). For Nasr, this 'knowledge', or primordial tradition, which is metaphysical, pervades the cosmos and all the great religions of the world, binding each both to 'the Source' and 'to each other' (Aslan 1998: 50). All philosophy, says Nasr, 'originates from the lamp of prophecy' (1994: 206), while true science is 'not based on purely human reason ... but ... belongs to the supra-human realm' (p. 100). Like al-Faruqi, Nasr believes that co-operation is possible between Muslims and Christians but also like al-Faruqi he is not uncritical of Christianity, arguing that it lacks a *Shari'ah* and overstresses religion's next-worldly dimension at the expense of this world. Judaism, he says, is the religion of law and of this world, Christianity is the religion of the heart and of the next world, while Islam perfectly balances 'law and spirit, body and soul' (1994: 69, 34).

Bucaillism: the Qur'an as a scientific text

Maurice Bucaille (born 1922) was chief of the surgical clinic at the University of Paris. In 1976, after ten years of study, he addressed the French Academy of Medicine on science and the Qu'ran. He argued that the Qur'an accurately describes scientific phenomena long before modern scientists had discovered, or rather rediscovered, them. In his *The Bible, The Qur'an and Science* (1978) he examines the Bible and the Qur'an for scientific reliability, looking for example at their creation narratives, and concludes that the Bible contains statements that are 'scientifically unacceptable' while the Qur'an is 'in perfect agreement with modern data'. In his view, the presence of data in the Qur'an of which scientists had been ignorant until modern times confirmed for him the Qur'an's status as Revelation. In contrast, the Bible's scientific errors proved that its revelatory claims are false. His ideas are highly controversial and are often referred to as 'Bucaillism'.

Von Denffer comments how classical scholars had pointed out that statements in the Qur'an about 'the nature of things, the material environment, etc' contain information that does not 'conflict with man's perspective and experience' (1983: 155). However, he points out that some more recent writers go further in arguing that the Qur'an 'contains information on scientific facts which are in perfect agreement with the findings of' science. The problem, he suggests, with this as a criterion for the genuineness of the non-human origin of the Qur'an is that in the future science, which is 'after all the human perspective on the true nature of things' might 'describe its findings entirely differently from the way it presents its "truths" today' (p. 157). The Qur'an is 'guidance from Allah under any circumstances irrespective of whether science, which changes continuously, seems to be in support of it or not' (*ibid.*). Sardar (1989) criticizes Bucaille for elevating science to the 'realm of the sacred' and for making 'Divine Revelation subject to the verification of Western science', which is unacceptable (p. 36). The claims of Bucaille are debated on rival internet sites, *www.answering-islam.org* and *www.answering-christianity.com*. One issue is whether Bucaille is a Muslim or not. Certainly, his book is very popular within the Muslim world, where he has visited and lectured widely. The book is easily available on the net; see for example *home. swipnet.se/islam/quran-bible.htm* and *http://sultan.org/articles/QScience.html.*

Sardar: a critique of al-Faruqi and Nasr

Inayatullah and Boxwell, editors of *The Sardar Reader*, claim that 'more than any other scholar of our time, Sardar has shaped and led the renaissance in Islamic intellectual thought, the project of rescuing Islamic epistemology from tyrants and traditionalists, modernists and secularists, postmodernists and political opportunists' (2003: 1). Sardar wants to end what he calls the West's epistemological imperialism by revitalizing Islamic thought, a goal he shares with al-Faruqi and Nasr. Like them, he thinks that Western science and learning has wrongly and dangerously separated 'ethics and morality from its epistemology' (1985: 104). He shares their concern to Islamize knowledge and argues very strongly in favour of the Muslim world developing its own paradigms as an alternative to the West's, which cannot meet the needs of Muslims (p. 105). He argues in favour of a pluralist world in which different cultures work out 'their own ways of being, doing and knowing', construct their 'own science and technologies', undertake 'their own civilizational project' instead of copying the West (1989: 7). He believes that no civilization can retain its vitality if it does not possess its own science and argues that just as American science can be said to be 'different in character from European science', being more entrepreneurial, so Islam can imbue science with its own values and character (p. 62). Indeed, fundamental to Sardar's argument is that while Western science claims to be 'neutral' and 'value-free' (p. 48), it is not. Rather, it is profoundly secular and deeply rooted in Western free-market values, which are both alien to Islam.

Further, he argues that what might be called the infrastructure of Western epistemology, with its disciplines and divisions of knowledge, is flawed, since 'neither nature nor human activities are divided into watertight compartments marked "sociology", "psychology"' (p. 99). Nor is the West to be imitated for elevating one way of studying nature, that is 'the pursuit of objective truth' (p. 55), above all others; 'science was never the dominant way of knowing' in Islam, he says, 'but always existed alongside other ways' (p. 21).

The problem was that, although those Muslims who first developed a rational philosophy did so to defend justice, they made the mistake of making revelation redundant and of substituting the infallibility of the Qur'an with that of Plato. To their opponents, it looked as if the rationalists were claiming that reason 'alone could lead to absolute truth' (p. 16) thus al-Ghazzali (d. 1111) argued that instead of deriving their teaching from the Qur'an they merely appended 'their views to the Qur'an', citing 'numerous Qur'anic verses to pretend that their doctrines' were genuinely Islamic. The accusation that they honoured Plato more than Muhammad easily lent credibility to the charge that their teaching was 'foreign' and 'alien' (p. 16). Instead of a much-praised synthesis between Greek philosophy and Islam, often presented as Islam's 'major achievement', the rationalists 'came to believe in the absolute validity of Aristotelian logic'

(p. 14). Here, Sardar refers to Ibn Farabi (870–950) and to the Mu'taza-lites. Consequently, use of independent reasoning was declared danger-ous, and imitation (*taqlid*) of the past, of the *Sunnah*, became the duty of all good Muslims.

Sardar argues that the victory of Asharite theology led to the emergence of three divergent tendencies in Islam, which all shared 'two basic char-acteristics, blind imitation and authoritarianism' (p. 17). These three tendencies were the mystical or Gnostic (Sufi) tendency, that reduced everything to mysticism, the philosophical tendency that reduced every-thing to 'rational categories' and the legal, that reduced everything to the *Sunnah*, while all three demanded 'unquestioning acceptance' (p. 18). Thereafter, 'the tyrannical attitude of passive acceptance' became 'the dominant paradigm of Muslim civilization' and with this 'closing of the gates of *ijtihad*', 'Islamic science truly became a matter of history' (p. 18). Not only did science suffer as a result of the 'passive dependence on authority' but so did art and literature, which all lost their former 'vitality and independence' (1987: 42). A 'spirit of enquiry' thus gave way to 'the straitjacket of scholastic theology' and led to the 'decay of Muslim civili-zation'. Sardar is as adamant as Nasr that Islam must not be reduced to an ideology of any kind. Traditionalists do not merely want to 'reconstruct Islamic society through the re-establishment of external legal and social norms' but 'through inner purification' (p. 84). For Nasr, the task of Islamization begins with 'the spiritual, inward and esoteric aspects of religion', not with the 'exoteric' (Nasr 1990: 310). He criticizes 'funda-mentalism' for turning Islam into an 'ideology which serves a particular movement or regime'. 'Ideology', he says, 'is a Western concept' (p. 306). Sardar (1985) describes 'ideology as the antithesis of Islam', an 'enterprise of suppression and not a force for liberation'. 'Ideology', he says, closes down 'thought and analysis' and 'ensures that mistakes and errors are perpetuated', while Islam 'requires an open attitude' (pp. 81–2).

Muslims from the right, such as Mawdudi, and from the left, such as Tibi, all want Muslims to revive *ijtihad*. However, for the right the areas in which any new interpretation may be developed are limited to certain civil matters, such as taxation and banking (excluding personal and criminal law), while for the left what emerges as Islamic law will be radically dif-ferent from traditional *Shari'ah*, as an-Na'im says, so that 'every aspect' of Islamic law 'including personal law' can be brought 'into complete con-formity with human rights standards' (1998: 234).

Aaaron Segal (1996) points out that while the Muslim world constitutes about 20 per cent of the world's population, it produces about 5 per cent of its science (measured by the number of citations of articles published in international science journals written by Muslim scientists resident in the Muslim world). Segal does think that the tension between faith and reason that exists for many Muslims contributes to the dearth of science in the Muslim world but he suggests that, more significantly, authoritarian regimes that 'deny freedom of inquiry or dissent lie behind the lack of scientific activity'. Bernard Lewis (2003: 100) has a 'table of active research scientists, frequently cited articles, and frequently cited papers per million inhabitants' with the USA followed by Switzerland at the top and Egypt and Algeria at the bottom.

Discussion topic

- Historically, both Christian and Islamic authorities have exercised censorship. At times, both have regarded scientific enquiry as dangerous. However, is it plausible to argue that religion *per se* was responsible for this attitude? Or, did the elite adopt this attitude to protect their interests and to retain control over the academy? How would a postmodernist approach this question?

Operational and non-operational knowledge

Sardar argued that what passes for science in the Muslim world today is science that has been imported from the West. Such science fails to meet the needs of Muslim countries because it originates from a worldview that has divorced enquiry from such core values as justice and humanity's trusteeship of nature, which in his opinion are central planks of Islamic belief and essential to the pursuit of science in the Muslim world (1985: 100). However, while Muslim scientists give notional support to the value-system or 'non-operational knowledge' that ought to be informing their production and practice of science, that is, to Islam's values, they are unable to 'incorporate' these values 'into their work' so suffer 'acute schizophrenia', trapped between their operational and non-operational knowledge (1989: 24). His criticism of al-Faruqi's Islamization of knowledge project is that it accepts the divisions of knowledge, the disciplines, of Western epistemology and thus 'makes Islam subordinate to Western civilization' (1985: 101). Disciplines are 'not made in heaven' but 'develop within particular historical and cultural milieu and only have meaning within the world-view of their origin and evolution' (p. 101). Muslim scientists use what he calls Western 'operational knowledge', that is, technical know-how to build bridges or to design computer programmes, says Sardar. Al-Faruqi calls for a synthesis between the best that Western science offers and Islamic values but fails to produce a viable methodology to enable this (Sardar 1989: 96). Sardar's books contain diagrams that set out his plan to further the project of Islamizing knowledge. Even al-Faruqi's first principle, the 'unity of truth and knowledge', is flawed, since quantum physics and relativity show that 'truth' is not necessarily singular. Al-Faruqi's equation of knowledge with truth is noble, 'but superfluous' in helping to develop a pragmatic epistemology.

Sardar offers a similar criticism of Nasr. Nasr's view that the goal of knowledge is salvation is, to put it bluntly, silly, since much knowledge has more mundane goals, such as the production of clean water or the construction of an environmentally friendly transport system (see 1989: 126–7). Nasr reduces science to a 'magical system for removing the hidden veil of reality', whereas for Sardar it is a problem-solving instrument. Nasr is so preoccupied with his 'particular brand of Sufism' (1985: 174) that even his much praised survey of Muslim scientific achievement is so dominated by such areas as astrology, alchemy and 'occult sciences' that it neglects much more significant areas, such as 'the determination of the *qiblah*, a task that occupied Muslim astronomers for over a hundred years' (1989: 120). Nasr attributes all sorts of inventions and discoveries to 'outstanding Persians' while truly significant figures go unnoticed. Whether Nasr is writing on Islamic art, science or religion he 'essentially says the same thing', which is 'why he is so prolific' (p. 116). Nasr makes side issues and the unimportant his 'main focus and hence the norm of Islam' (p. 124). Sardar characterizes Nasr's thought as Ismaili but he also suggests that Nasr find all he needs for his *religio perennis* philosophy in ancient Pythagorean theosophy (p. 119). The strength of Nasr's contribution, says Sardar, lies in his depiction of Islamic science as serving and promoting Islamic values and as distinctive from Western science (1985: 174), but in the end Nasr is a 'nowhere man' occupying a 'nowhere land' and his discourse is 'neither about Islam, nor about science' but ultimately is part of a 'totalitarian enterprise' that would submit all knowledge to the 'authority of the Gnostics and others who know the truth' (1989: 128–9). Sardar frequently draws on popular culture to illustrate his ideas. Reportedly, Nasr has dismissed Sardar as 'uneducated' but does not appear to have responded in print.

Sardar's Ijmali epistemology

Sardar advocates an Ijmali (from *ijma'*, social consensus and *jml*, beauty/wholeness) approach that seeks to synthesize 'pure knowledge' with 'moral knowledge'. Its guiding principles are social consensus (*ijma'*), trusteeship (*khilafah*), public welfare (*istilah*) and reason (*adl*). That which is wasteful or destructive (*dhiya*) as well as tyrannical (*zalim*), is alien – science must serve the public good, not harm or dominate people. This approach does not seek 'to discover absolute truths' nor some 'ready made system', but aims to develop distinctive Islamic 'paradigms' and 'bodies of knowledge' that can meet 'the needs of contemporary Muslim societies' (1985: 104, 1989: 112). This represents a programme of action that is at the same time inherently pragmatic, not merely idealistic, and which is also a form of worship. As noted in Chapter One, Sardar hopes for a 'new type of intellectual: deeply committed to Islam' on the one hand but on the other 'ready to see good in other systems of thought and action, and even ready to borrow those ideas which he can synthesize with the world-view of Islam' (1985: 323). Presumably, these scholars would be less sympathetic towards Islam's Sufi tradition than the 'new scholars' for whom Nasr also calls. For Sardar, what is borrowed from the West is to be integrated into an Islamic framework, instead of existing as an import, essentially alien and exotic. Islam, not the West, is to be the arbiter of what is valuable and necessary. His criticism of the Muslim modernists was that they made Islam subordinate to Western thought by 'substituting the blind following on the part of early Muslims' with 'unquestioning imitation of the Occident' (1987: 56). Their project had been the 'Occidentization of Muslim societies' (p. 58).

Usefully, Sardar contrasts the principles of Western science with what he sees as those of Islamic science (1989: 95–7). He often uses the environment as an example, claiming that Islamic science would treat the environment with more respect than Western science, exercising stewardship as a divine duty. His chart is summarized in Figure 5.1.

Western Science	Islamic Science
Puts its faith in rationality	Places its faith in revelation
Values science for the sake of science	Sees science as a form of worship which has a spiritual and a moral function
Posits one all-powerful method as the only way of knowing reality	Uses many methods based on reason as well as revelation
Claims impartiality – to be value free; a scientist is not responsible for the use to which his/her work is put	Claims partiality – towards the truth; consequences must be morally good
Claims the absence of bias	Admits the presence of subjectivity
Reduces the world to what can be empirically verified	Admits the reality of the spiritual dimension
Is fragmented into disciplines	Values synthesis, is multi-disciplinary but holistic in its approach

Figure 5.1 Western/Islamic Science

Reviving the Mu'tazalite heritage

Sardar (1989) also contrasts the main dogmas of the Mu'tazalites and the Aharites, identifying five main postulants for each school.

One of the most vocal Muslim contributors on whether Muslims can adopt ideas from 'outside' Islam is the Iranian scholar, Hossein Dabbagh, who writes as Abdul Karim Soroush. Like Nasr, Soroush combined a Western education with some traditional Muslim schooling (his PhD in

Mu'tazalites	Asharites
1. rejection of all attributes in consideration of the Oneness of God	1. the uniqueness of the characteristics of God which are inapplicable to human beings
2. God is not responsible for human acts which result in evil and, consequently, ... man has free will ... to do as he wills	2. man has free will but not the ability to create anything
3. nobody is in a position to see God, neither will anyone ever see Him	3. the possibility of seeing God
4. ability of the human mind to perceive the truth without revelation	4. God sits on His Throne
5. the Qur'an was created and revealed under the impact of circumstances and spontaneously	5. the eternity and uncreatedness of the Qur'an

See Peters (1994: 365–6) on 'The Fundamentalist Position, Without Knowing v. Dialectical Theology'.

Figure 5.2 The Mu'tazalites v the Asharites (adapted from Sardar 1989: 16–17)

the philosophy of science is from London). This enables him to speak the language of the religious traditionalists, who are intellectually very influential in Iran. Perhaps his main achievement has been the translation of ideas about the civil society into the type of language that traditionally-trained religious scholars can understand. President Khattami has spoken and written about civil society (see 2000). Tamimi, though, considers the term civil (*madani* or *ahli* in Arabic) society 'like democracy and secularism ... an intruder into Islamic political thought' (2000b: 127). Soroush (2001) characterizes the Sunni reformist agenda as a reviving of the Mu'tazalite heritage. Progressives, ranging from pioneers such as Sir Sayyed Ahmed Khan to Mernissi (see below), have identified strongly with Mu'tazalite and rationalist Islam. He stated:

> What most reformist thinkers in the *Sunni* world are trying to do [he names Arkoun and Abu Zaid] is revive the *Mu'tazalite* school of thought. Their goal is to show that rationality *per se* is acceptable in the Islamic milieu, even when not based on religion. They strive to demonstrate that there are values that need not be derived from religion.

Soroush believes 'that the Muslim world needs the re-invention and rethinking of Mu'tazalite tradition'. As noted, Nasr charges the Mu'tazalites with the elevation of reason over revelation. Rahman, unlike Nasr no admirer of the Sufis (see Chapter Two), shares his negative estimate of the Mu'tazalite legacy, although he falls short of saying that they elevated reason above revelation. Rahman says that they 'made reason equal to revelation' and transformed God from being a Person to being a Principle 'whose nature and purpose can be known by philosophical reasoning' (Denny, 1991: 101). On the other hand, he says, Asharite theology represents 'an almost total distortion of Islam' and had simply reacted against 'Mu'tazalite rationalist theology' (Rahman 1998: 306; 1982: 133). Esack criticizes the Mu'tazalites, suggesting that they are not quite the enlightened liberals that modernist Muslims and Western admirers take them to be. Referring to the Mu'tazalites 'overwhelming arrogance and self-righteousness,' he says that they held the common people 'unbelievers due to their lack of scholarly sophistication'. One Mu'tazalite, Abu Musa al-Murdar, believed that only 'he and three of his disciples' would enter Paradise (Esack 2002: 110, n. 10). Soroush thinks that Shi'a Islam has 'few epistemological obstacles' in the way of reformist thinkers (as *ijtihad* has remained part of the classical tradition) apart from some dogmatists in the *Hawsa*. The vast majority of Iranians do not share the 'worldview of the dogmatists, so stimulating dialogues and lively philosophical debates are common in Iran among the religious classes as well as in university circles' (Soroush 2001), he says.

His arguments develop from his thesis on the 'contraction and expansion of religious knowledge'. This posits that 'religious knowledge', like any other form of knowledge, 'is human, fallible, evolving and most important of all . . . constantly in the process of exchange with other forms of knowledge' (2000: 16), whatever their source. In Chapter 11 of his *Reason, Freedom and Democracy in Islam* (2000), 'What the University Expects from the Hawzeh', he discusses the relationship between seminary and the university. God's revelation is infallible, he says, but our interpretation of it is not; 'It is up to God to reveal a religion, but up to us to understand and realize it. It is at this point,' he says, 'that religious knowledge is born, entirely human and subject to all the dictates of human knowledge' (p. 31). Soroush argues that the provenance of an 'idea' is unimportant – its 'truthfulness' is. Truth, he argues, is always compatible with truth. One of his heroes was 'Ali Shari'ati (1933–77) whom he believed successfully reconciled his religious faith with 'knowledge sought and attained outside the confines of a traditional Islamic culture' (Cooper, 1998: 48). Soroush admires 'Ali Shari'ati. He had wanted rule by the learned but thought the clergy too rigid. He extended the role of leadership to all who 'have the necessary knowledge and commitment to rule' (Tamadonfar 1989: 109. See Shari'ati 1998; Sachedina 1983).

Mernissi's appraisal of the Mu'tazalites is probably the most positive. She depicts their version of Islam, 'the way of '*aql*, glorifying reason' as an alternative to 'the way of rebellion taken by the Kharijites'. The question was, 'what should Muslims do if the Khalif acts unjustly?' The Kharijites said 'rebel'. The Mu'tazalites, instead of 'preaching violence', took the view that 'a thinking individual could serve as a barrier against arbitrary rule' (1994: 32). This alternative, she says, has been forgotten by Muslims today which is 'why outlining it is so critical'. By stressing reason, the Mu'tazalites democratized politics, since in addition to 'two actors, the Imam and the rebel leader' they enlisted 'all believers who are capable of reasoning' (p. 33). Their intervention into politics also introduced the concept of *i'tizal*, or taking a middle position. For example, instead of condemning someone who sinned, the Mu'tazalites adopted a neutral position, arguing that without mature reflection, judgement is risky. Thus, says Mernissi, when the 'Abbasids adopted the Mu'tazalite theology for more than a century, their rule was characterized by toleration and openness. Thus, 'all human knowledge, including the scientific treatises and Greek philosophy now translated into Arabic' was embraced (p. 35).

The Mu'tazalites excelled not only as philosophers but also as 'mathematicians, engineers, doctors, and astronomers' (p. 34). 'All the great names of scientific and philosophical learning', she says, belong to this period (p. 36). Baghdad, known then as the city of peace (*Madinat as-Salám*), was a beacon of enlightenment throughout the empire and beyond.

Mernissi argues that unlike Christianity in its early days, Islam had not been opposed to scientific investigation. In a passage that Nasr might have written, she remarks that 'in the beginning scientific investigation was necessarily linked to the flowering of mystical reflection, in that the best homage one could render to God was the good use of one's mind' (p. 34).

The backlash was also political. Fearing the people's ability to argue in favour of justice and to challenge despotic rule, the Khalifs started to recruit 'their thinkers from the tradition of knowledge based on *ta'a* (obedience)' (p. 37). To serve the needs of tyrants, *Shari'ah* 'was stripped of its speculative dimension' and *ra'y* (personal opinion), *ihdath* (innovation) and *ibda'* (creation) were condemned as foreign and blasphemous (p. 40). Subsequently, the only type of opposition that has been 'capable of playing a credible role' in the Muslim world is that which 'preaches violence' (p. 34). Mernissi argues that it was Shahrastani (d. 1153), the Iranian Asharite theologian (who has, though, been accused of Ismaili tendencies), who put the final nail in the coffin of reason: 'he who gives priority to their own opinions', he said, 'is a modernizing innovator and a creator' (p. 40). Any expression of dissent was thereafter equated with *fitnah* (social disorder). The Asharite answer to such questions as how were Qur'anic references to God's seeing, hearing and sitting to be understood was that Muslims should 'believe in these traditions' but 'without asking how' (*bila kayfa*). Ibn Hanbal and the Asharites contended that as the Qur'an says that God sees, sits and hears, Muslims should accept that God does so 'without going beyond His description, nor removing from Him any of His attributes' (see Peters 1994: 366). Esack describes this formula as an 'all-purpose doctrinal weapon' in the hands of the Asharites, who now demanded unquestioning acceptance of their dogmatic position (2002: 110).

Those modern Muslims who have tried, like the Mu'tazalites, to 'spread the philosophy of the Enlightenment' have been 'harassed, condemned and denounced as blasphemers' and as 'servants of the West', says Mernissi (1994: 41). The Muslim world 'rumbled on in its obscurantism'. Its 'enlightened intellectuals' have been 'systematically condemned' and its people reduced to apathy (p. 37). Islam will only be able to survive in the twenty-first century when the *ummah* 'roots its security somewhere other than in the ban on free thought', sheds its links with 'state tyranny' (p. 91) and thereby frees people to opt for Islam by choice, not compulsion (see p. 65). Mernissi wants 'fewer weapons and more learning' (p. 170).

Like Nasr, Tibi finds it odd that modernists and fundamentalists, usually on opposite sides of any argument, both view the acquisition of Western science and technology as an 'act of retrieval or re-possession' (2001: 11, 44, 140) and both 'cite the Koranic notion of *'ilm* (knowledge) to articulate the conviction that the Koran is the foremost source of all knowledge, including modern science' (p. 142). Tibi points out that fundamentalists' desire to adopt the instruments of modernity in order to 'confront the evils of modernity', which 'produced them', is a somewhat 'intellectually schizoid program' (1998: 68; see also p. 74 and 2001: 142–4).

The problem for Tibi is that fundamentalists divorce the instruments of modernity from the worldview that created them. Sayyid Qutb believed that the whole project of modernity had to be dismantled but that Muslims could borrow science from the West. However, no true Islamic concepts could be found in the work of Ibn Sina, Ibn Rushd or al-Farabi, whose 'philosophy is no more than a shadow of the Greek philosophy which is in its essence foreign to the spirit of Islam' (1976: 118). The belief that Islam is the 'very source of all science is', says Tibi, 'certainly among the peculiarities of Islamism and even of reformism' (2001: 15). He is highly critical of the tendency to see the Qur'an as the source of all knowledge, so that even the principles of modern management are said to be found there and a Muslim can claim that the 'US had adapted it from there' (2001: 44). The argument is that as the Qur'an is 'the complete and final revelation' there is 'no other knowledge – except [that] based upon it and pointing to it' (2001: 185, 94). In Tibi's view the claim that all knowledge, including science, is to be found in the Qur'an is dangerous, since 'scientific knowledge is socially determined, and is never divine' (2001: 12). Disavowing 'the Koran as an inexhaustible encyclopaedia of science', comments Tibi, 'involves the danger of being accused of unbelief' (2001: 184). 'Scholarly knowledge', he says, is 'universal, and human' (2001: 107). For Tibi, the Qur'an is 'source of a divine ethic which belongs to the realm of inwardness', not of law. In his view, his approach to the Qur'an derigidifies its 'scholastic understanding' (2001: 62).

Tibi goes so far as to suggest that the claim that all knowledge is found in the Qur'an, which is often linked to the notion that Muslims are the best community (Q3: 110; *khair umma ukhrijat li*), effectively serves as a psychological barrier dividing Muslims from humanity, preventing Muslims from 'seeing the other and the different as equal in value' (2001: 184; Qutb 1988: 10 cites this verse, arguing that consequently Islam's mission is world domination). Insistence on their own superiority and on what Tibi calls Islam's 'claim to absolutism' must be abandoned (2001: 55; see also 1998: 209). Only civilizational confrontation can result from Muslims divorcing themselves from the rest of humanity (2001: 204). Muslims feel able to borrow and use the content of Western science, its technological tools, while rejecting its context (2001: 177, 184), says Tibi, but in his view it is wrong to separate 'technological goods' from the social context and attitudes that produced them. Fundamentalists 'fail to understand that the worldview that drives modernity is essential to its capacity for producing modern science and technology' (1998: 74). Divorced from its context, such knowledge is either 'handed down' or 'adopted in a cumulative fashion' as a 'ready made, imported product'. It is learnt by rote by students in the Muslim world so that they gain certificates but not knowledge 'that can be usefully applied to the developmental needs' of society. The upgrading, too, of foreign degrees over home degrees is 'far from conducive to the developmental process' (p. 177; see also Ramadan 2001: 288 on a 'deadening programme of learning' that leaves children 'the choice of repetition, cramming or failing').

Tibi argues that before the triumph of Asharite orthodoxy, Islam had been more open to plurality of interpretation and to the use of reason in critical enquiry. Plurality of opinion, for example, allowed the differentiation that produced the four legal schools (p. 162). There is a *hadith* that says, 'Difference of opinion in my community is a mercy for people' (*ikhtilafu ummati rahmatun li an-nas*) and another that says 'the people of knowledge are the people of flexibility (*tawsi'a*)' and that 'those who give *fatwas* never cease to differ, and so this one permits something while that one forbids it, without finding fault with the other when he knows of his position'.

Tibi describes two types of educational institutions in early Islam, the madrassa or religious school and the less formally organized *dar-ul-ulum*, where philosophy and natural science were taught. Known as *ulum-al-qudawa*, or foreign science, this was frowned upon in the madrassa. Initially, madrassas had been privately funded (*waqf*) and 'some diversity of opinion was allowed', but with the introduction of the paid, state-appointed *mufti*, with 'the right to pronounce generally valid and binding fatwas ... room for manoeuvre' came to an end (1998: 172). Thereafter, madrassas were no longer concerned with 'a process of reason-based investigation or unrestrained enquiry but with a learning process in the sacred sense' (p. 169). Tibi argues that the retention-based style of teaching and learning that became characteristic of Muslim education has its roots in the Islamic conviction that only God creates (p. 173). The human responsibility is to transmit revelation. Thus, the learning and copying of texts accurately is the dominant task: 'the testing of memory by being checked by another or reciting a text in front of someone else (*mudhakara*); and writing down the words of the teacher'. However, knowledge gained by rote learning cannot be retained, 'what remains is a valueless piece of paper, and ensuing unemployment' (p. 179). The *dar-ul-ulum* failed to become institutionalized in the Muslim world, and eventually died. Benefactors were afraid to sponsor what was perceived to be heretical and foreign.

Tibi praised the Hellenized philosophers (al Farabi, Ibn Rushd, Ibn Sina) and the Mu'tazalites who all distinguished 'religious' from 'philosophical truth' and 'gave each its proper space' (2001: 62). This Hellenized tradition was intellectually open to 'cultural borrowing' from other civilizations, which Tibi describes as 'one of the great sources for enriching humanity' (p. 139). This rationalist tradition saw knowledge as universal (p. 136). Tibi rejects the Islamists claim that knowledge is peculiar to Islam and instead champions the view that the pursuit and construction of knowledge is the task of all humanity. He is fully aware that the very Muslim rationalists that both he and the West praise were 'charged with *takfir* (apostasy)' and are 'condemned by Muslim orthodoxy even today' (2001: 160; see also p. 49). The problem is that, *fiqh* (jurisprudence), which is a post-Qur'anic, human construct, is treated as if it is itself infallible and divinely revealed; 'Islamic law is post-Koranic and constructed but it was and still is to this day perceived as a *lex divina*' (2001: 63).

Arkoun (1988b), like Mernissi, wants to restore imagination to the centre of Islamic epistemology. In his *L'Islam, morale et politique* (1986), he comments that the theological and philosophical tradition in Islam imposed an ontological weakness on the imagination, which was supported by the Qur'an's attack on 'the poets whom the erring follow' (Q26: 224–6) (p. 12). The ability and freedom to imagine is crucial to the task that Muslims face in order to determine their destiny and their identity (p. 219). Arkoun shares with postmodernists the conviction that what passes as Islamic orthodoxy was constructed to serve the needs of the dominant group at the time it was formulated (1998b: 210). Now, a new epistemology is required that recognizes the relationship between 'ideological discourse' and 'identity, power and protection' and that revisits the tradition and its texts in order to exercise 'social imaginaire', that is, to construct an identity that meets contemporary needs. Similarly, Rahman (1998) recognized the need to reinterpret Islam within changing social contexts. Thus, the study of the Qur'an is actually a social science, and the 'study of the social sciences is a process, not something that is established once and for all ... for its subject matter – social behaviour – is constantly in the process of creation' (p. 318). However, while Rahman, like Tibi, Arkoun, Soroush, Mernissi *et al.*, wanted to humanize Islamic epistemology, he was not in favour of a secular state. In his view, Muslim secularists deny Islam's spiritual dimension, in which they are just as mistaken as are the conservatives for denying its dynamism (Sonn 1995: 408).

On imagination: an ally from the world of science

Dawkins (1989) also argues that imagination is an important tool in the process of human development, enabling us to rebel against our own selfishness: 'We are built as gene machines and cultures as <u>meme</u> machines [<u>memes</u> for Dawkins are cultural constructs passed on by non-biological vehicles, such as books, fables] but we have power to turn against our creators' (p. 201). This power to 'rebel', says Dawkins, is related to our ability to imagine, 'our ability to simulate the future in imagination' (p. 200).

Further discussion topics

- Are technology and science neutral?
- Can another culture adopt the instruments and applications of science that a different culture has produced without also subscribing to that culture's values and worldview?
- Comment on Sardar's view that 'no civilization is possible without its own science' (1989: 62).
- It is interesting that many contributors to the Islamization of Knowledge debate, including al-Faruqi, S. H. Nasr, Bassam Tibi, Muhammad Arkoun and Ziaudin Sardar all teach or taught in Europe or the USA. There may be a link here with the issue of Muslims living in Diaspora serving as leaders of Islam's intellectual tradition (see further discussion in Chapter Eight). Can such Muslims, themselves all operating within secular contexts, be seen as coming to the defence of the Islamic tradition as perceived in the West, that is, as intellectually stagnant and backwards in orientation, rather than as a dynamic, forward-looking tradition? Much of Sardar's writing addresses Islam's future, for example.
- Respond to Tibi's question 'is the validity of the primacy of reason not universal? Is it culturally relative?' (2001: 9).
- When Nasr and Sardar speak about knowledge, are they talking about the same thing? True science for Nasr is 'not based on purely human reason but on the Intellect which belongs to the supra-human level of reality' (1994: 100). For Sardar, science is 'approximate, provisional, problem-solving' (1989: 119).
- El Saadawi wrote: 'books are controlled by the global and local powers of domination and exploitation, and they help to veil our brains with one myth after another. We have to acquire this knowledge by ourselves, from our own experience in the daily struggle against those powers globally, locally and in the family. This is creativity ... Discovering new ways of thinking and acting, of creating a system based on more and more justice, freedom, love and compassion. If you are creative, you must be dissident. You discover what others have not yet discovered' (1997: 160). In your opinion, do autocratic regimes fear

literature? Is there a link between how liberal, free and democratic a society is and the willingness of government to tolerate freedom of thought, as Mernissi, El Saadawi and others suggest?

- Tibi calls Sardar a 'fundamentalist' because he wrote to free 'Muslims from the "epistemological imperialism of the West"' (Tibi, 2001: 8). Do you agree with Tibi's description of Sardar?

- Do you think it is correct to read any significance into the fact that many reformist Muslim thinkers live outside the Muslim world? Not all reformist thinkers live in the West. For example, Mernissi, Soroush, Talbi live in the Muslim world.

- Progressive Muslim thought, from the time of Iqbal and 'Abduh onwards, has been labelled as too Western and as lacking Islamic *bone fides*. Sardar thinks that al-Faruqi made Islam subordinate to Western thought. Do you think that any of the progressive contributions reviewed in this chapter succeeded in establishing authenticity on Islamic grounds?

- Where will the revitalization of Muslim intellectual life stem from? Nasr does not view this as primarily a juridical task. Iqbal thought that legal scholars had a vital role. Sardar wants to encourage scientific development. Mernissi writes, 'A Galileo challenging the authority of Islam must not be a scientist but an essayist or novelist, a Salman Rushdie, and exploration of the psyche will surely be the arena of all future sedition' (1994: 134). What in your view is the most necessary area of intellectual life that requires development? Do you agree with the assumption of many of the Muslim scholars reviewed in this chapter that significant change is needed?

6 Muslim Voices on Gender in Islam

This book is a vessel journeying back in time in order to find a fabulous wind that will swell our sails and send us gliding toward new worlds, towards the time both far away and near at the beginning of the Hejira, when the Prophet could be a lover and a leader hostile to all hierarchies, when women had their place as unquestioned partners in a revolution that made the mosque an open place and the household a temple of debate.

(Mernissi 1991: 10)

Introducing the debate

Much writing on gender in Islam, as on minorities in the Muslim world, qualifies as apologetic and polemical, even when written by serious scholars. This is true for Muslim and for non-Muslim contributions. The idea that women are routinely maltreated and oppressed in Muslim societies, and that Islam is intrinsically misogynist and chauvinist, is a popular Western image of Islam. It contributes towards the Islamophobia that characterizes much Western thinking on Islam. Nor is this a new development. Leila Ahmed cites Lord Cromer, Egypt's colonial administrator, that Islam was a manifest failure as a social system first and foremost because of its ill-treatment of women, which was a 'canker' eating 'into the whole system of Islam'. Cromer's authority here was Stanley Lane Poole, whom Ahmed describes as 'the pre-eminent British Orientalist of his day' (1992: 153). Cromer believed that Egyptians had to imbibe the 'true spirit of Western civilization' by force or persuasion if they were to improve their moral standards and character. Above all, the abolition of the veil and female seclusion was a priority (p. 154). However, he discouraged the training of women doctors on the basis that 'throughout the civilized world, attendance by medical men is still the rule', and by raising school fees he made it difficult for boys as well as girls to access education. Ahmed points out that for all Cromer's rhetoric about the baneful effect of seclusion and veiling, in England he was a 'founding member and sometimes President of the Men's League for Opposing Women's Suffrage' (p. 153).

Mawdudi's classical contribution (1939, 1972) offers the traditionalist view that gender relations in Islam represent the divine and the human ideal. Legal reform is not needed. In addition to Badawi (1976) another easily accessible traditional text is Sherif Abdel Azeem (1995). He wrote this popular article after reading a 1990 essay by El Saadawi. In contrast, Mernissi, representing a leftist (or centre-left) contribution and offering what can be described as an Islamic feminist position, sees much that is wrong in Muslim societies and much that requires change if women are to enjoy full human rights. Radical legal change, as well as a change in outlook, is required. She sees Islam's classical settlement of the gender issue as a corruption of what the Qur'an and Muhammad really intended. In her view, the true spirit of the Qur'an confers women with dignity and freedom. The term 'Islamic feminism' was coined by Western academics to describe the approach of such Muslim women as Mernissi and Leila Ahmed (1992). However, it is not inappropriate, since these women regard themselves as working within Islam to reformulate and reinterpret a tradition whose dominant paradigms were produced by a patriarchal elite. Ahmed describes Mernissi as representing 'the aspirations of women who, while remaining Muslims, wish to live in modernity' (cited in Kurzman 1998: 112). Mernissi's 1991 text is also published as *The Veil and the Male Elite: A Feminist Interpretation of Women's Rights in Islam*. Shirin Ebadi, the 2003 Nobel Peace Laureate, similarly aims at a reformation of Islam from within. She does not reject Islamic law but tries to resolve what she perceives as its contradictions.

Akbar Ahmed's *Paradise Lies at the Feet of the Mother* (TV and video programme) represents a more centrist (centre-right) position. The film invites non-Muslim critics to look again at some aspects of what passes as orthodox Muslim praxis that Mernissi and Ahmed and others would either abolish or reform. In addition to these female reformist voices, such male voices as Esack's, Taha's and an-Na'im's among others also call for legal reform. Moghissi (1999) is much more sceptical that an authentically Islamic feminism is possible, and is critical of attempts to pursue this. Similarly, Tasrina Nasrin, who, though brought up in Muslim Bangladesh, now defines herself as a humanist, represents a post-Islamic response. A signatory to the 1997 Declaration of Women's Rights in Islamic Societies, her slogan is 'let humanism be the new name of religion'. Moghissi, Nasrin and others who share their approach contend that Islam is inherently misogynistic and they cannot agree that Islam can provide a solution when it is itself the problem. Islam alone can do little to improve the lot of women, given its unapologetic discrimination 'against women and minorities' (Moghissi 1999: 141). The solution lies outside Islam (p. 136), the very reverse of the fundamentalists' slogan of *al-hull-al-Islami*.

Two novels, Nawal El Saadawi's *The Fall of the Imam* (1988) and Naguib Mahfouz's *The Palace Walk* (1990), part one of his Cairo Trilogy, are reviewed in a literary case study following this chapter, which also briefly examines the *Arabian Nights* as a 'feminist' text.

Internet resources for and about Muslim women

http://islamworld.net (see section on Women, Family and Marriage)
www.islamfortoday.com/women.htm (Women in Islam)
www.ias.org/departments/sufiwomen.html (this is the Sufi Women's Organization's page on the International Association of Sufism site)
www.wluml.org (the Women Living Under Muslim Law Network's home-
page. This group was founded in 1984 in response to incidents concerning
women in Algeria)
www.mwlusa.org/ (The Muslim Women's League, USA, works to implement the values of Islam thereby reclaiming the status of women as free
and vital contributors to society)
www.islam21.net/pages/keyissues/key2.htm (The Women Issues section of the
International Forum for Islamic Dialogue)
See also the Women in Islam page at University of Southern California,
www.usc.edu/dept/MSA/humanrelations/womeninislam

Discussion topic

Roxanne D. Marcotte of the University of Queensland, Australia,
comments that Muslim women are increasingly using the Internet to
'promote their own vision and version of Islam' and to 're-
appropriate religious interpretation of matters that affect their own
personal lives'.

Walter W. Powell (1992) writes 'The publication system is a type of
control system. A number of factors – prestige, tradition, and networks of affiliation – limit access and restrict diversity' (p. 346). This
can make it difficult for ideas that challenge decision makers' vested
interests, such as their own scholarly output, to get into conventional
print.

- Is Internet 'theology' a bottom-up, people's movement that can
  challenge the vested interests that control religious interpretation and publishing?

Mawdudi: equal but different

Mawdudi's text evidences the degree to which a contemporary fundamentalist or traditionalist writer addressing gender consciously responds
to popular Western images of Muslim women. His *Purdah and The Status of
Women in Islam* was written in 1939 and has been repeatedly reprinted.
This analysis is based on a 1972 edition. While not a contemporary text as
such, this Mawdudi classic remains hugely influential and in many respects
sets the pattern for subsequent traditionalist Muslim writing on gender.
Mawdudi begins his text with sections on the status of women in different
ages and in other civilizations (pp. 4–17). He then proceeds to describe

Left	Centre left	Centre right	Right
Humanist position: reject the view that Islam is not to blame for the oppression and exploitation of Muslim women or that a reinterpretation of the tradition is the remedy. Rather, equality, dignity and freedom for women reside in the humanist option. Humanism itself needs to become people's religion.	Feminist position: Islam as practised is the product of a male elite. A gender neutral reinterpretation of the Qur'an and *hadith* will lead to the rediscovery of freedom and equality for women and men in Islam. Radical revision of practice and teaching, including legal precepts, follows from this but this is in reality a return to original Islam.	Centrist position: ignorance of Islam's true teaching causes some mistreatment of women and denial of their rights but this is not to be confused with the need for any radical change in Islamic practice or teaching. The West can learn from Islam's respect for women, who it exploits as sex objects and fashion fodder.	Conservative position: Islam is the natural religion that ascribes to men and women the rights and duties that are appropriate to their different roles and biological capabilities. Women are honoured in Islam while in the West they are exploited and ascribed inappropriate roles that God did not intend for women.

Figure 6.1 The main positions on gender relations explored in this chapter

how women had, in pre-Islamic times and until the modern period in Western society, no freedom, no rights and no dignity.

Mawdudi characterizes the modern view of the equality of the sexes as unnatural, producing women who are 'unmindful of their natural function' (p. 12). Historically, female dependence on males crushed them 'economically' (p. 10) while the free intermingling of the sexes in contemporary Western society 'has brought in its wake an ever growing tendency towards showing off, nudeness and perversion' (p. 15). Mawdudi denounced at length the West's 'nude pictures, sexual literature, love romances, nude ballroom dancing, sex-inciting films' which all serve to intensify 'the same fire which the wrong social system has kindled in every heart'. To save their faces, the Westerners 'call it "art"' (p. 15). Mawdudi explains that he used the word 'Purdah' in his title because this signifies the whole set of injunctions that 'constitute the most important part of the Islamic community life', which he later explains (p. 19). Unfortunately, people within the Muslim world have enthusiastically adopted 'drinking, gambling, lottery system, horse-racing, theatre, music, dancing and other evils of the Western civilization' (*ibid.*). In the 'face of faultfinding by the enemies of Islam', Muslims had started to apologize for their own practices or rather for what Westerners stated was Islamic practice. Thus, 'they found fault with slavery and the Muslims averred that it was absolutely unlawful ... they object to polygamy and the Muslims at once closed their eyes to a clear verse of the Qur'an ... they said that Islam disfavoured art, the Muslims stated that Islam had always been patronizing music and dancing, painting and sculpture' (p. 20). Islam and Western civilization, said Mawdudi, 'are poles apart in their objectives' and social systems (p. 23). Mawdudi argued that in France especially, sexual debauchery is so extensive and entrenched in the national character that a loss in physical strength has resulted (p. 51). Prostitution and venereal disease are rampant (p. 63). The rapid rise in rates of divorce and of marital separation in the West 'shows that man is resorting to animosity'. Similarly, Sayyid Qutb, as noted in the Introduction, saw sexual depravity as rampant in Western society so much so that he accused non-Muslims of failing to distinguish 'man from animal' (1988: 184). 'Free sexual intercourse and illegitimate children' are the basis of Western society, where women's 'role is merely to be attractive, sexy and flirtatious'. Islamic society, with its 'division of labour between husband and wife' is truly civilized, curbing the downward 'degeneration toward animalism' (pp. 182–3). Under official Islam, women can initiate divorce but only after recourse to a third party judicial authority: men need only recite 'I divorce you' three times (albeit this right is subject to certain conditions; see Q65 on *talaq*, divorce). Q4: 128 says that if a wife fears cruelty or desertion, she should reach an amicable settlement with her husband. Official Islam does allow women to stipulate the right to initiate divorce in their marriage contract but Ahmed's historical survey shows that this has rarely happened (1992: 106).

Islam ennobles women

Mawdudi argues that, in contrast to the above sorry state of affairs in the Western world, Islam, in the seventh century, brought with it principles and practices that ennoble both women and men, and introduced a social system within which gender relations and roles take due 'cognizance of all the demands of man's nature, his temperament and his physiological structure' (Mawdudi 1972: 123). He thus contrasts the status of women in the non-Muslim world with that of women in the Muslim world, and finds them more elevated in the latter. Mawdudi contends that the Qur'an guarantees women rights that Western society has traditionally denied, and that even today Muslim women are better off than their non-Muslim sisters. He claims that Islam introduced reforms and rights that vastly improved the status of women in Arabia, who in the age of ignorance had very few rights. Infanticide, vehemently condemned in the Qur'an (Q16: 59, 43: 17, 81: 8–9), was practised widely and girls were often compelled to marry without giving consent, which Islam forbids, while the *mahr* (bridal price) which is given to the wife guarantees protection and financial security. Under Islamic Law, brides are not sold, as in many other cultures. In place of the unlimited polygamy (some believe polyandry) of pre-Islamic Arabia, Islam regulated polygamy (see below). Thus, polygamy helps to prevent promiscuousness, fornication and adultery and might even be considered as a 'viable solution to some of the social ills of modern societies' (Parekh 2000 rejects the view that a liberal society can condone polygamy, see below). Mawdudi describes the Islamic provision as 'conditional polygamy' (up to four wives and each must be treated equally) (see 1976: 163). To reject polygamy is to oppose what the Qur'an clearly permits.

In the West, women have the right to own property and to work but this actually burdens them with responsibilities that Muslim women lack. Mawdudi writes extensively about the division of labour and of responsibility between men and women; men are responsible for 'all outdoor duties including the duty of supporting and protecting the family'. If a woman is 'loaded with economic and social responsibilities along with the man' as in the West, she 'will throw off the burden of her natural duties' of 'bringing up children, looking after the domestic affairs and making home life sweet, pleasant and peaceful' (p. 121). Mawdudi also says that Islam grants women educational rights but stresses that female education should be appropriate for the female role, thus a woman should be 'trained primarily in those branches of knowledge that make her more useful' in the domestic sphere (p. 152). The influential Deobandi movement in Pakistan shares many of Mawdudi's views on the status of women, such as that veiling is compulsory, that women and men should not mix in public, that men are 'in charge of women' (and are more intelligent) but unlike Mawdudi teach that women should not be educated after age 8. Caner (2003) describes an inscription on a mosque in Kabul, claiming to cite 'Umar, which reads 'Prevent the women from learning to write! Say no to their capricious ways' as evidence that Islam is the cause of women's oppression, for if it were not 'why have these words not been eradicated?' (p. 11).

Women and men, then, are equal but different, with distinctive roles and responsibilities. Women, said Mawdudi, are not suitable to undertake tasks that require physical strength because monthly menstruation renders them unfit for 'responsibilities ... involving physical or mental exertion' (1976: 118). Women are prone to be more 'tender and plastic' than men, who are 'tough and rigid', thus to 'drag women' into certain 'fields of activity' abuses women and these 'fields of activity themselves' (p. 120). To enter 'the police, the judicial, administrative, foreign, railway, industrial and commercial services' merely 'defeminizes' women and treats them like men (p. 119). Women's 'mental and physical state becomes unstable' once every month (p. 120). Mawdudi states that it is 'an impossibility that geniuses like Aristotle, Ibn-i-Sina, Kant, Hegel, Khayyam, Shakespeare, Alexander ... will ever come forth among women' just as no man could be even a 'most ordinary mother' (p. 120). Mawdudi wrote that only 'foolish and senseless people' mix up 'the different fields of activity of the two sexes' (p. 122). Islam guaranteed women's right to earn centuries beforehand, although Mawdudi did not believe that women should be expected to work, nor did he regard paid work as women's natural or appropriate role, which is domestic duty. Mawdudi accepts that Islam allows men to marry up to four wives, provided that they treat them fairly. He sees this as a pragmatic measure, given that in many societies women outnumber men but require caring for, while many want to fulfil their natural roles as child bearers and up-bringers.

The veil: a symbol of honour and respect

Akbar Ahmed's film *Paradise Lies at the Feet of the Mother* and Production Co-ordinator Mary Walker's article 'A World Where Womanhood Reigns Supreme' (1995) are examples of the argument that the choice to wear the veil empowers and liberates Muslim women. Kabbani (1989) comments:

> Wearing the *hijab* can be a liberation, freeing women from being sexual objects, releasing them from the traps of Western dress and the dictates of Western fashion ... since all women look the same in it, it is a most effective social equalizer. (p. 27)

Feminist Muslim responses

Muslim feminists reject the contention that traditional Islam treats women fairly, arguing instead that it is misogynist and that reform is needed. They especially think that traditional or classical Islam is unfair to women in their rights of divorce, legal testimony, political participation and access to employment. Traditional Islamic law also values the life of women as half that of men in cases where 'blood money' (compensation) is payable (while the life of a non-Muslim is valued at one twelfth of a Muslim's). However, they do not believe that Islam's true spirit is misogynist or that its ill-treatment of women derives from an authentic reading of its foundational texts.

Rather, they argue that, as formulated, Islamic law and Islamic tradition serve the needs of a patriarchal elite. Much of their work consists of revisiting texts and historical contexts to deconstruct patriarchal interpretations and to construct feminist alternatives. However, their aim is not to replace interpretations that serve male interests over-and-against female interests with those that privilege women, but to render the tradition fair to both genders. For these writers, the veil is neither the traditionalists' symbol of honour and respect nor the centrists' symbol of liberation, but signifies women's subservience and bondage. These writers agree with the centrists that to wear the veil is to make a political statement but they differ in what that statement says. For the centrists, it affirms that traditional Islam honours and respects women, for the feminists it is an admission of servitude: 'The *hijab*', says Mernissi, 'is manna from heaven for politicians facing a crisis ... it sends women back to the kitchen' (1994: 165). According to Mernissi, it effectively silences women. Rulers who want, for example, to manipulate unemployment statistics can do so simply by 'appealing to the *shari'a* in its meaning as despotic caliphate tradition', that is, by declaring that women should be secluded and enforcing this via the *Muttaween* (religious police).

The Forgotten Queens of Islam

Following the election of Benazir Bhutto as Pakistan's Prime Minister in 1988 (she served until 1990 and then for a second term 1993–96), Fatima Mernissi heard many Muslims declare that a woman could not be a leader of Muslims. Many cited the *hadith* 'those who entrust their affairs to a woman will never know prosperity' (or 'never will such a nation succeed as makes a woman their ruler', Bukhari, Vol. 9, Bk 88, Ch. 18, *hadith* 119, Khan 1987: 170–1). Mernissi observed that this *hadith* is 'omnipresent and all-embracing' and that any attempt to discuss the issue of women's involvement in politics or public life is 'swallowed up by the debate on this *hadith*'. Therefore, in her *Women and Islam* (1991) Mernissi set out to critique this and other oft-cited misogynist *hadith* with a view to establishing whether or not they represent Muhammad's authentic voice. In her 1993 book, *The Forgotten Queens of Islam*, Mernissi responded to the claim that Bhutto's election had no precedent in Islamic history, asking whether women had in fact exercised power in Muslim states, even though this runs counter to Islam's social-cultural-religious norms. Discovering evidence that women have occupied seats of power, Mernissi argues that their songs are not sung because their stories have largely been 'rubbed out of official history' (p. 2) although it was in yellowed old books that she discovered these women, who 'paraded through the silent rooms of libraries' (p. 3). What interested her especially was how these women achieved power without 'frightening the men? What strategies did they use to tame them?' (p. 5)

Modern Muslim women leaders

Megawati Sukarnoputri became President of Indonesia in 2001. She may be the first woman to serve as Head of State in a Muslim country. Benazir Bhutto was Prime Minister of Pakistan 1988–90 and 1993 until 1996. Sheikh Hasina was Prime Minister of Bangladesh 1996–2001; Khaleda Zia was Prime Minister of Bangladesh 1991–1996 and from 2001. Turkey elected a woman, Tansu Ciller, in 1993. She was PM until 1996.

Mernissi recounts the stories of no few women who at different times in Muslim history have exercised power. Mernissi argues that the women who did succeed in ruling did so against the odds. Many were involved in intrigue. No few met untimely deaths. Of course, male rulers of Muslims have also indulged in plots and counter-plots and many have died violently. However, in achieving positions of authority, women extended the boundaries, the *hudud*, and did so on two fronts. First, they broke the conventions that excluded women from public life, symbolized by the veil. Second, they also shattered the veil (*hijab*) that had been set up between the Khalif and the ordinary people, the *'amma* (earthly masses). As the 'Abbasids lost political power, they increased their own spiritual mystique. Consequently, they drew apart from the people, protected by the *hajib* (official who controlled access to the Khalif; see Chapter Two). Ironically, this also involved moving out of the mosque into the palace. Mernissi suggests that this innovation was inspired by the desire to 'avoid the anxiety of direct contact with the group', whose opinions the Khalif no longer wished to hear (1993: 79). The people's job was to obey, not to offer political commentary. Women's job was to remain veiled, and silent. The original idea of an enlightened Khalif 'attentive to his people, who were close to him in a mosque' was replaced by the reality known as *mulk* (earthly power; p. 183).

The entry of women into politics, says Mernissi, especially Bhutto's election, 'represented the dual emergence on the political scene of that which is veiled and that which is obscene: the will of women and that of the people' (p. 178). Women who dare to tread the public stage intrude into a space that men have reserved for themselves, where heaven and earth meet (p. 67). It was the prophet's wife 'A'isha who first transgressed the *hudud* (limits) when she led the 'armed insurrection in 36/658 against the fourth orthodox Caliph, 'Ali Ibn Abi Talib' and lost. As a result, says

Mernissi, women's political intervention has been regarded as *fitna* (disorder and destruction), and has consequently been feared, just as has the voice of the people (p. 66). When the people's voice is heard, it may result in centuries of despotic *mulk* being replaced with 'so-called aberrations like the election of a Muslim woman' (p. 185). Interestingly, Bhutto, Sheikh Hasina, Zia and Sukarnoputri all belong to political dynasties (three through fathers, one through a husband).

True and false traditions

In her *Women and Islam* (1991), Mernissi embarked on a detailed study of the *hadith* and other religious texts, since simply by quoting such a *hadith* as 'those who entrust their affairs to a woman' can silence all further discussion of women in politics. She comments that such a text has 'extraordinary power over the ordinary citizens of a modern state' (p. 2) and that it is not unsurprising that the critical study of such texts has tended to be the prerogative of a comparatively small number of people, 'the mullahs and Imams' given the 'overwhelming ... number of volumes' of such literature. Mernissi identifies the conversation stopping *hadith* cited above as one that has passed the traditional tests of authenticity. It is found in Bukhari's *Sahih* (collection of sound *hadiths*) as well as in the *Musnad* of Ahmad ibn Hanbal, founder of the Hanbali legal school (*Madhhab*) (p. 4). She describes how the classical traditionalists authenticated *hadith* by investigating each link in the chain of narration to establish 'who uttered it, and in what circumstances and with what object in mind' (p. 3). Mernissi describes the techniques that were developed to investigate the *isnads* (chain of transmission) as resembling 'fieldwork and interview technique' and says that they would 'turn late nineteenth century anthropologists green with envy' (p. 9). Ibn Qayyim al-Jawziya established rules for examining the content (*matn*) of *hadith*, aware that *hadith* had already become weapons in the mouths of those who wanted to legitimate certain privileges or attitudes (p. 9). From the seventh century onwards, power in Muslim societies has been legitimated by the manipulation of sacred texts (pp. 8–9; see p. 43).

To pass off a false *hadith* as authentic imbues whatever action or attitude it describes with divine authority. Thus, 'the present day is no exception when it comes to misrepresenting privileges and interests in the name of the Prophet' (p. 9). On the one hand, Mernissi points out that textual investigation and historical reconstruction in Islam have been carefully supervised activities 'for all of us, men and women' since the imams want to control and manage 'memory and history' (p. 10). On the other hand, she also points out that questioning the authenticity of *hadith* has an honourable history in Islam. It is a tradition, says Mernissi, to 'question everything and everybody'. Bukhari had always begun his work 'by asking for Allah's help and acknowledging that only He is infallible' (p. 76). It was because Muslims were aware that *hadith* were being fabricated that 'experts felt the need to establish a technique for detection of false traditions' (p. 9). Much of Islam's true message has been obscured yet access to memory has never been completely denied, she says, and a careful listening to dead and silent voices can 'animate the present' (p. 10). In place of the official story of a Prophet who excluded women from leadership, a different story emerges of 'a Prophet-lover who, in the middle of the desert, spoke in a strange language to his mother-tribe ... of absurd things: non-violence and equality' (p. 10). The problem was, argues Mernissi, that people were not ready for this message, so they manipulated their 'texts in such a way as to maintain their privileges' (p. 125). Islam's tradition of misogyny has been justified by using sacred texts as political weapons, she says. Misogyny does not derive from the discourse of Muhammad but from the later editing of those elite men who were unprepared for Muhammad's message.

Turning to specific misogynist *hadith*, Mernissi is able to use traditional methodology as well as a feminist approach to question their authenticity. Traditional *hadith* criticism placed great stress on establishing the personal integrity of the narrator, as well as establishing plausibility of content. When she examined the oft-quoted, conversation-stopping 'Those who entrust their affairs to a woman will never know prosperity', she found that its narrator, Abu Bakra, had first 'remembered' these putative words of Muhammad 25 years after they were supposed to have been said by him at the battle of al-Jarnal, when Muhammad heard that the Persians had 'made the daughter of Khosrau their Queen' (Khan 1987: Vol. 9, Bk 88, 219, p. 171). Abu Bakra narrated this convenient *hadith*, she says, immediately after the 'A'isha-led rebellion against Ali had been crushed at the Battle of the Camel (1998: 115). Did he, she surmises, really remember this *hadith* or was it fabricated as a posthumous justification for his decision not to support the revolt (1991: 50–1). The same narrator, Mernissi discovered, had been found guilty of and punished for lying by Khalif 'Umar (1991: 60, 1998: 119), who was himself very reluctant to recite *hadith*, since he considered the human memory 'dangerously fallible' (1991: 70, 1998: 125).

She points out how Muslim men have used the failure of 'A'isha's revolt, which is described as *fitna* (civil strife), ever since as proof enough that when a women takes the lead, disaster follows. In her 1991 'Introduction' (reproduced in part in Kurzman 1998), Mernissi cites some recent male writers on women in Islam for whom the whole episode of the Battle of the Camel 'proves that woman was not created for poking her nose into politics' (p. 6). Thus, these writers represent 'A'isha's action as contrary to Muhammad's *Sunnah*; moreover, it was, they say, denounced by all the companions as well as by Muhammad's other wives (p. 5). Such 'errant behaviour' was *bi'da,* a 'scandalous violation of the sacred tradition' (*ibid.*). Other writers accept the authenticity of this *hadith* but not its traditional interpretation. They argue that Muhammad was not legislating for all time that no woman could rule but was predicting that in this particular historical instance, Persia would not flourish since following King Khosrau's murder by his own son, a succession of princes succeeded each other over the next five years while anarchy reigned. Muhammad may thus have foreseen the likely outcome of rule by inexperienced women in such turbulent times. In fact, two queens, Purandukht and Azarmidukht, each ruled briefly, only to be overthrown by a grandson of Khosrau. Still others point out that Muhammad was referring here to Zoroastrian, not Muslim, rulers. Others point out that for Muhammad to have denied that women could rule would be contrary to the Qur'an, in which the Queen of Sheba is praised for her acumen, judgement and purity of faith, with no suggestion that God disapproved of her role (Q27: 23–44; see Maqsood at *http://www.themodernreligion.com/women/w-hell.html*).

Turning to the Qur'anic verse that traditionalists interpret as prescribing the veil for all women for all time, the Verse of *Hijab*, Q33: 53, which instructs Muhammad's male companions to approach his wives 'from behind a curtain', Mernissi argues that this was intended at the time to 'intimate to the Companions certain niceties, like not entering a dwelling without asking permission' (1991: 92). There is some suggestion here that the companions were becoming overly casual and informal in their behaviour within the Prophet's household. As 'mothers of the believers', Muhammad's wives were to be respected and honoured. This interpretation sees the verse as setting down a rule of etiquette, instead of legislating that women must always be segregated from men, which is Mawdudi's interpretation.

Mernissi argues that such rights as rejecting proposals of marriage, inheriting money and property and retaining their own earnings (see Q3: 195, 4: 32, 9: 71, 33: 35–6), which Muhammad's message guaranteed women, upset and distressed men, since they diminished their control over women and also affected them financially. In response, men used the device of interpretation to distort the meaning of texts and manipulate them 'in such a way as to maintain their privileges' (1991: 125). For example, they interpreted the verse 'give not unto the foolish your wealth' as applying to women, since they deemed women 'foolish' (p. 126). Islam's true message was thus one of gender equality. Muhammad consulted women, held them in high esteem and could even be considered a feminist. His message held out the hope of equality in the treatment of women but despite this, as Islam developed after Muhammad's death, misogyny 'very quickly reasserted itself' (1991: 75, 1998: 123; see Q58: 1 and 60: 10–12 for women's participation in discussion). While misogyny became enshrined in official Islam, it is absent in true Islam. Official Islam is the Islam of the palaces, bereft of its rational and ethical element (see 1991: 37). Mernissi distinguishes between what she calls 'political Islam', or 'Islam as the practice of power', an Islam 'animated by passions and motivated by interest', and 'spiritual Islam', or '*Islam Risala*, the divine message, the ideal recorded in the Koran' (1993: 5).

Mernissi argues that male superiority was so 'ingrained in the people of the Arabian area, before and after the Prophet', that some scholars tried very hard to protect Muhammad's revolutionary message from those who set out to distort it, whose efforts largely succeeded (*ibid.*). Such scholars were swimming against the tide yet some of their work has survived. Mernissi makes much use of a text by the fourteenth-century scholar, Imam Zarkashi, called *Collection of 'A'isha's Corrections to the Statements of the Companions* (*Al-Ijaba li 'irad ma Istadrakathu 'A'isha ala al-Sahaba*), that records some of the work of earlier *fuqaha* 'who saw in misogyny the danger of betrayal of the prophet' (1991: 75, 1998: 123). Zarkashi's collection remained in 'manuscript form until 1930' (1991: 77, 1998: 124).

Turning to other popular misogynist *hadith*, Mernissi found that the narrator was often Abu Hurayra and that while Bukhari records only one version of these *hadith* (although often with more than one source), corrected versions appear in Zarkashi. She further discovered that a long-standing feud existed between Abu Hurayra and 'A'isha. He criticized the prophet's young wife (she was nine when they married, six when betrothed) for spending too much time on cosmetics and jewellery, implying that she was thus frivolously engaged while he was attentive to the prophet's every word, memorizing them for posterity (1991: 72, 1998: 121). Hurayra liked to spend time in Muhammad's company and 'sometimes helped out in the women's apartments' (*ibid.*). He turned down an offer of employment from 'Umar because he preferred to 'follow the Prophet everywhere' (1991: 80, 1998: 125). His name, which translates as 'Father of the Little Female Cat', had been given him by Muhammad to replace his pagan name of 'Abd al-Shams (Servant of the Sun) (1991: 71, 1998: 121). Muhammad was renowned for his love of female cats, so much so that Abu Hurayra may have invented *hadith* in which female cats 'come off much better than ... women' (1991: 72, 1998: 121). For example, he cites Muhammad as saying that a woman had gone to hell 'because she starved a little female cat'. 'A'isha contradicted this: 'A believer', she said, 'is too valuable in the eyes of God for Him to torture a person because of a cat'. She rebuked Abu Hurayra for false reporting (1991: 73, 1998: 121). Abu Hurayra also reported that Muhammad said 'three things bring bad luck: house, woman and horse', which A'isha disputed. 'What the Prophet said was, "May Allah refute the Jews; they say three things bring bad luck ..."' (1991: 76, 1998: 123). According to 'A'isha, Abu Hurayra had only overheard part of Muhammad's words. She similarly disputed the *hadith*, 'three things interrupt prayer, dogs, asses and women', saying that she had seen Muhammad at prayer while she was 'lying on the bed between him and the *qibla*' (*qiblah* = direction of prayer, towards Makkah; 1991: 70, 1998: 120).

While Bukhari included Abu Hurayra's misogynist *hadith* in his collection, he did note that 'people say that he recounted too many *hadith*' (1991: 79, 1998: 125). In his three years spent in the company of Muhammad, Abu Hurayra memorized 5,300 *hadith*. 'A'isha, herself an important narrator of *hadith*, only recounted 1,200 but was also recognized to be one of the *Sunnah*'s most careful interpreters and an expert on *fiqh*. Chiragh 'Ali, the Indian reformer, considered her to be the founder of a *madhhab*' (2002: 278). Muhammad advised his followers to learn a part of their religion from 'A'isha (Mernissi 1991: 79, 1998: 124). 'Inspiration', he said, 'does not come to me when I am under the cover of a wife, except that wife be 'A'isha' (MM, 2, p. 1762). We read that the believers never asked 'A'isha 'about a tradition regarding which they were in doubt without finding that she had some knowledge of it' (MM, 2, p. 1762).

Bukhari's own attitude towards women, Mernissi suggests, may well have been biased, since he sometimes includes several versions of disputed *hadith* 'with a different transmission chain', which 'generally strengthens a *hadith*' by giving 'the impression of consensus concerning it' (multiple attestation of *hadith* was a traditional criterion of authenticity; 1991: 76, 1998: 123). 'Abdullah was another source of misogynist *hadith* included in Bukhari, to whom he attributes 'I took a look at heaven, and noticed that the majority of people there were poor. I took a look at hell, and noticed that there women were the majority' (1991: 76, 1998: 123; Bukhari, Vol. 8, Bk 76, Ch. 16, *hadith* 456, Khan 1987: 306; some commentators suggest that Muhammad may have said this but in jest; see Ruqaiyyah Waris Maqsood's 'Are there more women than men in hell?' at *http://www.the-modern religion.com/women/w-hell.html*). Mernissi concludes that 'even the authentic *hadith* must be vigilantly examined with a magnifying glass' in order to 'disinter our true tradition from the centuries of oblivion that have managed to obscure it' (1991: 76–7, 1998: 123–4). Muhammad himself, renowned for his fondness of women, was a feminist. Mernissi also points out that women did contribute to the creation of Islam's early texts, even though they were later excluded, which, she claims, is possibly unique among religious traditions (1991: 64, p 73; see 'Women Scholars of *Hadith*' by Dr Muhammad Zubayr Siddiqi, Chapter 6, pp. 142–53, 1961, available at *http://www.islamfortoday.com/womenscholars.htm*).

Male contributions

Some humanists and feminists reject Mernissi's and Ahmed's version of Islam as untenable but there is considerable overlap between their arguments and those of reformist male writers. One of the earliest texts advocating gender equality was Qasim Amin's *tahrir-al-mar'a* (the liberation of women) published in 1899. He believed that unveiling was the 'key to social transformation' for women (Ahmed 1992: 145). While Amin (1863–1908) subscribed to the 'colonial thesis of the inferiority of Islam' and promoted Westernization (*ibid.*, p 162), his book, says Mernissi (1991), nonetheless put debate 'on the equality of the sexes' firmly on the agenda 'as far back as the 1880s' (p. 23; see 'The Emancipation of Women', pp. 61–9, Kurzman 2002). Amin graduated in law and worked with al-Afghani and 'Abduh on their journal, *al-Urwa al-wuthya* (The Strongest Link), while studying in Paris. 'Abduh championed female education and schools founded by his benevolent societies educated more boys as well as more girls than did government schools under Lord Cromer's administration (Ahmed 1992: 138). 'Abduh argued that the 'Qur'anic verse on the equal rewards of labour showed that "men and women are equal before God in the matter of reward", and that thus "there is no difference between them in regard to humanity, and no superiority of one over the other in works" '(p. 139). Polygamy, and other 'backward' and 'degraded' practices had their origin 'not in Islam but in the corruption and misinterpretation that had beset Islam over the centuries' (p. 140). Q4: 3 had only permitted polygamy because of the 'conditions of the day, although monogamy was clearly the Qur'an's ideal' (p. 140). Q4: 3 refers to 'widows and orphans', of which there were many following the Battle of Badr (624 CE) after which this verse was revealed, and the need to care for them and also to treat all wives equally. Many Muslims point out that since this is virtually impossible for most men, polygamy is not an option. Technically, the correct term for men marrying more than one wife is polygyny. Polygamy includes women marrying more than one man, or polyandry. However, following common usage, except where quoting, this book uses the inclusive term.

Among reformist and progressive male scholars whose writing has featured in discussion elsewhere in this book, Esack, Talbi, Taha, an-Na'im and Soroush among others advocate gender equality. Esack, Talbi, Taha and an-Na'im all argue that those verses of the Qur'an that speak of the equality of men and women before God abrogate (and not vice-versa as classical scholars argued) those that uphold (or appear to uphold) male superiority. Taha's 'Second Message of Islam' argues (as noted elsewhere in this book) that all the pragmatic edicts of the Madinah period are temporary, situational applications of the eternal and universal norms contained in the Madinan verses. Thus, when these later, situational texts were made the basis of *Shari'ah* it was inevitable that Islamic law evolved as a discriminatory system; an-Na'im states bluntly 'The fact that *Shari'a* does not treat women and non-Muslims equally with male Muslims is beyond dispute' (1987: 12). An-Na'im would equalize divorce for women and men, as opposed to the traditional right of men to pronounce divorce. Taha argues that polygamy, divorce, veiling and seclusion were not meant to be eternal, universal principles in Islam but that all were temporary, pragmatic provisions for the Madinan period (subsidiary verses). The Madinah message lowered the standards of the Makkan 'to suit the times and serve society' (1987: 145). Islam's original principle was '*al-sufur*' (unveiling) and veiling was introduced because of the misuse of this freedom by Muhammad's immature followers. All these writers argue that by recognizing that historical *Shari'ah* 'is not the whole of Islam but merely the level of Islamic law that suited the previous generation', the circumstantial verses on which it was based can be replaced 'as having served their transitional purpose' by 'other texts of Qur'an and *sunnah*' (*ibid.*: 23; see 1998: 234).

Esack (1997), former Chair of the South Africa Government's Commission on Gender Equality, calls for a gender *jihad*, arguing that demands by some Muslims living as minorities in non-Muslim states for legal recognition for Muslim Personal law represents an attempt to legitimate the illegitimate (p. 241). Such law derives from the period of Islam's decline, when women were marginalized and emerged as one of the most oppressed of all groups. It was in Pakistan that Esack first became aware of the 'many similarities between the oppression of women in Muslim society and that of Blacks in South Africa' (p. 5). As summarized in Chapter Three, he sees the up-lifting of the oppressed and marginalized (*mustad'afun*) as Islam's primary task, thus 'for Muslims' such as those involved in the anti-racist struggle in South Africa, to 'succumb to interpretations of the *shari'ah* that perpetuated the subjugation of women, was tantamount to legitimizing the illegitimate' (p. 242). Such interpretations need to yield to those that uphold gender equality, argues Esack (see below for Esack on minorities). See Figure 6.2 on the Ethical versus the Pragmatic Voices of the Qur'an from a 'left' and a 'right' perspective.

Islamic feminism: human rights and humanist critiques

Moghissi, an Iranian émigré, currently teaches sociology at York University's Atkinson College, Toronto. After graduating from Teheran University she took her masters and doctorate at Queens University, Ontario. Her 1999 book, which won the Choice Outstanding Academic Books Award in 2000, begins with a critique of Western views of Islam, borrowing from Edward Said. She argues that Islam alone can do little to improve the lot of women, given its unapologetic discrimination 'against women and minorities' (p. 141). Rather, 'change in Muslim societies ... has to start, perhaps, with the rule of law, state accountability and separation of church and state' (p. 142). While she is aware of (and cites) Muslim women who argue for improved status and for equal rights from within Islam (see pp. 125–48) such as Ahmed and Mernissi, unlike them she finds it difficult to concede the viability of Islamic feminism, since she is convinced that the solution resides outside Islam within human rights discourse (p. 136). Despite the West's tendency to insist that Islam is 'all there is' in Islamic contexts, the reality is much more complex (p. 135), she says. Culture, history, politics, class, economics and many other factors contribute to women's and men's experiences in Muslim countries.

She describes two versions – the Muslim world as fanatic, irrational, totalitarian, immoral and as offering, for men at least, sexual possibilities denied in Europe. Double standards applied. What was regarded as 'appropriate in Europe', for example 'female domesticity', was condemned as 'sexual slavery' in the Muslim world (p. 15). However, she proceeds to describe the position of Muslim women in Islam as to all intents and purposes just that – sexual slaves, which perhaps suggests that the latter image was not altogether inaccurate. Muslim men, she says, fear

For Taha, an-Na'im, Talbi, Ahmed *et al.* the ethical voice cancels the pragmatic voice.

For Mawdudi and conservative Islam, the verses on the right take priority over those on the left (for progressives, those on the left are eternal principles, those on the right time-limited applications).

Ethical voice of the Qur'an/original precepts (unqualified gender equality)	Pragmatic voice/situational precepts not universally valid – qualify gender equality and privilege men
'The believers, men and women, are protectors, one of another: they enjoin what is just, and forbid what is evil, they observe regular prayers, practise regular charity, and obey Allah and His Messenger. On them will Allah pour His Mercy: for Allah is Exalted in power, Wise' (Q9: 71).	'As to those women on whose part you fear disloyalty and ill-conduct, (1) Admonish them, (2) refuse to share their beds, (3) beat them; but if they return to obedience seek not against them means of annoyance: For Allah is Most High, Great. (4) If you fear a break between them, appoint two arbiters, one from his family and the other from hers; If they wish for peace, Allah will cause their reconciliation' (Q4: 34–5).
'And their Lord answered them: Truly I will never cause to be lost the work of any of you, Be you a male or female, you are members one of another' (Q3: 195).	'O Prophet, tell your wives and daughters and the believing women that they should cast their outer garments over their bodies (when abroad) so that they should be known and not molested' (Q33: 59).
'Whoever works righteousness, man or woman, and has faith, verily to him/her we will give a new life that is good and pure, and we will bestow on such their reward according to the best of their actions' (Q16: 97).	'O ye who believe! When ye deal with each other, in transactions involving future obligations in a fixed period of time . . . and get two witnesses, out of your own men, and if there are not two men, then a man and two women, such as ye choose, for witnesses, so that if one of them errs, the other can remind her' (Q2: 282).
'To Allah belongs the dominion of the heavens and the earth. He creates what He wills. He bestows female children to whomever He wills and bestows male children to whomever He wills' (Q42: 49).	'And they (women) have rights similar to those (of men) over them, and men are a degree above them' (Q2: 228).
'And among His signs is that He created for you mates from among yourselves, that you may dwell in tranquillity with them and He has put love and mercy between your hearts: verily in that are signs for those who reflect' (Q30: 21).	'Men are the maintainers of women because Allah has made some of them to excel others and because they spend of their wealth (*anfaqu min amwalihim*) [for the support of women]' (Q4: 34).
	'Your wives are a tilth [or tillage] for you, so approach your tilth when and how you will' (Q2: 223).

'O mankind! reverence your Guardian-Lord, Who created you from a single person, and created of like nature his mate, and from them twain scattered (like seeds) countless men and women' (Q4: 1).

'To men is allotted what they earn, and to women what they earn' (Q4: 32).

'God (thus) direct you as regards your children's (inheritance): to the male, a portion equal to that of two females. If only daughters, two or more, their share is two-thirds of the inheritance. If only one, her share is a half. For parents, a sixth share of the inheritance to each, if the deceased left children. If no children, and the parents are the (only) heirs, the mother has a third. If the deceased has brothers (or sisters) the mother has a sixth' (Q4: 11).

'If you fear that you shall not be able to deal justly with the orphans, marry women of your choice, two or three or four; but if you fear that you shall not be able to deal justly with them, then only one' (Q4: 3). This verse can be interpreted as ethical and pragmatic. While it permits polygamy, which is pragmatic, it also places ethical constraints on this male privilege.

Figure 6.2 The Ethical v. the Pragmatic Voice of the Qur'an

the seductive power of women's sexuality and so seek to manipulate and to control it: 'woman's very existence is serving men, sexually and emotionally. Women are a "tillage" for the male believer, to go to when he wishes' (p. 22; see Q2: 223; Awde 2000: 85). Islam's 'obsession with sex, women and the human body', she says, 'borders on the pathological' (p. 46). The inequality of women and men before the law translates into the cheapness of women's lives: 'setting a higher price on a man's life ... means that rape and women's murder go unpunished' (p. 111).

Far from reforms in Iran promoting the cause of female equality, gains made under the former regime have been lost, she says (see especially pp. 104–109). The number of women in work may indeed have increased in Iran but mainly in low-paid jobs or in 'coercive apparatus designed to control and police other women' (p. 114). It may be true that some Muslim women voluntarily don the veil (hijab) as an affirmation of their Islamic identity, in protest against Western slavery to fashion. However, for many women in present-day Iran, where wearing the veil is legally enforced, it is far from empowering. 'Women who are persecuted, jailed and whipped for their non-compliance with hejab find the dress code anything but empowering', she says (p. 5). She dismisses images of veiled women and of harems as guaranteeing women's space and freedom, the centrist position described above, as romantic and naïve (see p. 87). Similarly, blaming everything on colonialism cannot get Islam off the hook. Colonial misdemeanours do not excuse the clerics who 'painstakingly protected' women 'for many centuries against modern ideas, institutions and relations' (p. 86). Moghissi refers to crimes against women as endemic throughout the Muslim world (see p. 105).

Universal ethical norms, including the discourse of human rights, must not become the victim of postmodernism's critique of meta-narratives, she argues. Too easily, she says, the subjugation of women by Muslim men, inside and outside the Muslim world, gets labelled as culturally appropriate; ' "they" have their ways, "we" have ours, and we should be "more accepting" of practices which are unacceptable here but admissible there' is ethically unacceptable (p. 5). This is the limit of postmodern analyses: 'Charmed by "difference", and secure from the bitter facts of the fundamentalist regime, outsiders do them [Muslim women] a disservice by clinging to the illusion of an Islamic path' (p. 121). Islamic fundamentalism would thus become 'the only conceivable future for societies of the Middle East where fundamentalists now rule' (p. 145). Referring to Mawdudi's writing, she comments that it 'can easily impress the reader'. However, she continues, his 'language is very misleading ... considering his very reactionary political practice, his views on women and non-Muslim minorities, his opposition to modernizing reforms, and finally his support for the most reactionary and brutal government of Pakistan, that of General Zia ul-Haq. This is why we can never depend on words alone' (p. 69).

Taslima Nasrin

From her own humanist perspective, the Bangladeshi exile Taslima Nasrin (2000) also argues that, since Islam is itself the problem, the solution to discrimination against women in Muslim societies cannot be found within Islam. Trained as a doctor, Nasrin started writing poetry, periodical articles and books that won literary recognition with such awards as India's *Ananda Puroshka*. From 1989 she wrote a regular column on the plight of women in rural Bangladesh, highlighting the role of religion. Following the publication of *Lajja* (Shame), a *fatwa* for her death was issued by fundamentalist *ulama* in Bangladesh. Helped by Western governments, she fled Bangladesh and since 1993 has lived in such countries as Sweden, France, Germany and the USA. In exile, she has identified with the humanist movement. She is a senior editor of the magazine *Free Enquiry*, and was given a humanist award by the International Humanist and Ethical Union as well as the Sakharov Prize for freedom of thought by the European Parliament. She rejects any law based on religion and criticizes Abu Zayd and other reformist thinkers for not going far enough, calling for modification to, rather than abolition of, Islamic Law. She cites him as saying that the UDHR is not suitable for Islamic countries and disagrees with his view that human rights are not universally applicable. She also rejects Mernissi's and Ahmed's attempt at a feminist reformation of Islam:

> Leila Ahmed and Fatima Mernissi are praised by many so-called liberal Muslims and also by Western intellectuals. They try to interpret the Qur'an in a new way, but I can't agree with them. How can one interpret the Qur'an positively on the question of women – when it says that men are superior to women, that men have the right to beat women, and that women should be submissive? In the matter of inheritance, women are not equal with men, and the testimony of women in a court of law is worth half that of men. In the Qur'an, it is written that men can have four wives. It is impossible to think that this is equality. I don't believe any positive interpretation of these verses is possible.

Her view is that 'Nothing will be gained by reforming the Qur'an; instead, what is needed is a uniform civil code of laws that is not based on religious dogmas, and that is equally applicable to men and women'. Islam is, she says, the root from which Islamic fundamentalism grows like a poisonous stem. She calls for the replacing of all religions with universal human values.

Reza Afshari (2003)

Muslim rationalists, liberals, socialists and feminists merely graft 'contemporary concepts ... onto the pre-modern Islamic paradigm' (p. 1), says Afshari, responding to whichever 'global trend' is flavour of the day (a point also made by Nasr). She does not find such reinterpretations of Islam at all convincing and comments that Mernissi's efforts to 'explain away' such 'highly restrictive verses' as Q33: 53 (the verse of veiling) (p. 6) any more convincing than their traditional, misogynist interpretation. What Mernissi and Ahmed are trying to do, she says, is to place ninth-century jurists and modern feminists 'on the same epistemological continuum' (p. 20) by reading into Islam's origins modern feminist and postmodern theories and assumptions, thus 'running the risk of anachronism by attributing contemporary political meaning to antecedents far removed in time'. She doubts that such terms as gender equality, egalitarianism or freedom of the individual (also central to Taha's reformed Islam), which, she says, are all derived from modern secular ideology, can be discovered in Islam's founding discourses. For her and others, Islamic feminism is an oxymoron.

Discussion topics

- Can Nasrin be criticized for seeming to confuse what the Qur'an says with what it has been traditionally understood to say, that is, is there a distinction between text and interpretation?

- Mawdudi takes it that the plain meaning of Q4: 3 is that men can marry up to four wives, but Ahmed shows that even among the classical jurists this plain meaning was open to different interpretation (1992 pp. 88–91). Do you agree that this text has a plain meaning or do you think that different interpretations are possible?

- Do you agree with the critics of Islamic feminism that any attempt to reform Islam by rereading texts is really nothing more than a projection of late twentieth-century ideas 'back to premodern Arabia' (Afshari 2003: 21), which is intellectually bankrupt?

- Do you find reformist thought on the possibility of an egalitarian Islam persuasive, or do you agree with those such as Nasrin who call for the abolition of all religion?

- Can the question of women's rights be removed from the sphere of religion in majority Muslim countries?

- Does the approach of Moghissi, Afshari and Nasrin elevate a version of Islam into an unchanging, definitive version above challenge? Can such a view of Islam be defended? Was Lord Cromer right when he said that Islam reformed is Islam no longer?

- According to Nasrin, Islam itself oppresses women, not a fallible and changeable interpretation or version of Islam, as Mernissi and others argue. Do you agree?

- Do you think that Islamic feminism is an oxymoron?

- When Westerners write about the status of women in the Muslim world, are their evaluations informed by an ideological assumption about the relationship between status and ability to exercise power in the public domain that imposes juxtaposition between the private and the public onto other cultures? In their collection of essays, *Muslim Women's Choices: Religious Belief and Social Reality* (1994), El-Solh and Mabro present a range of ethnographical sketches depicting Muslim women 'consciously as well as subconsciously negotiating their gender role within the situational context of their lives', in other words, exercising economic or domestic power within the home (pp. 8–9). The assumption of much Western writing is that unless power is also exercised in public, women are not equal to men. Do you agree? Or, in a society where gender roles are governed by distinctively different codes, with men leading in public and women exercising power in private ('equal but different') can women and men be fairly judged as equal?

Resource

See also Miriam Cook (2001) *Women Claim Islam: creating Islamic feminism through literature*, New York: Routledge.

Literary case study: two Egyptian novels and *Alf Laylah Wa Laylah*

The Palace Walk, *volume 1 of the Cairo Trilogy*

This book by Nobel Prize winner Naguib Mahfouz is the first of three novels telling the story of Cairo in the twentieth century through the eyes of a middle-class family, ruled over by a tyrannical but much loved and respected patriarch whose private life, however, differed radically from his more public life. Al-Sayyid Ahmed Abd al-Jawad was known to his family as a pious, conservative, often angry man who never smiled, sang or allowed his family to do so either, while his friends knew him as jovial, humorous, generous, the life and soul of any party and as a renowned womanizer and drinker. Al-Sayyid Ahmed Abd al-Jawad enjoyed serial adultery while confining his wife and daughters to the home. This seems to correspond with Leila Ahmed's contention that classical Islam divided women into two categories, those who were secluded and safe and those who were public and sexually available (1992: 79–80). Al-Jawad demanded absolute obedience from his wife: 'I'm the man. I'm the one who commands and forbids, I will not accept criticism of my behaviour. All I ask of you is to obey me'. His wife, Amina, 'became convinced that true manliness, tyranny, and staying out after midnight were common characteristics of a single entity' (p. 4). Yet the patriarch did not see anything wrong in 'having fun that harmed no one', nor why everything seemed permitted 'save these two things', that is sex outside marriage and alcohol (p. 43). He 'found within himself strong instincts, some directed towards God and tamed through worship and others set for pleasure quenched in play' (p. 42). He believed in God's mercy, and 'only allowed himself things he considered licit or within the bounds of minor offences', so 'he was content to select his lovers from unattached women or wait until a woman had ended her previous relationship' (p. 223) and he was fastidious in respecting the 'reputations of honourable people in general and of friends and neighbours in particular' (p. 222).

When Yasin, the oldest son, discovered the truth about his father, he too had no difficulty justifying such conduct: 'He sings. So what's wrong with singing? He gets drunk, and believe me, drinking is even better than eating. He has affairs and so did the Muslim caliphs. Read it in the ancient poems contained in Abu Tammam's anthology Diwan al-Hamasa or see its marginal glosses. Our father isn't doing anything sinful' (p. 271). Al-Jawad himself was certain that even if his family did find out about his affairs, 'their subservience to him and his domination over them' would assure that 'no convulsion would shake them' (p. 269). However, in his home, as his daughter-in-law says, 'what's licit is forbidden', such as showing joy on a wedding day (p. 317). When Amina ventured out of the house while al-Jawad was away, persuaded to do so by her children (to visit the shrine of Muhammad's grandson, al-Husayn) and was injured in the process, she is punished by banishment to her mother's house. Any hint that his daughters may have been glimpsed by men, or that they might have glimpsed men themselves through the windows of the house, resulted in rage and punishment.

Nawal El Saadawi's The Fall of the Imam (1988)

El Saadawi trained and worked as a doctor, specializing in psychiatry (reflected in her novels). Her husband, Sherif Hetata, who is also a doctor and a novelist of renown, translates many of her books into English. She was dismissed from her government post in 1972 following the publication of her first non-fiction book, The Hidden Face of Eve (1977), possibly her most famous work. It covered a host of controversial topics such as aggression against female children and female genital mutilation, prostitution, sexual relationships, marriage and divorce and Islamic fundamentalism. She was imprisoned in 1981 and released in 1982 after President Sadat's assassination. In 1991 the government closed her Arab Women's Solidarity Association, and handed its assets over to a conservative Muslim women's group. The motto of her Association was 'unveil the mind'. She writes (1997), 'we speak and write in Arabic ... we study our history, and try to redefine Islam in intellectual terms. We question the dominating Islamic tradition defined by men. There is nothing in Islam that prevents women from participating fully in ... political or religious activities ... [the] authentic identity of the Arab woman is not a straitjacket or dress, or veil. It is an active, living, changing process' (p. 98).

The Fall of the Imam, like much of her work, explores sexuality and the experiences of Muslim women. Set in an imaginary, fundamentalist Islamic state, it also tackles such issues as dissent, the freedom to imagine and political Islam. The central characters of the novel are the Imam of the State, who is supreme leader and in whose hands political and religious authority resides, and a young girl who is his illegitimate daughter. As she has no acknowledged father, she is called God's daughter, Bint Allah, and is raised as a ward of the state. The Imam speaks for God throughout the novel. It is necessary, we read, for loyal citizens to 'believe in the Imam, in the nation and in God' as in a single entity, 'either believe in all, or in nothing' (p. 174). The Imam represents God on earth and 'whoever opposes the Imam opposes God' (p. 145). He ruled, we read, according to the *Shari'ah* (pp. 1–2). However, while the daughter and father are the novel's central characters, other characters merge and mingle with theirs so that at times it is difficult to separate the different personalities involved. For example, the character of the daughter merges with that of her mother, with whose stoning for adultery the book begins and in a sense also ends, because the daughter's execution for refusing to 'obey' closes the book and these two events intermingle. Indeed, the stoning incident is a recurring theme in the book, although 'no one witnessed the crime. No one saw her drop to the ground' (p. 5). The very men who had used her stoned her mother. Q 24: 4 requires four witnesses to the actual act of adultery (*zina*) before a guilty verdict can be given and those who falsely charge are liable to the punishment of 80 strokes (revealed after 'A'isha was unjustly accused of betraying Muhammad).

Bint Allah is a 'child of sin', and her 'mother was stoned to death' (p. 1). Only her mother and her dog knew that the Imam was her father (p. 9). She is puzzled as to why her mother was stoned when the criminals (the stoners) were free (p. 13). Another character in the book is Gawaher, mistress to the Imam and, it seems, to all the other men in the novel as well. While the novel blurs the men's identities, Gawaher knows them all individually, since 'Once in the House of Joy and in her bed, they took off their rubber faces ... so she alone of all people had seen them without their clothes, or ... badges, or ... medals, and they all looked the same' (p. 173). The men in the novel are the Imam, the Imam's lookalike bodyguard or Chief of Security, who often doubles for him on ceremonial occasions (is this a reference to Saddam Hussein's famous double?), the Leader of the Opposition (whom the Imam appointed to give a semblance of democracy) and Great Writer, the Imam's school friend. All four characters appear to look the same, so that is it almost impossible 'to distinguish between one and the other, except by a badge on the chest or a star on the shoulder' because 'the face of all of them merged into a single face' (p. 168).

The Imam appointed both the party of God (*hizb allah*) and the opposition (*hizb shaitan*) since 'if Satan does not come and go freely among' his people, 'how are they going to know fear?' (p. 34). By appointing a Leader of the Opposition, he felt secure. His instruction was 'say no in front of my people and whisper yes' into his ear. The Opposition Leader could 'oppose all orders' except the Imam's, 'criticize all decrees' except the Imam's. 'I alone rule this land', said the Imam, 'and there is no one else besides me to decide'. The Assembly and Advisory Council were window dressing. Thus, the Imam's 'life was in the hands of the Chief of Security, his safe in the hands of the guard, democracy in the hands of the Official Leader of the Opposition and the cultural patrimony in hands of the Great Writer' (p. 116). As the common people can neither read nor write, they are confident that the Imam speaks God's word: 'It is God's word, they said. But, say I [Bint Allah], His word is written and you neither read nor write. So who told you that? . . . it is our Lord, the Imam, who has seen God and knows His word' (p. 23). Much of the novel describes the Imam's relationship with his Official Wife, with his mistress and his search for sexual gratification, which is a major preoccupation. The Imam is convinced that legal wives will not go to Paradise (p. 57) and that he will be greeted with either 70 or 77 virgins when he gets there. The men debate the exact number they are promised. Islam's misogynist tradition is reflected in such passages as 'woman was created from a twisted rib and is lacking in both faith and mind' (p. 124) and 'nothing is more important than ownership of women's bodies . . . without this . . . a child has no rights . . . and if a child is a girl her sin is double that of a boy, but she has only half the rights he is permitted to enjoy' (p. 136). Women's tongues are the 'source of all rumours, and should be cut off . . . in accordance with *shari'at*' (p. 148). While the 'treachery of men is allowable by divine law', that of women 'is inspired by Satan' (p. 59). Women, the novel says, can use 'magic to change a man into a cat or sheep', while a man's sexual arousal is a catastrophe, since 'when it is provoked nothing can stop it, neither the reason of the mind nor faith in God' (pp. 115–16). Women are therefore to blame for men's inability to control their sexual urges.

Throughout the book, the daughter seeks to confront her father, who fears for his safety. At the end of the novel, she is tried for treason. She is condemned to death for 'conspiracy, breach of honour and heresy' (p. 145). She refuses to repeat words that she is commanded to repeat by order of the Imam, and so is found guilty of opposing his will. She demands a public trial (which is a right enshrined in traditional Islamic law) 'and a proper defence' (pp. 154–5) to which the response is 'we have a legal opposition but we have never heard of a legal defence counsel' (p. 146). However, Bint Allah's real crime is her reason, which was to the men in power the 'more dangerous' (p. 175). Bint Allah was right to the end 'in complete control of her mind and what she says is reason itself. And her reason for them became more dangerous than any of her madness and they decided to condemn her to death' (p. 175). Even her silence, to the men, indicated that she was thinking, which 'indicates a lack of faith' (p.

174). Bint Allah, in words reminiscent of William Blake, declares that the men's paradise is her hell (p. 175). When she asked to whom she could complain, 'they said the Imam ... Can I complain to him about him?,' she asked.

'Reviving Our Cultural Heritage' (pp. 112–19)

In several passages, we learn that Bint Allah's favourite book is the *Thousand and One Nights*: 'The book which I enjoyed best of all was the *Thousand and One Nights*' (p. 112) while we learn that the 'old grandmother' in the orphanage would entertain the children with tales from *The Nights* (pp. 58–9). It may not be accidental that a modern novel challenging the sexual exploitation and social oppression of women refers positively to the *Alf Laylah wa Laylah,* or the *Thousand and One Nights,* also known as the *Arabian Nights.* The exact origin and date of the *Arabian Nights* is unknown but there are references to the tales as early as the tenth century. It existed for many years in oral form and although the narratives are set in Arabia during the rule of Khalif Harun al-Rashid (764–809 CE), an Indian source for much of the material has been suggested. The first major European translation of *The Nights* was by Antoine Galland (1646–1715), appearing in 1704. The manuscript that he worked from was from Syria, and dated from the fourteenth or fifteenth century. *The Nights* begins with the frame tale in which we learn of the cause of the King's mistrust of women, and of his decision to sleep with and then execute a different bride each night. The vizier's daughter, Shahrazad, volunteers. As her last wish, she requests the company of her sister. As previously arranged, her sister asks her to tell her 'one of her charming stories' before the sun rises, which she proceeds to do, engaging her husband's interest to such an extent that when she is unable to finish the story that night, he begs her to continue the next evening. There follows a thousand and one nights of storytelling, testimony to the power of the storyteller's imagination and creative ability.

It is thus Shahrazad's courage and wit that leads to the healing of the king's insanity and that saves the remaining virgins from death. Not only does a woman play the central role as narrator, but women feature throughout the text. On the one hand, many fit the stereotype of the obedient, submissive Muslim woman, but not all – there are women as well as men who take the initiative, including sexually, and women as well as men who break the rules of fidelity. The book can be read as a charming novel in which magic and absurdity serve to captivate and amuse us. However, it can also be read as a subversive text that challenged contemporary attitudes towards women and sexuality as well as attitudes towards fiction and literature at a time when narrative had to be nonfiction, that is, a description of real events. Muhammad's antipathy towards poetry made fiction a late development in Arabic literature.

Resource

See Beaumont 2002, especially the 'Introduction' available electronically at *http://www.arabiannights.org/index2.htm*, which also has a full text of the Andrew Lang version of *The Nights*.

7 Non-Muslims in the Muslim World: Voices and Views

If Muslims implement historical Shari'ah, they can not exercise their right to self-determination without violating the rights of others ... I strongly believe that the application of the public law of Islam will be counterproductive and detrimental to Muslims and to Islam itself.

(An-Na'im 1998: 238)

Four positions on Islam and non-Muslims

This chapter explores contemporary Muslim thinking about the rights of non-Muslim minorities living within the Muslim world. The issue of the status and rights of non-Muslim minorities in the Muslim world and that of women is related, as Leila Ahmed (1992) comments: 'the question of minorities has close notional ties to the question of women. In establishment Islamic thought, women, like minorities, are defined as different from and, in their legal rights, lesser than, Muslim men'. However, 'Unlike non-Muslim men, who might join the master-class by converting, woman's differentness and inferiority within this system', she says, 'are immutable' (p. 7). Esack (1997) also links treatment of minorities and of women in Islam when he describes women as 'the other component of the *mustad'afun*', who also 'demand their liberation' (p. 239). Among modern Muslim writers on the rights of non-Muslims, four positions can be identified along the left–right spectrum. On the far left, Nasrin would see the end of Islam as a religious and political system, while Muslims such as Mernissi, Tibi and Soroush on the centre left, who advocate secularism, see all faiths contributing to public and ethical debate, including Islam, which could influence legislative decisions by convincing others that its perspective is the best. Under this model, Muslims would exert more influence in states where they are the majority or where they are a large minority but they could also make their moral presence known in situations where they are a smaller minority, such as in the UK or Holland. On this spectrum, an-Na'im and Taha are classed as centre-right. Their version of an Islamic state would give non-Muslims and Muslims identical rights. They argue that the Makkan term *mu'minun* (believers) embraces the people of the book, which is also Esack's contention. The traditional concept of *dhimmi* (see below), or protected communities with fewer rights than Muslims, defended by writers on the far right and classically by Mawdudi, does not feature in their centre-right version of an Islamic State. The rights of Muslims as set out in the *hizb-ut-tahrir*'s Islamic Constitution (see Chapter Two) and as presently enshrined in the Iranian Constitution correspond almost exactly with Mawdudi's model. First, since the division of the world into Muslim and non-Muslim territory features prominently in this chapter, the historical background is explored. This discussion draws mainly from Khadduri (1955).

Two worlds

As the Islamic empire expanded, two different categories of territory ruled by Islam emerged, namely that acquired by force ('*anwatan*; this land is called *fay'* and is state owned) and that acquired by peace (this land is called *ghanima*), and a sword or a staff, indicating how the territory was acquired, 'was placed in the pulpit of the speaker on Fridays' (Khadduri 1955: 156). The fundamental distinction between *dar-al-islam* and *dar-al-harb* was, according to Khadduri, introduced as a pragmatic measure after the Battle of Tours (CE 732). This defeat prevented Islam's northerly advance through the Pyrenees at about the same time that expansion east into India was halted, although later Islam succeeded in expanding into India and beyond. Khadduri argues that in theory the world of Islam is engaged in perpetual conflict with the non-Muslim world since its mission is to convert the whole world; thus 'We have charged you to be a community of the middle way, so that you may bear witness [to the Truth] before all mankind and the Messenger may bear witness [to it] before you' (al-Baqarah 2: 143).

This conflict does not have to be understood in military terms but can be understood as one of peaceful persuasion, or missionary preaching. Some Muslims interpret this commission to justify the continued expansion of Islamic rule, or the extension of political power (see Khadduri 1955: 53). For those Muslims for whom Islam is a system of ethics and a spiritual tradition, peaceful persuasion is the only acceptable method (see Talbi 1998: 168). Muslims could enter temporary treaties with non-Muslim states as a pragmatic measure even though the ultimate aim of worldwide Islamic domination remained. Khadduri says that such treaties could be entered into either 'for expediency and because Islam suffered a setback'. Q9: 7 is cited as justification as is Muhammad's treaty with the Makkans (the treaty of Hudaybiya) (p. 202). In theory, non-Islamic states lack 'legal competency to enter into relations with *dar-al-islam* on the basis of equality', since they do not recognize God's law (p. 170; see Chapter Nine for references to Ibn Rushd's chapter on *jihad* in his *Bidayat al-Mudjtahid*, translated by R. Peters, 1977).

Historically, only non-Muslims who enjoy *dhimmi* status or temporary asylum as a *musta'min* (secured person) (see Q9: 6) can legally reside in *dar-al-Islam*. The latter can only remain for 12 months unless they undergo a change in status, either by becoming Muslim or a *dhimmi* (p. 165). If they die, relatives outside *dar-al-islam* have no right to claim their possessions. Classically (see below) the rights of a *dhimmi* were clearly defined, although sometimes differentially practised. A *harbi* who enters Muslim territory without *aman* 'was liable to be killed unless he adopted Islam' (p. 165). The status of Muslims who venture out of *dar-al-islam* into *dar-al-harb* is more problematical, as shall be discussed in more detail below. The rights and responsibilities of Muslims in the non-Muslim world are addressed in the classical texts (see Khadduri 1955: 170–4), but with the assumption that residence there is temporary (see below). Historically, other categories of territory also developed. *Haram* is territory where only Muslims can reside, such as Makkah, Madinah and by extension the whole of the Hijaz, from where Jews and Christians were expelled A.H. 15/636 CE under Khalif 'Umar, acting according to *hadith* on Muhammad's instructions (p. 160). Muhammad is reported to have said that two religions could not co-exist in the Hijaz, although the *hadith* usually cited to justify the exclusion of Jews and Christians from the Arabian peninsula reads, 'on his death bed, the Prophet' ordered 'expel the pagans from the Arabian peninsula' (Bukhari, Vol. 4, Bk 52, Ch. 176, *hadith* 288) and the term 'pagan' did not usually include the Scriptuaries. *Dar al-'ahd* refers to territory that enjoys a treaty with *dar-al-islam* (al Shafi'i introduced this category), *dar-al-hiyad* refers to neutral territory (traditionally, Ethiopia, where Muslims had taken refuge, based on a *hadith* in which Muhammad advises Muslims to leave the Abyssinians in peace as long as they left Muslims in peace), while Sayyid Ahmed Khan in British-ruled India used the term *dar-al-aman* (or *dar-al-sulh*) to refer to territory where Muslims were free to practise their faith without hindrance or restriction. S. H. Nasr draws attention to problems associated with the continued use of these traditional terms in the contemporary world, while Tibi (see below) calls for the abolition of these categories from Islamic discourse.

S. H. Nasr (1994) on the limitation of the classical terminology

'... *dar-al-sulh*, the abode of peace where Muslims live as the minority but where they are at peace, and can practise their religion freely and ... *dar-al-harb*, the abode of conflict, where Muslims are not only in a minority but where they are in a state of conflict with and struggle against the external social and political environment ... But today the situation is made complicated by the fact that, in many parts of *dar-al-islam*, non-Islamic forces have gained a footing, sometimes under the name of a foreign ideology or a Western form of nationalism and sometimes even under the name of Islam, which ... has been used in a cunning and sometimes insidious fashion to hide the real nature of the forces at work. Moreover, Muslims in both *dar-al-sulh* (such as India and parts of Africa), where they are in fact not always able to live in peace, and even *dar-al-harb* (such as Muslims in Europe and America, many of whom can live peacefully) have come to play an important role in *dar-al-islam* and modern means of communication have linked Muslims in the three "worlds" in a new fashion. It is, therefore, not so easy to define exactly what is meant by the Islamic world' (pp. 76–7).

This analysis begins with Mawdudi's contribution, arguing that this represents a classical model, and describes much of what has been the historical experience of non-Muslims in the Muslim world. Reference is also made to Khadduri (1955) for historical and legal background. What has been claimed for the Mawdudi model, that minorities have been 'fairly treated' in comparison with how they fared elsewhere in the world, has been challenged. Brief discussion of this issue refers to the controversial work of Bat Ye'or (1996). This analysis then outlines the centre-left approach of Taha, an-Na'im and Khan and the approaches of those further to the left. A literary case study reviews Nasrin's novel, *Lajja*, representing the far-left approach.

Mawdudi: theory and reality of the classical *dhimmi* model

Mawdudi's much cited 'Rights of Non-Muslims in an Islamic State' is available as a separate publication and as Appendix One of his *Islamic Law and Constitution* (1955), on which this analysis draws. Mawdudi was writing for those in power in his native Pakistan, whose task in his view was to transform the state into a legitimate, genuine Islamic state following pre-existing principles and legal provisions derived from the classical Islamic tradition. He did not regard his model of an Islamic state as 'a model among many' but as *the model*, a divine blueprint for the correct ordering of Muslim affairs. It represents the model of an Islamic state that movements such as *Jamaati-i-Islam* (which he founded), the Muslim Brotherhood and *hizb-ut-tahrir* want to establish and there is considerable overlap between his writing on minority rights and what has been written by other Muslims on the ideological right. While not as contemporary as some texts, it usefully sets out the classical position. This summary begins with an outline of the *dhimmi* system as described by Khadduri (1955: 175–201, Chapter Seventeen, 'Status of the *Dhimmis*'). What is clear is that Muhammad set some of the regulations concerning minorities down while others are from a later period, when the classical distinction (not found in the Qur'an or *Sunnah*) between the world of Islam and the world of rebellion or unbelief (or war) was developed. This leaves the classical system open to challenge from writers such as an-Na'im, Taha and Khan who prefer to take as their ideal more primitive Islamic models (see below).

The *dhimmi* concept has its origin in such Qur'anic passages as 9: 29: 'Fight against those to whom Scriptures have been given ... until they pay the *jizya* [tax], and they be humbled' (Khadduri 1955: 178) and in treaties

Left	Centre left	Centre right	Right
Minorities can never enjoy equal rights under Islamic law or in a society that privileges Muslims and excludes non-Muslims from high office. Only a secular society can guarantee minority rights. Far-left advocates of secularism such as Nasrin are anti-religious and want to see the abolition and end of all religions.	Centre-left advocates of secularism such as Soroush, Mernissi and Tibi contend that religion can have an ethical role to play within society, that it can influence political decisions and that a majority faith will in a democracy exert such an influence with or without constitutionally enshrined privileges.	Centre: a reformed Islam can fully accommodate minority and human rights. An Islamic state that rests on progressive Islam can treat all its citizens fairly, Muslims and non-Muslims who share the same human values and commitment to justice and equity (an-Na'im, Taha, Khan).	The classical Islamic pattern of tolerating religious minorities but of excluding them from certain posts in government and public service is a just and fair system, predicated on the superiority of Islam over all other beliefs and on the need for those who occupy the highest posts to be in full agreement with Islamic ideology (Mawdudi).

Figure 7.1 Non-Muslim minorities* in Muslim states

* the term *dhimmis* does not only apply to minorities but to non-Muslims who enter a compact with Muslim rulers. For example, in Spain and India, *dhimmis* were the majority of the population. It is best translated as 'protected communities' not 'minorities'.

made between Muhammad and Christians and Jews, especially the treaty with the Christians of Najran, which Khadduri cites on pp. 179–89. This document guarantees the Christians protection from attack, protection of their properties and places of worship, the right to practise their faith and the right to justice in return for goods and services (the *jizya*). Muhammad stated that he would afford oppression 'no support'. Such treaties were perpetually binding provided that *dhimmis* maintained good relations with the Muslim state. A much quoted *hadith*, 'Whoever wrongs a *dhimmi* and lays on him a burden beyond his strength, harms me', testifies to the sanctity of the *dhimmi* compact (see Mawdudi 1955: 178–9). This *hadith* is also understood to mean that the tax can only be levied from those who can afford to pay it and that, as Mawdudi writes, 'in the realization of *Jizyah* ... every kind of coercion is strictly forbidden' (p. 184). Mawdudi cites a source that protects *dhimmis*' 'pigs and liquor' from harm by Muslims (p. 180). 'Umar gave instructions that *dhimmis* must be protected and not taxed 'beyond their capability' (Bukhari, Vol. 4, Bk 52, Ch. 174, *hadith* 287) while Bk 52, Ch. 21, *hadith* 383 states that the level of *jizya* charged 'has been fixed on the degree of prosperity' (see Mawdudi 1955: 177).

The *jizya* (a head tax) was only levied on those who would have been capable of combat (it therefore excluded priests, monks, women, the disabled, the insane, children and the old; see Mawdudi 1955: 179). The Maliki school left it to the governor to set the amount payable while 'the Hanafi school classified the tax into three categories', namely the well-to-do (who paid 48 *dirhams*), the poor (who paid 12 *dirhams*) and those 'in between' (who paid 24) (Khadduri 1955: 196). Mawdudi says that the amount of tax is 'fixed in accordance with' a *dhimmi*'s financial means. He also recognizes the above three categories but adds that 'the very poor ... are exempt' (p. 177). However, in all *fay*' territory, the *kharaj* or land tax was payable by all who wished to cultivate their land, whether *dhimmis* or Muslim. According to Khadduri, although payment of both taxes became the rule, in the earliest period the Khalif 'exercised discretionary right' and could either collect only the *jizya* or levy both taxes (p. 192, see also p. 190 and p. 188). *Dhimmis* were exempt from paying *zakat* (2 ½ per cent of a Muslim's disposable income, distributed to the needy). Early treaties allowed *dhimmis* to wear whatever clothes they wished, except uniforms. They could not proselytize or 'ring their bells at the time of the call to prayer' (Khadduri, p. 186). Later treaties, such as the Pact of 'Umar, prohibited the building of new churches (but not the repairing of old) and placed many restrictions on *dhimmis*, such as not wearing the same clothes as or wearing their hair in the same style as Muslims (Khadduri, pp. 193–4). Khadduri expresses the view that this Pact was 'the work of later generations' since it departs from the instructions of tolerance and protection otherwise ascribed to 'Umar (p. 194). By the time that the classical legal texts were written, the twelve duties and disabilities of the *dhimmi* included not riding horses, wearing distinctive dress (the *ghiyar*, yellow patch, the *zunnar* or girdle and the *qalansura*, or tall hat), not drinking alcohol or eating pork in public (but they may do so privately), not assisting the enemy, showing respect towards Muhammad and the Qur'an, not building their homes higher than Muslim homes and not weeping loudly at their funerals (see Khadduri, pp. 196–8).

The statement at Q9: 29 that the *dhimmis* should pay the tax until they are humbled has been variously interpreted. Khadduri points out that while the earliest accounts of collecting *jizya* do not appear to involve anything that could be construed as humiliating (p. 185), later on different interpretations of Q9: 29 resulted in jurists advocating 'a humiliating treatment of the *dhimmis* for persistence in disbelief' (p. 200). Zamakhshari (1075–1144) ordered that the *dhimmis* must kneel before the collector, who is to seize him by the neck, demand payment then slap the *dhimmi* on the neck as reward for payment. Khadduri argues that while the 'original objective' of the *dhimmi* system 'reflected a genuine spirit of toleration and provided safe-guards for non-Muslim subjects who preferred to follow their own scriptures and practise their own rights', certain Khalifs proved to be 'both hard and brutal' (p. 200). He cites as examples of intolerance Mutawakkil (847–61), who 'ordered all the churches and synagogues built after the Islamic conquest' to be pulled down and al-Mansur, who 'removed all the *dhimmis* from the administration' (p. 199). Talbi (1998) also attributes mistreatment of *dhimmis* to Mutawakkil, pointing out that before his rule they had often enjoyed 'real prosperity' and held 'high office'. Mistreatment, he says, reached its zenith in Egypt under al-Hakim (966–1021). However, he may not have been sane (p. 165). Similarly, Zakaria (1988) argues that in the early period Christians and Jews enjoyed the Khalifs' confidence in key appointments, until 'Umar II reversed the process 'saying that the Qur'an had warned that the faithful should not be friends with' the people of the book (see below). His 'successors reverted to the old practice' of discrimination and oppression (p. 73). Some point out that even when *dhimmis* were ill-treated in parts of the Muslim world and had to flee, they were given refuge elsewhere. For example, during the Almohad's rule in Spain (1172–1212) the Jewish scholar and physician Maimonides fled to Egypt after Cordoba's capture (1148). Later, when Jews were expelled from Spain (1492) by the Christian reconquistadors, many found refuge in the Ottoman empire, including Bosnia, which Duran (1995) calls 'the other Andalusia'. Bernard Lewis (1984) cites a fifteenth-century Jew writing to Jews in Europe and urging them to migrate to Turkey: 'is it not better for you to live under Muslims than Christians? Here every man may dwell at peace under his own vine and fig tree. Here you are allowed to wear the most precious garments. In Christendom, on the contrary, you dare not even venture to clothe your children in red or blue – without exposing them to the insult of being beaten black and blue'. Jews in Germany are 'pursued even unto death' (pp. 135–6). 'Jewish reports on Turkish behaviour and Turkish attitudes are almost uniformly favourable', says Lewis (p. 135).

Mawdudi considers that *dhimmis* and Muslims are subject to the same law and 'are to be punished in the same manner', giving the example of theft: 'whether it is a *zhimmi* who steals or a Muslim, the hands of the thief will be chopped off in both cases' (pp. 179–80). The punishment for adultery (*zina*) is the same (although Mawdudi notes the dissenting opinion of Imam Malik, that cases 'should be referred to his co-religionists') but *dhimmis* are exempt from the punishment for consuming alcohol (p. 180). Generally, internal discipline within the *dhimmi* community was entrusted to the 'religious head, who, in turn, was responsible to the Muslim authorities' (Khadduri 1955: 198). All matters pertaining to marriage and divorce were governed by the *dhimmis'* own Personal Law except in any cases concerning a Muslim, when 'the case will have to be dealt with in accordance with Islamic *Shari'ah*' (Mawdudi, p. 182). A *dhimmi*, however, could not give evidence against a Muslim but required the corroborating testimony of a Muslim witness (Khadduri, p. 198). This is derived from Q9: 29–30's reference to fighting against Christians and Jews because they are liars, which was later elaborated by the law schools to exclude the validity of their testimony (Q5: 82 describes Jews as the most vehement in hostility towards Islam). A non-Muslim could not inherit from a Muslim nor receive a share of the *khums* (spoils of war). While his rights within his own community were fully protected, 'as a subject of the Muslim state' he suffered 'certain disabilities which reduced him to the status of a second-class citizen' (Khadduri, p. 198).

Mawdudi justifies differences between the rights of Muslims and of non-Muslims on the grounds that the Islamic state is an ideological state and that therefore 'the responsibility to run the State rests with those who believe in the Islamic ideology' (p. 171). Mawdudi clearly believed that non-Muslims were fairly treated (would be fairly treated in his state) but that while they can 'co-operate with the Muslims in the task of administration' they 'cannot be entrusted with the authority to make policy' (p. 172). On the issue of parliamentary representation, Mawdudi modified his earlier position. Initially, he thought that *dhimmis* could elect their own council to make representation on affairs affecting their welfare to the Muslim government. He points out that non-Muslims could not be members of a *Shura* Council. Later, he decided that since the state's constitution precludes the enacting of any legislation contrary to Islamic Law, *dhimmis* could be members of an Assembly. They could occupy 'general administrative posts' but not any posts that influence policy. The Head of State must be a Muslim (see 1976a: 167 and 1955: 189). However, for Mawdudi 'general administrative posts' included such senior jobs as 'Accounting General, Chief Engineer or Post-Master General of an Islamic State' and even non-combatant posts in the military could be 'thrown open to the *Zimmis*' (p. 192).

Rights granted non-Muslims by an Islamic state would not merely adorn the statute book but 'it shall be the duty of the State to translate them into actual practice' (p. 193). Non-Muslims in Pakistan were mistaken to believe that they would be better served by a secular constitution like

India's, where instead of their rights being upheld, non-Muslims are victims of a 'vicious cycle of injustice'. Would it not be better, he suggests, 'to try and test a system of life based on godliness, honesty and observance of unalterable ethical principles?' (p. 193). Here, Mawdudi sounds like Taha and an-Na'im, who also believe that the best guarantee of non-Muslim rights is not a secular but an Islamic state, but their centre-left model of an Islamic state makes no distinction between the rights of citizens 'based on colour, faith, race, or sex' (Taha 1987: 153). Esack (1997) comments that having grown up in South Africa as a member of a minority community, he was sensitive during his eight years in Pakistan 'to the religious and social persecution of the Christian and Hindu minorities' which suggests that the reality may not correspond to Mawdudi's ideal (p. 5). Pipes (2002) argues that many Islamic radicals would no longer leave 'non-Muslims to regulate their own conduct, as did traditional Islam' but would seek 'to intrude into their lives'. He chronicles incidents of non-Muslims being subjected to Muslim law: in Libya, all adulterers are stoned; in Saudi, non-Muslims are told to fast during Ramadan; in Iran, foreign women cannot wear nail polish; in Sudan, two million Christians 'must comply with virtually all the *Shari'ah* regulations'; in Palestine, 'Christian's pigs are mysteriously poisoned' (pp. 83–4). On the other hand, Iran has made moves to equalize the amount of blood money payable for non-Muslims and Muslims and some MPs are reportedly 'pressing for equality for non-Muslims in other areas' such as 'the right to testify in Islamic courts' (see *BBConline*, 'Iran Revalues Price of non-Muslim Lives', 4 November 2002). In Egypt (with a 6 per cent Christian population), Boutros Boutros Gali, former deputy Prime Minister and Secretary-General of the UN (1992–96), a Coptic Christian, was appointed to head a newly formed National Council on Human Rights in January 2003, partly in response to the criticism that Copts are victims of systematic discrimination.

The centre left and non-Muslims in an Islamic state

An-Na'im, Talbi and Taha all advocate an understanding of citizenship and belonging in an Islamic state that includes all peoples of the book as 'believers' (*mu'minun*), arguing that the restriction of full citizenship to Muslims was not an original precept in Islam. Similarly, Esack argues that 'there were *mu'minun* in the non-sociological sense of the word ... outside the Muhammad community' (1997: 124) and 'given that *iman* [faith] is ... a deeply personal response to God, it cannot be confined to a particular socio-religious community' (p. 124). According to Talbi, all 'forms of discrimination' must be denounced as 'crimes strictly and explicitly condemned by the Qur'an' (1998: 168) and any discriminatory practices that have featured in Islamic history were circumstantial. This derives from Talbi's conviction that what is eternally valid and universally applicable in the Qur'an is also humane and cannot therefore discriminate between people on the basis of their gender, faith or ethnicity (classically, Muslim regard Islam as *din-al-fitrah*, the natural religion). What the Qur'an yields are 'the universal human principles of goodness, mutual respect, equality of views and doctrines and peace' (Nettler, 1998 p. 152). Citing Q29: 46, which instructs Muslims not to argue with the people of the book, or Scriptuaries, unless in a 'most courteous manner', Talbi argues that 'to be true Muslim is to live in courteous dialogue with peoples of other faiths' (p. 164). Like Esack (1997), Talbi believes that the Qur'anic view of the human being is that he or she is innately a pluralist (*ta'addudi*) and that plurality of opinion is of the essence of religious thought. Islam is pluralist internally and Muslims must also respect the views of others. Diversity of religious opinion (*ikhitilaf*) is both natural and divinely sanctioned (Nettler, p. 135). Mohammed Talbi, who earned his doctorate from the Sorbonne in 1968, also argues in favour of a universal standard of human rights. Now professor emeritus of history at the University of Tunis, his human rights activism earned him the title 'the Tunisian Sakharov'. His writing on scriptural interpretation, interreligious dialogue and religious epistemology make him a significant figure in modern Islamic thought, under-exposed in this book.

Muslim defenders of religious pluralism and of the legal equality of Muslims and of peoples of the book also cite such Qur'anic verses as Q49: 13: 'O mankind, we created you from a single pair of a male and a female, and made you into nations and tribes, that ye may know each other', and Q5: 48: 'unto every one of you we have appointed a different law and way of life', as evidence that the Qur'an not only tolerates religious diversity but 'is explicit in its acceptance of religious pluralism' (Esack 1997: 159; see p. 87). Esack argues that the Qur'an derides and denounces attempts to appropriate God (a criticism that Q5: 18 levels at Jews and Christians), so much so that it cannot conceivably support any Muslim exclusivist claims or religious arrogance but instead 'makes it a condition of faith to believe in the genuineness of all revealed religion' (Q2: 136, 2: 285, 3: 84) (p. 159). Esack therefore contends that Muslims have been wrong to respect 'the laws of the religious Other' while rejecting 'their salvation', a view especially associated with 'the most conservative Muslims' (p. 159). He cites a *hadith* in which Muhammad is reported to have said to Salman the Farsi that Christians who 'hear of' him but who do not affirm his mission will perish, while those who 'died in the faith of Jesus' previously will not perish. Such classical scholars as al-Shahrastani endorsed this 'supercessionist theory' (p. 177, n.13).

Syed Mumtaz Ali (1993) takes it as axiomatic that Muslims extend 'the greatest equality possible to ... Muslims and to strangers (non-Muslims)' but that 'the former will be granted paradise while the latter will inherit hell' (p. 1). This anomaly has been justified, he says, by the application of the theory of abrogation to the Qur'anic text, so that the verses of friendship (*wilayah*) in which Muslims, Christians and Jews are said to stand on common ground are cancelled by verses of opprobrium that accuse Christians and Jews of theological arrogance, or of failing to accept signs from God (see Q3: 70–1, 3: 98) or of obscuring the truth (see Q3: 70, 3: 98–9; Esack 1997: 173). Thus, a text such as Q2: 62, 'Surely those who have faith and those who are Jews and Christians and Sabeans [the peoples of the book], whoever has faith in Allah and the Last Day and does good, they have their reward with the Lord, there is no fear for them, nor shall they grieve' (and similar verses), is cancelled by a verse such as Q3: 85, 'Whosoever desires a *din* [religion] other than *islam* shall not have it accepted from him' (p. 162).

Esack offers a different interpretation. He extends *islam* to include all who struggle in God's name to liberate the oppressed, and argues that the verses that criticize peoples of the book were not intended to abrogate the verses of friendship but to 'challenge them regarding their commitment to their own scriptures (Q5: 68), their deviation from these, and their distortion thereof' (Esack 1997: 173). Esack stresses that verses critical of the peoples of the book almost always qualify criticism with the phrase 'among them', implying that not all are guilty as accused (of, for example, corrupting their scriptures) but that some, who are hypocrites, are (see p. 147; Q2: 109, 5: 66, 22: 17, 57: 26). 'They are not all alike', says Q3: 113, 'among them is a group who stand for the right … they enjoin what is good and forbid what is wrong. And vie with one another in good deeds'. Such people are counted as 'righteous'. Esack argues that while the Qur'an castigates a 'section' of the 'people of the book' for *tahrif* it is 'silent about the extent and nature of … distortion' (p. 173). In Esack's view, since the Qur'an clearly states that, although God could have made people a single community (Q5: 48), he instead revealed for them different *shir'ah* and *minhaj*, and those who fulfil the obligations associated with their revelations are among the righteous (p. 170). All who uphold justice and compassion are *muslim*. Verses accusing Jews and Christians of corrupting their scriptures (the charge of *tahrif*, altering or distorting so that they failed to acknowledge the truth about Muhammad), such as Q4: 46, appear to refer to oral or interpretational distortion of meaning rather than wilful tampering with actual texts (a view pioneered by Sir Sayyid Ahmed Khan in his 1862 *Commentary on the Bible*). Classically, *tahrif* was taken to mean a deletion or addition to the Bible's text, which encouraged the view that the Qur'an criticizes the faith of Christians and Jews. However, as Esack argues, it can be understood to criticize those who distort their faith. In Q10: 94 Muhammad is instructed to consult the Scriptuaries if he was in doubt about the meaning of a revelation, which is a clear affirmation that their religious opinions are valid. Muhammad's mission is universal (Q7: 158) but his message addresses different people in different ways (p. 173).

The Muslim's duty is not to seek to convert the Other but to 'vie' with them 'in righteousness towards God' (p. 170). Esack is able to cite several Qur'anic verses that exhort all who believe to 'compete with one another in righteous deeds' to support this interpretation. Q5: 48 continues 'so vie with one another in virtuous deeds', since all will 'return to Allah, so that

Allah will inform' them of 'that wherein' they 'differed' (see also Q2: 148). However, towards the real *kufr*, those who maintain silence in the face of oppression and exploit the weak, the message is repentance and surrender to God as a Muslim (p. 137; see Q3: 21–2). The 'qur'anic islam is', says Esack, 'not the sole possession of those who identify with the historical *ummah* (community) of Islam' (p. 116). For Esack, being a *kufr* (denier, rejecter, ingrate) or a *muslim* (submitter to God) is not a nounal but a verbal matter (drawing on Wilfred Cantwell Smith), thus 'it is not labels that are counted by God, but actions that are weighed (Q2: 177, 99: 7–8)' (p. 144). Based on his analysis of the thought of S. H. Nasr, Aslan (1998) similarly concludes:

> that those who are outside the Islamic faith might possibly be saved if firstly they accomplish the ethical and religious requirements of their own traditions, and, secondly, if, when the truth is revealed to their inner being, they do not deliberately and consciously cover up that truth. (p. 196)

Support for rethinking how Muslims view non-believers can be found in the writing of a *Jamaati-i-Islam* activist, and champion of Islamic *da'wah*, Khurram Murad, who argues that the Qur'an never addresses people as *kufr* unless their opposition to Islam 'was demonstrated to be entrenched and deliberate' (1986, paragraph 6 – Internet version).

An-Na'im and Taha also reverse the classical view that the verses of opprobrium abrogate the verses of friendship, arguing instead that the former are subsidiary verses of the Qur'an with no universal validity, while the latter express its original principle of equality. All discriminatory practices in society must be abolished, as noted already, so that 'in the good society, people are judged according to their intellect and moral character, as reflected in their public and private lives and demonstrated in the spirit of public service at all times' (Taha 1987: 153). An-Na'im points out that while the traditional *dhimmi* was 'tolerated', he or she also suffered 'a variety of civil disqualifications in relation to competence to hold public office or testify in judicial proceedings', but that in the true nation of believers 'all discrimination against women and non-Muslims in Islamic Law' would be removed, not through a 'piecemeal reform' but as a result of the evolution of Islamic Law onto the totally 'fresh plane' that he and his mentor advocate (1987: 23).

Muqtedar Khan argues that Islamic states 'inevitably treat non-Muslim citizens as less than equal'. He cites blasphemy and apostasy laws as 'well known for the problems they cause minorities' and says that 'narrow interpretation of the role of women in Islamic societies has also restricted the scope of possibilities for non-Muslim women' (2003: 1). In his view, 'in seeking to impose Islamic Law and create an Islamic state', Islamists are 'in direct opposition to the spirit and letter of the Qur'an', which explicitly states 'there is no compulsion in religion' (Q2: 256) and exhorts peoples of the book to 'live by the laws revealed to them' (p. 2; Q5: 43, 5: 47). From 'these verses it is abundantly clear that an Islamic State must advocate

religious pluralism', he says. Like Taha, an-Na'im *et al.*, Khan argues that
the example Muslims should follow pre-dates the establishment of the
classical *dhimmi* system. For him, the ideal model is represented by the
federal state of Madinah, which was based on a 'real and actual social
contract agreed upon by Muslims, Jews and others that treated them as
equal citizens'. Divine law was applied but only after 'consultation and
with consent of all citizens regardless of their faith'. The difference
between this and 'contemporary Islamic states' is that the latter 'apply
Islamic Law without consent or consultation and often through coercion'
(p. 2).

Discussion topics

- Which interpretation of the Qur'anic verses relating to non-
  Muslims do you find convincing?

- Do you think that the only option for Muslims who want to be
  faithful to the Qur'an is to treat non-Muslims as *dhimmis*?

- Can Muslims interpret the Qur'an so that non-Muslim believers
  of other scriptural traditions are treated in every way as Muslims
  are, with identical rights?

The radical left

Champions of the secularization of Islamic society such as Soroush, Mernissi, Zakaria and Tibi, for whom Islam is an ethical, spiritual and cultural
but not a religious system, see this as the best way forward for guaranteeing
not only the rights of non-Muslim minorities but those of Muslims too. All
contend that in a democratic, pluralist society Muslims can contribute to
debate and even to the legislative process, but by winning the intellectual
and moral arguments in favour of their views and not by imposing these by
force or through constitutionally privileging Islam. Tibi argues that in
order to take their seat at the table of debate in a genuinely pluralist
society, Muslims need to abandon their claim to be a superior community
(2001: 185; see Chapter Two of this book). Arabs, he says – and by
extension he means Muslims – need to 'learn how to view human beings as
individuals, and not as obliged members of collective entities, which today
are virtually the functional equivalent of the old Arab tribes' (1998: 193).
Tibi clearly does not think that a Mawdudi-style Islamic state would treat
non-Muslims fairly, commenting that it was not only the 'secular Arab
tyrant of Baghdad' but 'fundamentalists in Sudan' and even 'fundamentalist oppositions in Egypt and Algeria' who 'violate human rights of
minorities', leading us to ask, 'what would fundamentalists do if they were
in power?' (1998: 193). Soroush (2000) suggests that a truly 'religious
community', would also be 'plural and pluralist by nature ... there are as

many paths to God as there are people', he says (p. 145). This is why he argues that the Islam of identity has to yield to the Islam of truth:

> the Islam of identity should yield to the Islam of truth. The latter can co-exist with other truths; the former, however, is, by its very nature, belligerent and bellicose. It is the Islam of war, not the Islam of peace. Two identities would fight each other, while two truths would co-operate. (2000: 24)

Tibi praises the period of Muslim ascendancy in Spain and the period when Hellenized learning thrived as examples of an Islam capable of embracing pluralism and of interacting culturally and intellectually with others (see Chapter Five). The way forward for Tibi is the formulation of a 'cross-cultural morality able to contribute to international peace' (2001: 221) and he calls Muslims to participate in an 'extended colloquium on cross-cultural morality' and to 'develop a consensus on human rights' (1998: 203). Akbar Ahmed also praises Muslim Spain as a model to which Europe could usefully look today, arguing that although lapses in good interreligious relations did occur, 'there were certainly long periods' when Mulims, Jews and Christians interacted positively. Alliances were made 'between Muslims and Christians' and there was 'a great deal of give and take at all levels' (1993 p. 67). Another example of Muslims embracing pluralism was Bosnia before the outbreak of war on 4 April 1992. Duran (1995) depicts Bosnia, with its 50 or 51 per cent Muslim population, as a model of the type of society that Tibi champions. Its Muslims were 'leading in democracy and modernity, in pluralism and secularization' (p. 33) and most favoured a 'state for all Bosnians regardless of their religious affiliation' (p. 31). Mosques, synagogues and churches, Muslims, Christians, Jews and gypsies lived side-by-side in Sarajevo. A traditionalist Muslim leader such as Hafiz Kamil Silaijich, Imam of Sarajevo's largest mosque, was 'in close and amicable contact with reformist groups' (p. 33). Mixed marriage was common. Islamic Law was not practised (p. 30). Muslims refused to 'promote the anti-Christian slogans handed out by Iran and the Islamist parties in Turkey' (p. 33). Duran describes Bosnian Islam as 'Islamic Humanism instead of Islamic fundamentalism' (p. 32). For Mahmutcehajic (1998) the West's delayed intervention in Bosnia was a strategy to turn its own anti-Muslim fears into reality. Muslims who wanted to be simply Bosnians were manipulated into becoming an Islamic republic (Islamic *jamahiriya*) (p. 181), with the result that Bosnian Muslims, confronted with the possibility of almost complete annihilation, developed an 'increasingly strident Islamic identity'. This was part of the enemy's plan 'to reduce the totality of Bosnia to that of her Muslims', then 'to portray her Muslims . . . as Islamic radicals' and 'as a potential threat to global stability' (p. 183).

For rightist contributors, verses on the right cancel those on the left. For leftist contributors, verses of the left cancel those on the right

Verses of Friendship	Verses of Opprobrium
Surely those who have faith and those who are Jews and Christians and Sabeans, whoever has faith in Allah and the Last Day, and does good, they have their reward with their Lord (Q2: 62)	They have taken their rabbis and their monks – as well as Christ, son of Mary – for their lords besides God, although they have been bidden to worship none besides God (Q9: 31)
And of the People of the Book there are those who have faith in Allah ... they have their reward with their Lord (Q3: 199)	And they say, None shall enter paradise unless he be a Jew or Christian. Those are their vain desires (Q2: 111)
For every one of you we have appointed a *shir'ah* and a *minhaj*. And if Allah pleased he could have made you one community, but that he might try you in what he gave you. So vie with one another in virtuous deeds (Q5: 48)	Don't take them [People of the Book] as your friends they are but allies of one another (*illa an tattaqu minhum tuqatun*) (Q5: 51)
And dispute ye not with the People of the Book, except with means better (Than mere disputation), unless it be with those of them; Who inflict wrong (and injury) But say, 'We believe in the Revelation which has come down to us and in that which came down to you: Our God and your God is One; and it is to Him We bow (in Islam)' (Qur'an Sura, 29: 46).	Fight those who believe not in Allah nor the Last Day, nor hold that forbidden which hath been forbidden by Allah and His Messenger, nor acknowledge the religion of Truth, (even if they are) of the People of the Book, until they pay the *jizya* with willing submission, and feel themselves subdued (Q9: 29)
Thou wilt find the most vehement of mankind in hostility to those who believe (to be) THE JEWS and the idolaters. And thou wilt find THE NEAREST OF THEM in affection TO THOSE WHO BELIEVE (to be) those who say: Lo! WE ARE CHRISTIANS. That is because there are among them priests and monks, and because they are not proud. When they listen to that which hath been revealed unto the messengers, thou seest their eyes overflow with tears because of their recognition of the Truth. They say: Our Lord, we believe. Inscribe us as among the witnesses (Q5: 82–3).	
An ambiguous verse with positive reference to Christians but negative reference to Jews. (For progressive, those on the left are eternal principles, those on the right time-limited applications.)	

Figure 7.2 Verses of friendship v. verses of opprobrium

Discussion topic

An Islamic time bomb or Nielsen's ogre
Duran (1995) concludes his chapter by citing the words of the former British PM, Margaret Thatcher, who urged President Bush (Senior) to 'intervene against Serbia in order to spare Europe the emergence of an "Islamic time bomb"'. Duran suggests that the two million 'traumatized Bosnian' refugees who are now dispersed as refugees throughout Europe may be 'a new potential for terrorism' that 'might surpass all such activity from the past' (p. 36). Bosnia, he says, might become 'another Palestine'.

● What does Duran mean by another Palestine?

Do modernists close their eyes to mistreatment of minorities?

Classical modernists, like Tibi, praised examples of harmonious intercultural relations between Muslims and others (not always minorities: for example, in Spain Muslims were never a majority), but they tended to avoid controversy about the rights or status of minorities in the Muslim world. This was probably because they wanted to attract support for their reformist agenda and thought that some sensitive issues were best left alone. Sivan (1985) comments that the modernists tended either to deny that any inequalities existed between Muslims and non-Muslims under traditional Islamic rule, or to minimize them, or to call for 'further evolution of the Islamic concept of tolerance' (p. 78). In practice, in the struggle for liberation from colonialism, the support of Christians 'was important'. During the period of British mandate in Palestine, for example, delegations to London usually included Christians. On the other hand, while Christians stressed what they held culturally and socially in common with their Muslim neighbours, many Muslims wanted to stress what religiously differentiated them. Christian Arabs were blamed for 'introducing modern ideologies to the Arab world' such as socialism, neo-Pharaonism, secularism and even the idea of a pan-Arab rather than a pan-Islamic nation. New radicals, says Sivan, started to call for laws that would 'not allow for exceptions', whether 'in criminal punishment, prohibition of alcohol, or interdiction of conversion to a non-Muslim religion' (p. 78). There is a tendency in discussion on the issue of treatment of minorities to claim that, when compared with how Europe has historically treated them minorities (such as Jews), Islam has treated them justly. Sivan (1985) also points out that for many Muslims 'the fact that so many Arab Christians (beginning with Michel Aflaq) were so prominent in Arab nationalism was a reason for alarm' (p. 36). Even the pan-Arab movement was problematic for some, at 'odds with the notion of Islamic *umma* because, on the one hand, it excluded all non-Arab Muslims (for example, those in Indonesia, the largest Islamic nation) from this entity and, on the other it included

Arab Christians (for example, those living in Lebanon and Egypt) as citizens and no longer as *dhimmis*/protected peoples, that is, minorities' (Tibi 1998: 144; see also p. 53 and 2001: 122).

A writer such as Zakaria (1988), no defender of the Islamic political system, argues that Islam has a history of tolerance of other faiths despite some blemishes on the historical record. Yet others see that record as a chronicle of cultural, social and religious destruction. Bat Ye'or (1996) has championed the view that what she calls *dhimmitude* is a 'history of oppression' that has 'engulfed in death many peoples and brilliant civilizations' (p. 263). Far from levying *jizya* according to means, she argues that it has been routinely 'extracted by torture' not only from able-bodied men but from 'children, women, widows, orphans, even the dead' (p. 78). Collaborators and intra-rivalry in the *dhimmi* communities share responsibility for this systematic destruction of whole communities, since 'the caliph' would give 'his seal to the appointment of the notable or patriarch who pledged to extort the highest tribute from his community' (p. 126). The aim was always to Islamize the Scriptuaries, she says, often through 'the utility of women ... *harems* filled with female prisoners and slaves' (p. 135). She dismisses 'as specious comparisons between the Orient and Europe' on the treatment of minorities, since comparison requires defining 'areas of comparison' and 'the segment of history', and to debate 'degrees and subtleties of tolerance' obscures the fact that *dhimmitude* represents a systematic, calculated tool to subjugate, oppress, exploit and humiliate whole communities of people (p. 247).

Some revivalists are of the view that by their stubborn resistance of Islam for centuries, peoples of the book no longer qualify for *dhimmi* status but must be forced to submit to Islam (see Sivan 1985: 80). Sayyid Qutb (2001) applied the term *kufr* to anyone who rejects God's law, including those who claim to be Muslim, 'For what use is a verbal claim of being a believer' if a person's 'action denies such a claim?' (Vol. IV, p. 123). Esack refers to some classical interpretations of the founding discourses that ascribed certain communities with innate evil by visiting on present members of these communities the sins of the past. Qur'anic verses referring to Jews as rejecting the prophets informed the 'notion that evil runs through' Jewish blood (1997: 140), which has implications not only for Muslim attitudes towards Jews generally but their attitudes towards the State of Israel in particular, which is perceived to be a Jewish state (see Chapter Five). Esack relates how as a youth growing up in South Africa, he was taught to greet non-Muslims with *samm alaykum* ('poison be on you') since it was commonly accepted by Muslims that except in rare circumstances 'Muslims should only associate with Muslims'. Friendship with people of other faiths was thought to be non-Islamic (Sonn 2002: 260). He says that in South Africa, Muslims whose views denied the 'potential for virtue in non-Islam' denounced Muslim participation in what they called 'the political organizations of the Kuffarr', such as the ANC, as 'following the path of *kufr* and *baatil* [falsehood]' (1997 p. 40). There is a *hadith* that has Muhammad saying that if Jews greet Muslims with *samm alaykum*, they should respond with *wa'alaikum* ('and on you') (Bukhari, Vol. 8, Bk 74, Ch. 22, *hadith* 273 and 274). In Akbar Ahmed's *Living Islam* series, in the episode *The Last Crusade* (1992), we see a burnt-out church in northern Nigeria, destroyed by Muslim *jihadists*, and hear Akbar Ahmed interviewing Christians who feel that they are targets of Muslim aggression.

On the other hand, as Esack (1997) points out, the first Qur'anic verse permitting the use of armed struggle specifically protected churches and synagogues: 'But for the fact that God continues to repel some people by means of others, cloisters, churches, synagogues and mosques wherein the name of God is mentioned, would be razed to the ground' (pp. 160–1). This verse clearly recognizes the sanctity of other places of worship, which makes any attack on a church by Muslims a very dubious enterprise. Prince Hassan of Jordan (1998 and various speeches) is an outspoken champion of interreligious friendship and collaboration and argues that not only have Christians made an enormous intellectual contribution to Arab culture and to the moral and material fabric of Islamic civilization in the past, but in the present they are often the conduit for new ideas, and as they share a common future with Muslim Arabs they should not fear Islam nor should Muslims fear them. Muslims and Christians can best work together to combat ignorance, poverty, extremist ideologies and unemployment and to achieve progress and a better standard of living for all. The Arab renaissance that he advocates needs to be built by all people working together to lay down the foundation of a civil society. He encourages Christians not to emigrate in the face of attempts by the media to create instability but to proudly assert their Arab patrimony. He calls for a code of common values that respects differences while also promoting justice for all.

Literary case study: Nasrin's *Lajja*

'Let the pavilions of religion be ground to bits'

Set in Bangladesh, *Lajja* describes how the Hindu majority in Bangladesh were affected by incidents in neighbouring India surrounding the event in December 1992 'when a 450-year-old mosque was razed to the ground by a mob of fanatic Hindus' (p. 7). This refers to the Babri Masjid in Ayodhia, which Hindus believed was built on the birthplace of their god, Ram. The novel tells the story of Suranjan and his sister, Maya. Much of the novel resembles newspaper reports of anti-Hindu atrocities and the text chronicles incident after incident of attacks on Hindus, confiscation of their property and desecration of their Temples.

See *Human Rights in Bangladesh* 1997, University Press, Dhaka, p. 118, for a list of 'Reported Incidents of Violence Against Religious Minorities'. Confiscations take place under the Vesting of Property and Assets Ordinance of 1972 and it is estimated that 1.64 million acres of Hindu property have been lost under this law, or 53 per cent of the total land owned by Hindus. Christians, Buddhists and Hindus through their Unity Council have campaigned for the law's abolition. In 1997, the Hindu population was 10.5 per cent, Christians 0.32 per cent and Buddhists 0.59 per cent, others (aboriginals) 0.26 per cent (p. 116).

Suranjan himself, like Nasrin, is a humanist and tends to see all the above as 'cases of the strong oppressing the poor', as he wryly comments 'if you are rich, it does not matter if you are Hindu or Muslim' (p. 77). Most of the time, he is hardly aware 'of his identity as a Hindu'. As a child he had not even realized that 'Hindu' was not an 'insult', but the name of 'a community of which he was a member'. However, Suranjan is critical of the way in which a programme of Islamization has hijacked originally secular Bangladesh, which had been meant to be a homeland for all Bangladeshis. Like other Hindus, he had fought for his freedom in the 'war of liberation' (p. 225). He recalls how his sister had used the name Farida in 1971 'to conceal her Hindu identity' (p. 79; Hindus were routinely killed by Pakistani soldiers, although Christians were usually spared, thus there were quite a few conversions during the war of liberation; source – the author's own conversations with relatives in Bangladesh). Now, he felt insecure 'in the place of his birth'. This presented him with a real dilemma, since if he lacked security in his homeland, which he would never leave, 'where else on earth' could he 'expect security' (p. 23). Bangladesh had become a 'homeland for the Muslims', with no Hindus 'in the post of secretary or even additional secretary' (in the civil service) and no 'high ranking army or police' officers. There was one Hindu High Court Judge (p. 41). He himself had 'done brilliantly at University' but 'couldn't get any job'. Teaching jobs all went to Muslims, even if their grades were poorer (p. 83). When Ershad 'declared Islam as the state religion', no one protested. Those who had fought for freedom for all Bangladesh had failed to raise their voices. On the other hand, during previous anti-Hindu disturbances, his Muslim friends had 'rushed to his side' (p. 46).

Muslims in India

Muslims in India make almost identical claims about their exclusion from the workforce and from high office, although they acknowledge some token appointments by way of appeasement. Both Gandhi (1986) and Akbar Ahmed (1993) describe how historically Hindu saints attracted Muslim admirers, and vice versa, so that 'if Islam rode across India with the sword and spoke from the throne, it also walked with the Sufis and spoke in gentler tones from the hut' (Gandhi, p. 12) Ahmed (1993) writes about how most pilgrims who visit the shrine of the Muslim mystic Chisti at Ajmeer in Rajasthan are Hindu. Chisti taught *suhl-i-kul* (peace to all; see *Living Islam,* episode *Among the Non-Believers*). At times, Hindus in India were exempted from paying *jizya*, at times its payment was enforced. Kabir (1998) argues that when the Hindus were oppressed by their Muslim rulers, the same rulers 'oppressed their Muslim subjects with equal gusto' (p. 148). The status of Hindus was often debated. Some Mulims classed them as *dhimmis*, since they possessed scriptures, others as *kufrs* since they venerated images (p. 154).

A colonial legacy

Suranjan comments that the legacy of intercommunal rivalry inherited by India/Pakistan/Bangladesh was largely a reality that the British had created; realizing 'that unless they could disrupt Hindu–Muslim unity and friendly relations, they wouldn't be able to keep India under colonial rule', 'from their cunning was born divide-and-rule policy' (p. 246). Riots break out in protest against the burning of the Mosque; 'as if it were the Hindus of Bangladesh who were responsible – business establishments were attacked and places of worship demolished' (p. 9). Then a gang of seven or eight Muslim youths (p. 203) abducts Maya and no one comes to their aid. He knows that she is being raped. Ironically, she is being raped because she is a Hindu, but unfortunately neither Ram nor Radha nor Krishna, all of who are 'mythical pictures', can 'rescue Maya from the harsh, rigid, merciless clutches of the fundamentalists' (p. 225). In rage, Suranjan pays a Muslim prostitute for sex and takes her savagely as an act of vengeance against Maya's rape: 'He dug his nails into the girl's abdomen and sank his teeth into her breast ... her cries gave him a strange pleasure' (p. 272). Afterwards, he felt remorse (p. 276). His only hope is that one day he will see the end of all religion:

> Let the pavilions of religion be ground to bits. Let the bricks of temples, mosques, gurudawaras, churches, be burned in blind fire, and upon these heaps of destruction let lovely flower gardens grow, spreading their fragrance. Let children's schools and study halls grow. For the welfare of humanity, let prayer halls now be turned into hospitals, orphanages, schools, universities. Let prayer halls now become academies of art, fine arts centres, scientific research institutes ... from now on let religion's other name be humanity. (p. 223)

Discussion topic

- In your view, can you legitimately compare how non-Muslims were treated in the Muslim world with how non-Christians were treated in Europe before the modern period (after the emancipation of the Jews and the emergence of pluralist democratic states)?

- How would you compare and contrast the experience of non-Muslims today in the Muslim world with the experience of religious minorities in the West? Is such a comparison legitimate?

- In any society where one religion has political and legal privileges, is it inevitable that other religious communities and individuals will enjoy fewer rights? Identify examples from European history as well as contemporary examples.

8 Muslims as Minorities: Voices and Views

The West has to face its intrinsic racism and rise above the Islamophobia that resides
so deeply and perniciously in its historical consciousness. Muslim communities in
the West need to expunge their sense of moral superiority and righteousness and seek
new ways of empowering themselves.
   (Sardar 1995: 15)

Three strategies

This chapter identifies and explores three strategies that Muslims in Diaspora adopt vis-à-vis their attitude towards the countries in which they
reside. These are described in Figure 8.1.

   This analysis begins with what the classical texts say about Muslims in
non-Muslim territory, drawing on Khadduri (1955) and on Doi (1987).
Next, it describes each of the three positions. India is used as a case study
and the novel *Brick Lane* is analysed as an example of literature that
explores the Muslim migrant condition.

Muslims in non-Muslim territory: what do the founding discourses say?

Khadduri (1955) says that the 'Islamic state ... refused to recognize the
coexistence of non-Muslim communities' (p. 51). However, it was 'not
considered inconsistent with' this 'ultimate objective' to enter temporary
treaties with non-Muslims for 'purposes of expediency or because Islam'
had 'suffered a setback' (p. 202; see p. 171). During such periods, Muslims
may enter non-Muslim territory by *aman*, for example as an ambassador or
diplomat or to trade. Even when in non-Muslim territory a Muslim is still
subject to the *Shari'ah*, but if there by *aman* he must 'abstain from doing
any harm or injury to non-Muslims as long as he enjoys the benefit of their
aman' and should not contravene the laws of the land (p. 172). He must
not engage in any activity that might strengthen 'that territory against *dar-
al-Islam*', such as giving intelligence or aiding in the production of weapons. Muslims in this situation are 'advised from marrying a *harbi* woman,
even if she were a Scriptuary, for such a marriage might result in leaving

Left	Centre	Right
Assimilationist/Pluralist	**Separatist/Siege Syndrome**	**Confrontational**
Islam is a progressive religion that can adapt to different cultural contexts. Muslims can be faithful citizens of non-Muslim countries and can collaborate with people of good will to pursue ethical and social goals. Islam can contribute to debates on social and political issues. Muslims can embrace cultural pluralism and accept Islam as a faith system, as a source of ethics and of inspiration, but it is not for Muslims in non-Muslim countries a political ideology. Such Muslims join existing political parties (e.g. Tibi, Zaki Badawi, the Muslim American Society).	Muslims should establish their own institutions and negotiate recognition of their distinct identity and personal law by the legal establishment in response to the hostile, Islamophobic society in which they find themselves, arguing that this is to assert their rights to cultural and religious freedom and to self-determination as a minority community. In the meantime, separate institutions are set up to serve the community. Only distinctly Muslim political affiliations can legitimately voice Muslim concerns (e.g. the Islamic Party of Britain, the Nation of Islam).	The only purpose for Muslims living in the West is to bring about its submission to Islam. The aim is to bring about, by whatever means possible, the West's eventual conversion to Islam not only as a religion but also as a political and legal system. In other words, the goal is to create Islamic states in Britain, the USA, etc. as parts of a worldwide Islamic entity. Some are members of or supporters of organizations that use or condone violence as a means towards achieving their goals (e.g. al-Muhajiroun in the UK).

Figure 8.1 Three strategies among Diaspora Muslims

his children in the service of *dar-al-harb*.' If a Muslim finds any conflict between Islamic law and the laws of the non-Muslim country he is in, 'there is no doubt as to what his choice must be', says Khadduri (p. 171). If a Muslim entered *dar-al-harb* without *aman*, he was not bound to obey the laws of the land since Islam does not recognize the legitimacy of non-Muslim governments. According to Khadduri, many of the classical jurists did not 'at all approve of international trade, namely, the exchange of commodities between *dar-al-Islam* and *dar-al-harb*'. Malik advised the Khalif to appoint border patrols to prevent Muslims from leaving *dar-al-Islam* (Ruthven 1991: 52), which Ibn Rushd also proposed. Ibn-Hazm (d. 1064), from Cordoba, forbade Muslims to take copies of the Qur'an, weapons, horses and other commodities which might strengthen the enemy against Muslims into *dar al-harb*. However, other Muslim scholars regard entry into *dar-al-harb* as legitimate if Muslims do so to propagate Islam (see below). Historically, whole populations were converted as a result of the missionary preaching of merchants and teachers as they travelled far beyond the borders of *dar-al-Islam*. According to most classical jurists, while resident in *dar-al-harb*, if *halal* food is not available, Muslims can eat food slaughtered by the peoples of the book (and say the *bismillah* before eating; see Doi 1987: 50), based on Q5: 5: 'the food of the people of the book is made lawful to you'. While Khadduri's chapter on the *dhimmis* is 26 pages long, his discussion of 'Muslims in Non-Muslim Territory' is only five pages, suggesting that, as Doi (1987) argues, there is lack of substantial discussion of Muslims as minorities in the classical texts, since when they were written 'no one then imagined that a time would come when Muslim empires would decline and some of the areas once ruled by Muslims would be ruled by non-Muslims and that Muslims would have to live as minorities under non-Muslim jurisdictions' (p. 43).

Doi argues that *ijtihad* is needed in order for the *ulama* to 'guide Muslims in this new and unprecedented situation' (*ibid.*). Doi adopts a flexible approach to the classical distinction between the Muslim and non-Muslim world, stating that where Muslims are able to build mosques, worship freely, fast during Ramadan, and 'uphold *amr bil ma'ruf* and *nahy 'anil munkar*' (enjoining the right and forbidding the wrong) it is inappropriate to call such countries *dar-al-harb*, even if they are ruled by non-Muslims (p. 44). Several contemporary Muslim scholars have similarly argued that wherever Muslims are free to observe their major religious obligations, such territory can be considered Islamic, which some even extend to the USA and Europe (for example the Moroccan scholar, 'Abd al-'Aziz ibn al-Siddiq, and al-Ghannouchi, who declared that France was Islamic in 1989 at the congress of the Union of Islamic Organizations in France). Doi says that even a secular state should not be seen by Muslims as automatically hostile, provided that its government does not try to force Muslim minorities to adopt the beliefs of the majority (p. 56). Muslims need to be 'weaned away' from the desire to 'dominate' and instead take part alongside others in building up the traditions of the nation-state, recognizing that they owe their loyalty to it since Islam represents God's message 'for the benefit of all mankind even before it represents the establishment of a state and political authority' (p. 57). Here Doi directly addresses an issue that has been raised by many non-Muslim commentators on Muslim communities in the non-Muslim world. That is, whether Muslims can really be trusted as fully loyal citizens in any confrontation with a Muslim country, or whether their true allegiance lies elsewhere. In the USA, post-Gulf War, the FBI has questioned many Muslim groups about their alleged knowledge of terrorist plans and has accused Muslims of funding terrorists. Some British Muslims fought on the side of the Taliban against British troops, encouraged by at least one Muslim preacher, Sheikh Omar Bakri Mohamed, the Syrian-born founder of al-Muhajiroun (see below). Doi (1933–99) was professor of Islamic Law at the International Islamic University, Malaysia (1989–93) then a Professor at Rand Afrikaans University, South Africa. Born in India and a graduate of Bombay and Cambridge Universities (his Cambridge PhD was gained under the supervision of Prof. A. J. Arberry, the Islamic scholar and Qur'an translator). Doi also taught at several Nigerian universities. He was author of the popular *Shari'ah: The Islamic Law* (1984) cited in Chapter Two and of several books on Islam in Africa. In contrast with his book on *Shari'ah*, which adopts a conservative approach, his article on Muslim minorities is progressive. This is yet another example of the difficulty of attaching labels to scholars.

India: a case study of the three strategies

Muslim power began in India with the creation of the Delhi Sultanate in 1210, and various Muslim dynasties ruled from then until 1526 when the Moghul Empire was established, which lasted until 1858. Muslims were always a minority in India, although they formed the majority in the north east and in the north west (which became Pakistan and Bangladesh), ruled in Hyderabad in the south and were roughly 50 per cent in Aligarh. From 1757, real power passed to the British East India Company. After 1857, direct rule from Westminster replaced the East India Company as the British Government's agent. As Muslim power waned and Britain's increased, Muslims in India had to come to terms with the change in their own status from a dominant minority to a subjugated one. Muslims see ascendancy as a blessing from God, proof of Islam's superiority. How were they to understand their subjugation? An early response, dating from the very beginning of the decline of Muslim power, was pioneered by Shah Waliullah (1703–62), who blamed Sufi practices and Hindu influence for Islam's change in fortune. Shi'a Islam was also denounced. One of his successors, Sayyid Ahmad Shaheed Barelvi (1776–1831), a disciple of Waliullah's son Abdul Aziz (1746–1822), led a movement called the *tehrik-i-mujahidin* who, on the basis that India was no longer *dar-al-islam*, trekked to the north west on *hijrah* (migration). In his view, Muslims who found themselves in non-Muslim territory were obliged to migrate to Muslim territory, from where a *jihad* could be conducted to restore Muslim dominance.

Barelvi waged a *jihad* initially against the nearest non-Muslims, the Sikhs who then ruled an independent state in the Punjab, although his eventual aim was to defeat the British. He was himself defeated and killed in 1831 when a Sikh army stormed his capital, Balakot. Barelvi wrote 'my real objective is the establishment of *jihad* and carrying war into Hindustan ... The Christian infidels who have gained possession over India are very artful' (Ahmad 1966: 358). Another revivalist movement that remains influential in the subcontinent and has a presence in Diaspora is the *Ahl-e-Hadith* (people of tradition), whom Sayyid Ahmad Shaeed Barelvi also inspired. This movement, which operates through some 17 affiliated organizations in Pakistan today, including the *Markazi Jami'at Ahle-e Hadith* (founded 1948) which has a centre in Small Heath, Birmingham, UK, controls some 6 per cent of Pakistan's seminaries. They do not recognize the four legal schools (although they are close to the Hanbalis) and base their version of Islam on Qur'an and *Sunnah*, also rejecting *qiyas*. They consider the 'rule of women' un-Islamic and have demanded separate voting lists for Muslims and non-Muslims. Some *Ahl-e-Hadith* participate in politics but some condemn the existing order as *batil* (false) and say that until the Khalifate is re-established, participation in politics is un-Islamic. Instead, *jihad* is to be pursued (see Chapter Nine). Several *Ahl-e-Hadith* groups were active in Afghanistan and are currently involved in the Kashmir struggle, perpetuating the confrontational response. These include the *Lashkar-e-Toiba* (or *Tayba*, Army of the Pure, founded 1990), a wing of the *Markaz Daw-Wal Irshad*, or the *Jamaat al-Dawa* (founded 1987), the *Harkat-ul-Mujahideen* (founded 1985) and the *Tehreek-al-Mujahideen* (founded 1989). The *Lashkar* accuse the *Markazi Jami'at Ahl-e-Hadith* of lacking commitment to *jihad*, that is, of not being sufficiently militant (*askari*). They teach that boys can go to *jihad* without parental permission. They have been accused of kidnapping Barelvi girls and of keeping them as slaves. The *Lashkar* were responsible for attacking the Indian Parliament in December 2001 and a crowded shopping centre in New Delhi in November 2002 on the eve of the Hindu festival of Diwali. Bin Laden is said to have paid for their parent organization's mosque on their 190-acre headquarters outside Lahore. The *Tehreek* claim that 500 of their 'warriors' have died fighting Indian soldiers. Said to be Saudi funded, the *Tehreek*'s military commander Abu Waseem Salafi was killed in 1999, but it has reportedly converted many Barelvis in Kashmir to the *Ahl-e-Hadith* version of Islam.

In January 2000 the *Majlis-e-Amal*, which brings various *Ahl-e-Hadith* groups together, denounced President Musharraf as representing the USA, not Islam. These movements (which have links with al-Qaeda, see Chapter Nine) are involved in the disputed territory of Kashmir, which, although a majority Muslim province, became part of India and not

Pakistan in 1947 (the princely ruler was Hindu). Various Kashmiri free-dom movements campaign for different goals – some for an independent Kashmir, some for union with Pakistan, some (including the above) for the restoration of Muslim power throughout South Asia, the creation of an Islamic Khalifate. The *Lashkar* aims to restore Muslim rule throughout India. The banned Student Islamic Movement of India (SIMI) shares this agenda and consists of young men who have been tested in the various armed conflicts in Afghanistan, both against Soviet occupation and in defence of the Taliban. Some of its leaders are from the southern state of Kerala, a long way from Kashmir. They aim to liberate Kashmir and also the Muslims of India. These movements are said to have close links with the Pakistani and Bangladeshi Intelligence Agencies and to receive funds from various overseas sources. SIMI may have had CIA funding when it was combating the Soviets. Suspicion that Indian Muslims are pro-Pakistani, anti-nationalist fifth columnists has been rampant among such Hindu nationalist groups as the Vishnu Hindi Parishad and the Bharatiya Janata Party (BJP). Newspapers accuse Muslims of planning to Islamize India by mass migration over the Pakistan and Bangladesh borders. The BJP, in power between 1988 (as leader of a 14-party coalition) and 2004, has close links with a number of Hindu organizations (usually called fundamen-talist) whose ultimate aim is to transform India from a secular to a Hindu state (*Hindutva*). The leader of the Shiv Sena Party, in power in Mumbai, makes 'no secret of his hostility towards Muslims', says Rushdie (1991: 31). India's Muslims constitute about 20 per cent of the population and is the second largest Muslim community in the world, which makes their experience very significant in terms of worldwide Islam.

Traditionally, many Muslims have supported the pro-secular Congress Party (returned to power May 2004). They argue that a secular govern-ment in India is the best guarantee that all religious communities will enjoy equal rights and freedoms (see below). Rafiq Zakaria (1988) and Humayun Kabir (1998), among other eminent Muslims, champion secu-larism. Zakaria's model is the Constitution of Madinah, which united Muslims and non-Muslims (p. 28). Kabir, who has served in the Indian cabinet, opposed partition, arguing that 'a secular state in India is not in the interests of the minorities alone' but of 'all the peoples of India' (p. 151). In a faith that has '330 million gods' and also 'some perfectly good Hindus who are atheists', he asks, 'which form of Hinduism' would a religious state enforce? (p. 50). Rushdie (1991) describes the Hindu nationalist movement as a 'new element in Indian communalism' that promotes a 'collective Hindu consciousness that transcends caste and that believes Hindus to be under threat from other Indian minorities' (p. 31). Secular Muslims believe that as long as Muslims are free to practise their main religious obligations, and preferably their Personal Law (aspects of which are incorporated into Indian law, based on the legal code devel-oped by the British in India), they can be loyal citizens of the country in which they live (the integrationist model). Historically it was Sir Sayyid

Ahmed Khan who pioneered this response, rejecting Sir W. W. Hunter's view (see Khan 1860). Sir W. W. Hunter (1840–1900), in his official 1871 report, was of the view that Muslims were bound by their faith to rebel against the Queen. In contrast, Sir Sayyid supported the British in the Muslim-led revolt of 1857, founded his MAO (Muhammad-Anglo-Oriental College) at Aligarh in 1875, co-operated with the British government and stressed that Islam was in every respect compatible with modern science and learning (see Kurzman 2002: 300). Many secular Muslims are members of Sufi orders. Their Islam is a progressive Islam capable of adaptation and change.

Still other Muslims in British India opted for what Pulcini (1995) describes as the subcultural response, which entails a 'certain separation . . . from the mainstream' (p. 183). Instead of co-operating with the British and embracing the concepts of secular, pluralist modernity, these Muslims kept themselves apart from British institutions and from government service and established their own training centres instead. While Islam as a unity of religion and politics is a tenet of their beliefs, in practice they withdrew from the political stage to concentrate on religious learning of a conservative, traditionalist (Wahhabi) variety. Maulana Mohamed Qasim Nanotyi founded the *Dar-ul-Uloom* (house of learning) at Deoband (the world's second largest Islamic college) in 1866, from where some 65,000 students have graduated. They enter at age 5 and leave at age 25. The study of Western science is prohibited. Students today may watch television but not movies. They can use computers but not the Internet (although the seminary has a webpage, *www.dauluoom-deoband.com/eng lish/index.html*). All non-Muslim influences are resisted. Outside of India, many Deobandi mosques and colleges ban television and the reading of newspapers. The curriculum is based on the reading and recitation of religious texts, mathematics, and some Greek logic. Sufi Islam is condemned. In Diaspora, Deobandi-related mosques and madrassas function within Muslim enclaves in large urban areas as more or less self-contained ghettoes, in what Tibi (2001) calls 'communitarian ghettoes' (p. 205). Of Pakistan's 20,000 or so seminaries, 64 per cent are Deobandi. Rana Kabbani (1989) also uses the term 'ghetto' to describe the self-imposed isolation from the mainstream of many British Muslims (p. 11). The *Dar-ul-Uloom* seminary in Bury was founded in 1973 (its Halcombe Hall premises were purchased with Saudi aid in 1976, see *www.inter-islam.org/new dex.html*). The Islam that is practised is the Islam of the village that was left behind in the subcontinent, which is regarded as unchangeable. Sardar (1995) calls this the 'frozen-clock syndrome' (p. 11).

Imams are usually invited from India, Pakistan or Bangladesh and have little contact with the mainstream, majority community (few therefore need to learn English). According to Raza (1991) such Imams 'know almost nothing about the context in which they are resident' so they 'cannot propose any solutions' to the problems faced by their communities. Any solutions they do offer are 'escapist or obscurantist', and their teaching is strongly sectarian and 'thrives on demeaning the doctrines of other sects' (p. 33). Such mosques, says Raza, are 'medieval sectarian fortresses'. Western dress is shunned in favour of Arab-style robes or *Salwa-Kameez*. Women wear complete *burkhah*. Muslims who do not conform to this dress code are ostracized. Conservative Muslims in France (mainly of African origin) also regard dress as a sign of one's Islamic *bone fides*. Or, says Sardar, writing in 2002, feeling that they do not belong to British society, Muslim youth look elsewhere for the symbols and sense of identity they need which they find in 'beards, turbans and the rhetoric of injustice' and even in joining *jihads* in such places as 'Afghanistan to right countless real and perceived wrongs' (p. 54). According to the *Guardian*, 41 per cent of Muslims under the age of 34 define themselves first and foremost as Muslim and are more likely than older Muslims to say their community is too integrated. At that time (17 June 2002), two-thirds of British Muslims disapproved of Britain's role in Afghanistan. 61 per cent said that relations with non-Muslims had deteriorated since 9/11 (Lelso and Vasager 2002). The movement for Pakistan as a separate state may also have its origins in this response.

The confrontational response in Diaspora Islam

Militant Islamist groups in the UK, such as the Supporters of the *Shari'ah* and *al-Muhajiroun* (a breakaway from *hizb-ut-tahrir*) also aim to establish a Muslim government and while they have not engaged in acts of violence in the UK itself, their members have fought against British troops in Afghanistan and leaders have defended attacks on US embassies, as well as 9/11. Omar Bakri, *al-Muhajiroun*'s founder, for whom the 9/11 hijackers are heroes, is said to approve the creation of an Islamic state in Britain 'by any means possible'. Allegedly, Bakri is the main British link to al-Qaeda. SOS's founder, Egyptian-born Abu Hamza al-Masri (Mustafa Kamal), lost his hands and an eye fighting against the Soviets in Afghanistan. He also aided Muslims in Bosnia in the mid-1990s in what he calls their *jihad*. He is said to have advocated the hijacking of planes to be used to attack the West as far back as 1999 and has actively recruited volunteers for *jihad*, including at least one Muslim now held in Guantanamo Bay. The Charity Commission presently bans him from preaching in his Finsbury Park Mosque. On 27 May 2004, he was arrested, facing extradition to the USA for terrorist related crimes. Abdullah el-Faisal, a Jamaican-born Saudi-trained Muslim preacher, found guilty in early 2003 of incitement to murder and racial hatred, is said to regard the UK, the USA and France as legitimate targets for attack using any means, including chemical weapons, and is alleged to see the conflict as between Islam and democracy, Allah and Satan.

Pipes (2002) is convinced that there are many Muslims in America whose goal is to establish Islamic law, and a Muslim majority, in the USA 'by 2020' (p. 122), citing Shamin A. Siddiqi. The non-violent route to achieve this goal is by 'increasing the number of Muslims' (p. 117), but Pipes cites some who legitimize the use of 'ways outside the law to guard their rights' (p. 22). Wahaj, he says, the 'first Muslim to deliver the daily prayer in Congress', aspires to 'take over the US' (p. 173). In 1995, says Pipes, Wahaj gave Omar Abdel Rahman a character reference at his trial for conspiracy against the USA and for masterminding the 1993 bombing of the World Trade Center. Abdelkader Bouziane, deported from France for his views on wife beating, is quoted as saying that he favours an Islamic republic 'not just for France' but 'the whole world'. In the USA, several Muslim charities have been shut down following accusations that they have funded terrorism and 'prominent members of the American Muslim middle classes have been detained or arrested' while an 'unknown number ... have been visited and questioned by the FBI'. Worldwide since 9/11, seventeen Islamic charities 'have had their assets frozen' (Laurie Goodstein, *The Muslim News*, 17 April 2003). Millions of 'Muslims ... love the flag' but some have 'worrisome aspirations for the US', says Pipes (p. 111).

The separatist response

Tibi, Sardar, Kabbani and others regard opting for the ghetto as inimical to the future of Muslims in the non-Muslim world. It may not seem to be a matter of choice for some Muslims. In France, for example, many Muslims feel that the option of assimilating into French society, of being French Muslims rather than Muslims in France, is not on offer to them, although they form approximately 10 per cent of the population (between 5 and 6 million). 60 per cent of Imams do not speak French. Many Muslims in France feel that they are living in an alien society that has not welcomed them, that views them with 'fear, suspicion and hatred' and is happier for them to remain in their ghettoes than to join the mainstream. Accusations of being fifth columnists, discrimination in the job market, harassment and intimidation, convince Muslims that they will never be other than second-class citizens. Modood (2001) describes Muslim experience in the USA in identical terms. The French Government's ban on public wearing of the headscarf and its establishing of the French Council for the Muslim Religion (December 2002) are interpreted as efforts to encourage and to foster a liberal, progressive French Islam and to counter radical Islam. Some Muslim leaders in France have responded to government threats to close down radical mosques with promises to self-police the community (*Newsnight*, BBC2, 8 October 2003, Allan Little reporting from France). According to some commentators, it is hoped that French Muslims might pioneer a 'secularizing revolution' in Islam, although Turkey may feel slighted by *Newsnight*'s comment that such a revolution has not yet occurred in Islam. What alarms some analysts is the fact that the headscarf ban was supported by left-wing as well as by right-wing politicians, who see the presence of an increasingly large Muslim population in France as a threat to its secular heritage of *laïcité*. Modood says that Islam's claim to regulate both public and private life presents an ideological challenge to French secularists, who see Muslims as inassimilable. He points out that while France happily grants citizenship to people, irrespective of their ethnic origin, who embrace French culture, they do not accept the idea of composite or multiple identity. For Muslims who also want to 'retain pride in their Algerian' identity, 'their claim to be French citizens is jeopardized' (2003: 3).

In the USA, the Black Muslim movement, the Nation of Islam (NOI), founded by Elijah Muhammad (1897–1975), evolved out of Marcus Garvey's 'black is beautiful' and 'look to Africa' message that sought to restore pride and self-confidence in America's black community. Christianity for many was the religion of the oppressors, the religion of those who had enslaved their ancestors and kidnapped them from Africa. For many, their real identities had been lost and Islam, with a large African following, appealed as the religion of choice, not of compulsion. Elijah Muhammad (previously Robert Poole) taught that the white race was evil, that Islam was the authentic faith of black people, and that ultimately the USA would be destroyed, a message derived as much from the Bible as from the Qur'an – prayer leaders are ministers, centres are temples. Like Garvey (1867–1949), he wanted to instil pride and self-sufficiency into his followers and his message also stressed the centrality of family, paternal responsibility and the dignity of work. Blacks should not depend on white handouts, on welfare. Black Christian preachers were sycophants, imitating whites with their blond, blue-eyed Jesus. Whites had systematically devalued and destroyed black culture, aided by Jews. Within the Nation of Islam, like Garvey's earlier UNIS (Universal Negro Improvement Society), Elijah Muhammad established ranks and grades. Members wear uniforms. The emphasis is on pride in your own self-image and identity. Women wear dresses similar to Christian nuns, men suits (often with bow ties). Sister Clara and Elijah Muhammad Schools were founded to educate children, since 'for the Muslim child to stay in the American educational mainstream is to lose his or her religious identity and to suffer moral corruption' (Pulcini 1995: 184). Pipes (2002) comments that the attitude converts adopt towards the USA depends largely on the 'sort of Islam' they adopt (p. 127) and that they are often 'influenced by the contempt for America that many immigrant Muslims bring from their homelands' (p. 130).

The ultimate aim of NOI is to achieve a separate nation, or state, for black American Muslims, which they believe is a right that the US authorities should grant. Elijah Muhammad told his members 'You are not American citizens' (Pipes 2002: 127). In the words of Louis Farrakhan, NOI's current Supreme Minister, 'an army of black men and women' will 'sit down with the President, whoever he may be, and negotiate for a separate state or territory of our own' (Pipes 2002: 128). The NOI represents a separatist or subcultural response that uses its own organizations to avoid the need for interaction with non-Muslim society on the one hand, while on the other demanding what Tibi (2001) calls the granting of minority 'rights and privileges'. Other Muslims in the USA in addition to the NOI (which does not attract universal recognition as a *bona fide* Muslim movement) also demand what Pipes and Tibi regard as privileges, such as state funding for Islamic schools, the right to pronounce the *bismillah* in public ceremonies (such as at graduations in the state system), provision of prayer space in public buildings, segregation of girls and boys and Islamic punishments for 'activities offensive to Islam', such as drinking alcohol and gambling (Pipes 2002: 119). Such Muslims, he says, also want to 'close down the critical analysis of Islam' (p. 120; Pipes claims that in 'majority Muslim countries it has become virtually impossible to comment critically about Islam', p. 172). Siddiqi believes that Muslims can 'transform' the USA without needing to challenge the existing political order (Pipes, p. 121). Siddiqi knew Mawdudi, whom he cites in his article 'Islamic Dawah in the US: Challenges and Opportunities' (*radianceweekly.com*), which concludes, 'O Allah help the Muslims of America to understand the realities of today and give them *Tawfeeq* to prepare themselves to forebear the responsibilities that are lying ahead of them in discharging the onerous task of leading the greatest and the mightiest nation of the world to its natural destiny in the near future'.

An argument used to support this demand is that of reciprocity – Muslim states grant minorities legal rights, so non-Muslim governments should reciprocate by granting Muslims such rights as to practise their Personal Laws, which the Muslim Parliament, UK, advocates. Thus, the Muslim system for regulating minority affairs is the best model for all to follow. Syed Mumtaz Ali (1993), a lawyer and President of the Canadian Society of Muslims, in his widely circulated *Treatment of Minorities: The Islamic Model*, suggests that 'it is up to Muslim States to see if their heritage could not be proposed to others with convincing arguments for universal application' (p. 8). Mawdudi (1939) remarked that the world has yet to see a system other than Islam that treats 'people of other faiths' with 'such magnanimity' (p. 28). Commenting on Muslim demands for change in European law to accommodate *Shari'ah*, Nielsen (1999) points out that while Islamic law deals with communities, Western law deals with individuals (p. 132), which creates a mismatch between Muslim aspiration and Western tradition. There are Muslims in the UK who engage with the government to secure rights for Muslims but who operate within established systems, such as the voluntary-aided school sector (which includes Christian and Jewish schools).

Such Muslims are fully integrated into society. One, Lord Ahmed of Rotherham, who chairs the al-Hijrah Education Trust in Birmingham which runs a primary and a secondary school, is a Labour Life Peer and says that he is proud to be a British Muslim. However, the Muslim Parliament in the UK, established in January 1992 under the leadership of Kalim Siddiqui (1931–96), has a separatist agenda. Siddiqui rose to prominence during the Rushdie controversy, which he says dragged him from his desk into community affairs. Born in British India, he moved to Pakistan in 1948 where he was a member of a group 'dedicated to establishing *Khilafah* in Pakistan' and went to Britain, with other members of the group, in 1954 as a journalism student (Siddiqui, 1996). After working for local newspapers, he was by 1964 a sub-editor at the *Guardian*. His doctorate, in international relations, was awarded by London University in 1972. In 1973, he founded the Islamic Institute (now the Institute of Contemporary Islamic Thought) to promote what he saw as Islam's global agenda. A sympathizer of the Iranian regime, he regarded the Islamic Republic of Iran as the first Islamic State of the modern era (see Siddiqui 1980). He envisaged the Muslim Parliament as an embryonic non-territorial state for British Muslims that could eventually run its own schools and hospitals. In a hostile environment it was futile for Muslims to work in or through the existing political establishment and they could only flourish 'separately from the main British state' (see K. Siddiqui 1973 and I. Siddiqui 1998). Its *Muslim Manifesto* (1990) explicitly rejects assimilation or integration as an option, and each section ends with 'we are Muslims first and last'. Muslims are duty bound to engage in *jihad*, either by taking part in armed struggle abroad or by materially assisting such struggle. Another refrain is 'Islam is our guide in all situations'. *Da'wah* (see below) is a duty incumbent on all Muslims (see the ICIT website for additional material, especially Iqbal Siddiqui's biography of Kalim Siddiqui (original 1996)). One of the successes of the Parliament was setting up the Halal Meat Authority that grants certificates to a network of approved abattoirs and shops throughout Britain. Dr Ghayasuddin Siddiqui, the Parliament's current leader, says that Muslims in Britain should settle for the meeting of what he calls minimum requirements not maximum demands. On the issue of Islamic dress, he describes wearing the *hijab* as a matter of personal choice. Women who choose not to wear it must not be labelled as bad Muslims (speech, 10 July 2004, as heard by this writer).

The integrationist mode

Doi (1987) advocates that, where possible, Muslims negotiate legal and educational provisions but the position he outlines is closer to an integrationist one than to a separatist one, since he wants Muslims to take a full part in public life and to address the 'common problem of the country they live in'. They should not hold themselves 'aloof' (pp. 56–7). Directly referring to an issue that remains controversial, whether Muslims can serve in the armies of non-Muslim countries, Doi emphatically says that they can and must 'if called upon to fight' and that should they kill a Muslim, they are not guilty of breaching the *Shari'ah* because they did not do so intentionally but had no choice (*ikhtiyar*) 'in the matter' (p. 52). Similarly, in October 2001 a 'group of prominent Islamic scholars', in response to a question from a Muslim Army Chaplain, issued a *fatwa* that 'Muslims serving in the US armed forces have a duty to fight for their country even if it means combat against other Muslims [The *fatwa* applied to British soldiers too]' (Murphy 2002). The *hizb-ut-tahrir* adopts the opposite view, arguing that Americans will always trust a Protestant American before they will trust a Muslim US citizen and that Muslims fool themselves if they think their citizenship is real ('Our Brotherhood is Real and their Citizenship is False', 2001).

In the UK, Egyptian-born Zaki Badawi has been in the forefront of developing a British Islam. Formerly Imam of the Regent's Park Mosque, London (1978–81), he founded the Muslim College, Ealing in 1986. Author of *The Hajj* (1976) and *Reformers of Egypt* (1977) (and co-editor of *Hajj Studies* with Ziaduddin Sardar (1978)) and of numerous newspaper articles, he has held visiting professorships at universities throughout the Muslim world, and is one of this writer's oldest Muslim acquaintances. An al-Azhar graduate, he came to the UK aged 29 to preach Islam. Since 1984, he has served as Chair of the Council of Mosques and Imams in the UK, which brings together mosques mainly from the Sufi and Barelvi traditions. The Barelvi movement constitutes the 'majority of Muslims in Britain'. Founded by Maulana Amad Raza Khan (1856–1931) in India, it is characterized by an 'overwhelming love of the Prophet Muhammad' whose honour it defends 'whenever ... under attack' (Raza 1991: 11). Barelvis believe that Muhammad had '*ilm-i-ghaib*', or knowledge of the unknown. The pro-Sufi Barelvis and the anti-Sufi Deobandis and *Ahl-e-Hadith* (who share much in common with Wahhabis) are bitterly opposed to each other. Some 25 per cent of Pakistan's seminaries are Barelvi. In the UK context, Saudi and Gulf-State funding is unavailable to Barelvis, unlike some 800 British mosques that receive petro-dollars. Raza (1991) says that petro-dollars only go to those who are willing to be 'the mouthpiece of foreign governments', and that the Saudis 'finance the mosque to get their own point of view put across' (p. 26). No money, he says, comes without strings. Badawi's move from the Regent's Park Mosque has been attributed to loss of support following Egypt's signing of the Camp David Peace Accord with Israel. In Birchfield, Birmingham, the former President Saddam Hussein Mosque, built with a million and a half pounds' 'donation from the Iraqi leader' had 'an interest in' Saddam's 'continued good health', as he had promised a further million. The name was retained until just after Saddam's downfall, when it was changed to Birmingham Jame Masjid (Raza, p. 50).

Badawi's own funding is from the Libyan Call Society. His College, whose courses are accredited by the University of London's Birkbeck College (see *www.muslimcollege.ac.uk*), aims 'to train a new class of Muslim leadership, freed from national traditions, educated in European cultures, and trained in the technologies of the new media' (Metcalf 1996: 19), the opposite of Deobandi seminaries and very much in the tradition of Sir Sayyid's Mahommedan Anglo Oriental College. Badawi, who drafted the *fatwa* referred to above, believes that British Muslims must be loyal to the state. While he disliked Rushdie's novel, he also rejected Khomeini's *fatwa* and volunteered to offer Rushdie refuge in his own home. He has actively promoted interreligious concord for many years (having served on committees with this writer), and openly speaks of the need for Muslims in Britain to enthusiastically adopt Britain's language, laws and culture if they are to prosper in this country. In his view, citizenship is not a buffet from which you can select what you want and leave the rest; it is all or nothing (see Combe 2001). Badawi thinks that it may be too late for many Muslims who have already settled in Britain to adopt British culture but says that newcomers can be helped to adapt. He thinks that Muslims are best advised to work within the existing political system, instead of attempting to set up their own system or party and described the Islamic Party of Britain as 'run by converts with few roots'. Syed Pasha of the more conservative Union of Muslim Organizations also considered the party 'counter-productive' and that Muslims would be better represented through existing parties (Raza, p. 41). On the other hand, Raza comments that one advantage of the involvement of converts is that no one can tell them to 'clear off back from whence they came' (p. 41). Raza also observes that while converts in the West face the problem of 'being between two cultures', they also help to 'clear confusion between traditions, cultures, customs and Islam' (p. 103).

Several eminent Muslims resident in the West have suggested that it will be émigré Muslims who lead the renewal of the whole of the Muslim world. Badawi, for example, suggests that the 'most profound formulations will come, not from the United States, where life is too easy', or 'from Britain ... but in France, where Muslims will be challenged by the hardness of life, the deep-held conviction of republican secularism, and the depth of racism' (Metcalf 1996: 19). Al-Faruqi (whom Pipes also cites, 2002: 113, 118) used language of *hijrah*, or migration, to justify Muslim presence in the West, as Metcalf explains:

> *Hijrah* may long have been understood as movement from a land where one could not lead an Islamic life, typically one of non-Muslim rule, to a land ruled by Muslims. Today, it can continue to mean physical movement, this time from a land of Muslim settlement, but of poverty, to a non-Muslim land of greater opportunity. (p. 19)

The idea that residence in the non-Muslim world can be regarded as *hijrah* is for many contingent on Muslims engaging in *da'wa*, or mission. Al-Faruqi argued that '*hijra* can only be justified if understood as a providential opportunity' both to invite non-Muslims to become Muslim and to reform 'Islam among Muslims as well' (cited by Metcalf, p. 19). Raza (1991) also argues that Muslims can only justify their residence in the West, where they originally migrated for purely economic reasons, 'if they work for Islam' (p. 110). He advocates 'a revolutionary perspective' that calls on Muslims to 'help the genuine Islamic groups committed to transforming the secular Muslim states (their countries of origin) into Islamic states' (p. 111). Shabbir Akhtar has argued 'that the freest Muslims live in the West', while 'everywhere else' except in Iran 'Islam is an out-lawed political force' (see Lewis 1994: 52). Such thinking has historical precedent in, among others, the thought of Ibn Taymiyya and al-Mawardi as well as the Shi'a Imam, Jafar al-Sadaq, who all suggested that Muslims might serve Islam better living with non-Muslims, while some Hanafi jurists thought that there might be enclaves of *dar-al-Islam* in *dar-al-harb*. Muslims associated with the *Jamaati-i-Islam* have also supported the idea that there is a necessary link between *hijrah* and *da'wa*. For example, see Khurram Murad's *Dawah Among Non-Muslims in the West* (1986), in which he bemoans lack of commitment to *da'wah* not only 'among non-Muslims in the West' but almost universally. However, while Murad's aim is eventually to convert the non-Muslim, he eschews polemic and what he calls 'emotive diatribe ... against the West' in favour of 'an objective, powerful critique of *Kufr*, of Western thought and society' such as that pursued by the Islamic Foundation, Leicester, of which he was Director-General, and in the writings of Khurshid Ahmad, the *Jamaati*'s current vice-president. Murad, an engineering graduate from Karachi (BEng. 1952) and from the University of Minnesota, USA (MSc. 1958), was *Jamaati* Vice-President (1987–96), directed its training programme, and since 1992 has edited its journal, *Tarjumanal Qur'an* (founded by Mawdudi in 1932). Other *da'wah* activists have no political goals to establish an Islamic government but offer Islam as an alternative to 'potential converts' who feel that 'Christianity or secularism ... have somehow failed them' (Werbner 2002: 180).

In the USA, according to Pulcini (1995), the integrationist strategy (he calls it 'Accommodationist') appeals to some Muslims who are 'not very observant' and whose 'Islamic specificity gives way to the vague generalizing American civil religion'. He argues that accommodationists 'oppose withdrawal and isolation' from the mainstream 'but differ ... regarding the extent to which they think children should be allowed to conform' (p. 190). According to Pipes (2002), integrationists in the USA are those who are typically grateful to be living there, who are thankful to be citizens of a democracy and who want to 'create an American Islam', as opposed to those Muslims who 'want an Islamic America' (p. 139). They are likely to 'go out into the world and involve themselves in non-Islamic activities', unlike Islamists (Pipes 2002: 207). Integrationists, whether in Europe, UK or the USA, are likely to wear Western dress. Doi says 'there is no definite Islamic dress as such and that prayer will be acceptable if offered in any suitably modest dress' (1987: 51). When W. W. Deen Muhammad succeeded his father as Supreme Minister of the NOI in 1975, inspired by Malcom X (1925–65), a former NOI deputy leader and spokesman who had converted to Sunni Islam by his own reading while in prison for refusing the draft (1961), he moved the majority of NOI members into mainstream Islam, renaming the movement the American Muslim Mission (AMM). In 1981, a breakaway group reconstituted the NOI under Louis Farrakhan, cited above, which conforms to the teachings of Elijah Muhammad. The AMM sent students to mainstream Islamic seminaries for training, and forged links with other Muslim organizations in North America and beyond, and has received funding from the United Arab Emirates to build mosques and schools. W. W. Deen Muhammad changed his title from Supreme Minister to Imam and the name of his movement to the World Community of al-Islam in the West. In 1985, each mosque became an independent trust but most remain affiliated to the new Muslim American Society, which sponsors a raft of organizations and businesses, schools and colleges. He retains his father's social ethic but rejects his teaching. Pipes (2002) suggests that the upwards economic mobility that Elijah's teaching of 'hard work' and 'thrift' inculcated in members enabled them 'to escape poverty', so that those who 'had moved ahead found normative Islam an attractive alternative' (p. 229). W. W. Deen urges his followers to identify themselves as American and as Muslims, and to participate in mainstream politics. According to Poston (1991), as a result of 'Warith Deen's change of policy', some Muslims have made 'serious efforts ... to engage in political life' (p. 245).

Tibi (2001) champions the concept of 'Euro Islam', not as a strategy for the whole Muslim world but for Muslims in Europe. Nonetheless, he sees Euro Islam as a cultural expression of Islam that represents a valid pattern for Muslims throughout the world. A Euro Islam would draw inspiration from Islam's rationalist tradition and from the Andalusian experience, which is 'a lasting indication of a Western-Islamic encounter in its best terms' and 'had a great impact on the making of Europe itself' (p. 204). Euro Islam is an 'interpretation of Islam that makes it compatible with four ... constitutional standards', namely, '*laicism* (that is, the separation of religion and politics), secular tolerance based on individual human rights, democratic pluralism and last but not least, civil society' (p. 226). In his view, citing India, the granting of special privileges impedes 'the political integration of these groups' (which these groups do not themselves desire) and entices 'the growth of right-wing radicalism', such as neo-fascist, nationalist and racist political parties (p. 208). Tibi has in mind the rise of such parties as the British National Party, which has won local council seats, and of neo-fascist parties in Germany. In India, the rise of the BJP, with its pro-Hindu policies between 1989 and 2004 (under Atal Behari Vajpayee) and the decline of the pro-secular Congress, can be seen as a backlash to perceived special treatment of Muslims, for example, the Muslim Women (Protection on Rights of Divorce) Act of 1986. Following the controversial Shah Bano case of 1985, this Act reversed the Supreme Court's award of alimony for which Islamic law does not provide, but which India's legal code did. This was interpreted as exempting Muslims from civil law on the one hand and as giving legal recognition to the *Shari'ah* on the other. Many Hindus found this objectionable, because their own conduct was judged under a secular, not a Hindu, code. The continued minority character of the Aligarh Muslim University, too, regarded by some Hindus as a breeding ground for Islamism, attracts criticism that while paid for by the state, it discriminates in favour of

Muslims. This perception, that the Congress government that had dominated India since independence was actually privileging Muslims, resulted
in its defeat. Rajiv Ghandi lost the 1989 election. The eruption of such
anti-Muslim sentiment that destroyed the Babri Mosque in 1992 has been
attributed to the perception that Rajiv had compromised India's secular
constitution. However, the BJP's pro-Hindu, anti-secular policies did not
convince the majority to re-elect them in 2004, when, despite a campaign
that demonized the foreign origin of Congress leader Sonia Gandhi,
Rajiv's widow (and former PM Indira's daughter-in law), the Congress
were returned to power. Many Indians felt that the BJP had neglected the
poor while making the wealthy richer. When Sonia declined the Prime
Ministerial nomination, it went instead to a Sikh, Manmohan Singh, who
became India's first non-Hindu PM.

As noted previously, the type of pluralism for which Tibi calls is different
from multiculturalism, which he says marginalizes communities by creating 'separate entities' and invites the toleration of practices that are not
tolerated in the mainstream, on the basis that 'their ways are not our ways',
which Moghissi also critiques. Multiculturalism strands Muslims as permanent 'aliens in their Diaspora ... opposed to Europe and to its norms
and values' (1999: 207). Muslims thus have a choice, between 'creating a
ghetto or being an inter-cultural bridge between Islam and the West' (p.
208). However, Tibi prefers to talk about political rather than cultural
integration, since the first implies the 'granting' of 'citizenship rights and
duties' and the 'demanding' from Muslims of loyalty to European laws,
while the latter implies 'a denial of the cultural identity of migrants' (p.
208). He calls on Muslims to abandon the distinction between *dar-al-islam*
and *dar-al-harb* 'which has never been revised' in favour of 'religious and
cultural pluralism' and the aim of becoming demographically 'the
majority in Europe', whether by migration (*hijrah*) or *da'wah* or *jihad*, thus
'the concept of migration (*hijrah*)' must not be linked 'with *da'wa*' (p. 227;
see p. 55, p. 116, p. 203, p. 208). The Qur'an clearly states, says Tibi,
'*Lakum dinakum wa liya din*', 'you have your religion and I have mine'
(p. 203).

Dannin (2002) argues that *hijrah* has been 'historically closely associated
with *jihad*', and is regarded by some Muslims as part of a strategy for
territorial expansion, when they factor 'the strength of the local Muslim
community' into their plans. Thus, 'both *jihad* and *hijrah* measure the
same social and demographic potential' (pp. 68–9). Pipes (2002) refers to
Jean Raspail's *The Camp of the Saints* (1973) that depicts 'a Muslim takeover
of Europe by an uncontrolled influx of Bangladeshis' (p. 22). Tibi, as
noted previously, calls for Muslims to give up their claim to 'absolutism';
belief in their own superiority, he says, prevents engagement in dialogue,
which for him is essential in a pluralist society, where, while representing
'different views', people remain 'strongly committed to common rules
and, above all, to mutual tolerance and mutual respect' (p. 209). Muslims
need to embrace 'religious pluralism' so that they can learn that 'their

belief is only one of many others' (p. 226). However, if Muslims 'need to reform', then Europeans need to 'give up exclusiveness and Eurocentrism', which is just as evil as Muslims' attitude of 'cultural superiority' (p. 202, p. 226, p. 229). Part of the problem, he says, is that too many Muslim leaders opt to set up 'obstacles in the way of integrating Muslim minorities' to further their own agendas. Many, he says, were criminals at home and reside in the West only by abusing the asylum system (p. 204). In Kureishi's film *My Son the Fanatic*, the fundamentalist Imam rants and raves about the decadent West but asks Parvez to use his connections to get him leave to remain in the UK: 'Your great long-beard friend wants to stay in this immoral country' (1997: 19), Parvez tells his son. Some Muslims in the West, as noted above, see their community as a moral fortress surrounded by immorality. Thus, much contact with the non-Muslim majority is undesirable (a view found among many Deobandis). The 'othering' of Muslims by themselves is as unacceptable as their 'othering' by the mainstream, which must offer Muslims viable alternatives to being a 'peripheral minority' (Tibi 2001: 205), or as Modood puts it, 'a "them" not one of "us"' (2003b: 2). Sardar (1995) also identifies Muslim 'sense of moral superiority' as a barrier to better relations with the mainstream: 'Muslim communities in the West need to expunge their sense of moral superiority and righteousness and seek new ways of empowering themselves' (p. 15). He favours the French *citoyen*, not the 'ethnic German *Staatsbürgerschaft* or the Islamic *ummah*' (p. 200).

In the British context, Tariq Modood (2003b) argues that a healthily multicultural society needs to accommodate religion as a valid social category – and to rethink Europe so that the Muslim 'them' becomes part of a plural 'us'. The political integration or incorporation of Muslims – remembering that there are more Muslims in the European Union than the combined populations of Finland, Ireland and Denmark – has not only become the most important goal of egalitarian multiculturalism but is now pivotal in shaping the security, indeed the destiny, of many peoples across the globe. The *Cantle Report* (2001) took the view that there is 'no single dominant and unchanging culture into which all must assimilate' and that a 'common sense of belonging' to society would follow from the identification and affirmation of 'shared values'. It invited debate 'about citizenship, civic identity, shared values, rights and responsibilities' to enable people 'from diverse backgrounds, faiths and cultural traditions' to 'unite', pointing out that the 'need to articulate a clear set of shared values ... has been brought into sharp focus by this summer's disorders [race-related riots in three north England cities May–July 2001] and increased community tensions following the terrorist attacks on New York and Washington DC' (pp. 19–20).

Literary case study: Monica Ali's *Brick Lane*

Just as scholars, Muslim and non-Muslim, find the Diaspora experience a fertile field for enquiry and for literary production, so do novelists and playwrights. *The Camp of the Saints* by Jean Raspail (1973) was referred to above (and by Pipes). Monica Ali's Booker-prize nominated *Brick Lane* (2003), her debut novel, is set in East London's Bangladeshi community (Ali was brought up in Bolton). Its central character, Nazneen, transported from Bangladesh to London by marriage, struggles to discover her identity as she faces the dilemma of choosing what she wants to retain from her upbringing, both social and religious, and what she wants to adopt from her new environment. Intergenerational difference with Nazeen's husband Chanu, whose dream is to return to *Shonar Bangla* (Golden Bangladesh), and Nazneen's own desire to find acceptance, despite her experience of racism, in her new context, emerges as a major theme. Throughout the novel, Nazneen explores her role as a woman, what her own culture expects from her and how she perceives the life of women in London.

Ali's book reflects her own experience. She was born in Bangladesh but brought up in the UK. Her family fled during the war of liberation, when she was three. Her Bangladeshi father, to whom the book is dedicated, imbued her with a love of literature and told her many stories of their native land. Ali's mother is English. It was after race riots that Ali first ventured into the Bangladeshi housing estates and discovered the poor conditions, and economic exploitation, that many experience. She also encountered a drug problem that she had not associated with the community, which challenged her own stereotype. In *Brick Lane*, Nazneen's husband Chanu's preoccupation is instilling a love of all things Bangladeshi into his children. Bangladeshis, he claims, citing research from LSE, are 'the happiest people in the world' (p. 290). Indeed, although he lived in the UK he never became 'of' the UK. He did not even 'see the sights of London' until 30 years after he arrived there (p. 239). Asked 'where's he from' by an American tourist, he replies 'Bangladesh' (p. 245). His doctor diagnosed him as suffering from 'Going Home Syndrome' (p. 381). At the end of the novel, he explodes what has been called 'the myth of return' by actually returning. Much of the novel revolves around Nazneen's friendship with Karim, who helps to found the Muslim youth group, Bengal Tigers. Nazneen also participates in the group, although women's presence in meetings does not pass without criticism: 'The Qur'an bids us to keep separate. What are you doing here anyway?' (p. 236). Music must be un-Islamic because the Taliban had banned it (p. 345). Karim and the group are anxious to support Muslims wherever they are suffering. They also respond to BNP propaganda and to racist incidents but much of the time their discussion often focuses on the call to *jihad* (racist thugs also feature in Kureishi's 1985 *My Beautiful Laundrette*). 'It's a worldwide struggle', says Karim, 'everywhere they are trying to do us down. We have to fight back. It's time to fight back', as he reads a magazine article inviting support for the *Mujahideen* in Chechnya (p. 200). Egypt's regime is 'a cowardly American-loving government' (p. 216). Sanctions against Iraq are 'the ... crime against humanity ... that exceeds all others in magnitude' (p. 235). President Bush is described as preparing a 'Crusade' (p. 311). Ali describes a community that is oppressed by racism and by the relative poverty of their lives and has little or no sense of belonging to the wider UK context. For them, their local struggle is part-and-parcel of a global struggle to restore Islam's glory. 'Think global but act local', said Karim (p. 238). Chanu advised his children to take pride in Islam's glorious past: 'Don't forget it. Take pride, or all is lost' (p. 177). 'It is written', we read, 'in the Qur'an that every Muslim must work towards one, unified Islamic state across the world.' 'It is written', states the speaker, 'that khilafah is fard' (p. 347). On the other hand, the group are adamant that Muslims cannot target civilians, women or 'innocent people' (p. 339) or commit suicide, and are thoroughly sceptical that any Muslim was involved in the events of 9/11: 'One of the hijacker's passports survived the fire – heat of over one thousand degrees Fahrenheit. Found in the rubble of the World Trade Centre. What kind of fools does the FBI take us for?' (p. 318). Asked who was responsible, Karim replies, 'ask the right question. Who benefits?' 'It seemed to Nazneen', though, 'that no one benefited' (p. 318). Nazneen by no means abandons her culture or her faith but finds that she can no longer be only an obedient wife. As her anti-racist and community development interests blossom, she finds that she likes her new freedom. Ali's recent application for a visa to visit Bangladesh was refused.

See also Hanif Kureishi's *My Son the Fanatic* (1997) for an exploration of how a young Muslim, whose father has 'assimilated', finds this repugnant and turns to 'pure Islam' as an alternative. His father has swallowed 'the white and Jewish propaganda' (p. 69). The West is obsessed with sex (p. 64). Capitalism is all about 'taking advantage' (p. 69). It is nothing but the 'empty accountancy of things' (p. 70). The solution is to turn to Islam. 'They say integrate, but they live in pornography and filth' (p. 64), which echoes Mawdudi and Qutb.

Further discussion topics

- Akbar Ahmed asks whether there is conflict between loyalty to the worldwide *ummah*, and loyalty to the particular state in which a Muslim lives. How would you reply to this question?
- Do you think that Tibi's concept of Euro Islam is authentically Islamic? If so, how would you measure its Islamic legitimacy?
- Parekh (2000) argues that when pressure is exerted on communities to 'assimilate' this can have 'the opposite consequence'. He suggests that societies need to accommodate the genuine demands of their cultural minorities, unless they opt to define belonging in ethnocultural terms. What demands might be considered legitimate? Why

would these not represent the granting of the type of unequal 'privileges' that Tibi considers inappropriate and counter-productive?

- Immanuel Kant (1724–1804) was sceptical that a universal moral code could be established but Tibi is confident that an intercultural ethic can become the basis for achieving world peace. Is he too optimistic?

- Some have argued, in the UK context, that legislation in order to preserve the dominant culture is needed for the maintenance of social cohesion. Huntington sees a pluralist society as doomed to disintegrate, while Parekh and others see pluralism as a strength allowing for mutual cross-cultural enrichment. In Parekh's view, while a society does need a 'broadly shared culture to sustain it', in a pluralist society this will evolve by fusion and cross-fertilization (2000: 219). Obviously, no one can predict the end result. Is this what some people find threatening? Which view do you find the more persuasive? What, if any, measures would you propose to give your view legislative support?

- Parekh (2000) suggests that pluralist societies need public forums to enable minorities, who are often 'culturally and psychologically insecure', to voice concerns and to take part in national discussion on crucial issues, and that Parliament, divided on party lines, is not such a place (p. 306). What form might such forums take? Do any currently exist? Can you identify any? Could existing forums be put to better use, or reconstituted for this purpose?

- How would you critique Europe's response to the Bosnian crisis? Modood (2001) suggests that the USA and the West were slow to act because poor, not oil-rich Muslims, as in the Gulf, were the victims. Other Muslims saw US involvement as an attempt to impose its own agenda on Muslim people. What do you think?

- Are Tibi and Pipes fair to call on Muslims to abandon hopes of becoming a demographic majority in Europe and in the USA? Freedom to convert is a human right. It can be argued that people have the right to try to persuade others that their religion, or political ideology, is correct provided that they respect other opinions as well. Evangelical Christians believe that the Muslim world must be 'won for Jesus'. Would you defend or oppose Muslims' right to engage in missionary activity in the West, and why? Would you also defend or oppose the rights of Christians and of members of other religions to do the same, and why?

- Should Western states adopt aspects of the Islamic model for the treatment of minorities? If so, which? Or should they adopt the whole model?

- Do you think that reform of Islamic thought will come from the West? How will the views of such scholars as Tibi, Arkoun, Esack and Modood reach Muslims in the Muslim world? How will Muslims who agree with Lord Cromer, that Islam reformed is Islam no longer, reconcile themselves to new formulations of Islam? Do you agree that Islam can be constantly reinterpreted, or do you regard its meaning as fixed and unchangeable?

9   War and Peace in Islam: The Traditional View

Islam has the right to take the initiative ... God's rule on earth can be established only through the Islamic system.
   (Qutb 1988: 137)

Muslim understanding of war and peace

This chapter explores traditional understanding of war and peace. Qutb is taken to represent the traditionalist perspective, although he was not himself as radical as those whose actions he inspired, such as President Sadat's assassins and Osama bin Laden, whose activities and beliefs are described below. Palestine is used as a case study, chosen because many Islamist movements have roots in the Israel–Palestine conflict. Figure 9.1 describes three Muslim understandings of war and peace; two (the left and the centrist position) are discussed in the following chapter while the first is the focus of this chapter.

Sayyid Qutb on *jihad*

Qutb's *Milestones* (*ma'alim fil tariq*) (also called *Signposts*) was first published in 1964. Alongside Mawdudi's writing on *jihad*, it has been a hugely influential text. He also discussed *jihad* in Volumes 8 and 9 of his *In the Shadow of the Qu'ran* (2001) but *Milestones*, available in electronic medium on the Internet, is the most important and accessible of all Qutb's writing. Qutb references Mawdudi in two footnotes (p. 57 and p. 81). As a consequence of publishing this book, Qutb was imprisoned (1955). Following the intervention of the then President of Iraq, President Arif, he was released in 1964. Re-arrested in August 1965, he was executed in August 1966. The English translation of the book has 303 pages and is divided into 12 chapters. This analysis focuses on Chapter Four, entitled '*Jihaad* in the cause of God' (the more conventional rendering, *jihad*, will be substituted for this version's *jihaad*). The edition used is dated 1988 (Mawdudi texts are advertised on the fly cover). Other English editions appear to follow the same pagination (this author has traced references to other

Left	Centre	Right
Progressive	**Moderate/Liberal**	**Traditionalist/Revivalist**
Islam is opposed to use of violence and is a pacifist faith. The original *jihad* was spiritual and social, not military. War in Islam's classical period was permitted due to historical circumstances but there is no permanent permission for war in Islam. The verses of the Qur'an that uphold peace, persuasion and reconciliation are eternally binding. The 'sword verses' were temporary. **Aim:** for Muslims to embrace as equals those of whatever faith or of none who share their moral and spiritual values. **Representatives:** M. M. Taha, F. Esack, M. Talbi.	Islam permits only defensive war or war fought for a just cause, such as against oppression. Civilians must not be harmed, nor places of worship damaged. Islam aspires to be the religion and the political and social system of choice for the whole world but it expands by peaceful persuasion and the inner *jihad* of spiritual renewal. **Aim:** to win the intellectual and moral argument in favour of the claims to be the 'best path'. **Representatives:** Chiragh 'Ali, M. Shaltut, Y. Qaradawi.	Islam claims the whole earth. Territory not under Islamic rule is at war with the Muslim world. Temporary truces are permitted for pragmatic reasons but when opportunity and the means allow, *jihad* as military struggle is obligatory to bring the world under God's rule. The West is engaged in a Crusade against Islam, therefore the military–civilian distinction is void and any target is legitimate. **Aim:** world domination by any means. **Representatives:** Mawdudi, Qutb, Osama bin Laden.

Figure 9.1 Three Muslim understandings of war and peace

editions to the same page in this edition). First, this analysis places Chapter Four and Qutb's view of *jihad* in the wider context of his thought. Qutb is emphatic and dramatic in describing the relationship between true believers and the world around them as a battle. *Jahiliyyah* (literally 'period of pre-Islamic ignorance' but applied by Mawdudi and Qutb to their own societies and to the West) surrounds Muslims everywhere. This is 'perhaps even deeper' than during Islam's first phase: 'Our whole environment, people's beliefs and ideas, habits and art, rules and laws – is *jahiliyyah,* even to the extent that what we consider to be Islamic culture, Islamic sources, Islamic philosophy and Islamic thought, are also constructs of *Jahiliyyah*' (p. 32). 'All existing so-called Muslim societies are ... *jahili* societies', he says (p. 152). To escape from this pervasive influence, Muslims must return to the 'pure source', which is 'the Qur'an' and learn 'the total view of the universe which the Qur'an' teaches (p. 33). All Muslims must aim to 'change the *jahili* system at its very roots – this system which is fundamentally at variance with Islam' (p. 34) and the method they must use is that of the Qur'an (p. 37). Qutb is highly critical of those Muslims who argue that before Muslims act, they must 'first perfect Islam as a theory' (p. 70). This reduces Islam to 'the level of ordinary human theories and laws', 'a mere collection of abstracts and theories' (p. 60).

Such Muslims 'want a short-cut solution to satisfy their immediate desires'. They 'remove the Divine method and outlook from' Islam's 'character', treating it like a 'man-made system of thought' (p. 72). Their approach 'is extremely dangerous', says Qutb (p. 72). Those who pursue this method may call themselves Muslims 'or their birth certificates' may 'register them as Muslims' but they cannot be called Muslim in the true sense (p. 61). Qutb argues that once Muslims have submitted to God's law, and accept '*Shari'ah* without any question', rejecting all other 'laws in any shape or form' (p. 63), they are ready to 'materialize into a practical movement' (p. 73). Islam, he says, 'addresses only those people who in principle have already submitted themselves to its authority and have repudiated all other', that is, man-made 'rules and regulations' (p. 58). Qutb stresses that as a 'practical movement' Islam proceeds in stages, each of which uses resources that are appropriate according to 'the needs of the situation and prepares the ground for the next one' (p. 99). Islam must first become 'a living reality in' people's 'hearts' (p. 74). Only an active movement can combat *jahiliyyah*, which also 'takes the form not of a "theory" but of an active movement' (p. 82). As *jahiliyyah* is supported by a visible and distinct group, by a 'living and active organization', its opponents must also represent an 'organized and a viable group' (p. 83). Only when two such forces meet can battle ensue. It is absolutely essential that Islam's theoretical foundation, belief in God's sovereignty and in God's law, 'materialize in the form of an organized and active group' that separates itself from *jahili* society and works to replace it with the Islamic system (p. 84). When Muslims, with true conviction imprinted on their hearts, assume power, they will 'proceed to formulate laws and regulations for the existing practical needs according to the general teaching of Islam' not because they have already formulated theories but because this is consistent with the Qur'anic method (p. 62). This process may take time, since the Qur'an itself 'took thirteen years to construct and strengthen the structure of faith' (p. 76). Qutb's argument is that when Muslims sincerely love God, love of the Divine Law will follow as an automatic consequence (p. 63). Muslims can trust this law to guide them in all matters, so they can act to establish its supremacy. Only the *Shari'ah* harmonizes human life, external behaviour and internal nature (p. 167). It is not necessary or possible to fully understand divine law, but it is necessary to 'obey' it (p. 165). The *'Sharia'h* which God has given to man to organize his life is also a universal law'. 'Related to the general law of the universe', it is 'harmonious with it' (p. 165). From the very instant the Islamic movement 'comes into being,' says Qutb, it 'should become a real representation and an accurate mirror of its beliefs' (p. 73). In this view, movements such as the *Jamaati-i-Islam* and the *Ikhwan-ul-Muslimin* are vanguards of right-believing and right-acting Muslims ready to assume leadership of the Muslim world when the time arises. Qutb wrote that it is 'necessary that there should be a vanguard which sets out with determination' along the road, knowing 'the starting place, the nature, the responsibilities and the ultimate purpose of' the long journey that will result in the assumption of world leadership (p. 17). This vanguard will know all the milestones along the path. Qutb stressed the importance of leadership within the ideal 'practical movement' (p. 73), at the centre of which must be a 'new leadership which first came in the person of the Prophet ... and after him was delegated to those who strove for bringing people back to God's sovereignty' (p. 84). This leadership will be totally 'independent of the *jahili* leadership' (p. 85), dedicated to abolishing all *jahili* influences on the lives of Muslims. Any member of the practical movement must 'cut off his relationship of loyalty from the *jahili* society, which he has forsaken, and from *jahili* leadership' and 'give his complete loyalty to the new Islamic movement and to the Muslim leadership' (p. 85). Qutb's representation of a battle between belief and unbelief, *jahili* societies and true Islam, is also of a battle between backwardness and civilization. Reversing the idea that Europe and the USA are advanced and the Muslim world backward, he sees the former as ignorant and uncivilized and the latter as 'by its very nature, the only civilized society' (p. 175). *Jahili* societies are backward because neither 'the *Shari'ah* nor the values prescribed by God and ordained by Him as eternal and invariable, find any place' there (p. 174). Only in Muslim society are people truly free from servitude (p. 178). Only a society that 'places the highest value on the "humanity" of man and honours the noble "human" characteristic is truly civilized' (p. 179). Only Muslim society nurtures and strengthens human values and 'characteristics progressively and guards against degeneration towards animalism' (p. 182). Only in a Muslim society are people truly free, because 'only in the Islamic way of life do all men become free from the servitude of some men to others and devote themselves to the worship of God alone' (p. 15). Only 'when all individuals are equally subject to a law which is not man-made but made by their creator' can humans claim to fulfil their highest purpose, that is, of worshipping God (p. 179). Qutb, as noted earlier, saw Western society as immoral and promiscuous, however scientifically advanced it claims to be. Islam, unlike the West, does not elevate the material over the spiritual (p. 186). Unlike the West, Islamic social life revolves around 'the family,' with proper rules about relations between men and women (p. 182). In the West, a woman's role is merely to be 'sexy and flirtatious', while in Islam it is the upbringing of children (p. 182). In short, the West, which is ruled by desire and animalistic passion, qualifies as retrogressive while Islam 'implants ... human values and morals, nurtures and strengthens them' and 'develops human characteristics progressively' (p. 182). Western democracy is too 'sterile' to lead humanity towards fulfilling human destiny. Western leadership is 'on the decline' and only a new leadership, the leadership of Islam, can take humanity forward. No man-made theory can suffice (p. 10). Citing Q3: 110, 'you are the best community', Qutb argues that it is Islam's God-given duty to assume the 'leadership of mankind' (p. 13). However, in order to assume this role, Islam must first be revived (p. 12) so that at least one Muslim country can show to the world what a genuinely Islamic society has to offer. Only then will the 'beauty of' the Islamic system be appreciated, because it will have taken 'concrete form' (p. 16). 'Only such a revivalist movement', said Qutb, 'will eventually attain to the status of world leadership, whether the distance is near or far' (p. 16).

Jihad as a gradual strategy

Qutb's chapter on Islam begins with a summary of how Muhammad received the divine 'command for *jihad*'. At first, Muhammad was called to invite his near relatives to believe in God, then his fellow residents of Makkah 'through preaching, without fighting' (p. 94). He was commanded to 'restrain himself'. Then he was 'commanded to migrate, and later permission was given to fight those who fought him', while restraining from fighting 'those who did not make war with him' (pp. 94–5). Finally, he was commanded to fight unbelief until 'God's religion was fully established'. The command for *jihad*, says Qutb, involved three categories, those 'with whom there was peace', 'the people with whom the Muslims were at war', and 'the *Dhimmis*' (p. 985). As long as those with whom a treaty existed kept it, they could not be attacked but if, despite notice being served that they had broken it, 'they persisted, then he should fight with them'. *Jihad* should be declared against Scriptuaries who openly defied Islam 'until they agree to pay *Jizyah* [tax] or accept Islam' (p. 96). According to Qutb, Muhammad was commanded not to renew an expired treaty but to 'give four months' notice of expiration' before commencing hostilities (p. 97). In this view, once the treaties that

Muhammad had ratified expired, they were not to be renewed. A permanent state of hostility then ensued between Muslims and non-Muslims, which only ends when non-Muslims accept either Islam or the status of a subjugated people. Qutb interprets the Qur'anic revelation as progressive and practical.

The early restriction of Islam's mission to preaching recognized the reality of the context in which Muhammad lived, which was a 'stage of training and preparation' (p. 118). There was at that time no 'organized government' and had permission been given for Muslims to fight, 'every house would have become a battlefield' and people would have said 'So, this is Islam' (p. 120). After the migration to Madinah, initially 'fighting was also prohibited'. The Prophet wanted to 'conserve all his efforts to combat the Quraishi, whose relentless opposition was a great obstacle in spreading Islam' (p. 123). When permission was given to Muhammad to fight against all who refused to accept Islam (Q9: 5) the Muslims were ready to engage in offensive action in the cause of God. Thus, Muslims were 'first restrained from fighting; then they were permitted to fight; they were commanded to fight against aggressors; and finally they were commanded to fight against all polytheists' (p. 115). Verses associated with each stage must be seen as part of a progressive revelation and must not be clumsily mixed or treated as if 'every verse of the Qur'an ... were the final principle of this religion' (p. 100). By arguing that a verse permitting only defensive war (such as Q2: 190) or only war against oppression (2: 193), or a verse that permits only preaching, represents the totality of the Islamic position, Muslims lay 'down their spiritual and rational arms in defeat' (p. 100). The 'command to refrain from fighting ... was a temporary stage in a long journey' (p. 117). Restraint was a 'question of strategy rather than of principle' (p. 139) and the idea that Muslims can never commit aggression ('udwan), says Qutb, is misguided and dangerous. Rather, the jihad bis saif (striving through sword; p. 110) is a legitimate instrument in the hands of Muslims, who have a 'God-given right to step forward and take control of the political authority' (p. 139) and to pursue the goal of securing 'complete freedom for every man throughout the world by releasing him from servitude to other human beings so that he may serve his God, who is One and Who has no associates' (p. 128). This 'is in itself sufficient reason for jihad' (ibid.). Qutb argues that the term 'polytheist' or 'infidel', identified as legitimate targets of jihad in Q9: 5, includes those who worship their nation, or man-made laws. Like Mawdudi, Qutb dismisses the view that jihad can only be defensive. Here, like Mawdudi, he directs his argument against liberal Muslims as well as against Orientalist scholars. He sees both as enemies of revivalist Islam, and regards them as allies of each other (p. 138). Muslims whose 'defeated mentality' leads them to claim that Islam only has a right to defend itself but never to take the initiative have 'adopted the Western concept of "religion" which is merely a name for "belief" of the heart', with 'no relation to the practical affairs of life' (p. 138). Islam is rather a total system of life, and jihad 'a name for striving to make this system of life dominant in the world' (p. 139). This system cannot be confined to 'geographical and racial limits' (p. 134) nor is it 'a heritage of any particular race or country', but is 'God's religion ... for the whole world'. As such, it has the right to 'destroy all obstacles in the form of institutions and traditions which limit man's freedom of choice' (p. 136), and it also has the right to 'take the initiative' (p. 136). No doubt Muslims must defend themselves against aggression (p. 132) since *jahili* society will always 'rise against' Islam 'for its own preservation'. However, to reduce *jihad* to self-defence is to 'diminish the greatness of the Islamic way of life' (p. 130) and leaves open the possibility that mankind will be left 'on the whole earth in evil, in chaos and in servitude to lords other than God' (p. 133). *Jihad* does not have to be justified by any particular condition; rather, *jihad* is justifiable as the instrument of choice for establishing God's authority on earth, for arranging human affairs according to the true guidance provided by God and for abolishing 'all Satanic forces' (p. 127). Its 'reason exists in the nature of ... the actual conditions it finds in human society, and not merely in the necessity for defence, which may be temporary and of limited extent' (p. 129). Qutb sees Q4: 74–6, 8: 38–40, 9: 5 and 9: 29–32 (pp. 125–7) as a 'clear' mandate for *jihad*, and says that 'taking the initiative' is of the 'very nature of Islam' (p. 133).

Islam and enforced conversion

Qutb responds to the often-repeated criticism that the sword spread Islam, as the Orientalists argue: 'The Orientalists have painted a picture of Islam as a violent movement which imposed its beliefs upon people by the sword' (p. 138). He argues that this is a non-issue. The Qur'an prohibits forced conversion (Q2: 256) but not the use of the sword to extend Muslim rule, or to 'annihilate all those political and material powers which stand between people and Islam' (p. 102). The charge that Islam spread by the sword is a very old criticism, found in al-Kindy, the ninth-century Christian apologist, who had it that Muhammad 'used no other argument ... but the sword' (1882: 100). Nineteenth-century Christian literature characterized Islam as the religion of the sword and Christianity as the religion of peace. Karl Pfander (1803–66), a German-born Church of England missionary in India and Turkey, concluded his famous *Mizan-al-Haq* (Balance of Truth) (original 1829) with an invitation to choose between Jesus Christ who had gone around 'doing good' and who said 'love your enemies', and Muhammad the Prophet of 'the sword' who said 'slay your enemies' (1910: 368; an electronic version is available at *http://answering-islam.org/Books/Pfander/Balance/p366.htm*. Arnold's *The Preaching of Islam* (1913), however, refuted the charge: 'The spread of' Islam 'over so vast a portion of the globe' was 'due to various causes, social, political and religious: but among these, one of the most powerful factors at work in the production of this stupendous result, has been the un-remitted labours of

Muslim missionaries' (p. 3). Qutb argues that Muslims who, in order to refute Orientalist criticism, reduced Islamic *jihad* to defensive war, misunderstand the basic 'nature of Islam' (that is, as a unity of religion and state) and its 'function', and deny that Islam 'has a right to take the initiative for human freedom' (p. 138).

Mawdudi's and Qutb's impact on contemporary Muslim life

Mawdudi and Qutb are credited with being the inspiration behind much Islamist activity, including terrorism. Ruthven (2002) identifies Qutb as 'the intellectual father of modern Islamist terrorism' (p. 71) and as the 'inspiration' behind 9/11. 'Mawdudi's writings', he says, 'exercised an important influence on Sayyid Qutb'. Mawdudi and Qutb advocated that Muslims living under any government that did not implement *Shari'ah* could legitimately oppose that regime, a Kharijite doctrine that Ibn Taymiyya did much to revive. Qutb especially emphasized that Muslims can take the initiative in using violence and do not have to wait until they are attacked. Qutb and Mawdudi spent much of their lives in opposition to the governments of Egypt and Pakistan. Both were imprisoned. Both were sentenced to death, although Mawdudi's death sentence was commuted to life imprisonment. However, neither man was personally involved in violent actions or in the planning of violent acts. Their respective movements, too, use constitutional means to pursue their Islamist agendas, and have won seats in elections (the Jamaati currently share power in Bangladesh). Sometimes, both parties have been banned. It is apt to describe Mawdudi and Qutb, as Ruthven does, as intellectual fathers of terrorism rather than as actors in any violent episode, although Qutb was accused of plotting to assassinate President Nasser. Their understanding of *jihad* sees the sword verses abrogating the verses of persuasion, which Peters (1977) describes as the view of the majority of Muslim scholars (see Figure 10.1 below) (pp. 82–3, n. 35). They justify action against Muslims whom they deem have forfeited the right to be called 'Muslim'. They justify unprovoked attacks, although in this understanding, such attacks are in fact provoked by the active and continual opposition of the non-Muslim world to Islam. Bin Laden soaked up the ideas of Qutb when he first made contact with the Muslim Brotherhood as a student at the King Abdul-Aziz University (he graduated in 1981). Bergen identifies this as 'the ideological underpinning of bin Laden's followers, who target not only the West but also such Muslim regimes as Saudi Arabia, which they regard as apostates' (2001: 52). Ruthven (2002) points out that other *jihads* also inspire contemporary Islamists, such as the Sudanese *jihad* of Mahdi Muhammad Ahmad of 1882 against the British and the Ottomans. The Mahdi (al-Sadiq's grandfather) condemned the Ottomans for judging 'by other than God's revelation', thus they could be fought as if they were unbelievers (p. 44).

Islamic Jihad and al-Qaeda

Two of the earliest men to translate Qutb's ideology into action were Abd al-Salam Faraj and Ayman al-Zawahiri. Faraj broke away from the Muslim Brotherhood in 1979 when he penned the tract *The Neglected Obligation* (*al-Farida al-Gha'ibah*) and founded the Islamic Jihad organization because the Brotherhood was not sufficiently militant. A major theme of *al-Farida* is the re-establishment of the Khalifate. On 6 October 1981, Jihad group member Khalid Islambouli assassinated President Sadat, exclaiming 'I have killed Pharaoh, and I do not fear death' (Bergen. 2001: 219). A copy of the tract was found on his body. Sadat's assassins also cited Ibn Taymiyya in defence of their act of killing an 'apostate'. Sadat's signing of the 1979 Camp David Peace accord with Israel was regarded as treason. Al-Zawahiri, a medical graduate, joined the Brotherhood at age 15 and may have been involved in a 1965 assassination attempt on Nasser. In 1980 he became a leading member of Jihad. Imprisoned for three years after Sadat's assassination, he reconvened Jihad on his release in 1985, moving to Saudi Arabia and then to Pakistan, where Islambouli's brother joined him. Assisting in aiding the Taliban and other *mujahideen* in Afghanistan, he joined forces with Bin Laden's al-Qaeda. Bin Laden, with his privileged and wealthy background, was then travelling backwards and forwards between Saudi and Afghanistan with equipment and Arab funds to finance the anti-Soviet *jihad*. His originally Yemeni family own a construction company worth in excess of $5 billion; al-Qaeda's annual budget is $30 million (*9/11 Report*, p. 14). According to some sources, bin Laden had contact at this time with the USA's CIA and may have received training from them (disputed by Bergen 2001, p. 69). Bin Laden founded al-Qaeda (the base) in 1989 as a recruiting and training organization, which also has a coordinating role linking other Islamist groups in a global network. With the end of Russian involvement in Afghanistan, bin Laden was interested in pursuing new jihadist agendas elsewhere in the Muslin world. Recruits are attracted not only from the Muslim world but also from the Muslim Diaspora. Bin Laden grew increasingly critical of the Saudi Government's alliance with the USA, especially of the presence of US troops on Saudi territory and of the Saudis' involvement in the Gulf War. By 1991 he was banned from entering Saudi. That year, he moved his headquarters to the Sudan. In several *fatwas* (also signed by al-Zawahiri) he called for a universal Muslim *jihad* against the USA. Like many revivalists, he regards traditional *ulama* as discredited, assuming their role himself. Muslims, he says, must terrorize and kill Americans and plunder their money wherever they find them. Citing Ibn Taymiyya, he calls on Muslims to 'join forces and support each other and to get rid of the main *Kufr* who is controlling the countries of the Islamic world' (1996). Man-made laws have been 'put forward in Saudi' permitting what Islam forbids and within 'the vicinity of the Holy Mosque in the Holy Land' itself. Civilians are not to be exempted. The aim of US aggression towards Iraq is to divert attention away from

Jerusalem and the mistreatment of Muslims there. The USA is in alliance with the Jew's state. The al-Aqsa Mosque must be liberated from the grip of the Jews and their US allies. He cites the sword verses. In 1998, he established the World Islamic Front for Jihad against the Jews and the Crusaders and Islamic Jihad formally affiliated with al-Qaeda (Bergen, p. 104). In his 1996 *fatwa*, he argued that any treaty that exists between the Saudi state and the USA is cancelled because Americans have shed Muslim blood in their aggression against Iraq. 'Terrorizing' Americans, while 'they are carrying arms on our land, is a legitimate and morally demanded duty', said the *fatwa*. Eventually expelled from Sudan in 1996, he returned to Afghanistan. He described this as a *hijrah*, as migration from an inhospitable to a hospitable land and to one from where *jihad* can be conducted. He urged Muslims to cause Americans and Israelis 'as much harm as can be possibly achieved' (Bergen, p. 103). After the US and allied invasion of Afghanistan in 2001, al-Qaeda has been driven underground and bin Laden's whereabouts are unknown. Al-Zawahiri (who often interprets for bin Laden) is credited as the chief strategist of al-Qaeda, and is said to have masterminded its terrorist programme. Bin Laden is the organization's charismatic leader and bankroller (see Erikson 2002). As well as fighting against the Soviets and the USA and allies in Afghanistan, al-Qaeda aided the Muslims of Bosnia (see Bergen, p. 93) and is currently involved in Chechnya where one of the leading Muslim combatants, known as Khattab, is said to enjoy a 'father–son relationship with bin Laden' (Bergen, p. 238). Al-Qaeda has been credited with the following acts of violence against US and other targets:

- 1993: the bombing attack on the World Trade Center, New York, for which Sheikh Omar Abdel Rahman was convicted. A leader of Egyptian Jihad, Omar received CIA assistance while recruiting for the anti-Soviet war in Afghanistan.
- 1995: truck bomb attack on the Egyptian Embassy in Pakistan
- 1996: 19 US soldiers killed in Saudi Arabia
- 1997: an attack in Luxor, Egypt. 60 tourists died.
- 1998: bombing of US embassies in Kenya and Tanzania
- 2000: attack on the USS Cole in the Yemen
- 2001: suicide attacks on the World Trade Center, New York, and the Pentagon, Washington, DC. The manual, which bin Laden is believed to have written, found among the terrorists' possessions, exhorted them to recite the Qur'an and to remember that there was but a short time before 'their marriage in heaven' (with the promised virgins). Qutb stressed that the *jihadist* will already have won a battle in his heart between self and Satan (1988: 131). After touching the Qur'an, they were to touch their passports, bodies and possessions in order to bless the enterprise.
- 2003: four simultaneous bomb attacks in Riyadh

The Egyptian Jihad has been credited with the attempted assassination of

Egypt's Foreign Minister Hassan al-Alfi in August 1993 and of Prime Minister Atef Sedky in November 1993. An attack on the US embassy in 1998 was thwarted. The Jemaah Islamiah group, affiliated to al-Qaeda, carried out the Bali bombing on 12 October 2002, in which 202 people died. Over 30 Islamic militants have recently been tried and convicted on terrorist-related charges in Indonesia. The Saudi al-Qaeda cell's beheading of captured US civilian worker Paul Johnson in Saudi Arabia on 18 June 2004 was justified by citing Q47: 3–6: 'When you encounter the infidels, strike off their heads till you have made great slaughter among them'. Classically, some scholars have interpreted this verse as of universal validity while others restrict it to the context of the battle of Badr (in which it was revealed). Others regard it as applicable to anyone captured in war. Ruthven (2002) points out that al-Qaeda enjoys considerable support in Saudi and comments that a disproportionate number (fifteen) of the nineteen terrorists who died on 9/11 'were Saudi citizens from the mountainous province of Asir, a formerly semi-independent Sultanate conquered by Faisal ibn 'Abd al-'Aziz Sa'ud (later King Faisal) in the 1920s and annexed by the Kingdom in 1930' (p. 289). He suggests that such men have good reason to dislike the Saudi regime, in addition to their different ideological understanding of how an Islamic state should be governed. Bin Laden considered the Taliban regime (in power (1996–2002) under Mullah Omar, whose interpretation of *Shari'ah* was absolute, to be the world's only legitimate Islamic state.

A global network

Other Islamist groups that share both al-Qaeda's goal, to establish a worldwide Islamic entity governed by traditional *Shari'ah*, and its method, violent acts against the enemy, include the Palestinian Hamas organization, the various *Ahl-e-Hadith* movements active in Kashmir, the Egyptian Jihad, the Lebanese Hezbollah, the Algerian GIA and Abu Sayyaf in the Philippines. Upwards of eight organizations are active among Thailand's 4 per cent Muslim population, demanding an independent Muslim state in the south-west. The immediate aim of an organization is often the overthrow of an existing political order and the establishment of an Islamic government in a specific context, such as in the Lebanon, Algeria, Kashmir or Egypt, or the creation of an independent Muslim state such as on Mindanao or in the south-west of Thailand (see Kuppuswamy 2004). Many of these local or regional organizations share the wider aim of re-establishing the universal Islamic Khalifate, perhaps region by region. In their own understanding, aggression against civilian targets (such as those who died on 9/11) is justified, as they interpret Q9: 5 as permitting the killing of any 'enemy' whether or not they are armed or engaged in direct military action. Lewis (2003) says that bin Laden himself has aspiration to the Khalifate (p. xvii).

Discussion topics

- How would you define terrorism?

- Is one person's terrorist another's freedom fighter?

- Can you identify any groups that you would consider to be freedom fighters that others regard as terrorist? What are your reasons for describing the group as freedom fighters?

- Do you regard the suicide missions of Palestinian youths as terrorism? If not, why?

- How would you categorize assassinations and attempted assassinations that have been carried out by Western intelligence and security agents? The CIA's 25-year-old ban on assassinations does not apply, according to Bush, to the war on terrorism. In November 2002 the CIA claimed to have assassinated al-Qaeda suspects in the Yemen. Peace and Justice activists condemned this as a blatant use of terrorist methods by the world's most powerful state. What do you think?

The case of Palestine

The entry of the term terrorist into modern vocabulary is largely the result of the 1968 hijacking of the first commercial airliner by the Popular Front for the Liberation of Palestine. Several Islamist organizations linked with terrorism emerged as a result of the Palestinian situation. The Palestinian situation is a critical issue throughout the Muslim world, as indicated by Mahathir Mohamad, the Malaysian Prime Minister's speech at the 10th Islamic Summit Conference, Putrajaya, 16 October 2003, when he castigated the world's 1.3 billion Muslims for their failure to unite or to restore the honour of Islam or to defeat 'a few million Jews'. The 'Palestinian issue' can be summed up as the creation of the State of Israel in 1948, the capture in 1967 by Israel of Jerusalem and the West Bank (as well as Sinai), and as Muslim demands for the creation of a Palestinian state or for the total annihilation of Israel.

Competing myths

Two competing myths lie behind the Israeli–Palestinian conflict. Neither myth is wholly false but the stories they tell are biased and one-sided. One is broadly a pro-Israeli or pro-Jewish myth while the other is pro-Palestinian. The first myth is well told by Uris's 1984 novel that depicts Palestine as a forgotten, neglected and not very important province of the Ottoman Empire (before the start of the British mandate). In the novel, most of the land was unused and owned by distant landlords in Beirut or Damascus who were only too happy to sell to enterprising Jews. Uris writes:

> the Holy Land lay gasping, the rocks of her fields protruding like the baked bones of monolithic mastodons, or from mucky, diseased swamps. As a minor backwater district of the Syrian province, Palestine had been devalued to bastardy and orphanhood. (1984: 16).

These Jewish settlers soon turned desert into profitable farmland. Thus the expression 'a land without a people for a people without a land'. Arabs in the novel are deceitful, lazy, jealous and rather stupid while the Jews are courageous, kind, generous and very clever. In this version of history, there was no solid Palestinian identity before the creation of the state of Israel. Palestinians, however, would have been welcome to stay in the State of Israel, which was not to be a religious but a secular and democratic state. Unfortunately, their own leaders deceived the Palestinians, who were given false hope of a Palestinian state or of a state under Muslim control. The Grand Mufti of Jerusalem (who had hoped and worked for a German victory), in this myth, promised the Palestinians that the Arabs would drive the Jews into the sea by invading the fledgling Jewish state on all sides (from Syria, Jordan and Egypt). They were encouraged to vacate their land, so that the invading armies could sweep into Israel more easily. However, the combined Arab armies failed to defeat Israel in 1948 and again in 1967. Instead, the Israelis occupied territory on all three sides. Meanwhile, the Palestinians remained in refugee camps, receiving comparatively little help from their fellow Muslim and Arab hosts. The myth of a Palestinian identity and of a lost Palestinian state was created in order to feed and fuel resistance to Israeli occupation. The rhetoric of driving the Jews into the sea became a standard phrase of anti-Israeli vocabulary. The religious element, the claim that Palestine is sacred or holy for Muslims is, in this view, if not an invention (it is rarely denied that Jerusalem has some significance for Muslims), downplayed as a historical reality. It is depicted as a recent invention to match or to counter the Jewish claim that Israel is the land promised and given them by God, to which they have finally returned. This myth also stresses that Israel is a democracy, surrounded by countries with limited democracy or dictatorial rule. In this myth, the Israeli–Palestinian conflict is really about a local land dispute between two ethnic groups, Jews and Arabs, and the Islamic religious dimension is an invention of the Muslim Arabs to attract wider international support to what is essentially a nationalist cause, although that description is also suspect. Supporters of this myth suggest that Arabs who stayed in Israel in 1948 are much better off than those who left and stress that they are full and equal citizens of the State of Israel (about 18 per cent of Israelis are Arabs).

The second myth is that there was a very strong Palestinian attachment to the land prior to the creation of the State of Israel. As *al-Quds* (the Holy), Jerusalem is of immense religious importance. The refugees did not leave voluntarily but were forced to vacate their land by Jewish militants, who conducted mopping up operations. In this view, Palestinians were forced to flee by threats, intimidation and violence. In this view, the creation of Israel was a neo-colonial project. Zionism is as much a Western as a Jewish ideology. It was part of a systematic attempt by the West to destabilize and to fragment the Muslim world after the defeat of the Ottoman Empire. The Jewish state is strongly supported not only by the Jews of the West but by Christians too. This is at the expense of Islam. One of Islam's most sacred sites, the *haram* mosque of al-Aqsa (see Q17: 1), is under non-Muslim control. As part of *dar-al-Islam* that has become *dar-al-harb*, it is Muslims' duty to engage in a *jihad* to restore Islamic rule. Jerusalem's capture by Khalif 'Umar in 638 CE was a sign of divine blessing. Its loss to the Crusaders in 1099 was a sign of God's disfavour. Its loss to the Israelis in 1967 is an insult that must be avenged, as was the loss of 1099 when Saladin retook the city (1187). Thus, Bin Laden's 1996 *fatwa* uses the term Crusader for today's occupiers of Jerusalem:

> It should not be hidden from you that the people of Islam had suffered from aggression, iniquity and injustice imposed on them by the Zionist–Crusaders alliance and their collaborators.

Israel in this view is the creation and agent of the West and part of a concerted international effort to undermine Islam and its place in the world. Bin Laden also describes Saudi as America's 'agent'. Mahathir Mohamed (2003) argued that the West has only been able to 'excise Muslim land to create the state of Israel to solve their Jewish problem' because of Muslim disunity. Muslims are weak when divided. Regardless of what sect or school they belong to, they will be targets for Western aggression, 'they will attack and kill us, invade our lands, bring down our governments whether we are Sunnis or Syiahs [Shi'a], Alawait or Druze'. Positive thinking is required; Muslims must not believe that they will always be 'oppressed and dominated by the Europeans and the Jews' but should unite on at least this one issue. He also argued that Muslims need to 'use their brains' to solve the Palestinian problem, since they are 'up against a people who think', who survived 2,000 years of pogroms 'not by hitting back, but by thinking'. He strongly hinted that the Jews are responsible for controlling the international order and therefore for the economic and imperial marginalizing of Muslims. However, the Prime Minister said that not all non-Muslims are to be considered enemies; 'even among the Jews there are many who do not approve of what the Israelis are doing'.

Investigating the myths

The area that is now Israel–Palestine was under Ottoman rule from 1517 until 1917. For much of that period it was part of a larger administrative unit known as Greater Syria, governed from Damascus. This territory included modern Syria, Lebanon and Israel–Palestine. The chief officials were the Pashas of Sidon and Damascus. The former lived in Acre and governed the coastal area and Galilee. The Pasha of Damascus governed central Palestine and Jerusalem as well as Syria. In 1887–8, the province was divided into three: Acre, Nablus and Jerusalem. The latter was given special status because of its religious significance. Direct rule replaced rule from Damascus. Although ruled from a distance and as part of a larger province, the local Arabs referred to their region as *Filistin*, and had an emotional attachment to their land.

During World War I, when Sharif Hussein of Makkah, although a protégé of the Ottoman emperor, allied himself with the British, he did so because he was promised an Arab kingdom including Palestine in return. However, as Hedworth (2004) points out, the Sharif had no formal treaty to support this, only letters from Sir Henry MacMahon in Cairo (p. 4). After the end of the war, the allies divided the Ottoman Empire up between themselves, with Syria and the Lebanon under the French and what became Iraq, Jordan and Palestine under the British. Libya went to Italy. Lebanon gained independence in 1943, Syria in 1946 and Libya in 1951. The occupying powers had a brief to establish indigenous government in Syria and Lebanon. Britain carved Iraq and Jordan from out of its mandated territory as rewards for the Sharif's sons, whom they installed as kings. Palestine was from the start treated as a peculiar case. In 1917, Lord Balfour, British Foreign Secretary, who had been at the 1878 Conference in Berlin when Turkey's finances were subjected to European control and some territory was confiscated, penned his Declaration that Her Majesty's Government:

> view with favour the establishment in Palestine of a national home for the Jewish people, and will use their best endeavours to facilitate the achievement of this object, it being clearly understood that nothing shall be done which may prejudice the civil and religious rights of existing non-Jewish communities in Palestine, or the rights and political status enjoyed by Jews in any other country.

This is why Palestine has been called the 'twice promised' land – since the British promised it to the Arabs and to the Jews. Balfour's Declaration gave the Zionist movement's dream of a state secured by international law, preferably in Israel where the second *Aliyah* had only just finished, official backing. The second *Aliyah* was 1904–14; the first *Aliyah* was 1882–1904. Both saw Jewish migrants settle in Palestine. There has been much speculation about why Balfour decided to support the Zionist cause. Some think there was a history of British support for the idea of restoring Israel to the Jews for a complex variety of philosophical, religious and imperial motives. Some think that British Zionism (the idea that the British people will have a major role in the events of the End Time) played a part, or simply the imperialist desire to retain a foothold in the Middle East through the Jewish people with their strong business and cultural ties to Europe. The result was a mandate from the League of Nations (24 July 1922) that empowered the British government to put 'into effect the declaration originally made on November 2nd, 1917 by the Government of His Britannic Majesty, and adopted by' the allies 'in favour of the establishment in Palestine of a national home for the Jewish people', while not prejudicing the 'civil and religious rights of existing non-Jewish communities in Palestine'. This mandate attracted very little formal Arab recognition (Hedworth 2004: 7).

Throughout the mandate period, the British did relatively little to carry out the promise contained in the Balfour Declaration but made some effort to be even-handed in their treatment of the Jewish and non-Jewish communities. Many mandate officials were old Arab-hands (that is, had served in Arab countries), spoke Arabic (and not Hebrew) and if anything were sympathetic to Arab concerns. Arabs, Christians and Muslims opposed Zionism and the goal of a Jewish state and demanded independence at their Congresses in 1921, 1922 and 1923 (15 per cent of delegates were Christian; Hedworth, p. 13), as well as in delegations to London. In practice, the British may have become aware of the difficulty of protecting the rights of both communities if a Jewish state was established. Friction between the Jewish settlers and their Arab neighbours resulted in the formation of a Jewish defence force as early as 1907. Riots broke out in 1929. By 1936, the two parties were engaged in a guerrilla war. Hedworth (2004) argues that Arabs felt they were educationally and financially disadvantaged. The British only spent the little funding available from tax revenue on education and social welfare for the Arabs while Jews enjoyed the support of rich philanthropists from the Jewish Diaspora (pp. 25, 30). The British tried to curtail Jewish immigration after the end of the 1930s in a White Paper issued in 1939. In 1946, an Anglo–US Committee of Enquiry decided that a two-state solution would be better, with an international zone around Jerusalem. Britain asked the newly formed United Nations to resolve the issue, declaring that their mandate was now unworkable. The UN decided that the British mandate should end and drafted a resolution, 181, to put the two-state strategy into effect. A two-thirds majority passed Resolution 181 on 29 November 1947. Remorse for the Nazi extermination of 6 million Jews persuaded most countries to vote for the resolution. Others were planning to extend UN Trusteeship. However, on 14 May 1948, a provisional Israeli Government declared independence, based on resolution 181, and was immediately recognized by US President Truman, who reportedly said that he had hundreds of thousands of Zionists among his constituents but not the same number of Arabs. The size of the independent Israel was only a fraction of the original British mandate. The British abstained on Resolution 181 (with nine other countries) and withdrew their army on 15 May, the day the Arab invasion began. The Arab states rejected the UN plan (Afghanistan, Egypt, Iran, Iraq, Lebanon, Pakistan, Saudi Arabia, Syria, Turkey and Yemen voted against 181). Fighting ended in July when the UN threatened to cite the Arab nations with a breach of its Charter.

In 1958, Palestinians in Jordan, led by Yasser Arafat (who was born in

Cairo in 1929 of Palestinian parents), an engineering graduate from Cairo University, formed *al-Fatah* and advocated armed struggle against Israel. Arafat was involved in organizing raids into Israel. In 1964, the Arab League sponsored the formation of the Palestinian Liberation Organization, which initially favoured a more diplomatic approach than *al-Fatah*. Some see the early PLO as a puppet of the Arab regimes, which appeared to support the Palestinian cause but lacked any real intent of proactively working for a Palestinian state. However, the PLO effectively brought together disparate groups working for the Palestinian cause and gave the movement an international voice. In 1967, the 6-day war (June 5th to 10th) saw Israel capture and occupy the Gaza Strip, the West Bank, the Sinai and the Golan Heights. As a result, the Suez Canal was also closed to shipping for many years, at Egypt's cost. Fighting began when Syria fired at Israeli armoured vehicles in the demilitarized zone. Egypt then massed troops in the Sinai and blocked Israeli shipping in the Gulf of Aqaba. On 5 June 1967 Israel launched a pre-emptive strike against the Egyptian Air Force. Jordan and Syrian troops joined the Egyptian offensive. Resolution 242 called for Israeli withdrawal and proposed a 'land for peace' formula. Instead, Jewish settlements started to be built, and land farmed, in what was referred to as Greater Israel. Some Jews argued that all this land was historically part of their promised land. Following Arab humiliation in the 6-day war, the PLO adopted a more radical stance and *al-Fatah* emerged as the dominant group. Arafat was elected Chairman of the PLO in 1969.

In October 1973, in the Yom Kippur War, Egypt retook the Suez, Syria the Golan Heights but Israel retaliated and regained this territory. On 26 March 1979 President Anwar Sadat of Egypt and the Israelis signed a Peace Treaty (finalized under US President Jimmy Carter at Camp David) and the Sinai was returned to Egypt. Egypt recognized Israel's right to exist and full diplomatic, trade and travel arrangements followed between the two countries. Arafat had developed the PLO into an efficient organization, with its own militia. In 1971, following the assassination by members of the PLO faction, Black September, of Jordan's Prime Minister, Wasfi Tel, Arafat and the PLO were expelled from Jordan. They moved to Lebanon. Lewis (2003) links the following non-peaceful incidents with the PLO's Black September: the hijacking of three aircraft, one Swiss, one British, one American in 1970; the murder of Israeli athletes at the Munich Olympics in 1972; the seizure of the Saudi embassy in Sudan and the murder of two Americans and one Belgian in 1973; the takeover of the Italian cruise ship, *Achille Lauro*, in 1985 and the murder of a crippled passenger (p. 126). The PLO was forced to flee from Lebanon by the Israeli invasion of 1982.

The flood of Palestinian refugees from Israel into Lebanon resulted in an increase of the Muslim population and changed the historical balance between Christians and Muslims. A bitter civil war ensued (usually dated 1975–90) that pitted Druze, Shi'a, Sunnis and Christians against each other. War started on 13 April 1973 when a Palestinian bus was ambushed in a mainly Christian area of Beirut following the killing of Christian Phalangists (members of a political and military movement founded in 1936) earlier that day. In 1976, the Lebanese President called on Syrian and other Arab troops to help to end the war. As a result of the bitter conflict, the word 'Shi'a' also entered Western popular vocabulary. The Hizbullah (Party of Allah), or the Organization of the Oppressed on Earth, or the Islamic Jihad for the Liberation of Palestine, was one of the groups that developed out of the civil war, founded in 1982 by Shi'a supporters of the Iranian Islamic revolution with assistance from members of the Iranian Revolutionary Guard. Its leader, Sheikh Muhammad Hussein Fadlallah, is chief *mujtahid* of the Shi'a in Lebanon. It aims both to create an Iranian-style Islamic state in the Lebanon, followed by a pan-Islamic republic headed by religious scholars, and to destroy the State of Israel. Activities have included bombing the US Beirut embassy (1984), the kidnapping and detention of Western hostages and the attack on the Israeli embassy in Argentina in 1992. Its 1985 Political Platform includes eradication of Western influence as a goal. The Israeli army invaded in June 1982 (the invasion, called Operation Peace for Galilee by Israel, had Phalangist support) in retaliation for Hizbullah and PLO cross-border raids on Israel. The war ended in May 1983 after UN intervention, and by June 1985 most Israeli troops had been withdrawn. The Lebanese civil war ended officially in 1990 when Taif agreement transferred power from the traditionally Maronite Christian Presidency to a cabinet of Christian–Muslim representatives on a 50–50 basis. Although the agreement called for the withdrawal of foreign troops, some 35,000 Syrian troops and some Israeli troops remain. In 1981, Israel voted to permanently annex the Golan Heights. Consequently, Syria has indicated that it is only prepared to negotiate non-belligerence with Israel, not a comprehensive peace. Syria views the whole of Israel, not just the territory acquired in 1967, as 'occupied Arab territory'.

The PLO was not explicitly a religious organization. Christians as well as Muslims have been prominent members, although during its period in Lebanon it was accused of anti-Christian policies. According to some, it wants a Christian as well as a Jew-free Palestine. Sheikh Ahmed Yasin, a Muslim Brotherhood member, founded one of the most influential Islamist resistance movements, Hamas (Islamic Resistance Movement, or Harakat al-Muqawama al-Islamia), in 1987 at the start of the first *Intifada* (uprising). On 22 March 2004 a helicopter-launched missile killed Yassin as he left a mosque in the Gaza strip. Hamas aims to replace Israel with an Islamic state and has attacked civilian and military targets, often using suicide bombers. It has worked through mosques and social welfare institutions to recruit members. It is said to receive funds from Iran but most of its money comes from Palestinians living in Europe and North America.

Many felt that diplomacy was failing to achieve results, since little had changed in the refugee camps or in the economically deprived towns of the Gaza Strip and West Bank, despite Camp David. Frustrated, people took to the streets, throwing stones at Israeli soldiers, rioting and striking. Suicide bombings were directed at Israeli targets, civilian and military. Known as the first *Intifada* (uprising), this broke out in 1987, spearheaded by young men and boys. In retaliation, universities were closed, activists were deported and economic activities restricted. The international community's response was the Oslo Declaration of Principle, signed in Washington, DC, on 13 September 1993. By 1994, Arafat had received the Nobel Peace Prize together with Israeli Prime Minister, Yitzhak Rabin (1922–95) and Foreign Minister Shimon Peres. Arafat's relentless work and wide travels on behalf of the Palestinian people had made him something of an international celebrity. Heads of State and Government often treated him as if he was already a President. Negotiated by the Norwegians, the Oslo Accord saw Israel and the PLO agree to mutual recognition. The PLO agreed to remove reference to the destruction of Israel from its charter and to renounce violence. In fact, Arafat had pledged to do this in a speech he gave at the UN in Geneva in 1988, which gave impetus to the peace process. Some of this impetus was lost after 1991, when the PLO supported Iraq during the Gulf War. Arafat's commitment to peace, and his acceptance of Israel's right to exist, have both been questioned. For example, in 1994, in Johannesburg, South Africa, he spoke of a *jihad* to liberate Jerusalem, which he and PLO spokesmen later explained referred to a peaceful *jihad* for Jerusalem.

Nonetheless, the Oslo Accord saw the establishment of the Palestinian National Authority (West Bank and Gaza), of which Arafat was elected President (1996). On 26 October 1994, Israel and Jordan signed a peace treaty, settling the West Bank border and normalizing relations. In return, Jordan received billions in US aid. On 24 November 1995 a right-wing Israeli assassinated Rabin. In September 2000 violence broke out in the PNA in response to the visit of Israel's Prime Minister, Ariel Sharon, to the Temple Mount (al-Aqsa Mosque). During this second *Intifada*, over 2000 Palestinians lost their lives and at least 700 Israelis were victims of suicide bombings and car ambushes. Israeli retaliation killed 15 Israeli Arabs. In March 2002, Israel began to build a Defensive Wall around its West Bank Settlements. In May 2003 the USA, the European Union, the Russian Federation and the UN published its Road Map for Peace in the Middle East, which set out a timetable and goals to establish an independent, sovereign and secure Palestinian State while also protecting Israel's existence and security. It aims for a complete and comprehensive peace by 2005. Until shortly before his death in November 2004 when he was allowed to travel to Paris, Arafat was confined to his HQ bunker in Ramallah which had been repeatedly bombed by Israeli troops avenging suicide attacks. As the PNA grows weaker, Hamas is reported to be gathering more and more support among disillusioned Palestinians.

Analysis

The leadership of the PLO, the Israeli government and the leaders of Jordan and Saudi Arabia have endorsed the Road Map. However, Hamas, Hizbullah, al-Qaeda and many Muslims around the world still aim for the destruction of Israel, as does the Syrian and Iranian regimes. 'The battle is open and war between us and them is open,' said senior Hamas leader Abdul Aziz al Rantissi following the assassination of Sheikh Ahmed Yassin. 'Today they killed an Islamic symbol,' he added (BBC News, 22 March 2004). Hamas's charter declares that 'peace initiatives and so-called peaceful solutions' contravene the principles of what it calls the Islamic Resistance Movement. Only *jihad* can solve the problem, it says. The continued presence of Israeli settlements in what would be Palestinian sovereign territory under the Road Map has been described as a 'road-block'. Resolution of the status of Jerusalem, which both sides claim as their historic capital, too, remains problematic. The Map offers no detail although some involved in various Middle East peace initiatives suggest that Jerusalem be jointly controlled and overseen by an international committee, as a cultural patrimony of humanity.

Moderates on both sides may reach mutually acceptable compromise; hardliners are unlikely to budge much from their entrenched positions. On the Jewish side, these are: to retain all settlements in Greater Israel and full and sovereign control of Jerusalem as Israel's indivisible capital. On the Arab side: to drive all Jews into the sea and to secure full and exclusive Muslim ownership of Jerusalem. Some argue for the destruction of the State of Israel and the creation of an Islamic state in which Jews could remain as *dhimmis*, 'as covenanters with the Islamic state for peace' (al-Faruqi 1983: 266). Al-Faruqi (1983) argues that the 'pressure, blackmail, bribery, speculation and forced eviction of Palestinian farmers from lands which they had inherited for centuries from their ancestors' can only be atoned for by the dismantling of the State of Israel so that its 'wealth' can be 'confiscated to pay off its liabilities' (pp. 261–2). The obligation to undo this injustice rests with all Muslims, corporately and individually, although 'dismantling the Zionist state does not necessarily mean the destruction of Jewish lives or property'. On the other hand, 'it is a first Islamic principle that aggression and injustice be met with an identical proportion of the same (2: 194)' (*ibid.*).

The traditional Muslim view that treaties can only be entered into for up to ten years (Khadduri 1955: 219) and that they must not be 'incompatible with Islam's interests' (p. 221) leaves open the possibility for some Muslims to regard Israel's treaties with Egypt and Jordan as null and void. The Map also calls for resolution of all border and territorial disputes, including the Golan Heights dispute with Syria, but Syria has traditionally opposed the Jewish State. Talks between Israel and Syria to settle the Golan Heights dispute broke down in 2000 because Israel would not relinquish all occupied territory. This is why some 'hawks' are calling for 'regime change' in Syria and Iran along the lines of recent events in Iraq. However, according to a statement issued by the UN, 24 November 2004, President Bashir al-Assal of Syria is now prepared to negotiate for peace, based on the 'land for peace' principle, 'without conditions'. The PLO has officially renounced violence but other organizations and individuals have not. In the face of what people perceive as lack of progress (economic deprivation remains rampant in the PNA, which this author last visited in December 2003), diplomacy is seen as failing. Violence, however desperate – such as suicide bombing and stone throwing – seems to some to be the only way to express anger and frustration.

Further discussion topics

- Is Israel a stooge of the Western powers in the Middle East?

- Is the Saudi regime an agent of the USA?

- Is regime change in Iran and Syria a prerequisite for resolution of the Palestinian issue?

- Are the USA and her Allies, especially Britain, guilty of double-speak? On the one hand they invade Iraq on the grounds that Saddam Hussein allegedly possessed weapons of mass destruction (WMD) while on the other there is no action against Israel, which almost certainly has nuclear capability yet has not even been reprimanded.

- Are suicide bombings in the West Bank and Gaza justified as acts of desperation in the face of injustice and oppression?

- How can the status of Jerusalem be resolved?

- Is the conflict between Israel and the Palestinians a religious or an ethnic or a nationalist one, or a complex combination of all three dimensions?

- Can a viable Palestinian State be built within the existing borders of the PNA?

- Could an agreement be reached that allows Jewish settlements to remain in a Palestinian State? It has been suggested that their presence is of potential economic benefit to a future Palestine. Free movement across the border (at present the Israeli government does not permit its citizens to cross the PNA border) would enable Palestinians to work in Israel, staffing essential service industries.

10 Progressive and Moderate Muslims on War and Peace

Jihad literally means 'to struggle', 'to exert oneself' or 'to spend energy or wealth' ...
In the Qur'an, it is frequently followed by the expressions 'in the path of God' and
'with your wealth and your selves'. For Muslims, the term jihad has also come to
mean the 'sacralization of combat' ... Despite its popular meaning as a sacred
armed struggle or war, the term jihad was always understood by Muslims to embrace
a broader struggle to transform both oneself and society. The Qur'an itself uses the
word in its various meanings ranging from warfare (4: 90; 25: 52; 9: 41) to
contemplative spiritual struggle (22: 78; 29: 6) and even exhortation (19: 8; 31:
15).

(Esack 1997: 106–7)

Rethinking *jihad*

Contemporary or near-contemporary advocates of the moderate or liberal
Muslim understanding of war and peace in Islam include Yusuf al-Qaradawi and the late Sheikh of al-Azhar, Mahmud Shaltat. Chiragh 'Ali
(1844–95), a disciple of Sir Sayyid Ahmed Khan, pioneered this approach.
'Ali often responded to Orientalist and missionary writing that characterized Islam as incapable of reform. In his 1884 book, *All the Wars of*
Muhammad Were Defensive or, A Critical Exegesis of the Popular Jihad, he argues
that the Qur'an does not permit or promote 'religious war' but only allows
war in self-defence. On the issue of war, as on such issues as 'polygamy,
arbitrary divorce, slavery, concubinage', too, 'the strongest witness against
all these errors is the Qur'an itself' and he cites verses to support his views
(see 2002: 288). Mawdudi and Qutb had such a writer in mind when they
roundly condemned Muslims who restrict *jihad* to self-defence as stripping
Islam of its God-given instrument to fulfil its worldwide mandate. Peters
(1977) also places the 'defence' argument in the context of response to
Western criticism, commenting that:

> in order to counter the rather distorted view of the *jihad* that is commonly held in
> the West, modern Muslims especially emphasize the following aspect: claiming the
> right to *ijtihad*, the new interpretation of the sources, they profess that the *jihad* is

essentially defensive warfare, striving to protect ... Islam ... and to guarantee the propagation of the Islamic mission. (p. 5)

Moderate and liberal Muslims also refer to *hadith* in which Muhammad spoke of the *jihad* of the sword as the 'lesser *jihad*' (Asghar) and of the *jihad* of the heart (striving to live a pious Muslim life) as the 'greater *jihad*'. The *jihad* of the pen, about which Mawdudi wrote so scornfully, would also qualify as 'greater *jihad*' (Akbar). However, as Firestone (1999) points out, these *hadith* are not found in the classical collections, so it is difficult to attribute this view of *jihad* to the very early period (see p. 5). This does not mean that the only view that existed in that period was that a perpetual war existed between the world of Islam and the non-Muslim world (these terms are themselves from a later date). Firestone suggests that the progression theory of the Qur'an on fighting (argued by Qutb) is not the only way to read the text. The retention of verses that only justify self-defence in the text suggests that differences of opinion existed within early Islam on the issue of militarism. The moderates rejected the abrogation theory in which the sword verses cancel the verses of forgiveness in favour of a different reading of the Qur'an. This analysis begins with the late Sheikh Shaltut's treatise, then discusses al-Qaradawi's contribution. Some of his interventions responded to 9/11, the Bali bombing and to the invasion of Iraq and represent a Muslim response to these events. In discussing al-Qaradawi, reference will also be made to other Muslim response to 9/11 and to the charge that Islam and terrorism are natural allies. Brief reference is made to Talbi (1998). Finally, it offers a description of some non-Muslim responses to 9/11.

Shaltut's treatise on 'The Koran and Fighting'

Shaltut was born in Egypt in 1893. After a traditional Islamic education in Alexandria, he started to teach at al-Azhar. In 1931, he was accused of advocating reform and was dismissed from his job (Peters 1977: 7). In fact he identified with the reformist thought of 'Abduh and Rida. He first wrote on *jihad* in 1933. His *The Koran and Fighting* (*al-Qur'an wa-al-qital*) was first published in 1948 but written in 1940. This analysis is based on Peters' 1977 English translation. Returning to al-Azhar as Dean of the Shari'ah Faculty (al-Qaradawi's post in Qatar), he became Sheikh al-Azhar by Presidential decree in 1958. He died in 1963. His book remains an influential text, written with the authority that his position as Sheikh al-Azhar gave him (for some, the Sheikh al-Azhar is the leading authority in the Muslim world). The English version is 53 pages long. The book begins on page 26 of Peters' 1977 text and starts with a summary (Section One, pp. 26–7). He identifies the traditional doctrine of abrogation as the central issue, suggesting that the key to understanding what Islam has to say lies not in considering 'about 70 verses' abrogated, 'since they are incompatible with the legitimacy of fighting', but in examining all the verses concerned with the issue 'and analysing them' (p. 27). 'There is no need', he says, 'to squeeze any verse into an unsuitable interpretation' (p. 27). He had already applied this method to the question of 'The Koran and Women'. His current topic is the 'Koran and Fighting'. This gives the book its analytical structure. In one section, Section Three (pp. 39–52), he discusses the sword verses, while in another, Section Four (pp. 52–5), he turns to the verses of forgiveness. Section Two (pp. 28–39) sets out his understanding of the nature of the Islamic mission (*da'wah*) and provides philosophical and ideological background for his view of fighting. Other sections discuss the organization of fighting (Section Five, pp. 55–71) and its practical implications (Section Six, pp. 71–9).

In his section on the nature of the Islamic mission, Shaltut asks whether there is any aspect of that mission that makes it necessary for Muslims to 'force people to conversion' (p. 28). He stresses that Muhammad's mission was to warn and to persuade people (Q5: 19) and that the book that Muhammad received sets out how humanity can attain happiness. It calls on all people to 'judge by reason', it 'propagates science', it places great value on evidence, 'it preaches peace' and 'puts an end to distress' (p. 28). It 'disapproves of blind imitation to the ways of the forefathers' (p. 29) and promises paradise to the pious. It confirms earlier religions and messengers, all of which exhort humanity to 'do what is good and forbid to do what is reprehensible'. He describes Islam as the call to 'natural reason', which is 'not alien to the intellect', which shows his modernist credentials. He argues that to employ force as an 'instrument for conversion' wraps Islam in absurdity, since this withholds it 'from the human mind and hearts' (p. 31). He rejects the contention that any verse of the Qur'an can justify 'coercion in matters of faith' (p. 31). Allah only wants believers who arrive at their decision to embrace Islam as a result of 'study, reflection and contemplation' (p. 31). In his view, such verses as Q10: 99 and 11: 118 which say that God could have made humanity one community had he wished endorse the principle of religious liberty (p. 32). The Qu'ran itself is sufficient 'to make people believe in Mohammed's Mission.' and God does not want to force people to believe with 'awe-inspiring tokens.' (see Q29: 50–2; pp. 36–7). Having established that the Qur'an totally rejects enforced conversion, he asks 'what then is the significance of the verses of fighting in the Koran?' (p. 39).

Shaltut identifies two types of fighting considered in the Qur'an, fighting against Muslims and fighting against non-Muslims. He points out that the first is a matter of internal concern to a Muslim state 'with the exclusion of any other state' (p. 39). He sees Q49: 9–10 as authoritative here, instructing Muslims to 'set things right' between themselves rather than to resort to fighting, but allowing them to fight against Muslims 'who are oppressive' should negotiation fail (pp. 38–9). Shaltut says that the second type of fighting is addressed in 'many Koranic verses and chapters' which discuss 'causes which may lead to it, its aim, upon the attainment of which fighting must stop, the obligatory preparations for it by the Moslems and the necessary caution against an unexpected attack' (p. 41). Like Qutb, he points out that permission to fight was only given after the *hijrah*, and says that this permission (Q22: 39–41) 'was motivated by the fact that the Moslems suffered injustice and were forced to emigrate and to leave their dwellings without justification' (p. 42). This verse, he argues, does not justify use of violence to fulfil selfish motives, such as to acquire wealth. Nor does it justify use of violence to oppress. Turning to the verses of fighting in *Surah al-Baqarah* (Q2: 190–4), he argues that these verses 'order the Moslems to fight in the way of Allah those who fight them' and 'prohibit the provocation of hostility' (p. 44). Fighting in a holy place is prohibited as is 'expelling people from their homes ... and preventing them from living peacefully'. He repeats that none of these verses contains a 'trace ... of any idea of conversion by force' (p. 45). The aim of fighting is to stop the aggression or persecution directed against the Muslims and when this has been achieved, fighting must cease (p. 45). The same principles are found in such verses as Q4: 75, Q4: 84, Q4: 90–1, Q8: 39, Q9: 13–14 and Q9: 36. Talbi (1998) also rejects any connection between the Islamic mission to propagate Islam and conversion by force, arguing that while it is his 'right' and 'duty' to 'bear witness ... it is up to each person to respond or not' (pp. 167–8). The Qur'an only permits dialogue and reasoned debate as the vehicle for propagating Islam, he says. The Qur'an 'warns, advises but never resorts to the sword' (p. 166). Talbi, like Shaltut, argues that while the Qur'an permits fighting in certain circumstances, it never encourages it and authorizes 'Muslims ... to take up arms in only one case, self-defence, when they are attacked and their faith seriously jeopardized' (p. 164). The Qur'an, he says, clearly states that fighting (*al-qital*) though prescribed (*kutiba*) is disliked (*kurhun lakum*) (Q2: 194). God does not love aggressors (Q2: 190).

However, says Shaltut, two verses in Q9 appear to contradict the 'just mentioned principles concerning fighting'. He is referring to Q9: 29 and Q9: 123, which traditionally have been taken (see above) to abrogate all previous verses on fighting (p. 47). Shaltut rejects this view and also the interpretation that these verses justify unprovoked aggression, or the idea of a perpetual war with unbelief. He understands the words 'fight the unbelievers who are near to you' as pragmatic advice that, when 'the enemies are manifold, it is imperative to fight the nearest first of all' (p. 49). He argues that previous verses (9: 7–16) make clear that these 'unbelievers' had 'broken their pledges and hindered and assailed the propagation of the Islamic Mission', and that they were not to be fought simply because of their religious beliefs (p. 47). Q9: 13–14's 'will you not fight against a people who have violated their oaths ... and who took the initiative with you' provides, says Shaltut, the context for 9: 29's 'fight against those who do not believe in Allah' (p. 47). In other words, the 'unbelievers' who are to be fought are those 'hostile polytheists who fight the Moslems' (p. 50) and there is no justification for the view that the Qur'an authorizes fighting 'unbelievers in general, regardless of whether they have committed aggression or not'. The 'fight continuously' of Q9: 36 is a conditional command, thus 'fight continuously those who fight you continuously'. Traditionally, says Shaltut, the 'fight those who fight you' and the 'fight them until there is no persecution' of Q2: 190 and 2: 193 is taken as abrogated by Q2: 191, 'kill them wherever you find them', and Q9: 13–14's 'fight ... a people ... who took the initiative' is abrogated by Q9: 36's 'fight the polytheists continuously as they fight you continuously' (p. 53; or by 9: 5, see Ibn Rushd 1977: 16).

Arguing that all these verses are to be understood in the context of an ongoing conflict between Muslims and certain unbelievers, Shaltut's view is that all verses remain 'fixed and unassailable' (p. 54). Q60: 8, 'Allah does not forbid you to act virtuously towards those who have not fought against you', for Shaltut sets the tone for Islam's normal dealing with non-Muslims. Muhammad had only fought those who fought him and 'his fighting had no other aims than repelling oppression, warding off rebellion and aggression and putting an end to persecution' (p. 75). Discussing the practical application of Qur'anic verses on fighting, Shaltut argues that Muslims are bound to negotiate for peace whenever 'the enemy is inclined to it' (Q8: 61; p. 69) and captives must either be released 'out of kindness' or ransomed, but they must not be harmed (p. 69). Q9: 5, 'and when the sacred months are passed, slay the unbelievers wherever you find them', traditionally taken as an abrogating verse, could similarly be understood to refer to the recommencement of existing hostilities after a short truce (during the month of pilgrimage) and not as an unconditional order for Muslims to kill non-Muslims. Those who uphold the abrogation theory point out that Q9 was probably the very last revelation that Muhammad received, while Q2 was revealed soon after the *hijrah*, which may also explain why it is the only chapter that lacks the prefix 'In the Name of Allah, the Merciful Lord of Mercy', since Muhammad did not have time to leave instructions regarding the correct recitation of this verse. Others point out that the content of the chapter, fighting, may have been so distasteful to Allah, who permits but does not like violence ('Allah does not love those who provoke hostility' (2: 190)), that the *bismillah* was deliberately omitted. Shaltut's view that Muslims have only ever attacked those who 'showed a spirit of hostility, opposition and resistance against' their mission (p. 78), and that they should never initiate hostility, contradicts Mawdudi's and Qutb's view that fighting is a God-given instrument in Muslim hands for the fulfilment of Islam's universal mandate to establish *Shari'ah* as the sole law throughout the world.

Al-Qaradawi and *jihad*

Al-Qaradawi prefers moderate leadership and avoiding extremes (see 1998). On the issue of violence, he has also adopted a moderate stance. On this issue, he has distanced himself from some who share his conservative views of the need to return to 'true Islam' and to reject all 'foreign solutions', as well as his criticism of the Islamic *bone fides* of many Islamic regimes. In several speeches and broadcasts since 9/11, al-Qaradawi has condemned the use of unprovoked violence, attacks on civilians and terrorist tactics, including hostage taking, all of which have been perpetrated by various Islamist groups. Condemning both 9/11 and the Bali bombings as heinous crimes under Islamic law (he called this *hirubah* in juristic terms), he explicitly rejected the targeting of civilians as a legitimate tactic. 'Our hearts bleed', he said, 'for the attacks that have targeted the World Trade Center', and such 'haphazard killing where the rough is taken with the smooth and where innocents are killed with wrongdoers is totally forbidden in Islam' (*islam-online.net/English/News/ 2001-09/13/article25.shtml*). He was speaking on 13 September 2001. He was expressing his condemnation for 9/11, he said, 'despite our strong oppositions to the American biased policy towards Israel on the military, political and economic fronts'. Muslims who kill innocent people are a threat to Islam and a distinction needs to be made between what Islam teaches and some peoples' 'narrow minded view of Islam'. He stressed that even in times of war, Islam prohibits the killing of non-combatants such as women and children. To launch an attack on non-Muslims who have not first attacked Muslims is 'a form of justice that is ... prohibited and abhorred by the Qur'an', he said. Islam prohibits indiscriminate attacks on life, property and on people's honour (*islamonline*, 15 October 2002).

Here, al-Qaradawi sides with Shaltut and is in total opposition to the view popularized by Qutb that Muslims are entitled to take the initiative. The ill-treatment of prisoners is un-Islamic, says al-Qaradawi. Muslim scholars meeting in Saudi Arabia in January 2002 similarly condemned terrorism as 'alien to Islam'. Like al-Qaradawi, they commented that Islam upholds the sanctity of 'religion, life, property and honour'. They described any 'unjustified act of violence or threat ... designed to terrorize people or endanger their lives or security' as contrary to Islam. They rejected any equation between *jihad* and 'terrorism', seeing the former as justifiable struggle against oppression, occupation and injustice and the latter as 'murder and banditry'. Islam forbids the targeting or the destruction of buildings or installations that are not 'related to the fighting'. Statements by such influential scholars as the Sheikh al-Azhar, Muhammad Sa'id Tantawi and the Imam of the Grand Mosque at Makkah, Sheikh Muhammad bin 'Abdullah, have also declared attacks on innocent people unlawful in Islam (see *al-Akhbar*, Cairo, 15 December 2000; Malka 2003). However, as does al-Qaradawi, they described 'acts by the Palestinians against the Israeli occupation as a form of *jihad* and legitimate self-defence' ('What is *jihad*? What is Terrorism?' Statement by Muslim Scholars, *Middle East Online*, 11 January 2002, *www.religionscope.com/info/doc/ jihad/2002_scholars_definition.htm*).

Al-Qaradawi defends attacks on Israeli civilians as legitimate. He argues that all Israelis are not civilians but combatants in a war of occupation against Palestinians. He says that the whole of Israeli society has a military mentality that pits the state against Muslim Arabs. Indeed, this writer frequently heard the phrase 'every Israeli is a front-line soldier' when he was first in Israel between October 1982 and January 1983. Al-Qaradawi also argues that in a military situation such as the Israel–Palestinian conflict, the killing and maiming of women and children is acceptable, although not deliberate. Responding to the charge that Palestinian suicide bombers are terrorists, he dismissed this and announced that if 'everyone who defends his land, and dies defending his sacred symbols is considered a terrorist, then I wish to be in the forefront of terrorists' (Daba 2004). He contends that in the Palestinian context, *jihad* has ceased to be a collective duty (*fard kifaayah*) but is an individual obligation (*fard 'ayn*) as in all situations when Muslims are under attack. Al-Qaradawi rejected the *fatwas* of those Imams, such as the Grand Imam of Makkah, who ruled out the killing of civilians in all circumstances, 'even in Israel'. However, he also rejects the view of some that Muslims are engaged in a war with all Jews throughout the world. The war, he says, is only with those who occupy Palestinian land. Here he parts company from Qutb who spoke of the 'pernicious role' played by Jews 'in the war against Islam'. He also blamed Jews for the destruction of the family and for 'the disruption of the holy bonds of society' (cited in Lewis 2003: 145).

Al-Qaradawi has condemned the targeting of Americans in America as un-Islamic, since he does not believe that the whole American nation is at war with Islam (although its 'arrogant' government is), but he sides with *hizb-ut-tahrir* and al-Qaeda in describing resistance to the Allied invasion of Iraq as a *jihad*, just as Palestinian resistance to Israeli occupation is a *jihad*. Anyone killed in an 'operation aimed at expelling American forces from the Gulf is a martyr due to his good intention', he says (*Uwaydidi*, 29 January 2003). The USA is in danger, though, of setting itself up as a 'god to be worshipped away from Allah'. 'When a Muslim defends his land', said al-Qaradawi, 'he is not just defending mere soil, he is actually defending the land of Islam' (*ibid.*). Al-Qaradawi has criticized the USA for victimizing Muslim organizations and individuals since 9/11. For example, the International Institute of Islamic Thought (see Chapter Three) and the Islamic Fiqh Council have been raided, and over a thousand people detained with no charges made (according to the BBC, citing the US Justice Department, the majority of detentions were for immigration violations). Al-Qaradawi's multiple-entry US visa has been cancelled. However, he has recently visited the UK (July 2004) where his presence raised questions about the desirability of introducing a new law against incitement to religious hatred. The Commission for Racial Equality and, among others, Tariq Modood called for this law over a decade ago but it had the support of the former British Home Secretary, David Blunkett. His visit also resulted in a debate on *Newsnight* (BBC2, 7 July 2004) about his comments on suicide bombers and on whether the Home Secretary should have admitted him to the UK. It was pointed out that while al-Qaradawi called suicide bombers martyrs, he did not encourage such bombings.

Lisbeth Lindeborg describes al-Qaradawi (born in 1926), currently Dean of the Faculty of Shari'ah and Islamic Studies at Qatar University, as 'Islam's foremost contemporary ideologue' (2002). Qaradawi's regular broadcast on *Al Jazeera* television is the station's most popular programme and the only one that is subtitled in English. It is said to reach 45 million viewers. *www.qaradawi.net* is one of the most popular Islamic sites.

Muslims on 9/11

Margaret Thatcher, the former British Prime Minister, complained in the *Guardian* on 3 October 2001 that too few Muslims had spoken out against the atrocities of 9/11. However, on 4 October the *Guardian* published an article entitled 'How Muslim leaders responded to September 11' that included condemnatory remarks, all dated prior to her comments, by Dr Ghayasuddin Siddiqui, leader of the Muslim Parliament of the UK (12 September 2001) and Dr Zaki Badawi, Principal of the Muslim College, London (joint statement with the Archbishops of Canterbury and Westminster and the Chief Rabbi). Dr Siddiqui has also called the al-Muhajiroun the 'lunatic fringe of Islam' and says that the Muslim Parliament has been condemning their acts for a long time.

Shaykh Abdul Aziz al-Ashaikh, Grand Mufti of Saudi Arabia and Chairman of the Senior Ulama, said on 15 September 2001: 'Hijacking planes, terrorizing innocent people and shedding blood constitute a form of injustice that cannot be tolerated by Islam, which views them as gross crimes and sinful acts.'

On the first anniversary of 9/11, 199 prominent Muslims and scholars of Islam signed a statement published by the Centre for the Study of Islam and Democracy, which included the following: 'We wish again to state unequivocally that neither the al-Qaeda organization nor Osama bin Laden represents Islam or reflects Muslim beliefs and practice. Rather, groups like al-Qaeda have misused and abused Islam in order to fit their own radical and indeed anti-Islamic agenda. Osama bin Laden and al-Qaeda's actions are criminal, misguided and counter to the true teachings of Islam. We call on people of all faiths not to judge Islam by the actions of a few' ('American Muslims and Scholars Denounce Terrorism', Statement from the Center for the Study of Islam and Democracy, *The American Muslim*, Sept–Oct 2002).

On 10 October 2001 the Organization of the Islamic Conference (OIC) meeting in Qatar condemned 9/11. They also drew a distinction between acts of terrorism, which are unacceptable, and legitimate resistance to occupation, which is acceptable. The OIC called for a UN-backed conference to look at the causes of terrorism. At the conference, Yasser Arafat criticized Israel for using the crisis caused by 9/11 to launch new attacks on his people.

Sardar (2004) writes 'On 11 September 2001 it became clear that Muslim civilization was being offered suicide, both as method and metaphor ... (p. 332) ... When metaphors are taken literally, should it surprise us that they lead to madness' (p. 334). Sardar (2002) pointed out that especially in the USA, Muslims post 9/11 are reduced to two 'kinds ... the terrorist (who has declared war on the West) and the apologist (who claims to be a liberal and defends Islam as a peaceful religion)' (p. 51). It has, he says, become impossible for a Muslim to claim on the one hand to affirm American values while on the other opposing US foreign policy and action in Afghanistan and elsewhere.

However, the British based al-Muhajiroun celebrated the anniversary of 9/11 as a Muslim martyrs' day, calling those Muslims who died 'the magnificent 19' (a word play on the 1960 film, *The Magnificent Seven*).

Resources for teaching about 9/11

www.teaching9-11.org, Clarke Center for the Study of Contemporary Issues, Dickinson College, Carlisle, PA
www.september11news.com
www.911digitalarchive.org, American Social History Project Center for Media and Learning, City University, New York, and the Center for History and New Media, George Mason University
http://www.homeoffice.gov.uk/terrorism/index.html, the UK Home Office terrorism page
www.clintonbennett.net/waron terrorism.html, a resource page on 9/11
http://www.cfr.org/index.php, Council on Foreign Relations (USA) Terrorism: Questions and Answers site
http://www.fbi.gov/terrorinfo/terrorism.htm, the USA's FBI terrorism site
http://www.9-11commission.gov/, the Report of the independent Commission, July 2004.

The issue of suicide

Traditionally, Islam regards suicide as a mortal sin, based on Q4: 29–30, 'do not kill yourselves, for truly Allah has been most merciful to you', and of *hadith* such as that cited by Lewis (2003), 'whoever kills himself ... will be tormented ... in the fires of hell' (p. 130). Q17: 33, which prohibits the taking of life without just cause, can also be cited to rule out the acceptability of a suicide mission such as 9/11, although those who perpetrated the act believe that they had just cause. However, Bernard Lewis (2003) suggests that the line is blurred between suicide and martyrdom in cases where the latter involves 'facing certain death at the hands of the enemy' (p. 33). On the other hand, he points out that while the *jihadist* (including the medieval Assassins) died at the hands of the enemy, the modern-day suicide bomber or plane hijacker 'dies by his own hand' (p. 130). According to the manual found among the hijackers' personal effects, they regarded themselves as *jihadists* facing the promise of paradise that awaits a martyr, not the punishment of hell that awaits those who commit suicide. Asking whether such a view can be 'justified in terms of Islam', Lewis says 'the answer must be a clear no' (p. 131).

Malka (2003) argues that until 9/11 suicide attacks enjoyed 'almost unquestioning support in the Arab world', and that despite condemnations of attacks on innocent civilians in the USA and Bali, Muslim opinion on the legitimacy of suicide missions remains divided. He cites Muslim authorities who condemn attacks, such as 9/11, aimed at civilians, but who express support for Palestinian suicide attackers: 'We support the families of Palestinian martyrs without differentiating between whether the Palestinian was a bomber or was killed by Israeli troops', said the Chair of a Saudi fund-raising committee (*Arab News*, Jidda, 27 May 2002). Those Muslims who express approval for the attacks of 9/11 do so by applying to all Americans the charge of which al-Qaradawi finds all Israelis guilty, that is, of being at war with Islam, or, as *hizb-ut-tahrir* and al-Qaeda express this, as engaged in a crusade against Islam. Bin Laden's *fatwas* urge Muslims to 'kill the Americans and their allies, civilians and military'.

Progressive Muslims on pacifist Islam

Progressive Muslims may accept that there are occasions when defensive war is justifiable but their overall positions can be characterized as pacifist. Taha (1987) argued that *jihad* was not an original precept in Islam and advocated that the Qur'an permitted fighting 'only when absolutely necessary' (p. 135). Applying his theory that those Qur'anic laws revealed during the Madinan period were temporary and abrogated by the earlier Makkan revelations, he elevates the verses of persuasion and mercy over and above the sword verses. For him, Q16: 125, 'propagate the path of your Lord in wisdom and peaceable advice', takes priority over all other verses. Use of the sword was permitted after the *hijrah*, which Taha describes as like 'a surgeon's lancet and not a butcher's knife', since it was designed to cut out evil (p. 134). Taha rejects the contention, though, that all Islamic wars 'were purely defensive', which he also (like Mawdudi and Qutb) describes as a 'mistaken belief prompted by ... keenness to refute claims by the Orientalists that Islam was spread by means of the sword' (*ibid.*). Rather, the sword, he says, 'was used to curtail the abuse of freedom'. Nonetheless, the granting of permission to fight represented a descent from the original principles of the religion (p. 136). Islam's original precept is that 'there can be no hostility except against wrongdoers' (p. 136). Citing the traditional view that 'all the verses of persuasion' were abrogated or repealed by the verses of compulsion (*jihad*), Taha explains that this was 'necessitated by the circumstances of the time and the inadequacy of the human capability to discharge properly the duty of freedom at that time' (p. 134). Muslims need to reflect on the whole of the Qu'ran so that they can return to its 'original principle, which they were unable to implement at the beginning' (p. 137). See Figure 10.1 on the abrogation argument.

Taha, like Talbi and Esack, rejects any idea that Muslims are compelled to regard all non-Muslims as enemies, arguing that the term *mu'minin* (believer) in its truest meaning embraces all who truly worship Allah and act justly, with whom collaboration is not only possible but mandated by the Qur'an. Esack (2002 and 2003) directly addressed the contention, often repeated since 9/11, that the Qur'an and Islam are themselves 'responsible for violence by Muslim terrorists'. In this view, the 'text by itself is the problem' (2002: 191). As noted in Chapter Three, Esack points out that Osama bin Laden fires off Qur'anic verse after verse like 'angry bullets at the "infidel" occupiers of the holy land and their Muslim allies' (p. 192). On the other hand, the state-paid *'ulama* 'fired an equal number of verses at Osama and his followers denouncing them as the ultimate destroyers of the faith' (2002: 192). Thus, the text of the Qur'an is read by some Muslims to justify 9/11 and it is, he says, plausible to argue that 9/11 was 'inspired by Islam', since 'the Qur'an is open to diverse readings' (2003: 92). He argues, however, that the weight of the Qur'anic witness supports the peaceful resolution of differences of opinion and the openness of Islam to collaboration with all people who share a passion for justice and equality before God. Muslim scholars and thinkers need to 'expose and oppose the theological and textual basis' of bin Laden's and others' arguments (2003: 92). Esack encourages those who care about the earth to 'find each other' and to co-operate 'before Bush, the Corporations and Bin Laden destroy us all' (2003: 93).

Esack repeats his contention that the Qur'an is 'contested scripture' in danger of manipulation by its readers to provide the answers they want to hear to the questions that they put to the text. In his discussion of '*Jihad*' (1997: 106–10), which he interprets as 'struggle and praxis', Esack stresses that the purpose of *jihad* is to achieve justice and not to establish Islam as a religious system or to 'replace one dominant group with another' (p. 107). To engage in *jihad* means to identify with the poor and the oppressed, against all that dehumanizes (p. 108), which is, says Esack, 'the very opposite' of invoking the Qur'an 'in a court of law as legitimation for the armed struggle' or 'when God is fervently petitioned before a raid on a government building or on the eve of the outcome of a trial on charges of terrorism' (p. 110). *Taqwa* (God-consciousness, which Fazlur Rahman saw as the essential feature of true Muslim obedience; see Esack 1997: 68) is in the Qur'an always associated with 'care for others' (p. 87). Adopting the term popularized by Christian (mainly Roman Catholic) liberation theologians (the preferential option for the poor), he writes of Muslims opting preferentially for 'the oppressed and marginalized' (p. 110). While *jihad* has been used in order to 'sacralize combat' (p. 107), the use of the term in the Qur'an to include 'contemplative spiritual struggle' (Q22: 78, 29: 6) and even exhortation (Q29: 8, 31: 15) opens up the possibility of viewing *jihad* as 'essentially non-violent uprising'. *Jihad*, though, is perpetual; it is a 'ceaseless, continuous, super conscious and effective struggle for justice' (citing a *Qibla* tract, p. 107; *Qibla*, established in 1981, was to the political right of Esack's Call of Islam organization of progressive Muslims in South Africa, but essentially shared its liberational perspective, see p. 42).

Discussion topic

- Esack writes, 'Texts, we know, answer to questions asked of them and in the same manner that the *taliban* are not innocent and void of a context, similarly the text is also not free from a history and a context (2002: 192). **How then can we know that a progressive reading, such as Esack's, is more correct than bin Laden's reading?**

Those Muslims, such as Tibi, Taha and Mernissi among others who, like Esack, regard Islam as endorsing religious pluralism, all reject the view that a perpetual enmity exists between the world of Islam and the non-Muslim world. Tibi calls on Muslims to discard these categories. Calling *jihad* 'militarily waged civilizational war' (2001: 224), Tibi says that it 'has to be abandoned' (p. 203). Tibi calls on Muslims to abandon the dogma that world peace can only be achieved by expanding *dar-al-Islam* to embrace the whole world (p. 220), but he is equally insistent that the West must also abandon its neo-imperial project, since this is no less dangerous. His goal of inter-civilizational peace can only be achieved by mediation (p. 225). In support of the view that these categories should be abandoned, it has been pointed out that they do not derive from the Qur'an but from the pragmatic decisions of the early jurists.

The first edition of Khadduri's book was published in 1941 and 'confined itself to a study of the principles and practices in early Islam' (1955: viii). In 1955, the extended edition added to the original aim of formulating 'from diverse sources a consistent legal theory and practice of Islam's relations with other nations' a discussion of recent developments among Muslims 'at adapting Islam to the principles and purpose of the modern community of nations'. In particular, Khadduri was interested in Muslim participation in the United Nations, which at the time of writing ten Muslim states had joined. Khadduri was born in Mosul in Iraq in 1908. In 1932 he graduated from the American University of Beirut and proceeded from there to Chicago where he completed his PhD in political science and international law. Between 1939 and 1947 he worked for the Ministry of Education in Baghdad, where he also taught law at the Higher Teachers Colleges. At the end of World War II, he was seconded to represent Iraq at the founding of the United Nations in San Francisco, where he helped to draft the Charter, although 'not the most senior member of the delegation' (Killgore 1996: 23). Khadduri subsequently served as Professor of Middle East Studies (1949–70) and as Distinguished Research Professor (1970–80) at Johns Hopkins University. He has held many visiting professorships and in 1957 was a co-founder and Dean of the

University of Libya. Killgore (1996) describes him as the 'grand old man among Middle East experts' in the US capital (see Khadduri and Ghareeb 1997 on the Gulf War).

His 1955 book, on which this analysis is based, presents a traditional Islamic understanding of war and peace, or, as he describes it, 'the classical legal theory of Islam' (p. vii). His purpose is to describe, and he has no brief to defend what he reconstructs from the sources. However, what he describes is essentially identical with what writers such as Mawdudi and Qutb claim to be the authentic Muslim position. His text divides into three 'books'. Book One (pp. 3–48) identifies the 'Fundamental Concepts of Islamic Law'. Book Two (pp. 51–137) describes Islam's 'Law of War', or 'jihad', while Book Three examines Islam's 'Law of Peace' (pp. 141–267). This chapter includes material on 'Muslims in Non-Muslim Territory' and on the 'Status of the Dhimmis' referenced in Chapter Four of this book. In the 'Epilogue' (pp. 268–96) Khadduri explores progressive Muslim thinking on the relationships between the Muslim and non-Muslim worlds. In his description of the classical tradition, Khadduri stresses that Islamic thought presupposes that the Islamic is an 'ever expanding state'. Recognizing no law other than Divine Law, Islam regards non-Muslim entities not so much as legitimate states but as territory awaiting conquest. Thus, Muhammad's 'early successors ... were determined to embark on a ceaseless war of conquest in the name of Islam' and employed jihad as 'an instrument for both the universalization of religion and the establishment of an imperial world state' (p. 51). From the outset, the aim of the Islamic entity was to 'establish Islam as the dominant reigning ideology over the entire world' (p. 51). However, like other imperial projects, it was impossible for the Islamic one 'to extend ad infinitum' and expansion north into Europe was halted at the Battle of Tours (732 CE) and eastwards at the borders of India (although later expansion continued further to the east).

In practice, the Islamic state 'did not correspond to the then known world' and outside or beyond its borders there remained communities governed by non-Islamic law 'which the Muslim authorities had to deal with', even if only temporarily (p. 52). It was pragmatism, he suggests, that prompted the four Imams to use the terms dar-al-Islam and dar-al-harb to distinguish territory under Muslim rule whose population was Muslim or members of tolerated religions from all the communities 'outside the world of Islam' from territory whose populations were 'infidels' or 'unbelievers' (p. 53; dar-al-islam is derived from Q10: 25's 'abode of peace'). Since Islam's 'ultimate aim was worldwide', in theory, a perpetual war exists between dar-al-islam and dar-al-harb, 'thus the jihad, reflecting the normal war relations existing between Muslims and non-Muslims, was the state's instrument for transforming the dar-al-harb into dar-al-Islam' (p. 53). Khadduri argues that war is therefore the normal relationship between the world of Islam and non-Muslim territories and that short intervals when war is suspended, which in theory 'should not exceed ten years – are

periods of peace'. Ultimately, says Khadduri, *dar-al-harb* is 'outlawed under
the Islamic jural order' (p. 64). In theory, non-Muslim states are not
recognized as legitimate but only as 'necessary', that is, 'necessary for the
survival of society' until Islamic rule can be established (p. 171). For
pragmatic reasons described below, Muslim government takes 'cognisance
of the authority that exists in countries which are not under Muslim rule'
but this does not 'constitute recognition in the modern sense of the term'
(*ibid.*). Jurists stress the obligatory and binding nature of *jihad* as long as
dar-al-harb remains a reality. Ibn Khaldun wrote, 'In the Muslim community, the holy war is a religious duty, because of the universalism of the
mission and the obligation to convert everybody to Islam either by persuasion or by force' (1958: 165).

The *jihad* between Islam and the non-Muslim world, which aims to turn
'all people into believers, if not in the prophethood of Muhammad (as in
the case of the *dhimmis*), at least in the belief in God' is the 'permanent
basis of Islam's relations with its neighbours'. This does not necessarily
mean constant war but it does mean that Islam is always in a 'state of war'
until 'the *dar-al-harb* is reduced to non-existence' and communities that
prefer to remain non-Muslims have submitted 'to Islamic rule and reside
in the *dar-al-Islam*' (p. 64). Until this has been achieved, 'the *dar-al-Islam* is
permanently under *jihad* obligation'. From the verb *jadada* (exertion),
jihad does not only refer to 'war or fighting, since exertion in Allah's path
may be achieved by peaceful as well as violent means' (p. 46). Khadduri
points out that 'the ultimate object of Islam was not war *per se*, but the
ultimate establishment of peace' (p. 141). In the Makkan period the
emphasis was mainly on persuasion, while 'in the Madinan revelations, the
jihad is often expressed in terms of strife'. In 'certain verses the conception
of *jihad* is synonymous with the words war and fighting', as in Q2: 216, 8:
41, 49: 15, 61: 11 and 66: 9.

Jihad *as holy war*

Texts contain much discussion about the meaning of the word *jihad*. It is
often and rightly argued that the word does not mean 'war' but 'striving',
and includes many types of striving to establish Islam, including the inner
struggle against temptation. *Jihad* when used in the Qur'an is usually followed by *fi sabil Illah* (in the path of Allah). However, texts also point out
that *jihad* can denote armed struggle and that when used without a qualification, such as 'of the heart' it usually means war on behalf of Islam.
Peters (1977) comments that 'it may be questioned whether the term
"Holy War" is an adequate translation of the concept of *jihad*' since a Holy
War is one fought 'exclusively for religious reasons' and *jihad* in Islam has
historically been more politically motivated, such as by the 'wish for
expansion of territory'. However, Islam makes no distinction between
religion and politics and *jihad* 'is subject to Islamic Law' (pp. 3–4).

Jurists distinguish four ways in which *jihad* can be pursued, namely by the heart, by the tongue, by the hand and by the sword (p. 56). *Jihad* must be waged for 'justifiable reasons' and it has to 'be *pium*, that is, in accordance with the sanction of religion' (p. 57). Since the aim of *jihad* is to establish 'Muslim sovereignty' it must 'be enforced by the state' (p. 60). *Jihad*'s purpose was 'religious', 'to enforce God's law', and secular war is regarded in Islam as evil, 'to be avoided' (p. 71). Secular war is prohibited, as is war between Muslims. That is, the whole community led by the Khalif wages *jihad*, and not individuals pursuing independent initiatives. This does not mean that all members of the community must engage in *jihad*, but those who do so act on behalf of the whole. Q9: 122 advises that a 'party from each section' of the believers do so unless necessity demands that all must fight (Q4: 71; see Shaltut 1977: 66–7). Ibn Rushd comments that 'the Prophet never went to battle without leaving some people behind' (1977: 10). *Jihadists* have to be economically independent so that their dependants can be supported, they must be 'mature and sound-minded' (p. 84), male (p. 85), able-bodied, and Muslim (Hanafis allow the employment of non-believers since Muhammad 'sought the support of non-believers' (p. 84)). While fighting they must be obedient and loyal to their 'commanders' decisions in matters of military affairs', including the distribution of spoil (p. 85).

Early rules set out certain conventions, such as not harming civilians, women, children, destroying crops or damaging places of worship (p. 102; Abu Bakr's address to 'the first Syrian expedition'), although there was discussion about 'the extent to which injury may be inflicted upon the person of the enemy' says Ibn Rushd (1977: 18). Malik 'allowed the felling of trees, the picking of fruits and the demolishing of buildings but not the slaughter of cattle and the burning of date-palms' (p. 18). Abu Hanifa 'laid down the rule that everything that the *jihadists* cannot bring under their control must be destroyed, including the houses, churches, trees, flocks and herds' (Khadduri 1955: 103). Shaf'i allowed the destruction of 'everything which is lifeless'. 'According to all scholars', says Ibn Rushd, 'the prerequisite for warfare is that the enemy must have heard the summons to Islam' (Rushd, p. 19). Khadduri observes, however, that jurists differed in matters of details, such as whether an invitation has to be sent just once, leaving open the possibility of a renewed attack 'without notification' (pp. 97–8). However, 'it has been related irrefutably that the Prophet repeatedly made sudden attacks upon the enemy at night', that is, without prior warning (p. 20). It was generally accepted that only able-bodied men among the enemy should be slain and that monks and hermits should be spared, based on *hadith* related by Ibn 'Abbas, 'Do not slay hermits', and 'do not slay old and decrepit, children or women' (p. 16). Q9: 5 'Then when the sacred months are slipped away, slay the polytheists wherever you find them' was taken by some to justify killing any polytheist, including 'monks' (*ibid.*). Q47: 4, 'when you meet those who have disbelieved, let there be slaughter until ... you have made havoc of them', has been cited to justify slaying captives.

Ibn Rushd pointed out that Q9: 5 was interpreted as giving blanket permission to kill polytheists whether or not they had actually fought against or opposed Muslims, maintaining that Q2: 190, 'fight in the way of Allah against those who fight you, but do not provoke hostility', has been abrogated by Q9: 5, which 'gives a rule without exception' (p. 16). *Jihad*, unlike prayer or fasting (which are obligatory for individuals) is a collective duty (*fard al-kifaya*). This 'made possible the employment of the *jihad* as a community ... and consequently a state instrument' (Khadduri, p. 61). The Qur'an itself promises that 'those who are killed in the path of Allah' are not to be thought dead but 'alive with their Lord' (Q3: 169; see such as Q9: 111). Martyrs who die in battle do not have to be ritually washed, as is normal for a dead Muslim before burial, but 'are buried where they fall' (p. 62). *Jihadists* die believing that they will enter Paradise immediately, based on both Qur'anic verses and on *hadith*. *Jihadists* who die in action are martyrs, or *shahid* (derived from the word for witness). Not all calls to *jihad* have been successful. As Ruthven (2002) points out, when the last Ottoman Khalif declared that *jihad* against the allies was *fard 'ain* (or *ayn*, an individual obligation) in November 1914, this had little effect. Although many scholars ratified the *jihad*, Sharif Hussein of Makkah, who aided the British, rejected it (p. 67).

In his 'Epilogue', turning to argue in favour of a progressive approach, Khadduri points out that just as *ijtihad* was used to develop the categories of *dar-al-Islam* and *dar-al-harb*, so Muslims in the modern era have used *ijtihad* to adapt Islam to the 'principles and purposes of the modern community of nations' (1955: viii). For Khadduri, this means joining the international order that the UN represents, with its principle of the peaceful negotiation of conflict and war as a last resort. Khadduri argues that pragmatically, Muslims accept the 'change in character of the state from Islamic to national' (p. 288) and also that religion should be separate from politics (p. 293). 'The secular approach to foreign affairs', he says, 'has been accepted by almost all Muslim states whether completely secularised in their internal structure, as in the case of Turkey, or still recognizing *shari'a* as their basic law, as in the Arabian peninsula' (p. 292). He argues that the participation of Muslim nations in the UN demonstrates that 'the *dar-al-Islam* has at last reconciled itself to a peaceful co-existence with *dar-al-harb*' (*ibid.*). The desire of Muslims to serve on the International Court of Justice and on several international commissions is testimony to 'the fact that Islam' has accepted 'its integration into the larger international community' (p. 203). He adds that almost all Muslim jurist-theologians, even those who object to secularism, have 'repudiated any claim that the *jihad* is offensive in character', referencing Rida (1938: 293).

Peace Verses (Progressive Islam)	Defensive (Just War) Verses (Moderate Islam)	Sword Verses (Radical Islam)
Invite all to the way of the Lord with wisdom and beautiful preaching, and argue with them in ways that are best and most gracious (Q16: 125)	To those against whom war is made (li-alladhin yuqatilun)*, permission is given to fight, because they have been wronged (Q22: 39–40)	Fighting is prescribed for you, and you dislike it (Q2: 216)
Nor can goodness and evil be equal. Repel evil with what is better and those who were your enemy will be as your friends (Q41: 34)	Fight in the way of Allah those who fight you, but do not provoke hostility – God does not love aggressors (Q2: 190)	And when the sacred months are passed, slay the unbelievers wherever you find them … beleaguer them, and lay in wait for them in every stratagem of war (Q9: 5)**
Thou art indeed a warner (Q88:21)	And if they incline to make peace, incline thou to it (Q8: 61).	Fight those who do not believe in Allah or the Last Day … until they pay the poll tax (Q9: 29)
The verses of peace represent Islam's true stance and fighting is only permitted in the most extreme circumstances of self-defence or against oppression and injustice	These verses, which permit only defensive war and express distaste for war, qualify the verses on the right, that is, they only allow Muslims to fight unbelievers who fight them.	Traditional view – these verses abrogate the earlier texts and justify a perpetual war, employing all means, against unbelief. This is a corporate duty for the Muslim world (heretical Muslims also qualify as targets).

* Shaltut renders this as 'to those who are fighting' (li-alladhin yuqatilun) p. 85, n. 60

** is used by some to justify 'terror' tactics, that is, non-regular war against any unbeliever, civilian as well as military

Figure 10.1 The Verses of Fighting v. the Verses of Persuasion: some key Qur'anic texts

Some non-Muslims respond to 9/11 and Islamic terrorism

Bernard Lewis (2003)

Said named Lewis as a lackey of the West in his representation of Muslim history and society (see 1978 for example, pp. 314–15). Yoffe (2001) describes him as 'The Islam scholar US politicians listen to'. Some dub him 'Lewis of Arabia'. From 1974 until his retirement in 1986 he was Professor of Near Eastern Studies at Princeton. During World War II he was attached to Britain's Intelligence Service, qualifying him as an example of what Said sees as scholarship in the service of Empire. Jewish by birth, he is charged with Zionist sympathies. His 2003 book has been an international bestseller. Lewis argues that future collision between Islam and the West can be avoided if Muslims who 'sympathise with us, and would like to share our way of life' succeed in 'establishing democratic systems' (p. 140). He suggests that 'even if we cannot help such people, we should at least not hinder them'. He points out that with the collapse of the Soviet Union, one element in the equation is no longer present. Whereas in the past Muslim militants turned to the West's enemies, such as Germany and the USSR, for help, there is now 'no such useful enemy'. Bin Laden is alone (p. 137).

In 'Double Standards' (pp. 89–96) he points out how the USA's foreign policy of dealing with 'the devil you know' rather than with the 'devil you do not know' (p. 91) results in support of dictatorial regimes. The USA's assumption seems to be that since Muslims are incapable of running democracies and have little regard for human rights, they will always end up being ruled by tyrants. The USA's role is not to 'change them, but merely to ensure' that 'the despots are friendly' towards the West (p. 91). All extremist groups, says Lewis, justify their acts with reference to Islamic sources and all 'claim to represent a truer, purer, and more authentic Islam than that currently practised by the vast majority of Muslims' (p. 118). Muslims, he says, are not commanded in the Qur'an to 'turn the other cheek' when attacked (p. 122). However, the attacks of 9/11 have 'no precedent in Islamic history' (p. 132). Lewis identifies the desire to 'gain publicity and to inspire fear' as the main aim of contemporary terrorism (p. 125). Yet, says Lewis, even as the full horrors of 9/11 became clear and Muslims joined in the condemnation of the atrocity, many at the same time took 'the opportunity to point out that the Americans have brought it on themselves' (p. 134).

Giles Kepel (2002)

Kepel is a professor at the Institut d'Etudes Politiques of Paris. Kepel's thesis is that 9/11 was 'a desperate symbol of the isolation, fragmentation, and decline of the Islamist movement, not a sign of its strength and irrepressible might' (p. 375). Islamism, he says, is fragmented and dying. Islamists' own appalling track record wherever they have gained power alienates more Muslims than it attracts. Kepel hears Islamists today talking about the need to seek for Islam's democratic essence (p. 368) rather than of the need to overthrow regimes violently. Muslims no longer see Islamism as the road to utopia and are becoming more open to the 'world and to democracy' (p. 373). He cites the Sudanese scholar, Abdel wahhab el-Affendi who, with other like-minded Islamist intellectuals, is ready to ally himself 'with mainstream secular society' (p. 362). El-Affendi, who opposes the Islamist regime in Sudan, attributes the failure of Islamists to three factors: they failed to resolve internal conflicts in the Islamist movement; they allowed the acquisition of power to deflate the utopian dream and they failed to establish democratic procedures (p. 362).

Ruthven (2002)

Ruthven offers a detailed analysis of Islamist thought, including the roles of Mawdudi and Qutb as well as the significance of Wahhabism, which went further than Ibn Taymiyya in denouncing Muslims who 'took part in religiously reprehensible practices' as infidel. Saudi Islam, he says, is symptomatic of the Islamist worldview that suffers from epistemological schizophrenia; it lives in the modern world while trying to deny that it really exists. Ruthven accuses the Saudi regime of supporting terrorism throughout the Muslim world (p. 270). He links the technological background of many leading Islamists with their literal, often proof-text approach to the Qur'an. They also bypass most classical scholars. He sees 9/11 less as an act of Islamic heroism than as 'an Outrage, a fury for God, the Baader-Meinhof slogan Don't Argue, Destroy, could well have been their own' (p. 133). Ruthven thinks there is hope for peace in the Muslim world if some of the stimuli that fuel Islamism can be removed, if its threat can be weakened and if Muslims can be steered to develop the democratic systems advocated by such men as Adbel wahab el-Affendi (p. 291).

Esposito (2003) and Pipes (2002)

These two scholars have been critical of each other. Esposito, who heads the Center for Muslim–Christian Understanding at Georgetown University, Washington, DC regards Pipes, head of the Middle East Forum (www.meforum.org), as pro-Israeli. Pipes regards Esposito as too soft on radical Islam. Esposito (2003) argues that terrorists distort Islam to support their views, although he also identifies Ibn Taymiyya's 'fatwa on the Mongols' as hugely influential (p. 46). The Wahhabis, Qutb, Sadat's assassins and bin Laden have used the same logic to call for jihad 'against un-Islamic Muslim rulers and elites and against the West' (ibid.). However, bin Laden has failed to 'effectively mobilize the Islamic world in his unholy war', he says (p. 128), and Islamic history 'makes abundantly clear' that 'mainstream Islam, in law and theology as well as in practice, in the end has always marginalized extremists and terrorists from the Kharijites and Assassins to contemporary radical movements such as Al-Qaeda' (pp. 128–9). Muslims, he says, like 'every global community', are diverse. Pipes (2002) sees radical Islam as a much more serious threat than any of the other writers but he also concludes that the West needs to help Muslims with compatible views 'to secure victory against the militants' (p. 256). In 2003, President Bush controversially appointed Pipes to the board of the US Institute for Peace. Zionists and evangelical Christians, whose role in influencing US policy Ruthven also critiques, supported him against Democrat critics. (In early 2005, the US Senate failed to confirm his re-appointment.)

Peter Bergen (2001)

Bergen offers detailed descriptions of the events of 9/11, traces bin Laden's career and influences on him and details the global network and activities of al-Qaeda. Throughout, he stresses the political nature of the Islamists' anti-Western agenda. Bergen conducted an interview with bin Laden (March 1997). He concludes by asking will 'bin Laden's group, and those holy warriors who continue to arrive in Afghanistan for *jihad* training, follow the Assassins into the history books as a bloody footnote?' (p. 248).

Further discussion topics

- Is there a distinction between the suicide bombings of 9/11 and those committed against Israeli targets by Palestinians?
- Discuss whether the term 'Muslim terrorist' should be banned from our vocabulary?
- Does the media, by giving men such as Bakri the 'oxygen of publicity' (see Ahmed 2004) serve the public well or badly?
- The Qur'an is cited to justify the killing of civilians and the beheading of captives and also to denounce such acts. Which is the more convincing interpretation?
- How realistic is Tibi's call for Muslims to abandon the concepts of *hijrah, jihad* and *dar-al-islam?*
- *The 9/11 Commission Report* calls on the USA to define the message and to stand as an example of moral leadership in the world and to communicate and defend the American ideals in the Islamic world, through much stronger public diplomacy to reach more people, including students and leaders outside government. What else should the USA do in order to counter what Bergen describes as bin Laden's 'political war with the US' (p. 242)?
- Esposito and Pipes have both been accused of partisan scholarship. In your view, are all opinions partisan?
- Ruthven suggests that an Islamist takeover in Saudi might actually serve the Saudi people better, allowing them to work out their own

destiny without the eternal pressure of oil companies and arms manufacturers. Is he too optimistic or is this a viable strategy for the West to follow?

- Behind much debate about *jihad* of the sword is the argument that Islam is inherently violent, that Islam, and not a particular version of Islam, is the problem. How would you respond to someone who offers this argument to justify the view that Muslims everywhere need to be persuaded to abandon Islam in favour of some alternative, such as Christianity or secular humanism?

- Bergen asks, 'Were bin Laden and his Afghan rebels a creation of the US government?' Can any blame be attributed to the USA's own foreign policy in arming Saddam against Iran and the Afghan rebels against the Soviets in the 'creation of bin Laden' (see Bergen 2001: 69).

- Reference to Huntington's 'clash of civilizations' thesis has recurred throughout this book. In your view, has it raised important issues or is it of limited or no use as an analytical tool in helping us to understand Muslim disillusionment with the West's influence throughout the globe?

Resources

www.danielpipes.org
www.peterbergen.com

11 Algeria: A Study in Islamic Resurgence, and Bangladesh: Culture v. Islam

Democracy is a movable feast ... desirable only when the pro-western side wins an election in a non-western country. It can be 'cancelled', to the applause of the West, as it was in Algeria, when the undesirable 'Islamic fundamentalists' won.
   (Sardar 1998: 58)

Algeria's colonial legacy

Algeria usefully parallels Muslim colonial and post-colonial experiences, their struggles for self-determination and for the recovery of suppressed identities in many parts of the Muslim world, hence its choice as a case study. French colonization of Algeria began in 1830 with France's annexation of Algerian ports. In 1848, Algeria was proclaimed a 'department' of France, that is, an integral part of French territory. The French saw Algeria as an extension of France into North Africa. As the *www.arab.net* history of Algeria says, 'The concept of French Algeria became ingrained in the French mind'. The French, however, regarded the Arabs as an 'underclass that had to be tightly controlled'. European style institutions were 'imposed'. Mosques and madrassas were nationalized and sometimes even Islamic schools were staffed with French teachers. Children were taught that France was their 'mother country', that Algeria and France shared a common heritage, that the 'Gauls' were their 'ancestors' (*http://www.arab.net/algeria/history/algeria_history.html*). Nothing was taught about the 1300 years or so of pre-colonial Algerian history. Few Algerians bought this. However, the French appear to have succeeded in convincing themselves that Algeria and France were indivisibly united. Consequently, the French always viewed the 'Algerian question' in a distinctively different way from how they saw the independence aspirations of other French colonies. When French *colons* left Algeria in 1962, they saw themselves as political refugees fleeing from their own land, not as victims of decolonization.

The French tried to create a class of Arabs who would become their allies, a Western-educated, francophone and francophile elite known as the *évolvés* (the evolved ones). The *évolvés* correspond to 'Macauley's minute men' in British India, who would form a 'class who may be interpreters between us and the millions we govern – a class of persons Indian in blood and colour but English in taste, in opinions, in morals, and in intellect'. See Rushdie 1996 pp. 165–6 for the term 'Macauley's minute men' (a 'bunch of English-medium misfits'). Like the French in Algeria, the British in India looked upon India as 'British'. In Richard Attenborough's film *Gandhi* (1982), there is a scene in which Gandhi tells the Viceroy that the British should leave India. Then, it will be Indians, not a foreign power, that would have the job of solving India's problems, including the position of her Muslim minority. The Viceroy replied, incredulously, that Britain was hardly a foreign power, since India was British! The process by which non-French could (and can) gain citizenship has been called 'Frenchification', and the French have tended to accept such people as authentically French, although Oommen (1997) comments that:

> There is a hierarchy of citizens/nationals even in France; the white, catholic, French-speaking citizen from France at the top, and the 'Frenchified', Black, Muslim 'immigrant citizen' at the bottom. (p. 145)

Bhabha (1991) says that in England becoming Anglified is not quite the same as being English. The element of 'mimicry' discernible in Macauley's minute men means they are always '*Almost the same but not white*' (p. 89, his italics). This 'mimicry' is well portrayed by the character Aziz in David Lean's film *A Passage to India* (1984). Leila Ahmed (2000) tells how her childhood experience in Egypt was of being on the edge of different identities – Arab, Egyptian and European through the colonial influence and an Anglophile middle-class upbringing. At her English school, where her best friend was Edward Said's sister, Jean, she found it impossible to distinguish between Palestinian Christians and Egyptian Muslims, since all shared common attitudes and values. Nor had such terms as 'Imperialism' or 'The West' acquired the negative connotations of today, or were yet associated with oppression and exploitation. It was taken for granted that Europe had much to offer. Later, her views changed when she realized that Western scholars had, even if inadvertently, 'reproduced and therefore endorsed dominant Islam's view of itself as the sole and only legitimate version of Islam' (1992: 278). She describes Orientalism as the West's 'mode of representing and misrepresenting the Islamic world as a domain of Otherness and inferiority' and as a 'field of domination' (p. 279).

Al-Jaza'ir 'Arabiyya wa al-Islam dinuha (Algeria is Arab and Islam is its religion)

Soon after World War I, some Algerians began to campaign for civil rights. Soldiers returning from active duty in France reported on better standards of living and on democratic rights enjoyed by the French but not by Arabs.

Moves to grant Arabs equal rights were blocked in the French National Assembly by representatives of the Algerian colonialists. At this stage, an Arab Algerian could become a French citizen only by renouncing Islam. From the start of Algeria's anti-colonial movement, Muslim identity was a vital component. In 1931, the Association of Algerian *Ulama* adopted 'Islam is my religion, Arabic is my language, Algeria is my Fatherland' as its motto. 1933–36 saw a series of political protests, culminating in the drawing up of a Charter of Demands by the Muslim Congress. Meanwhile, Algerian French prospered while the social-economic gap between them and Algerian Arabs widened. Much more revenue was spent on educating French Algerians, for example, than was allocated to the inadequately equipped Muslim schools. 80 per cent of Arab children did not even attend school. By 1939, when a vehemently anti-French movement known as the Friends of the Manifesto and Liberty was formed, the goal of equal citizenship had for many given way to autonomy, if not independence. This group pursued a partly socialist, partly Islamic agenda. On VE Day in 1945, anti-French sentiment resulted in a series of incidents during which some 80 French and about 50,000 Arabs lost their lives (Cornwell 1980: 319). In 1946 Arab Algerians were granted full citizenship. However, the election of 1948 was rigged to favour the *colons*, which weakened the hand of those who were demanding autonomy within France and strengthened the hand of those arguing for complete independence. By 1954, the FLN (National Liberation Front) was leading a guerilla war against the French, with 'Algérie Musulmane' as its slogan. Esposito (1999) says that 'the struggle was called a *jihad*: its fighters were called *mujahidun* (holy warriors) and its journal *El Moudjahid* (The Holy Warrior)' (p. 172). After a bloody, protracted war, Algeria achieved independence in 1962.

Literary case study: Camus's *L'Etranger*

A fictional view of colonial Algeria

Albert Camus (1913–60) is widely recognized as one of France's most acclaimed writers of the twentieth century. He was born in Algeria, where he locates his main works of fiction. Camus was raised not far from the Arab quarter, so he was certainly familiar with Algerian poverty. He knew and loved the landscape of his country of birth. However, he was thoroughly French, a product of French culture and language, and believed in the superiority of French culture over Arab and in the absolute Frenchness of Algeria. In the year of his birth, the governor-general of Algeria 'elaborated' the French mission as 'to substitute "civilization and common sense for barbarism and fanaticism, which means the assimilation, unification and Frenchifying of the races"' (cited by Mairowitz and Korkos 2001: *http://www.geocities.com/Athens/Aegean/1311/algeria.html*). Dying two years short of Algerian independence, Camus opposed the very concept of a separate Algerian nation. In his view, 'as far as Algeria is concerned, national independence is a formula driven by nothing other than passion. There has never yet been an Algerian nation. The Jews, Turks, Greeks, Italians, or Berbers would be as entitled to claim the leadership of this potential nation. As things stand, the Arabs do not comprise the whole of Algeria ... The French of Algeria are also natives, in the strong sense of the word. Moreover, a purely Arab Algeria could not achieve that economic independence without which political independence is nothing but an illusion. However inadequate the French efforts have been, it is of such proportions that no other country would today agree to take over the responsibility' (cited by Said 1993: 179).

Edward Said encourages the reading of colonial texts to see 'what went into' them 'and what' their authors 'excluded' (p. 67). With reference to Camus, he also points out that the intended audience of Camus's books was exclusively European, even though their context was Algeria. For Camus, he suggests, Algeria existed for Europeans, who in a sense (and this is implied in the above cited passage) had created Algeria. Camus's *L'Etranger* was published in 1942. The independence struggle, although not yet the bloodshed it later became, was already well under way, yet any reference to Algerian political aspirations or to the realities of colonial rule are conspicuous by their absence. Thus, we should read into *L'Etranger* 'what was once forcibly excluded ... the whole previous history of France's colonialism and its destruction of the Algerian state, and the later emergence of an independent Algeria (which Camus opposed)' (*ibid.*). In this way, the text becomes a tool for voicing 'what is silent or marginally present or ideologically represented in' such a work (*ibid.*).

Although set in Algeria, no few commentators regard the real context of *L'Etranger* to be Nazi-occupied France. The text reflects the darkness and the moral malaise that many experienced during that period. Camus was an existentialist and the book is concerned with its chief character's own dilemmas and conflicts, his seemingly unnatural attitude towards his own lack of a moral conscience. 'Love' has no meaning for him (Camus 1989: 44). At the start of the novel, he cannot mourn his mother's death (see p. 79). He did not remember his mother's age (p. 19). Then he shoots an Arab (who, like all Arabs in the novel, has no name) and has no remorse for this act. In the court scene, he is criticized for swimming and for going out with his girlfriend on the day his mother had died (p. 118). The prosecutor describes him as 'devoid of the least spark of human feeling' (p. 129), since he can only answer questions clinically and factually. He shows no emotion. Even though the central event of the novel is an Arab's murder, there is no reference to any probable cause, except that Meursault's friend, Raymond, appears to have been followed by some Arabs (see p. 61) who may have 'had a grudge' against him. They are merely ciphers, lacking personality or substance, unlike the European characters. Islam is totally absent from the text.

Arabs in the text: some examples

p. 5: 'An Arab woman, a nurse, I supposed – was sitting beside the bier; she was wearing a blue smock and had a rather gaudy scarf wound round her hair.'

p. 67: 'I noticed two Arabs in blue dungarees ... coming in our direction ... they walked slowly.'

p. 67: 'A fight ensues, "he's got a knife". I spoke too late. The man had gashed Raymond's arm and mouth.'

p. 69: 'The two natives backed away slowly, keeping us at bay with the knife and never taking their eyes off us.'

p. 71: 'The Arab with the reed went on playing, and both of them watched our movements.'

p. 72: 'the Arabs vanished; they'd slipped like lizards under cover of the rock.'

p. 75: 'the Arab didn't move ... I waited ... then the Arab drew his knife ... I fired four shots into the inert body.'

p. 89: 'they asked me what I'd done. I told them I'd killed an Arab, and they kept mum for a while. But presently night began to fall, and one of them explained to me how to lay out my sleeping mat.'

Discussion topics

- Can readers learn anything about French attitudes towards Algeria from this text? Respond to the way in which Arabs are represented in the text. Are they only 'objects' of French action?

- Is this a text that, to adapt a term used by Chinua Achebe of Joseph Conrad's *Heart of Darkness*, 'should not be read', or is Said right to suggest that such a text can be converted into a useful tool for critiquing colonial assumptions?

- Do you think the text provides any useful insight into or information on Algeria's anti-colonial struggle?

- How might an Algerian today evaluate this novel? Would they share the common French view that this is one of the classics of modern French literature?

Post-independence

The leaders of the FLN were of the *évolvé* class and although they condemned French colonialism and used Islam as a badge of identity, they were committed to socialist and nationalist policies that would, they believed, modernize Algeria. 'In the guise of Islamic socialism', says Esposito, the FLN 'pursued an essentially secular path of political and economic development implemented by a Western-oriented ruling elite' (Esposito 1999: 173). Ahmad (1983) describes the Western-educated and Western-oriented elite throughout the post-colonial Muslim world as a leadership that 'held the reigns of power but ... did not enjoy the trust and confidence of the people', from whom they 'were alienated' (p. 219). As under the French, mosques and Islamic schools were run by the state. In 1965, President Ahmad Ben Bella was overthrown by a military coup under General Houari Boumédienne, who ruled until his death in 1978. Chadli Benjedid succeeded him. Algeria, at this point, was a one-party system. It was not until 1989 that, with the promise of multiparty elections, other parties, including Islamic ones, were legalized.

Algeria's post-colonial situation resembles the Pakistani experience. During the independence struggle, Westernized leaders used Islam to mobilize and to inspire their followers. After independence, however, in a Pakistan whose systems and policies reflected Western models, Islam was relegated to the private sphere, although it still functioned as the state's badge of identity. In the Algerian and Pakistani contexts, it was products of the Frenchification and Anglification policies that led the independence struggle. Both drew on Islam to rally support but remained committed to a secular worldview. Pakistan's founder, Muhammad Ali Jinnah (1876–1948), advocated the 'two nation' theory and used 'Islam in danger' as a slogan but could only be properly described as culturally a Muslim. Opening Pakistan's first Constituent Assembly on 11 August 1947, Jinnah, who only spoke fluently in English, said, 'You are free, you are free to go to your temples, you are free to go to your mosques or any other place of worship in this state of Pakistan. You may belong to any religion or caste or creed – that has nothing to do with the business of the State' (cited in Zakaria 1988: 228). In both contexts, post-colonial politics has seen a power struggle between Western-oriented secularists and those for whom Islam is more than a source of morals or of cultural values. In Algeria, 'battle lines' were often drawn along the lines of French culture versus Islam, for example in the 'debate that raged 1975–1984' over 'family law reforms ... students and women's organizations demonstrated and clashed' (Esposito 1999: 174).

As Mawdudi and his Jamaat in Pakistan campaigned for a return to true Islam, so did groups and individuals in Algeria where the Islamic Salvation Front (FIS) became the most dynamic and popular organization. This coincided with a change in Algeria's economic situation. Revenue from her oil fell, which left the elite relatively unaffected but 'exacerbated social tensions between' the rulers 'and the majority of the population' (*ibid.*). Borrowing language from other Muslim revivalists, the FIS preached that the FLN, who were merely a neo-colonial, pro-Westernized continuation of French power (although its rhetoric remained anti-imperialist), was failing to deliver what independence had promised, a fairer distribution of resources. The best jobs still went to those with a French education (Esposito: 1999: 174). Ahmed (1993) describes the FLN regime as 'a morass of corruption' (p. 132). Instead of either capitalism or socialism, preached the FIS, Islam was the answer. On the one hand, the FLN were 'apparently hostile to the USA', while on the other 'they would sign immense natural gas deals with American companies' (Cornwell 1980: 321).

Islam the total answer

In her novel, *The Fall of the Imam* (1988), Nawal El Saadawi depicts a dictatorial Muslim ruler, the Imam, whose word is equated with Allah's word and who 'ruled according to the laws of God's *shar'iat*' so that citizens must believe equally and at the same time in 'the Imam, in the nation and in God' as a single entity. They must 'either believe in all, or in nothing' (p. 174). One of her characters is a foreigner who arrives in the country to win back his former sweetheart, who is now the Imam's official wife, but finds himself employed by the state as a 'foreign expert' to help solve its many problems. However, instead of applying foreign solutions he soon discovers that the best way to gain favour with leader and people alike is to refer to Islam in all matters, so he converts and becomes instead 'the expert believer':

> I had answers to every question and solutions to every problem ... the whole matter was very simple since all we needed ... was a return to religion and an unlimited belief in God and his prophet Muhammad. They would ask me: and now, Expert Believer, what do you think of nuclear radiations ... Pray five times each day and fast the month of Ramadan [I replied].

The Imam bestowed on him the title 'Philosopher' (p. 106). See literary case study in Chapter Six.

Like Mawdudi, the FIS's founder and leader, Abassi Madani, presents Islam as a ready-made, fully comprehensive, complete system (Esposito 1999: 178). Madani stresses that Islam is a religion of social justice and that the basis of this is the *Shari'ah* (p. 175). The *Shari'ah*, in his view, provides the perfect balance between the rights of individuals and those of society. He often presents, says Esposito, 'an Islamic ideal in which the world is one of white and black, right and wrong, self-interest and altruism. It is a world of transcendent principles and "shoulds"' (p. 179). He views secularism as a 'major cause for Muslim decline and impotence' (p. 180). He is outspoken in his condemnation of America's greed and self-interested foreign policy. However, he is open to 'constructive co-operation' with the USA provided that Algeria's 'autonomy', its 'right and that of the

Muslim world to determine its destiny' is properly recognized (p. 180). Madani believes that an Islamic state can hold elections, and that minority rights must be safeguarded. However, he criticizes political parties for desiring power for power's sake, not for the good of the people.

The demand for autonomy

Sardar (1998) criticizes the 'West' for denying other cultures freedom and autonomy, asking 'Who will be there to dialogue with once the earth and humanity are completely Westernized'. The West should abandon its project of 'turning all cultures into ahistorical, liberal, free markets' (p. 279). Similarly, Madani wants the USA to honour and respect Algeria's and the Muslim world's autonomy. As outlined in this book's Introduction, Samuel P. Huntington's 'clash of civilizations' thesis predicts that the next global fault line and conflict will not be between ideologies (unlike the cold war between Western capitalism and Eastern communism) but between civilizations, or cultures. Projecting emerging alignments, he posits a clash between Islam and the non-Muslim world:

> The governments of Muslim countries are likely to continue to become less friendly to the West, and intermittent low-intensity and at times perhaps high-intensity violence will occur between Islamic groups and Western societies. (1996: 238; see his figure on p. 245).

Does the Muslim world represent a military threat to Western civilization? Despite some anti-Western terrorism and the anti-Western sentiment of a number of Muslim regimes, most scholars who have analysed the 'threat' conclude that:

> there cannot be a great 'Islamic challenge', not only because the Islamic states are, and will remain, much weaker than those of the West, but also because they do not represent a coherent, internationally constituted alliance. (Halliday 1996: 119)

Esposito (1999) agrees, although he does warn that the West's attitudes and actions may 'risk ... creating a self-fulfilling' prophecy (p. 289). He points out that while some Islamists 'advocate violent rebellion' and an anti-Western policy, others 'do not'. Islamists 'are not necessarily anti-Western, anti-American and anti-democratic' and many do not 'threaten US interests', he says (p. 289). Zakaria (1988) writes that 'There is ... no basis to the bogey of Muslims ganging up against non-Muslims' (p. 297). Tibi (1998) says that 'claims ... made for forming a world bloc based on Islamic civilization ... are heedless of the significant regional differences within that civilization' (p. 52). 'I fail to see', he writes, 'the "Islamic threat" to the West' (2001: 22). However, he thinks that 'despite its deplorable shortcomings', Huntington's book rightly identifies the issue of 'culture' as of significance within world affairs (p. 16). He argues that the politicization of religion, in various parts of the world, puts cultural claims at the centre of several existing conflicts (p. 17). Pipes (2002) asks

'Does Islam threaten the West?' and answers 'No, it does not. But militant Islam does threaten it in many and profound ways', continuing, 'There is, indeed, no comparable danger in the world today' (p. 3). He suggests that the violence of Islamists towards Muslims who disagree with them is evidence that the current conflict is not a battle between civilizations but a battle within a civilization, Islam – a battle for the soul of Islam 'between Islamists and ... moderate Muslims' (pp. 251, 249). Sardar (1998) describes Huntington's solution as doing what the West has always done, 'support other civilization groups sympathetic to Western values and interests', that is, 'divide and rule' (p. 84). Yet a close reading of Huntington (1996) shows that he also suggests another strategy and that this one is surprisingly close to Sardar's and Madani's call for recognition of Others' cultural and political autonomy.

Huntington reprimands the West for assuming that the rest of the world either needs or wants its 'culture', 'values, institutions and practices' (1996: 78). He criticizes the notion that 'Westernization and modernization reinforce each other and have to go together' (p. 73). 'Non Western societies', he says, 'can modernize without abandoning their own cultures' (p. 78). When peoples and nations think their 'cultures' are threatened, they respond by retreating into some form of cultural isolationism, or by affirming their identity over-and-against the West's. This explains the anti-Western stance of many Islamists, since 'what Westerners herald as benign global integration, such as the proliferation of worldwide media, non-Westerners denounce as nefarious Western imperialism' (p. 66). Huntington's solution is for Westerners to accept 'their civilization as unique not universal and' to unite 'to renew peace' (p. 20–1).

Discussion topic

- Can you see common ground between Muslims and Huntington on cultural autonomy?

Resources

See Huntington's 1996 journal abstract of his book. Huntington is a professor at Harvard and Director of the Harvard Academy for International and Area Studies. His Bradley Lecture at the American Enterprise Institute (11 May 1998) on 'Global Perspectives on War and Peace, or Transiting a Uni-Multi Polar World' is also a useful summary of his theory. This is available at: *http://www.aei.org/news/newsID.16661/news_detail.asp.*

Democracy as a movable feast

The plight of Algeria and Tunisia are not dissimilar. For in both cases when the democratic choice of the people is not in favour of the secularist elite, undemocratic measures become acceptable. (al-Ghannouchi 2000: 104)

In 1991, the FIS won the largest share of the votes, pushing the FLN into third place. The FLN had campaigned vigorously against the FIS, warning that its victory would have dire consequences for 'democracy, pluralism and women's rights' (*ibid.*, p. 181). The FLN argued that Madani's apparent commitment to democracy was ingenuous, a pragmatic ploy to gain power (see p. 184). In early 1992, the military intervened, aborted the election process, detained thousands of Islamist activists, banned the FIS and set up its own Council of State. It appears that the military had at least the implicit support of the French government in suppressing what it called 'radical Islam'.

Reaction from around the globe was swift and ambiguous. On the one hand, the cancelling of an elected party's democratic victory attracted censure. On the other, the Western powers did nothing to reverse the situation, apparently happier with a pro-Western military regime than with democratically elected Muslim 'fundamentalists' who might reduce women to slavery! As Sardar says, 'Democracy is a movable feast ... desirable only when the pro-western side wins an election in a non-western country. It can be "cancelled", to the applause of the West, as it was in Algeria, when the undesirable "Islamic fundamentalists" won' (1998: 58). Similarly, Ahmed (1993) complains about 'democracy and double standards'. Following the Islamic victory, the West, he says, was

> put to the test. What would its attitude be? Would it wait and give the FIS a chance to run things in the way it wished? Or would it be pleased if the FIS was frustrated and power denied? For better or for worse, the FIS was poised to win the election and take power. At this juncture the elections were postponed and the military moved its tanks into the streets ... the West was jubilant. The beatings and the killings, even in the mosques, the arrests and the harassment did not appear to dim Western joy. The main news was that another Islamic movement had been stopped. There were no tears for the death of democracy. (p. 133)

Subsequently, what had been a constitutional and democratic campaign for Islamization became an armed struggle. The FIS itself split into factions, of which the more militant 'reject participation in the parliamentary process and espouse armed struggle (*jihad*) and terrorism' (Esposito 1999: 187). Ahmed (1993) points out that the FIS had not, as already noted, advocated a totally negative attitude towards the West. Its leaders had spoken in 'conciliatory terms of encouraging Western investments and maintaining close contacts with the European Community' (p. 133). Consequently, 'The double standards cause Muslims to ask, "Why is the West constantly hostile to us?" They point to Algeria. If Algeria is not so far inclined to an extreme Islamic position – for all kinds of social and sectarian reasons – this manner of negative Western response will provoke a virulently anti-West position' (*ibid.*). It has. In Algeria, a civil war developed between the military government and a range of Islamist groups. Government troops 'saw the beard and head scarf as symbols of fundamentalist terrorism', and took action, while the 'militants now targeted women in Western dress and secular intellectuals as symbols of a Western-oriented state despotism and repression' (Esposito 1999: 188). Attacks on civilians characterized the 'spiral of violence' on both sides. In 1997, following agreement between some of the opposition groups and the government, elections were held. The FIS was excluded. International observers alleged fraud. The military-backed National Democratic Rally won the largest number of seats but the MSP (Movement of Society for Peace) received the second highest number. A moderate Muslim party that rejects violence, MSP was awarded four (out of thirty) places in the new cabinet following which several opposition groups also 'declared a cease fire and a desire to pursue a dialogue with the army' (Esposito 1999: 191). Violence, however, continues. The Armed Islamic Group (GIA) is still committed to 'an all out war to achieve its goals' (p. 191). Some Algerian Muslims have apparently become more extreme following the failure of the democratic process to deliver power. Others, faced with continued violence and bloodshed, appear disenchanted with extremism. They want to stress Islam's ability to promote rational discussion and to achieve their aims by negotiation and dialogue.

Discussion topic

- Discuss Ahmed's contention that Muslims who advocate democracy have a harder job in the Muslim world as a result of what took place in Algeria.

    Muslims were appalled at the double standards of the West. Had there been a similar military action, say in Pakistan, the Western media would have become hysterical with stories of the tyranny of martial law. They would have paraded the old arguments about the death of democracy in Muslim society, the inherent predilection of Muslims for authoritarian rule. But here was a situation where the West was gloating over the denial of power to the duly elected FIS. (1993b: 233).

Tamimi (2000a) points out that when the tanks 'crushed the ballot boxes' in Algeria, it was Westernized secularists who cheered them on, claiming to 'protect democracy from the majority, because ... the majority could not be trusted'. When polls do not produce the result that self-proclaimed democrats want, they behave very undemocratically. Ironically, says Tamimi, 'free democratic elections have proven secularism to be very unpopular with the masses' (p. 27).

Summary of the Algerian Islamist agenda

a. the *Shari'ah*, not existing laws, is the only true basis for social justice.
b. The existing regime is pro-Western and anti-Islamic.
c. Islam is the source of all answers to Algeria's social, economic and political problems.
d. Original Islam must be revived.
e. Secularism is a major cause of Muslim decline.

Bangladesh: a case study

Bangladesh was originally part of what Sardar (1985) calls 'the first state in contemporary history to be created solely for the sake of Islam' (p. 135), Pakistan. In that state, says V. S. Naipaul (1998), 'Islam should have been identity enough for everybody' (p. 325). It wasn't. Bangladesh separated almost entirely to assert cultural independence. The struggle in Bangladesh between democrats, pluralists and Islamic activists (the *Jamaati-i-Islam* is a member of the present government, elected in 2001), as well as the role of elites and of patrimonialism, which all feature in this case study, are equally important in understanding how authority is exercised in other parts of the Muslim world, including Saudi Arabia (see Chapter Two).

Bangladesh achieved independence in 1971, after a civil war. The State of Pakistan, formed in 1947 as the British left India, had consisted of two provinces, East and West, separated by roughly 1,000 miles of Indian soil. Pakistan was intended to be the homeland for those Muslims who believed that they had no future in a Hindu-dominated India and was created by partitioning off from India the two most populous Muslim areas, the North West and the eastern part of the historical province of Bengal. Muslims who campaigned for Pakistan had always envisioned an Islamic state, with Islam as the unifying factor holding its two provinces, with their different languages and cultures, together. There were always those, however, who doubted the wisdom of partitioning Bengal, where despite a Hindu majority in the west and a Muslim majority in the east, a tradition of tolerance and of love for Bengali language, poetry, and literature all but bridged the religious divide between Bengali Hindus and Bengali Muslims. The eastern province, too, would still be left with a large Hindu population (some 15 per cent), while the west would have a substantial Muslim minority. The reality of the Pakistan experience did not prove popular in the east. Bengali Islam dates from the thirteenth century, when Sufi preachers followed by Muslim invaders, who supplanted Hindu and Buddhist dynasties, introduced Islam. The religion that took root was from the start imbued with Sufi notions and practices and some religious teachers could attract Hindu as well as Muslim devotees. Muslims in West Pakistan regarded Bengali Islam as deviant and corrupt, the type of Islam that had caused the loss of Islam's political and cultural ascendancy. Wahhabi influence can be detected here. Others said that Bengali was an unsuitable language for Muslims, compared with Urdu (which combines Arabic and Hindi). The latter resulted in the imposition of Urdu as the official language of Pakistan.

In East Pakistan, a pro-Bengali language movement was launched, largely student-led. On 21 February 1951 four protestors were shot (Pakistan had passed a law prohibiting public gatherings of more than four people). One of the protestors arrested at the time was Sheikh Mujibur Rahman (1920–75; later dubbed *Bangabandhu*, or friend of Bengal) who, elected to the National Assembly in 1954, emerged as the spokesman for East Pakistan's demands for cultural and linguistic freedom. He was a founder of the Awami League. With other politicians in the East, he believed that a separate party was needed in the face of the East's monopoly of power and resources. He was elected to the Provincial Assembly in the same year (1949). Mujibur spent a year and a half in prison (1958–59) and six months in 1962. He was arrested several times in 1966 and kept in detention for 21 months. Increasingly, the League campaigned for greater economic and political autonomy. Pakistan enjoyed only short periods of civilian, democratic government between longer periods of military rule. In 1971, the Awami League won 160 of 300 seats in the National Assembly, which should have enabled Mujibur to form a government. Instead, he was arrested yet again, Parliament dissolved and political parties disbanded. The war of liberation followed. Against all odds (and aided by India), Bangladesh won. Hussain and Khan (1998) claim that 'with the independence of Bangladesh in 1971, for the first time in history, a demand was made for politics and culture to coalesce' (p. 198).

The new Constitution provided for a Prime Minister-style government, a bicameral assembly and enshrined nationalism, socialism, secularism and democracy as the State's guiding principles. Elections held in 1973 gave the Awami League a large majority, with the charismatic father of the nation Mujibur as Prime Minister. Islam had been the sole ingredient in Pakistani identity and nationhood; Bangladesh's was language and culture. This also recognized the role played by Hindus and other minorities in the independence struggle. The slogan 'Islam in Danger' had rallied Muslims to the cause of Pakistan; in Bangladesh, the rallying slogan is *Joy Bangla* (Victory for Bangla). Rabindranath Tagore, the poet of the Bengali renaissance and a Hindu, penned the National Anthem (as he did India's)!

Mujibur, once elected, embarked on a centralizing project that abrogated more and more powers for himself. In 1974 he proclaimed a state of emergency, assumed the Presidency and banned all parties except his own. In August 1975 he was assassinated, together with ten members of his family. A series of military coups followed. Ziaur Rahman, initially Chief Martial Law Administrator, was ratified as President in an uncontested election (1978). Pledging to restore civilian rule, Zia removed restrictions on political activity and held multi-party elections in 1979. His own newly formed BNP won 207 of the 300 seats. Zia was assassinated in 1981. When the weak provisional government was unable to restore stability, military intervention followed under General Hussain M. Ershad, who banned political activity. Political pluralism was restored in 1986, when Ershad stood for election as President under his own newly formed Jatiyo Party. No major party's candidate stood against him. In the largely uncontested parliamentary elections of 1988, the Jatiyo won 251 seats. Islam was declared to be the religion of the state. This may have been a ploy to attract more aid from richer Muslim countries. Others think it inevitable that Bangladesh would at some point reassert its Islamic identity to distinguish itself from the culture of its neighbour, the Indian State of West Bengal (now Bangla), with whom reunification seemed logical to some.

In 1990, Bangladesh was crippled by strikes and rallies against Ershad, who, charged and found guilty of corruption, resigned in December. Elections followed in 1991. Khaleda Zia, Zia's widow, became Prime Minister in a coalition government that included the *Jamaati-i-Islam*. The amended constitution restored a Prime Minister-style system and left the President (elected by Parliament) with mainly ceremonial duties but with special powers in situations where the government is unable to function effectively. The Awami League alleged electoral malpractice. In 1994, opposition members resigned *en masse*, forcing the President to take emergency measures. Parliament was dissolved, a caretaker government installed and fresh elections scheduled. In February 1996 the BNP won a landslide second term. However, allegations of vote rigging brought the country to a standstill and a second election was held in June. This time, the Awami League won and Mujibur's daughter Hasina (only two daughters had survived the massacre) became Prime Minister. Her government became the first to complete its full tenure in office, although opposition members rarely attended parliament. In the election of 2001, Khaleda Zia was returned to power, again as leader of a coalition that includes the *Jamaati-i-Islam*. The Awami League is currently boycotting Parliament. 'Bengalis consider too much authoritarian rule as problematic', suggest Hussain and Khan (1998), and 'they [are also threatened] by the opposite of too much freedom ... so the lifting of authoritarian rule is also problematic' (p. 212). They also suggest that 'Bengalis have uprisings in almost every generation against oppressive rule, but being unable to handle the subsequent disorder, they set back to authoritarian rule again' (p. 212).

What role does Islam play in Bangladeshi identity and in Bangladesh's political arena?

On the one hand, democracy and political activity has had a long history in Bengal, where British power dates from 1757. Bengalis were the first to benefit from British education and the first to demand 'fair play' from the British, including the right to participate in the government of India. Political debate and activity is endemic in Bangladesh. On the other hand,

Bengal was governed for centuries by authoritarian rule from outside; first the Moghuls, then the British, then West Pakistan. This may have produced an unusual political culture, so that on the one hand there is a passion for participation while on the other there is also willingness to submit to authoritarian rule, especially if the ruler is also charismatic. Hussain and Khan (1998) suggest that the political culture of Bangladesh regards 'leadership' as something that is inherent in individuals, a quality that commands obedience, which does not depend on, or derive from, any electorate:

> Bengalis idealise power as something arising from human consent that is freely given. Authority stems from unquestioning recognition that some other person is superior ... and worthy of respect. (p. 208)

In their view, this explains why opposition leaders find it difficult to function, since the notion of a 'loyal opposition' is lacking in a culture that regards 'leaders' as 'superior': 'the political leaders of Bangladesh ... place themselves on an unequal position of hierarchy and fail to discuss nationally important issues as equals not as rivals' (p. 200). Leadership, too, may derive from holding or from inheriting positions of social or economic power (the landlords, or *jamindaris*). Hussain and Khan go so far as to say that 'Bengalis look for magical powers or charismatic qualities in a political leader' (p. 206). This is a type of 'patrimonialism', or elitism, perhaps not dissimilar to the traditional tribal leadership pattern found in the Gulf States and in areas of North Africa. This may explain why two women are so prominent in Bangladeshi politics: one is the Father of the Nation's daughter, the other a former President's widow (notwithstanding their abilities and achievements). On the other hand, a rumour that Mujibur intended to establish a monarchy, with himself as king, something that the Bengali appetite for participatory politics could not countenance, may have motivated his assassins. Power cannot be permanent. It 'moves' from person to person.

Islam remains the dominant religion and although minorities (now approximately 12 per cent) experience some discrimination (and occasional attacks on people and property), relations are generally good. The Constitution guarantees freedom of religion and non-discrimination on the grounds of religion, gender or ethnicity. An unusually large number of Muslims report friendships across religious grounds (see Banu, 1992 p. 163). Hussain and Khan (1998) cite research conducted in 1984–85 and 1988–90 that suggests that 'the majority ... do not opt for either religious or left radical parties' but 'for moderate or moderately secular parties ... Almost all respondents said that their choice was on the basis of liking for the leader of the party ... [their] knowledge of ideology, programmes and organizational structure was minimal' (pp. 210–11).

Research suggests that while Islam is the 'religion' of the majority, and the source of their morality, few want what could be called an 'Islamic State' or regard religion as the main ingredient of national identity (*ibid.*).

Islamic parties have not performed well in the polls and although the *Jamaati-i-Islam* is a member of the present government it is unlikely, in the near future, to win enough votes to form a government of its own. The 1988 amendment to the Constitution, too, was controversial at the time and arguably changed little in practice. The legal system is still largely derived from English law. The *Jamaati*'s *Manifesto* for the 2001 elections describes the party as unlike other parties since its aim is not merely to gain power but to 'establish a complete equitable and well-rounded social order in the world on the basis of the Qur'an and *Sunnah* uprooting all sorts of man's oppression over man including the oppressed from the world through introducing the law of Allah on His earth'. Islam, not any other ideology, is the answer to Bangladesh's economic and social problems. The party pledges itself to improve welfare, curb exploitation and to achieve social emancipation for all people, regardless of 'caste, creed and colour'. However, the *Manifesto* nowhere spells out in detail what 'establishing Allah's *Deen* and freeing humanity' would mean in practice for Bangladesh, for its laws, Constitution or for non-Muslim citizens. It does promise to work with all 'democracy-loving and patriotic' forces, pointing out that it had 'first mooted' the concept of a caretaker government (used between the dissolution of parliament and elections in 1996 and 2001). With 130 million citizens, Bangladesh remains (to date) a Muslim country where democracy, multi-party politics and a secular orientation (in practice, though no longer enshrined in the Constitution) are part and parcel of the prevailing political climate. See literary case study on Nasrin's *Lajja* (Chapter Seven).

Forty-eight per cent of the world's approximately 1.5 billion Muslims live in the four South Asian countries of Indonesia, Bangladesh, Pakistan and India.

Discussion topics

Tibi, referring to the Middle East states, comments that they are 'only nominally nation states' and lack the 'basic institutions required for establishing a democratically designed political community'. Their 'Neo-patriarchal political cultures' create 'obstacles to democratization' (1998: 192). On the other hand, merely imposing democracy (and human rights) is no solution either. Cultures, he says, must learn to speak the language of democracy 'in their own tongues' (p. 180).

- How can the right conditions for democratization be established in contexts where people are used to autocratic rule?

- Bangladeshis have talked about democracy for a long time and have democratic structures in place. In your opinion, has democracy taken root in Bangladesh's cultural environment? Where would you locate Bangladesh in terms of the 'left–right' spectrum? How would you describe the role of religion within the State?

- Has Bangladesh passed Huntington's test for democracy?

Bibliography

'Abduh, Muhammad (2002) 'Laws Should Change in Accordance with the Conditions of Nations *and* the Theology of Unity', pp. 50–60 in Kurzman, Charles (ed.), *Modernist Islam, 1840–1940: A Sourcebook*. New York: OUP.

Adams, Charles J. (1983) 'Mawdudi and the Islamic State', pp. 99–133 in Esposito, John L. (ed.), *Voices of Resurgent Islam*. New York: OUP.

El-Affendi, Abdelwahab (ed.) (2001) *Rethinking Islam and Modernity: Essays in Honour of Fathi Osman*. Leicester: The Islamic Foundation.

al-Afghani, Sayyid Jamal al-Din (2002) 'Lecture on Teaching and Learning *and* Answer to Renan', pp. 103–10 in Kurzman, Charles (ed.), *Modernist Islam, 1840–1940: A Sourcebook*. New York: OUP.

Afshari, Reza (2003) 'Egalitarian Islam and Misogynist Islamic Tradition: A Critique of the Feminist Reinterpretation of Islamic History and Heritage'. Institute for the Secularization of Islamic Society, www.isisforum.com/women/afshari.htm

Ahmad, Khurshid (ed.) (1976a, 2nd edn, 3rd edn 2001) *Islam: Its Meaning and Message*. Leicester: The Islamic Foundation.

Ahmad, Khurshid (1976b) 'Islam: Basic Principles and Characteristics', pp. 27–44 in Ahmad, Khurshid (ed.), *Islam: Its Meaning and Message*. Leicester: The Islamic Foundation.

Ahmad, Khurshid (1983) 'The Nature of the Islamic Resurgence', pp. 218–29 in Esposito, John L. (ed.), *Voices of Resurgent Islam*. Oxford: OUP.

Ahmad, Khurshid and Ansari, Zafar Ishaq (eds) (1979) *Islamic Perspectives: Studies in Honour of Mawlana Sayyid Abul Al'a Mawdudi*. Leicester: The Islamic Foundation.

Ahmad, Mumtaz (ed.) (1986) *State and Politics in Islam*. Washington: American Trust Publication.

Ahmad, Qeyamuddin (1966) *The Wahabi Movement in India*. Delhi: Manohar.

Ahmed, Akbar (1988) *Discovering Islam: Making Sense of Muslim History and Society*. London: Routledge.

Ahmed, Akbar (1992a) *Postmodernism and Islam: Predicament and Promise*. London: Routledge.

Ahmed, Akbar (1992b) *Living Islam.* BBC2 series.

Ahmed, Akbar (1993) *Living Islam: From Samarkand to Stornoway.* London: BBC Book.

Ahmed, Akbar (1999) Review of Bassam Tibi's *The Challenge of Fundamentalism: Political Islam and the New World Disorder,* in *International Affairs* Vol. 75: 3, p. 694.

Ahmed, Akbar (2003) *Islam Under Siege: Living Dangerously in a Post-Honor World.* Cambridge: Polity Press.

Ahmed, Akbar (2004) 'A Message of Violence and Hatred', the *Independent,* July 1.

Ahmed, Leila (1978) *Edward W. Lane: A Study of His Life and Works and of British Ideas of the Middle East in the Nineteenth Century.* London: Longman.

Ahmed, Leila (1992) *Women and Gender in Islam: Historical Roots of a Modern Debate.* New Haven, CT: Yale University Press.

Ahmed, Leila (2000) *A Border Passage: From Cairo to America: a woman's journey.* New York: Farrar, Strauss and Giroux.

al-Ahsan, Abdullah (1992) *Ummah or Nation: Identity Crises in Contemporary Muslim Society.* Leicester: The Islamic Foundation.

Akhtar, Shabbir (1989) *Be Careful with Muhammad: The Salman Rushdie Affair.* London: Bellew.

Akhtar, Shabbir (1991) 'An Islamic Model of Revelation', pp. 95–106 in *Islam and Christian-Muslim Relations* Vol. 2, No 1.

'Ali, Abdullah Yusuf (1989) *The Meaning of the Holy Qur'an* (new edn, revised by Ismail al-Faruqi; 9th edn 1996). Beltsville, MD: Amana Publications.

'Ali, Chiragh (1984; original publication 1885) *A Critical Exposition of the Popular 'Jihad'.* Delhi: Idareh-i Adabiyyat-i Delli.

'Ali, Chiragh (2002) 'The Proposed Political, Legal and Social Reforms', pp. 277–303 in Kurzman, Charles (ed.), *Modernist Islam, 1840–1940: A Sourcebook.* New York: OUP.

Ali, Monica (2003) *Brick Lane.* London: Transworld Publishers.

Ali, Syed Mumtaz (1993) 'Treatment of Minorities: The Islamic Model'. *www.muslim-canada.org/minorities.html.*

Anderson, Benedict (1991) *Imagined Communities.* London: Virago.

Anderson, Lisa (1983) 'Qaddafi's Islam', pp. 134–48 in Esposito, John L. (ed.), *Voices of Resurgent Islam.* New York: OUP.

Arkoun, Mohammed (1986) *L'Islam, morale et politique.* Paris: Desclée de Brouwer.

Arkoun, Mohammed (1994) *Rethinking Islam: common questions, uncommon answers.* Boulder, CA: Westview Press.

Arkoun, Mohammed (1994) 'Back to the Rushdie Affair Once More', pp. 45–50, in Brazilier, George (ed) *For Rushdie,* London: G. Brazilier.

Arkoun, Mohammed (1998a) 'Islam, Europe, the West: Meanings-at-Stake and the Will-to-Power', pp. 172–89 in Cooper, John, Nettler, Ronald and Mahmoud, Mohamed (1998), *Islam and Modernity: Muslim Intellectuals Respond.* London: I. B. Tauris.

Arkoun, Mohammed (1998b) 'Rethinking Islam Today,' pp. 205–21 in Kurzman, Charles (ed.) *Liberal Islam: A Sourcebook.* New York: OUP.

Arnold, Sir Thomas (1913) *The Preaching of Islam.* London: Constable & Co.

'Ashmawi, Muhamamd Sa'id (1998) 'Al-Shariah: The Codification of Islamic Law', pp. 49–56, in Kurzman, Charles (ed.), *Liberal Islam: A Sourcebook.* New York: OUP.

Aslan, Adnan (1998) *Religious Pluralism in Christian and Islamic Philosophy: The Thought of John Hick and Seyyed Hossain Nasr.* London: Curzon Press.

Awde, Nicholas (2000) *Women in Islam: An Anthology from the Qur'an and Hadiths.* New York: St Martin's Press.

Azeem, Sherif Abdel (1995) *Women in Islam Versus Women in the Judaeo-Christian Tradition: The Myth and the Reality* at *http://www.usc.edu/dept/MSA/humanrelations/womeninislam/womeninjud_chr.html* (hardcopy published by WAMY, Dammam, Saudi Arabia 1996).

Al-Azim, Sadik J. (1994) 'Is the Fatwa a Fatwa', pp. 21–3 in Brazilier, George (ed.), *For Rushdie: essays by Arab and Muslim writers in defense of free speech.* London: G. Brazilier.

al-Azmeh, Aziz (1993) *Islams and Modernities.* London: Verso.

al-Azmeh, Aziz 'Rushdie the Traitor', pp. 24–7, in Brazilier, George (ed) *For Rushdie,* London: G. Brazilier.

Badawi, M. A. Zaki (1976) *The Hajj.* London: Croom Helm.

Badawi, Gamal A. (1976) 'Woman in Islam', pp. 131–45 in Ahmad, Khurshid (ed.), *Islam: Its Meaning and Message.* Leicester: The Islamic Foundation. Available electronically at *http://www.iad.org/books/S-women.html.*

Badawi, M. A. Zaki (1977) *Reformers of Egypt.* London: Croom Helm.

Badawi, M. A. Zaki and Sardar, Ziauddun (1978) *Hajj Studies.* London: Croom Helm.

Bagabas, Abdullah (1998) 'A Look Into the Future: Is A Clash Between Islam and the West Imminent', pp. 65–87 in *Encounters: Journal of Inter-Cultural Perspectives,* Vol. 4, No. 1, March.

al-Banna, Hassan (1979) 'Five Tracts of Hasan al-Banna', translated by Charles Wendell. Berkeley: University of California Press.

Banu, Razia Akter U. A. B (1992) *Islam in Bangladesh.* Leiden: E. J. Brill.

Barber, Benjamin (1992) 'Jihad v McWorld', pp. 53–65 in *The Atlantic Monthly,* Vol. 269, No. 3, March.

Beaumont, Daniel (2002) *Slave of Desire: Sex, Love, and Death in the 1001 Nights.* New York: Fairleigh Dickinson University Press.

Ben-Yunusa, Mohammed (1995) 'Secularism and Religion', pp 78–85 in Mitri, Tarek (ed.), *Religion, Law and Society: A Christian–Muslim Discussion.* Geneva: WCC Publications.

Bergen, Peter L. (2001) *Holy War, Inc: Inside the Secret World of Osama bin Laden.* London: Weidenfeld and Nicolson.

Best, Steven and Kellner, Douglas (1991) *Postmodern Theory: Critical Interrogations.* New York: The Guilford Press.

Bhabbha, Homi K. (1991) *The Location of Culture.* London: Routledge.

Bhutto, Benazir (1998) 'Politics and the Muslim Woman', pp. 107–11 in Kurzman, Charles (ed.), *Liberal Islam: A Sourcebook.* New York: OUP.

Bielefeldt, Heiner (1995) 'Muslim Voices in the Human Rights Debate', pp. 587–617 in *Human Rights Quarterly*, Vol. 7, No. 4 (online at *www.soc. umn.edu/~boyle/17.4bielefeldt.html*).

Blake, William (1966) *Complete Writings*, edited by Sir Geoffrey Keynes. Oxford: OUP.

Brazilier, George (ed.) (1994) *For Rushdie: essays by Arab and Muslim writers in defense of free speech.* London: G. Brazilier.

Brohi, Allahbukhsh K. (1976) 'The Qur'an and its Impact on Human History', pp. 81–97 in Ahmad, Khurshid (ed.), *Islam: Its Meaning and Message.* Leicester: The Islamic Foundation.

Brooks, Geraldine (1994) *Nine Parts of Desire: The Hidden World of Islamic Women.* New York: Anchor Books.

Brown, Daniel (1999) *Rethinking Traditions in Modern Islamic Thought.* Cambridge: CUP.

Brown, J. A. (1963) *Techniques of Persuasion: From Propaganda to Brainwashing.* Harmondsworth: Penguin.

Bucaille, Maurice (1978) *The Bible, The Qur'an and Science.* Paris: Seghers.

Camus, Albert (reissue 1989) *The Stranger.* London: Viking.

Caner, Ergun Mehmet (ed.) (2003) *Voices Behind the Veil: The World of Islam Through the Eyes of Women.* Grand Rapids MI: Kregel Publications.

Cantle, Fred (chairman of the review team) (2001) *Community Cohesion: A Report of the Independent Review Team.* London: The Home Office.

Centre for the Study of Islam and Democracy (2002) 'American Muslims and Scholars Denounce Terrorism', *The American Muslim*, Sept–Oct 2002 (*http://www.theamericanmuslim.org/2002sept_comments.php?id=132_0_14_0_C*).

Combe, Victoria (2001) 'September 11 Will Bring Us All Closer Together: Dr Zaki Badawi talks to Victoria Combe', the *Telegraph*, 22 December 2001.

Conrad, Joseph (1994 edn; original 1902) *Heart of Darkness.* Harmondsworth: Penguin Classics.

Cook, Miriam (2001) *Women Claim Islam: creating Islamic feminism through literature.* New York: Routledge.

Cooper, John (1998) 'The Limits of the Sacred: The Epistemology of 'Abd al-Karim Soroush', pp. 38–56 in Cooper, John, Nettler, Ronald and Mahmoud, Mohamed, *Islam and Modernity: Muslim Intellectuals Respond.* London: I. B. Tauris.

Cooper, John, Nettler, Ronald and Mahmoud, Mohamed (1998) *Islam and Modernity: Muslim Intellectuals Respond.* London: I. B. Tauris.

Cornwell, R. D. (1980) *World History in the Twentieth Century.* London: Longman.

Cragg, Kenneth (1971) *The Event of the Qur'an: Islam in its Scripture.* London: Allen and Unwin.

Cragg, Kenneth (1973) *The Mind of the Qur'an.* London: Allen and Unwin.

Crone, Patricia and Cook, Michael (1977) *Hagarism: The Making of the Islamic World.* Cambridge: Cambridge University Press.

Crone, Patricia and Hinds, Martin (1986) *God's Caliph: religious authority in the first centuries of Islam.* Cambridge: Cambridge University Press.

Cundy, Catherine (1997) *Salman Rushdie.* London: Palgrave Macmillan.

Daba, Hasan Ali (2004) 'Sheikh Qaradawi's Jumu'ah Khutbah: I am a Terrorist', *www.mediareviewnet.com/Sheikh%20QARADAWIs%20lecture.htm.*

Dannin, Robert M. (2002) 'The Greatest Migration?', pp. 59–76 in Haddad, Yvonne Y. and Smith, Jane I. (eds), *Muslim Minorities in the West: visible and invisible.* New York: Altamira Press.

Davis, Brian L. (1990) *Qaddafi, Terrorism and the Origins of the US Attack on Libya.* New York: Praeger.

Dawkins, Richard (2nd edn, 1989) *The Selfish Gene.* Oxford: Oxford University Press.

Dawkins, Richard (2001) 'Time to Stand Up'. Freedom From Religion Foundation, September 2001, *http://www.ffrf.org/dawkins.html.*

A Declaration of Women's Rights in Islamic Societies (1997) *Free Inquiry* Vol. 17, No. 4, *http://www.secularhumanism.org/library/fi/women_17_4. html.*

Denffer, Ahmad von (1983) *'Ulum Al-Qur'an: An Introduction to the Sciences of the Qur'an.* Leicester: The Islamic Foundation.

Denny, Frederick Mathewson (1991) 'The Legacy of Fazlur Rahman', pp. 96–108 in Haddad, Yvonne Y. (ed.), *The Muslims of America.* New York: OUP.

Dewey, John (1934; new edn 1999) *A Common Faith.* New Haven CT: Yale University Press.

Doi, Abdur Rahman (1984) *Shari'ah: The Islamic Law.* London: Ta Ha Publishers.

Doi, Abdur Rahman (1987) 'An Islamic Agenda for Muslim Minorities: Duties and Responsibilities of Minorities in Non-Muslims States – A Point of View', pp. 43–61 in *Journal of Muslim Minority Affairs*, Vol. VIII, No. 1, January.

Duran, Khalid (1995) 'Bosnia: The Other Andalusia', pp 25–36 in Abedin, Syed Z. and Sarder, Ziaudin (eds), *Muslim Minorities in the West.* London: Grey Seal.

Eaton, Gai (1985) *Islam and the Destiny of Man.* Albany NY: SUNY Press.

Erikson, Marc (2002) 'Islamism, fascism and terrorism', *Asia Timesonline*, 5 December, *www.atimes.com/Middle_East/DK05ak01.html.*

Esack, Farid (1997) *Qur'an, Liberalism and Pluralism: An Islamic Perspective on Interreligious Solidarity Against Oppression.* Oxford: Oneworld.

Esack, Farid (2002) *The Qur'an: A Short Introduction.* Oxford: Oneworld.

Esack, Farid (2003) 'In search of progressive Islam beyond 9/11', pp. 78–97 in Safi, Omid (ed.), *Progressive Muslims on Justice, Gender and Pluralism.* Oxford: Oneworld.

Esposito, John (1983) *Voices of Resurgent Islam.* Oxford: OUP.

Esposito, John (1991) *Islam: The Straight Path.* New York and London: OUP.

Esposito, John (1st edn 1992; 2nd edn 1999) *The Islamic Threat? Myth or Reality.* New York: OUP.

Esposito, John L. (2001) 'Ismail Ragi al-Faruqi: Pioneer in Muslim–Christian Relations', pp. 23–38 in Esposito, John and Voll, John (eds), *Makers of Contemporary Islam.* New York: OUP.

Esposito, John L. (2002) *Unholy War: Terror in the Name of Islam.* New York: OUP.

Esposito, John L. and Tamimi, Azzam (ed.) (2000) *Islam and Secularization in the Middle East.* London: Hurst and Company.

Esposito, John L. and Voll, John (1991, 3rd edn) *Islam and Politics.* New York: Syracuse University Press.

Esposito, John L. and Voll, John (1996) *Islam and Democracy.* New York and London: OUP.

Esposito, John L. and Voll, John (eds) (2001) *Makers of Contemporary Islam.* New York: OUP.

Faraj,'Abd al-Salam (1986) *The Neglected Duty: The Creed of Sadat's Assassins and Islamic Resurgence in the Middle East,* trans. Jansen, Johannes. New York: Macmillan.

al-Faruqi, Ismail R. (1962) *Urubuh and Religion: A Study of the Fundamental Ideas of Arabism and Islam.* Amsterdam: Djambatan.

al-Faruqi, Ismail R. (1974) *Historical Atlas of the Religions of the World.* New York: Macmillan.

al-Faruqi, Ismail R. (1983) 'Islam and Zionism', pp. 261–7 in Esposito, John L. (ed.), *Voices of Resurgent Islam.* New York: OUP.

al-Faruqi, Ismail R. (1986) *Towards Islamic English.* Herndon VA: International Institute of Islamic Thought.

al-Faruqi, Ismail R. (1992, 2nd edn) *Tawhid: Its Implications for Thought and Life.* Hendon VA: International Institute of Islamic Thought.

Firestone, Reuven (1999) *Jihad: The Origins of Holy War in Islam.* Oxford: OUP.

Foucault, Michel (1961) *Madness and Civilization.* London: Routledge.

Foucault, Michel (1972) *The Archaeology of Knowledge.* London: Tavistock Books.

Foucault, Michel (1973) *The Birth of the Clinic.* London: Allen Lane.

Foucault, Michel (1979) *Discipline and Punish: The Birth of the Prison.* London: Allen Lane.

Gandhi, Rajmohan (1986) *Eight Lives: A Study of the Hindu–Muslim Encounter.* New Delhi: Roli Books Pvt. Ltd.

Geertz, Clifford (1968) *Islam Observed: Religious Development in Morocco and Indonesia.* Chicago: The University of Chicago Press.

Geertz, Clifford (1973) *The Interpretation of Cultures.* New York: Basic Books.

Geiger, Abraham (1896) *Judaism and Islam: A Prize Essay,* translated by F. M. Young. Madras: Cambridge Mission. Available at *http://www.answering-islam.org/Books/Geiger/Judaism/index.htm.*

Gergen, Kenneth K. (1999) *An Invitation to Social Constructivism.* London: Sage.

al-Ghannouchi, Rachid (1998) 'Participation in Non Islamic Government', pp. 89–95, in Kurzman, Charles (ed.) *Liberal Islam: A Sourcebook*. New York: OUP (also at the Muslim Public Affairs Committee website *http://www.mpacuk.org/mpac/data/262e0d7a/262e0d7a.jsp*).

al-Ghannouchi, Rachid (2000) 'Secularism in the Arab Meghreb', pp. 97–123 in Esposito, John L. and Tamimi, Azzam (eds), *Islam and Secularization in the Middle East*. London: Hurst and Company.

Gibb, Sir Hamilton (1949, 3rd edn 1978) *Mohammedanism: An Historical Survey*. Oxford: OUP.

Giroux, Henry A. (1991) *Postmodernism, Feminism, and Cultural Politics: Redrawing Educational Boundaries*. New York: SUNY Press.

Graham, A. William (1984) 'The Earliest Meaning of Qur'an', pp. 361–77 in *Die Welt des Islams*, 23–4.

Guillaume, Alfred (1955) *The Life of Muhammad: A Translation of Ibn Ishaq's Sirat Rasul Allah*. Oxford: OUP.

Haddad, Yvonne (ed.) 1991) *The Muslims of America*. New York: OUP.

Haddad, Yvonne Y. and Smith, Jane I. (eds) (2002) *Muslim Minorities in the West: visible and invisible*. New York: Altamira Press.

Hader, Leon T. (1992) *The Green Peril: Creating the Islamic Fundamentalist Threat* (Policy Analysis No. 177, 27 August, The Cato Institute at *http://www.cato.org/pubs/pas/pa-177.html*).

Halliday, Fred (1996; 2nd edn 2003) *Islam and the Myth of Confrontation: Religion and Politics in the Middle East*. London: I. B. Tauris.

Hamdi, Mohamed Elhachmi (1996) 'Islam and Liberal Democracy: The Limits Of The Western Model', *Journal of Democracy* Vol. 7, No. 2, pp. 81–5.

Hammersley, Martyn and Atkinson, Paul (1995) *Ethnography: Principles in Practice*. London: Routledge.

Hamzeh, Nizar A. and Dekmejian, Hrair R. (1996) 'A Sufi Response to Political Islamism', pp. 217–29 in *International Journal of Middle East Studies*, 28.

Hartwig, Mark (2004) *Spread by the Sword?* at *www.inplainsite.org/"* and *http://www.answering-islam.org/Terrorism/by_the_sword.html*.

Hassan Bin Tallal, Prince (1998) *Christianity in the Arab World*. London: SCM Press.

Hawkey, Ian (1995) 'Ambassador for Islam', *CAM, The University of Cambridge Alumni Magazine 1995*, pp. 16–17.

Hedworth, Donald H. (2004) *The British Response to Religious and Ethnic Conflict in Mandate Palestine, 1928–1931*, unpublished MA thesis, Cambridge, Centre for Jewish–Christian Relations (Anglia Polytechnic University).

Helicke, James (2002) 'Turks in Germany: Muslim Identity "Between States"', pp. 175–91 in Haddad, Yvonne Y. and Smith, Jane I. (eds), *Muslim Minorities in the West: visible and invisible*. New York: Altamira Press.

Hiro, Dilip (2002) *War Without End: The Rise of Islamic Terrorism and Global Response*. London and New York: Routledge.

Hizb-ut-tahrir (1962) *The System of Islam* at *http://www.hizb-ut-tahrir.org/english/books/*

Hizb-ut-tahrir (1996) *The American Campaign to Suppress Islam*. London: Al-Khilafah Publications.

Hopwood, Derek (1998) 'Introduction: The Culture of Modernity in Islam and the Middle East', pp. 1–9, in Cooper, John, Nettler, Ronald and Mahmoud, Mohamed, *Islam and Modernity: Muslim Intellectuals Respond*. London: I. B. Tauris.

Hudson, D. Dennis (2000) *Protestant Origins in India*. Grand Rapids: Eerdemans.

Hunter, Sir William Wilson (1871) *The Musalmans of India: Are they Bound in Conscience to Rebel Against the Queen?* London: Trubner & Co.

Huntington, Samuel P. (1996a) 'The West: Unique Not Universal', pp. 28–40 in *Foreign Affairs*, November/December.

Huntington, Samuel P. (1996b) *The Clash of Civilizations and the Remaking of World Order*. New York: Simon & Schuster.

Hussain, Naseem A. and Khan, M. Salimullah (1998) 'Culture and Politics in Bangladesh: Some Reflections', pp. 197–216 in Bayes, Abdul and Muhammad, Anu (eds), *Bangladesh at 25: An Analytical Discourse on Development*. Dhaka: The University Press.

Inayatullah, Sohail and Boxwell, Gail (2003) *Islam, Postmodernity and Other Futures: A Ziauddin Sardar Reader*. London: Pluto Press.

Iqbal, Javid (1983) 'Democracy and the Modern Islamic State', pp. 252–60 in Esposito, John L. (ed.) *Voices of Resurgent Islam*. New York: OUP.

Iqbal, Javid (1986) 'The Concept of State in Islam', pp. 37–50 in Ahmad, Mumtaz (ed.), *State and Politics in Islam*. Washington: American Trust Publication.

Iqbal, Sir Muhammad (1930) *The Reconstruction of Religious Thought in Islam*. Oxford: OUP.

Iqbal, Sir Muhammad (1998) 'The Reconstruction of Religious Thought', pp. 255–69 in Kurzman, Charles (ed.), *Liberal Islam: A Sourcebook*. New York: OUP.

Irfani, Suroush (1983) *Revolutionary Islam in Iran: Popular Liberation or Religious Dictatorship*. London: Zed Books.

Irvine, Martin (1998) 'The Po-Mo Page' on Georgetown University website. *http://www.georgetown.edu/irvinemj/technoculture/pomo.html*.

The Islamic Institute (1990) *The Muslim Manifesto*. London: The Islamic Institute.

Islamonline, 'Qaradawi Rejects Al-Qaeda's Killing of Innocents', 15 October 2002 at *www.islamonline.net/English/News/2002-06/23/article02.shtml*.

Jansen, Godfrey H. (1980) *Militant Islam*. New York: Harper.

Kabbani, Rana (1986) *Europe's Myths of Orient: Devise and Rule*. London: Macmillan.

Kabbani, Rana (1989) *Letter to Christendom*. London: Virago.

Kabbani, Rana (1994) *Imperial Fictions: Europe's Myths of Orient*. London: Pandora.

Kabbani, Rana (2001) *Letter to America*. BBC2, 9 December ('From Our Correspondent').

Kabir, Humayun (1998) 'Minorities in a Democracy', pp. 145–54 in Kurzman, Charles, *Liberal Islam: A Sourcebook*. New York: OUP.

Kane, Cheikh Hamidou (English translation, 1972) *Ambiguous Adventure*, translated by Katherine Woods. London: Heineman.

Kassem, Hassem (2003) 'Hizb-ut-tahrir-al-Islamic (The Islamic Liberation Party)', *EastWest Record*, 28 July at *www.eastwestrecord.com*.

Kepel, Giles (2002) *Jihad: The Trial of Political Islam*. Cambridge: Harvard University Press.

Khadduri, Majid (1955) *War and Peace in the Law of Islam*. Baltimore MD: Johns Hopkins University Press.

Khadduri, Majid and Ghareeb, Edmond (1997) *War in the Gulf: 1990–1991: The Iraq–Kuwait Conflict and Its Inspirations*. Oxford: OUP.

Khaldun, Ibn (1958) *The Muqudimmah: An Introduction to History* Vol. 1, translated by Franz Rosenthal. New York: Routledge & Kegan Paul.

Khan, Muhammad Muhsin (revised edn 1987) *The Translation of the Meaning of Sahih al-Bukhari – Arabic–English* (9 Vols). New Delhi: Kitab Bhavan.

Khan, Muqtedar (2001a) 'Islam and the Two Faces of the West', *The Globalist*, 11 October.

Khan, Muqtedar (2001b) *Islam and Democracy: The Struggle Continues*, 2nd annual conference, Centre for the Study of Islam and Democracy, Georgetown University, Washington DC, 7 April 2001.

Khan, Muqtedar (2003) 'The Islamic State and Religious Minorities', at *www.islamfortoday.com/khan06.htm*.

Khan, Sir Sayyid Ahmed (1860–66; English 1887) *Tabîyyan al-kalâm fi'l-tafsîr al-tawrâ wa'l-injîl χalâ millat al-islam: The Mohammedan Commentary on the Bible*, 3 parts. Ghazipur: Scientific Society.

Khan, Sir Sayyid Ahmed (1960–61) *An Account of the Loyal Mohammedans of India*. Meerut, privately printed for the author.

Khan, Sir Sayyid Ahmed (2002) 'Lecture on Islam', pp 291–303, in Kurzman, Charles (ed.), *Modernist Islam, 1840–1940: A Sourcebook*. New York: OUP.

Khattami, Mohammad Ayatollah (2000) *Islam, Dialogue and Civil Society*. Canberra AU: Centre for Arab and Islam Studies A.N.U.

Killgore, Andrew I. (1996) 'Personality: Professor Majid Khadduri', p. 23 in *Washington Report on Middle East Affairs*, July.

al-Kindy (1882) *The Apology of Al-Kindy*, translated by Sir William Muir, London: SPCK.

Kuppuswamy, C. S. (2004) *Thailand: Troubled By Terrorists*. South Asia Analysis Group paper no. 925 at *www.saag.org*.

Kurdi, Abdulrahman Abdulkadir (1984) *The Islamic State: A Study Based on the Holy Constitution*. London: Mansell.

Kureishi, Hanif (1985; DVD 2001) *My Beautiful Laundrette*. London: Channel Four; MGM Home Entertainment.

Kureishi, Hanif (1995) *The Black Album*. London: Faber and Faber.

Kureishi, Hanif (1997) *My Son the Fanatic*. London: Faber and Faber.

Kureishi, Hanif (2002) *Dreaming and Scheming: reflections on writing and politics*. London: Faber and Faber.

Kurzman, Charles (ed.) (1998) *Liberal Islam: A Sourcebook*. New York: OUP.

Kurzman, Charles (1999) 'Liberal Islam: Prospects and Challenges', *MERIAonline* Vol. 3, No. 3.

Kurzman, Charles (ed.) (2002) *Progressive Islam (1840–1940): A Sourcebook*. New York: OUP.

Bin Laden, Osama (1996) 'Fatwa', *Al-Quds al-'Arabi*, August. At *http://www.pbs.org/newshour/terrorism/international/fatwa_1996.html*.

Bin Laden, Osama (1998) 'Fatwa', *Al Quds al-'Arabi*, 28 February. At *http://www.emergency.com/bladen98.htm*. Fatwa can be Found at *www.clinton bennet.net/Lectures/fatwa.html*.

Lane, Edward W. (2003) *An Account of the Manners and Customs of the Modern Egyptian*. Cairo: American University Press (original edition 1836).

Lang, Andrew (1993) *Tales from the Arabian Nights*. Ware, Hertfordshire: Wordsworth Classics.

Lelso, Paul and Vasager, Jeevan (2002) 'Muslims reject image of separate society', the *Guardian*, 17 June.

Lester, Toby (1998) 'What is the Koran?', pp. 43–56 in *The Atlantic Monthly*, Vol. 283, No. 1, January.

Lewis, Bernard (1966; new edn 2001) *The Assassins: A Radical Sect in Islam*. New York: Weidenfeld and Nicolson.

Lewis, Bernard (1984) *The Jews of Islam*. London: Routledge and Kegan Paul.

Lewis, Bernard (1994) *The Shaping of the Modern Middle East*. Oxford: OUP.

Lewis, Bernard (1996) 'Islam and Liberal Democracy: A Historical Overview', in *Journal of Democracy* 7.2, pp. 52–63.

Lewis, Bernard (1999) 'The Roots of Muslim Rage', pp. 47–60 in *The Atlantic Monthly*, September.

Lewis, Bernard (2002a) 'What Went Wrong?', pp. 43–5 in *The Atlantic Monthly*, Vol. 289, No. 1, January.

Lewis, Bernard (2002b) *What Went Wrong: Western Impact and Middle Eastern Response*. New York: OUP.

Lewis, Bernard (2003) *The Crises of Islam: Holy War and Unholy Terror*. London: Phoenix.

Lewis, Philip (1994) *Islamic Britain: Religion, Politics and Identity among British Muslims*. London: I. B. Tauris.

Lindeborg, Lisbeth (2002) 'The Intellectual Fathers of Fundamentalism: Osama's Library', *World Press Review*, Vol. 49, No. 1.

Lindholm, Charles (1996) *The Islamic Middle East: an historical anthropology*. Oxford: Blackwell Publishers.

Lings, Martin (1983) *Muhammad: His Life Based on the Earliest Sources.* London: George Allen and Unwin.

al-Mahdi, al-Sadiq (1983) 'Islam – Society and Change', pp. 230–40 in Esposito, John L. (ed.), *Voices of Resurgent Islam.* New York: OUP.

Mahfouz, Naguib (1990) *The Palace Walk,* translated from the Arabic by William M. Hutchins. New York: Doubleday.

Mahmutcehajic, Rusmir (1998) 'The Downhill Path and Defense, not Surrender', pp. 179–84 in Kurzman, Charles (ed.), *Liberal Islam: A Sourcebook.* New York: OUP.

Mailer, Norman (2003) 'Only In America', *New York Review of Books,* 5, pp. 49–53, 27 March.

Majeed, Javed (1998) 'Nature, Hyperbole and the Colonial State', pp. 10–27 in Cooper, John, Nettler, Ronald and Mahmoud, Mohamed (eds), *Islam and Modernity: Muslim Intellectuals Respond.* London: I. B. Tauris.

Malka, Haim (2003) 'Must Innocents Die?: The Islamic Debate over Suicide Attacks', *Middle East Quarterly,* Spring.

Marcotte, Roxanne D. (2003) 'Feminism and Muslim Women in Cyber Space', at *www.emsah.uq.edu.au/conferences/of/abstracts/Marcotte.html.*

Matinuddin, Kamal (1999) *The Taliban Phenomenon: Afghanistan (1994–1997.* Oxford: OUP.

Mawdudi, Syed Abu'l A'la (1st edn 1930, 15th edn 1996) *Jihad in Islam.* Kuwait: International Islamic Federation of Student Organizations.

Mawdudi, Syed Abu'l A'la (1st edn 1939, 2nd edn 1972) *Purdah and the Status of Women in Islam,* translated and edited by al-Ash'ar'ri. Lahore: Islamic Publication Ltd.

Mawdudi, Syed Abu'l A'la (1955) *Islamic Law and Constitution,* edited by Khurshid Ahmad. Karachi: Jamaat-e-Islami Publications.

Mawdudi, Syed Abu'l A'la (1967–79) *The Meaning of the Qur'an,* 9 Vols. Lahore: Islamic Publications.

Mawdudi, Syed Abu'l A'la (1974) *Fundamentals of Islam.* Lahore: Jamaat-e-Islami Publications.

Mawdudi, Syed Abu'l A'la (1975) *The Rights of Non-Muslims in Islamic States.* Karachi: Kazi Publishers.

Mawdudi, Syed Abu'l A'la (1976a) 'Political Theory of Islam', pp. 147–71 in Ahmad, Khurshid (ed.), *Islam: Its Meaning and Message.* Leicester, The Islamic Foundation.

Mawdudi, Abu'l A'la (1976b) 'Human Rights in Islam', *Al-Tawhid Journal,* 14: 3.

Mawdudi, Syed Abu'l A'la (1980) 'The Essentiality of Knowledge for being a Muslim', Part One of Chapter One, 'Imam', of *Fundamentals of Islam* at *http://www.witness-pioneer.org/vil/Books/M_foi/index.html.*

Mawdudi, Syed Abu'l A'la (1986) *The Islamic Way of Life,* translated and edited by Khurshid Ahmad. Leicester: The Islamic Foundation.

Mernissi, Fatima (1991) *Women and Islam: A Theological and Historical Enquiry.* Oxford: Basil Blackwell.

Mernissi, Fatima (1993) *The Forgotten Queens of Islam*, translated by Mary Joe Lakeland. Cambridge, UK: Polity Press.

Mernissi, Fatima (1994; revised 2002) *Islam and Democracy: Fear of the Modern World.* London: Virago.

Mernissi, Fatima (1998) 'A Feminist Interpretation of Women's Rights in Islam', pp. 112–26, in Kurzman, Charles (ed.), *Liberal Islam: A Sourcebook.* New York: OUP.

Metcalf, Barbara Daly (ed.) (1996) *Making Muslim Space In North America and Europe.* Berkeley: University of California Press.

Metcalf, Barbara Daly (1996) 'New Medinas: The Tablighi Jama'at in America and Europe', pp. 110–27 in Metcalf, Barbara Daly (ed.), *Making Muslim Space In North America and Europe.* Berkeley: University of California Press.

Modood, Tariq (1992) *Not Easy Being British: colour, culture and citizenship.* London: The Runnymede Trust.

Modood, Tariq (2001) 'Muslims in the West: A Positive Asset', the *Observer*, 30 September 2001 (*www.guardian.co.uk*).

Modood, Tariq (2003a) 'Multiculturalism, Muslims and the British State', *The American Muslim*, May–June 2003 (*http://www.theamericanmuslim.org/2003may_comments.php?id=134_0_20_0_C*).

Modood, Tariq (2003b) 'Muslims and European Multiculturalism', *OpenDemocracy, www.opendemocracy.com, 15.05.*

Moghissi, Haideh (1999) *Feminism and Islamic Fundamentalism: The Limits of Postmodern Analysis.* London and New York: Zed Books.

Mohamad, Mahathir (2003) 'Speech by Prime Minister Mahathir Mohamad', 16 October, Anti-Defamation League website, *www.adl.org.*

Monbiot, George (2003) 'Comment and Analysis: America as Religion' in the *Guardian*, 28 July 2003.

Mostyn, Trevor (2003) *Censorship in Islamic Societies.* London: Saqi.

Mousavi, Ahmad (1986) 'The Theory of Vilayat-I-Faqih', pp. 97–113 in Ahmad, Mumtaz (ed.), *State and Politics in Islam.* Washington: American Trust Publication.

Muir, Sir William (1858–60) *The Life of Mahomet*, 4 Vols. London: Smith, Elder & Co. See also *http://www.answering-islam.org/Books/Muir/index.htm.*

Muir, Sir William (1878) *The Coran. Its composition and teaching and the testimony it bears to the Holy Scripture.* London: S.P.C.K.

Muir, Sir William (2nd edn 1891, 3rd edn 1899) *The Caliphate: Its Rise, Decline and Fall.* London: Smith, Elder & Co. For 3rd edn, see *http://www.answering-islam.org/Books/Muir/index.htm.*

Muir, Sir William (1894) *Life of Mahomet* (abridged). London: Smith, Elder & Co.

Murad, Khurram (1986) *Dawah Among Non-Muslims in the West* at *http://masmn.org/Books/Khurram_Murad/Dawah_Among_Non_Muslims_in_the_West/.*

Murphy, Caryle (2002) 'Islamic Scholars Say US Muslims Soldiers Must Fight for their Country' in the *Washington Post*, 11 October 2002, p. A22.

Nahai, Gina B. (1991) *Cry of the Peacock*. New York: Simon and Schuster.

an-Na'im, 'Abdullahi A. (1987) 'Translator's Introduction', pp. 1–30 in Taha, Mahmud Mohamed, *The Second Message of Islam*, translated by Abdullahi an-Na'im. New York: Syracuse University Press.

an-Na'im, 'Abdullahi Ahmed (1990) *Towards an Islamic Reformation: Civil Liberties, Human Rights and International Law*. New York: Syracuse University Press.

an-Na'im, 'Abdullahi Ahmed (1998) 'Shari'a and Basic Human Rights Concerns', pp. 222–38 in Kurzman, Charles (ed.), *Liberal Islam: A Sourcebook*. New York: OUP.

Naipaul, V. S. (1998) *Among the Non-Believers: An Islamic Journey*. London: Peter Smith.

Naipaul, V. S. (2001) *Half A Man*. London: Picador.

Nasr, Seyyed Hossain (1968) *Islamic Science: An Illustrated Guide*, photographs by Roland Michaud. London: World of Islam Festival Publishing Co. Ltd.

Nasr, Seyyed Hossain (1976) 'The Western World and Its Challenge to Islam,' pp. 217–41 in Ahmad, Khurshid *Islam: Its Meaning and Message*. Leicester: The Islamic Foundation.

Nasr, Seyyed Hossain (1990) *Traditional Islam in the Modern World*, London: Kegan Paul International.

Nasr, Seyyed Hossain (1994) *Ideas and Realities of Islam*, London: The Aquarian Press.

Nasrin, Taslima (1997) *Shame: A novel*. Amherst NY: Prometheous Books.

Nasrin, Taslima (2000) 'They Wanted to Kill Me', *Middle East Quarterly*, Vol. 1, No. 3, September; *www.meforum.org/article/73*.

Nettler, Robert (1998) 'Mohamed Talbi's Ideas on Islam and Politics: A Conception of Islam for the Modern World', pp. 129–53 in Cooper, John, Nettler, Ronald and Mahmoud, Mohamed, *Islam and Modernity: Muslim Intellectuals Respond*. London: I. B. Tauris.

Neuman, Lawrence W. (1994) *Social Research Methods: Quantitative and Qualitative Approaches*. Boston: Allyn & Bacon.

Nielsen, Jørgen (1999) *Towards A European Islam*. London and New York: Macmillan and St Martin's Press.

Nielsen, Jørgen (2004, 3rd edn) *Muslims in Western Europe*, Edinburgh: Edinburgh University Press.

Oommen, T. K. (ed.) (1997) *Citizenship and National Identity: From Colonialism to Globalism*. New Delhi: Sage.

Osman, Fathi (1986) '*Bai'at-al-Iman*: The Contract for the Appointment of the Head of an Islamic State', pp. 51–85 in Ahmad, Mumtaz (ed.), *State and Politics in Islam*. Washington: American Trust Publication.

Parekh, Bhikhu (2000) *Rethinking Multiculturalism: Cultural Diversity and Political Theory*. New York: Palgrave.

Peters, F. E. (1994) *A Reader on Classical Islam*. Princeton NJ: Princeton University Press.

Peters, Rudolph (1977) *Jihad in Medieval and Modern Islam: The Chapter on*

Jihad from Averroes Legal Handbook 'Bidayat al-Mujtahid' and the Treatise 'Koran and Fighting' by the Late Shaykh of Azhar Mahmud Shaltut. Leiden: E. J. Brill.

Peters, Rudolf (1996) *Jihad in Classical and Modern Islam*. Princeton NJ: Princeton University Press.

Pfander, Karl (1910; reprint 1986) *The Balance of Truth*, revised and translated by William St Clair-Tisdall. London: RTS; Villach: Light of Life.

Pipes, Daniel (2002) *Militant Islam Reaches America*. New York: W. N. Norton.

Poston, Larry A. (1991) 'Da'wa in the West', pp. 125–35 in Haddad, Yvonne Y. (ed.), *The Muslims of America*. New York: OUP.

Powell, Walter W. (1992) 'The Social Embeddedness of Getting into Print', pp. 334–50 in Zey, Mary (ed.), *Decision Making: Alternatives to Rational Choice Theory*. London: Sage.

Pulcini, Theodore (1995) 'Values Conflict among US Muslim Youth', pp. 178–208 in Sardar, Ziauddin and Abedin, Syed X. (eds), *Muslim Minorities in the West*. London: Grey Seal.

al-Qaradawi, Yusuf (1st edn 1960, revised edn 2003) *The Lawful and the Prohibited in Islam*. London: al-Birr Foundation.

al-Qaradawi, Yusuf (1998) 'Extremism', pp. 196–204 in Kurzman, Charles (ed.), *Liberal Islam: A Sourcebook*. New York: OUP.

al-Qaradawi, Yusuf (2001) *Fiqh-al-zakat*. Beirut: Mu'assarat al-Rissalah.

al-Qaradawi, Yusuf (2002) *Towards a Sound Awakening: Renovating Religion and Promoting Life* at *http://www.ymofmd.com/books/tsa/* and at *http://www.witness-pioneer.org/vil/Books/Q_awake/*).

Qutb, Sayyid (1952) *The Struggle Between Islam and Capitalism*. Cairo: Dar-al-Shuruq.

Qutb, Sayyid (1964; 1988) *Milestones*. Delhi: Markazi Maktaba Islami (and electronically at *http://masmn.org/Books/Syed_Qutb/Milestones/* and *http://www.youngmuslims.ca/online_library/books/milestones/index_2.asp*).

Qutb, Sayyid (1976) 'Islamic Approach to Social Justice', pp. 117–30 in Ahmad, Khurshi (ed.), *Islam: Its Meaning and Message*. Leicester: The Islamic Foundation.

Qutb, Sayyid (2001) *In the Shadow of the Qur'an*, 9 Volumes. Leicester: The Islamic Foundation.

Rahman, Fazlur (1982) *Islam and Modernity*. Chicago: Chicago University Press.

Rahman, Fazlur (1986) 'Principles of Shura and the Role of the Ummah', pp. 87–96 in Ahmad, Mumtaz (ed.), *State and Politics in Islam*. Washington: American Trust Publication.

Rahman, Fazlur (1998) 'Islam and Modernity', pp. 304–18 in Kurzman, Charles (ed.), *Liberal Islam: A Sourcebook*. New York: OUP.

Ramadan, Tariq (1999) *To Be A European Muslim*, Leicester: The Islamic Foundation.

Ramadan, Tariq (2001) *Islam, The West and the Challenges of Modernity*. Leicester: The Islamic Foundation.

Rashid, Ahmed (2000) 'Inside the Jihad: interview with Akash Kapur', *The*

Atlantic Monthlyonline, 10 August, *http://www.theatlantic.com/unbound/interviews/ba2000-08-09.htm*.

Raspail, Jean (1973) *The Camp of the Saints*. Petoskey MI: The Social Contract Press.

Raza, Mohamed S. (1991) *Islam in Britain: Past, Present and the Future*. Leicester: Volcano Press.

al-Raziq, 'Ali 'Abd (1998) 'Message Not Government, Religion Not State', pp. 29–36 in Kurzman, Charles (ed.), *Liberal Islam: A Sourcebook*. New York: OUP.

Reeves, Minou (2000) *Muhammad in Europe: A Thousand Years of Western Myth-Making*. New York: New York University Press.

Renan, Ernest Joseph (1866) *Averroes et L'avverro: essai historique*. Paris: Michel Levy.

Rida, Rashid (1938) *Le Califat*, translated by Henri Laoust. Beirut: L'Institut de Français de Damas.

Robson, James (1963) *Mishkat-al-Masabih*. Lahore: Ashraf Publishers.

Rockefeller (1991) *John Dewey: Religious Faith and Democratic Humanism*. New York: Columbia University Press.

Rodinson, Maxime (1980) *Muhammad*, translated by Anne Carter. Harmondsworth: Penguin

Ibn Rushd (1977) 'The Chapter on Jihad from Averroes' Legal handbook *Bidayat al-Mudjtahid*', pp. 9–25 in Peters, Rudolph, *Jihad in Medieval and Modern Islam*. Leiden: E. J. Brill.

Rushdie, Salman (1975; 1996) *Grimus*, Harmondsworth: Penguin.

Rushdie, Salman (1981) *Midnight's Children*. London: Cape.

Rushdie, Salman (1983) *Shame*. London: Picador.

Rushdie, Salman (1988) *The Satanic Verses*. London: Viking.

Rushdie, Salman (1991) *Imaginary Homelands: Essays and Criticism 1981–1991*. London: Granta.

Rushdie, Salman (1996) *The Moor's Last Sigh*. London: Vintage.

Rushdie, Salman (2001) 'Yes – this is about Islam', *New York Times*, 2 November.

Ruthven, Malise (1991) *A Satanic Affair: Salman Rushdie and the Wrath of Islam*. London: Hogarth.

Ruthven, Malise (2002) *A Fury for God: The Islamist Attack on America*. London: Granta.

El Saadawi, Nawal (Arabic 1977; English 1980, 1982) *The Hidden Face of Eve: Women in the Arab World* (*Al-Wajh al-'Ari lil-Mar'a al-'Arabiyya* 1977) translated by Sherif Hetata. London: Zed Press, 1980, Beacon Press, 1982.

El Saadawi, Nawal (1988) *The Fall of The Imam*, translated by Sherif Hetata. London: Minerva.

El Saadawi, Nawal (1997) *The Nawal El Saadawi Reader*, London: Zed Books.

Sachedina, Abdulaziz (1983) 'Ali Shariati: Ideologue of the Iranian Revolution', pp. 191–214 in Esposito, John L. (ed.), *Voices of Resurgent Islam*. New York: OUP.

Sachedina, Abdulaziz (1986) 'A Just Social Order in Islam', pp. 115–31 in Ahmad, Mumtaz (ed.), *State and Politics in Islam*. Washington: American Trust Publications.

Sachedina, Abdulaziz (1999) 'Woman: Half the Man? Crisis of Male Epistemology in Islamic Jurisprudence', pp. 146–60 in Khare, R. S. (ed.), *Perspectives on Islamic Law, Justice and Society*. Lanham MD and Oxford: Rowman & Littlefield Publishers.

Sachedina, Abdulaziz and Montville, Joseph (2001) *The Islamic Roots of Democratic Pluralism*. Oxford: OUP.

Safi, Omid (ed.) (2003) *Progressive Muslims on Justice, Gender and Pluralism*. Oxford: Oneworld.

Said, Edward (1978) *Orientalism*. Harmondsworth: Penguin.

Said, Edward (1988) *Orientalism*. Harmondsworth: Penguin.

Said, Edward (1994) *Culture and Imperialism*. London: Vintage.

Said, Edward (rev edn 1997) *Covering Islam: How the Media and the Experts Determine How We See the Rest of the World*. London: Vintage.

Saif, Walid (1995) 'Shari'ah and Modernity', pp. 11–19 in Mitri, Tarek (ed.), *Religion, Law and Society: A Christian–Muslim Discussion*. Geneva: W. C. C. Publications.

Sardar, Ziauddin (1985) *Islamic Futures: The Shape of Ideas to Come*. London: Mansell.

Sardar, Ziauddin (2nd edn 1987) *The Future of Muslim Civilization*. London: Mansell.

Sardar, Ziauddin (1989) *Explorations in Islamic Science*. London: Mansell.

Sardar, Ziauddin (1995) 'Racism, Identity and Muslims in the West', pp. 1–17 in Sardar, Ziauddin and Abedin, Syed X. (eds), *Muslim Minorities in the West*. London: Grey Seal.

Sardar, Ziauddin (1998) *Postmodernism and the Other: The New Imperialism of Western Culture*. London: Pluto Press.

Sardar, Ziauddin (2001) 'My fatwa on the fanatics', the *Observer*, 23 September.

Sardar, Ziauddin (2002) 'The Excluded Minority: British Muslim Identity After 9/11', pp. 51–5 in Griffith, Phoebe and Leonard, Mark (eds), *Rethinking Britishness*. London: Foreign Policy Centre.

Sardar, Ziauddin (2004) *Desperately Seeking Paradise: Journeys of a Sceptical Muslim*. London: Granta Books.

Sardar, Ziauddin and Abedin, Syed X. (eds) (1995) *Muslim Minorities in the West*. London: Grey Seal.

Sardar, Ziauddin, Anees, Munawar Ahmad and Abedin, Syed Z. (1991) *Christian–Muslim Relations: yesterday, today, tomorrow*. London: Grey Seal.

Sardar, Ziauddin and Davies, Meryl Wyn (1990) *Distorted Imagination: Lessons from the Rushdie Affair*. London: Grey Seal.

Sardar, Ziauddin and Davies, Meryl Wyn (2003) *Why Do People Hate America?*. New York: The Disinformation Company.

Sayyid, Bobby (1998) *Fundamental Fear: Eurocentrism and the Emergence of Islamism*. London: Zed Books.

Schacht, Joseph (1964) *An Introduction to Islamic Law*. Oxford: Clarendon.
Segal, Aaaron (1996) 'Why Does the Muslim World Lag in Science' *Middle East Quarterly*, June 1996, Vol. 111, No. 2, pp. 61–70. *www.meforum.org/article/306*.
Shadid, Wasif and van Koningsveld, Sjoerd (1996) 'Loyalty to a Non-Muslim Government: An Analysis of the Views of Some Contemporary Islamicists', pp. 84–115 in Shadid, Wasif and van Koningsveld, P. S., *Political Participation and Identities in non-Muslim States*. Kamen: Kok Pharos.
Shaltut, Mahmud (1977) 'The Treatise "Koran and Fighting" ' pp. 26–79 in Peters, Rudolph, *Jihad in Medieval and Modern Islam*. Leiden: E. J. Brill.
Shari'ati, 'Ali (1998) 'Humanity and Islam', pp. 187–95 in Kurzman, Charles (ed.), *Liberal Islam: A Sourcebook*. New York: OUP.
Shehabuddin, Sarah (2000) 'Perils of Neglect', *www.bangla.2000.com*.
Siddiqui, Iqbal (1996) *A Life in the Islamic Movement: Dr Kalim Siddiqui (1931–1996)*. London: The Islamic Institute and the Muslim Parliament of Great Britain, and at *http://www.islamicthought.org/ks-bio-p1.html prologue*.
Siddiqui, Iqbal (1998) 'Kalim Siddiqui's Understanding of the Muslim Parliament as a "Minority Political System" ', *Crescent International*, 1–15 August and at *http://www.islamicthought.org/mp-is2.html*.
Siddiqui, Kalim (1973) *Towards A New Destiny*. London: Open Press.
Siddiqui, Kalim (1980) *The Islamic Revolution: achievements, obstacles and goals*. London: The Open Press.
Siddiqi, Muhammad Zubayr (1991) *Hadith Literature: Its Origin, Development, Special Features & Criticism*. Cambridge: Islamic Texts Society.
Sivan, Emmanuel (1985) *Radical Islam: Medieval Theology and Modern Politics*. New Haven CT: Yale University Press.
Slomp, Jan (1991) 'Mawdudi: Reformer and Ideologist of Resurgent Islam', pp. 28–38 in *Bulletin of the Henry Martyn Institute of Islamic Studies*, Vol. 10, No. 1, January–March.
Slomp, Jan (2003) 'The "Political Equation" in *Al-Jihad Fi Al-Islam* of Abu A'la Mawdudi (1903–1979)', pp. 237–51 in Thomas, David (ed.), *A Faithful Presence: Essays for Kenneth Cragg*. London: Fox Communication and Publishing.
Slomp, Jan (2004) 'Christianity and Lutheranism from the Perspective of Modern Islam', pp. 277–96 in Medick, Hans and Schmidt, Peer (eds), *Luther zwischen den Kulturen: Zeitgenossenschaft- und Weltwirkung*. Göttingen: Vandenhoeck & Ruprecht.
Smith, Jane I. (1991) 'Seyyed Hossain Nasr: Defender of the Sacred and Islamic Traditionalism', pp. 80–95 in Haddad, Yvonne Y. (ed.), *The Muslims of America*. New York: OUP.
Smith, Wilfred Cantwell (1945) *Modern Islam in India*. Lahore: Minerva.
Smith, Wilfred Cantwell (1957) *Islam in Modern History*. Princeton NJ: Princeton University Press.
Smith, Wilfred C. (1959) 'Comparative Religion: Whither and Why' in

Eliade, Mercea and Kitagawa, Joseph (eds), *The History of Religions: Essays on Methodology*. Chicago: University of Chicago Press.

Smith, Wilfred C. (1981) *Towards a World Theology*. Philadelphia: Westminster Press.

Smith, Wilfred C. (1993) *What is Scripture?: A Comparative Approach*. London: SCM Press.

El-Sohl, Camillia Fawzi and Mabro, Judy (1994) *Muslim Women's Choices: Religious Belief and Social Reality*. Oxford: Berg.

Sonn, Tamara (1995) 'Fazlur Rahman', p. 408 in Esposito, John (ed.), *The Oxford Encyclopaedia of the Modern Islamic World*. Oxford: OUP.

Sonn, Tamara (2002) 'Muslims in South Africa: A Very Visible Minority', pp. 244–55 in Haddad, Yvonne Y. and Smith, Jane I. (eds), *Muslim Minorities in the West*. New York: Altamira Press.

Soroush, Abdolkarim (1998) 'The Evolution and Devolution of Religious Knowledge', pp. 244–51 in Kurzman, Charles (ed.), *Liberal Islam: A Sourcebook*. New York: OUP.

Soroush, Abdolkarim (2000) *Reason, Freedom and Democracy in Islam*. Oxford: OUP.

Soroush, Abdolkarim (2001) 'Reason and Freedom in Islamic Thought', Keynote Address, Center for Islam and Democracy Conference 2001 (*http://www.islam-democracy.org/SoroushAddress.html*).

Soueif, Ahdaf (1999) *The Map of Love: A Novel*. London: Anchor.

Soueif, Ahdaf (1993) *In The Eye of the Sun: A Novel*. New York: Pantheon Books.

Spinner-Halev, Jeff (2000) *Surviving Diversity: Religion and Democratic Citizenship*. Baltimore MD: Johns Hopkins University Press.

Streusand, Douglas (1997) 'What does *jihad* mean?', *The Middle East Quarterly*, Vol. IV, No. 3, September, *www.meforum.org/article/357*.

Taha, Mahmud Mohamed (1987) *The Second Message of Islam*, translated by Abdullahi A. an-Na'im. New York: Syracuse University Press.

Taha, 'Mahmoud Mohamed (1998) 'The Second Message of Islam', pp. 270–83 in Kurzman, Charles (ed.), *Liberal Islam: A Sourcebook*. New York: OUP.

al-Tahtawi, Rifa'a Rafi' (2002) 'The Extraction of Gold, or an Overview of Paris and The Honest Guide for Girls and Boys', pp. 31–9 in Kurzman, Charles (ed.), *Modernist Islam, 1840–1940: A Sourcebook*. New York: OUP.

Talbi, Mohammed (1998) 'Religious Liberty', pp. 161–8 in Kurzman, Charles (ed.), *Modernist Islam, 1840–1940: A Sourcebook*. New York: OUP.

Tamadonfar, Mehran (1989) *The Islamic Polity and Political Leadership: Fundamentalism, Sectarianism and Pragmatism*. Boulder CA: Westview.

Tamimi, Azzam (2000a) 'The Origins of Arab Secularism', pp. 13–28 in Esposito, John L. and Tamimi, Azzam (eds), *Islam and Secularization in the Middle East*. London: Hurst and Company.

Tamimi, Azzam S (2000b) *Rachid Ghannouchi: A Democrat Within Islamism*. Oxford: OUP.

Tamimi, Azzam (2001) 'Democracy in Islamic Political Thought' available at *www.ii-pt.com/web/papers/democracy.htm.*

Tamimi, Azzam (2002) 'Review of Bassam Tibi's *Islam: Between Politics and Culture*', at *www.ii-pt.com.*

Tibi, Bassam (1998) *The Challenge of Fundamentalism: Political Islam and the New World Disorder.* Berkeley CA: University of California Press.

Tibi, Bassam (2001) *Islam Between Culture and Politics.* Basingstoke: Palgrave.

Tisdall, William St-Clair (1894) *The Religion of the Crescent.* London: SPCK.

Tisdall, William St-Clair (1905) *The Original Sources of the Qur'an.* London: SPCK.

al-Turabi, Hassan (1983) 'The Islamic State', pp. 241–51 in Esposito, John L. (ed.), *Voices of Resurgent Islam.* New York: OUP.

Uris, Leon (1984) *The Hajj.* New York: Doubleday.

al-Uwaydidi, Nur Eddin (2003) 'Those Who Die Fighting US Occupation Forces are Martyrs: Qaradawi', by *www.islamonline.net/english/news/2003-01/28/article08shtml.*

Vakili, Valla (2001) 'Abdolkarim Soroush and Critical Discourse in Islam', pp. 150–76 in Esposito, John and Voll J. (eds), *Makers of Contemporary Islam.* New York: OUP.

Voll, John O. (1983) 'Renewal and Reform in Islamic History: Tajdid and Islah', pp. 32–47 in Esposito, John L. (ed.), *Voices of Resurgent Islam.* New York: OUP.

Wahba, W. H. (1966a) *The Ordinances of Government of Al-Mawardi (974–1058).* Reading: Garnet Publishing for the Centre for Muslim Contribution to Civilization.

Wahba, W. H. (1966b) 'Introduction', pp. xiii–xvii in *The Ordinances of Government of Al-Mawardi (974–1058)*, translated and edited by W. Wahba. Reading: Garnet Publishing for the Centre for Muslim Contribution to Civilization.

Walker, Mary (1995) *A World Where Womanhood Reigns Supreme*, Call to Islam Website, *http://www.zawaj.com/articles/womanhood_supreme.html*

Wansborough, John (1977) *Quranic Studies: Sources and Methods of Scriptural Interpretation.* Oxford: OUP.

Wansborough, John (1978) *The Sectarian Milieu: Content and Composition of Islamic Salvation History.* Oxford: OUP.

Warrack, Ibn (2002) *What the Qur'an Really Says: Language, Text and Commentary.* Buffalo NY: Prometheous Books.

Watt, W. Montgomery (1953) *Muhammad at Mecca.* Oxford: OUP.

Watt, W. Montgomery (1968) *Islamic Political Thought.* Edinburgh: Edinburgh: University Press.

Watt, W. Montgomery (1988) *Islamic Fundamentalism and Modernity.* London: Routledge.

Werbner, Prina (2002) 'Stamping the Earth with the Name of Allah: Zikr and the Sacralizing of Space Among British Muslims', pp. 167–85 in

Metcalf, Barbara Daly (ed.), *Making Muslim Space In North America and Europe.* Berkeley CA: University of California Press.

Wright, Robin (1996) 'Islam and Liberal Democracy: Two Visions Of Reformation', *Journal of Democracy* 7.2, pp. 64–75.

Yahya, Harun (2003) *Islam Denounces Terrorism.* Elmhurst NY: Tahrike Tarsile Quran (full text online at *http://www.harunyahya.com/terrorism1.php*).

Yaqub, Shagufta (2001) 'Ambassador of Dialogue', *Q-News, The Muslim Magazine,* July, *www.q-news.com.*

Ye'or, Bat (1996) *The Decline of Eastern Christianity Under Islam: From Jihad to Dhimmitude.* Madison NJ: Farleigh Dickinson University Press.

Yoffe, Emily (2001) 'The Islam Scholar US Politicians Like to Listen To'. *Slate,* November. Available at *http://slate.msn.com/?id=2058632.*

Zaid, Nasr Hamid Abu (1998) 'Divine Attributes in the Qur'an: Some Poetic Aspects', pp. 190–211 in Cooper, John, Nettler, Ronald and Mahmoud, Mohamed, *Islam and Modernity: Muslim Intellectuals Respond.* London: I. B. Tauris.

Zaid, Nasr Hamid Abu and Nelson, Esther R. (2004) *Voice of an Exile: Reflections on Islam.* Westport CT: Praeger.

Zakaria, Rafiq (1988) *The Struggle Within Islam: The conflict between religion and politics.* Harmondsworth: Penguin.

Zarkashi, Badr al-Din (1958) *al-burhan fi ulum al-qur'an,* 4 Vols. Cairo: Halabi.

Zarkashi, Imam Badr al-Din (1980, 2nd edn) *Al-Ijaba li 'irad ma Istadrakathu 'A'isha ala al-Sahaba.* Beirut: al-Maktab al-Islami.

Zullum, Abdul Qadeem (1998) *How the Khalifate was Destroyed.* London: al-Khilafah Publications (and at *http://www.hizb-ut-tahrir.org/english/books/*).

Index

'Abbasids 47, 48, 96, 112, 123, 137
'Abduh, Muhammad 19–22, 40, 61, 128, 142, 143
King Abdul Aziz University, Jeddah 36, 205
Abu Bakr 46, 47, 50, 93
Abu Bakra 139
Abu Hamza al-Masri 184
Abu Hurayra 141
Abu Zayd, Nasr Hamid 65, 76–8, 86, 96, 102, 105, 121
Achebe, Chinua 244
Adam 50
Adultery (zina) 134, 150, 152, 163
Aga Khan, the 5, 47
al-Afghani, Sayyid Jamal al-Din 22, 142
El-Affendi, Abdelwahab 39, 237
Afghanistan 11, 43, 76, 184, 206, 207, 213, 238, 239
  Kabul 134
Aflaq, Michel 171
Afshari, Reza 148–9
Ahl al-hall wa al-'aqd 47, 54
Ahlu-e-Hadith 18,181, 189, 208
Ahmad, Khurshid xiv, 17, 18, 21, 26, 46, 49, 51, 86, 191, 245
Ahmad, Mumtaz 63
Ahmed, Akbar xii, 2, 3, 7, 9, 11, 16, 31–5, 36, 39, 130, 135, 168, 173, 174, 196, 238, 246, 249, 250
Ahmed, Leila 16, 129, 130, 133, 142, 144, 145, 148, 150, 156, 241
Ahmed, Lord Nazir of Rotherham 187
'A'isha 137, 139, 141, 152
Akhtar, Shabbir 79, 190–1
Algeria 22, 78, 168, 169, 240–51
  FIS 245–7, 249–50
  Independence movement 242
  Al-Qaeda links 169
'Ali, Chiragh 40, 142, 199, 219
'Ali, ibn Abi Talib 47, 93, 137
Ali, Monica 195–6
Ali, Syed Mumtaz 165, 187
'Ali, Yousef xiv
American science 116

Amin, Qasim 142–3
Anglo-Oriental Mohammedan College (now Aligarg Muslim University) 20, 183, 189, 192
answering-christianity.com 115
answering-islam.org xv–xvi, 99, 105, 114
Anthroplogy/ethnography vii, 8, 108–9, 150
'aql/i 70, 112, 122
Arab League 68
Arabi, ibn 77
Arabian Nights, The 130, 154–5
  Galland's version 154
  Lang's version 155
Arafat, Yasser 213–5, 226
Arberry, Arthur John (1905–1969) 180
Arkoun, Mohammed 13, 22, 24, 57, 80, 86, 100, 101, 105, 106, 107, 121, 126, 127, 197
Arnold, Sir Thomas (1864–1930) 204
Asharites 120–3, 125
Aslan, Adnan 114, 167
assassins 48, 227, 238
assimilation 82, 196
Atatürk, Mustafi Kemal 59
Azeem, Sherif Abdel 130
Al-Azim 79
Al-Azmeh, Aziz 4, 7–8, 10, 17, 32, 38, 53, 58, 80

Baatil (falsewhood) 172, 181
Babri Masjid, Ayodhia 173, 193
Badawi, Gamal A xv–xvi, 130
Badawi, Zaki 178, 189–90, 226
  Condemns 9/11 226
  Muslim College 189
Badr, Battle of 143, 208
Baghdad 123, 168
  Abu Ghraib jail 76
Balfour, Lord (1848–1930) 212
Bangladesh 34, 42, 130, 137, 148, 173–5, 182, 183, 193, 196–7, 251–6
  caretaker governments 255
  Christians in 174
  Hindus in 173–75
Al-Banna, Hasan xvi, 19, 22, 53
Bai'at 47, 53
Bakri Mohamed, Sheikh Omar 180, 184, 207, 238

Bali bombings   208, 220, 228
Barelvis   189
Ben-Yunusa, Mohammed   26
Beirut, 13
　American University   108, 230
Bergen, Peter L   14–15, 205, 206, 207, 238–9
Bhabbha, Homi K   241
Bhutto, Benazir   18, 136, 137, 138
Bhutto, Zulfikar Ali   52
Bible   25, 86, 115, 166, 186
　corruption (*tahrif*) of   88, 166
Bida (innovation)   21, 139
Bielefeldt, Helen   65, 66
Bila kayfa   123
Birmingham   181, 189
　University   31, 86
　Saddam Hussein Mosque   189
Blair, Tony   12
Blake, William (1757–1827)   83, 154
Blunkett, David   225
Bosnia   162, 168, 171, 184, 207
　Jews in   162, 171
　Muslims   169, 171
Boxwell, Gail   36, 116
Brohi, Allahbukhsh K   86, 97
Brooks, Geraldine   59
Bucaile, Maurice   107, 115
Al-Bukhari   xiv, 90, 138, 141, 142
Burckhardt, Titus   2
Burlusconi, Silvio   12
Bush, George (senior)   11
Bush, George W.   12, 16, 44, 196, 209, 229, 238

Cairo   10, 150–1, 224
　Al-Azhar University   22, 112, 189, 220, 224
　Ein Shams University   78
　University   77
Call of Islam (SA)   106, 230
Cambridge University   9, 20, 30, 73, 180
Camel, Battle of   139
Camp David Peace Accord   189, 206, 214
Camus, Albert   242–4
Caner, Ergun Mehmet   134–5
Capitalism/capitalist   11, 14, 25, 66, 67
Chechnya   196, 207
Chicago University   101, 108, 230
　East–West University, Chicago   36
China   112
Christians/Christianity   3, 24, 66, 108, 114,
　118, 123, 158, 161, 162, 163, 164, 165, 166,
　169, 170, 171, 172, 173, 174, 181, 211, 238,
　239, 241
　Christian–Muslim dialogue   110, 114
　expulsion from the Hijaz   158,
　of Najran   161
Christian liberation theology   6, 229
Ciler, Tansu   137
Civil Society   43, 121, 173
civilization/s   5, 12–14, 25, 26, 35, 36, 39, 42,
　69, 72, 80, 109, 110, 112, 116, 117, 118,
　125, 126, 127, 133, 173, 247
　Islam as   12–14, 80, 109, 110, 112, 116

Clinton, William Jefferson   42
Communism, demise of   11, 14, 67, 81
Conrad, Joseph   244
Constitution of Madinah   46, 162, 182
Cook, Michael   105
Cook, Miriam   150
Cragg, Kenneth   97, 105
Crone, Patricia   48, 105
Cromer, Lord   61–2, 129, 143, 149
crusades/crusaders   13, 211
culture/cultures   5, 12–14, 25, 247, 251, 253, 255
cultural relativity   37, 64, 71
Corbin, Henry   2

Dannin, Robert M.   193
Dar-al-Aman   158
Dar-al-Harb   70, 157, 158, 159, 179, 191, 193,
　211, 231, 232, 234, 238
Dar-al-Islam   70, 157, 158, 159, 177, 179, 191,
　193, 211, 230, 231, 232, 234, 238
Dar-ul-ulum   125–6
　Deoband   183
　Bury   183
Darwin, Charles   24
Dawkins, Richard   12–13, 127
Da'wa   67, 167, 187, 191, 193, 221
Davies, Meryl Wyn   79
Deedat, Ahmed   55
Deobandis   18, 20, 134, 183, 189, 194
Democracy   xii, 3, 15, 16, 40–62, 67, 69, 72,
　121, 152, 249, 253, 255–6
　Centre for the Study of Islam and   60, 226
　Western hypocrisy   41, 43, 72, 236, 249–50
Denffer, Ahmad von   85–98, 100, 105, 115
development/aid   6, 8, 25
Dewey, John   25, 27
Dhimmis
　57, 66, 157, 158, 159, 160, 161, 162, 167,
　168, 172, 175, 179, 202, 217, 231, 232
　Dhimmitude   172
　Regulations on dress   161, 162
Din (religion) Islam as   26
Din-dunya (religion/world)   21
Din-wa-dunya   58, 65
divorce   56, 133, 143
Doi, Abdur Rahman   52, 177, 179–80, 188
Duran, Khalid   162, 169, 171
Durham University, Centre for Middle East
　Studies   43

Eaton, Gai   18
Ebadi, Shirin   73, 130
Enlightenment   37, 111, 124
Egypt   3, 7, 15, 57, 61–2, 74, 77, 78, 129, 164,
　168, 172, 189, 196, 205, 207, 210, 213, 214,
　220, 241
　Egyptian Islamic Jihad   206, 207–8
　Pharoahs   50
Esack, Farid   22, 30, 60, 81, 85–101, 122, 123,
　130, 143–4, 156, 164–7, 172–3, 197, 199,
　219, 229–30
　on Qur'an   85–101

on gender 143–4
on minorities 166–7, 172–3
on jihad 106, 199, 219, 229–30
Euro Islam 7, 192, 196
European/Western Science 21, 110, 113, 114, 116, 119, 120
European Union/Community 59, 216, 249
Ershad, Hussain Mohammad 174
Esposito, John L. xiv, 11, 20, 23, 41, 42, 59, 60, 237–9, 244, 246, 247, 249–50
evolution, theory of 111
evolution of the law (tatwir-al-tashri') 56, 74, 75

Fard 52
Fahd, King 55
Fahmi, Abu-Ziad 55
El-Faisal, Abdullah 184, 208
Faisal, King 54
award for services to Islam 56, 65
Faraj, Abd al-Salam 206
Al-Farabi 117, 124, 126
Farrakhan, Louis 186, 191
Al-Faruqi, Ismail R xiv, 94, 107–109, 114, 116–17, 127, 128, 190
on Israel/Palestine 217
fatwa/s 79, 125, 148, 188–9, 225, 206, 225, 237
Fitnah 48, 123, 138, 139
Fiqh 126, 142
Firestone, Reuven 220
Foucault, Michel 29–30
Fouda, Farag 78
France, 133, 179, 184, 185, 186, 240, 243
Islam in 179, 184, 185, 190
French concept of citoyen 194, 241

Gali, Boutros-Boutros 164
Gabriel 89, 90, 91
Gandhi, Mahatma (1869–1948) 108, 241
Attenborough's Gandhi
Gandhi, Rajiv 193
Gandhi, Rajmohan 108, 174
Gandhi, Sonia 193
Al-Ghannouchi, Rachid 41, 42, 57, 179, 249
Gairdner, W. H. Temple (1873–1928) 61
Garvey, Marcus 186
Al-Ghazali, Sheikh Mohammed 78
Al-Ghazzali (1058–1111) 103, 116
Geertz, Clifford 5, 109
Gender xiii, xv, 3, 45, 66, 129–155
Germany 7, 86, 148, 192, 236
Gibb, Sir Hamilton Gibb (1895–1971) 111
Giroux, Henry A. xii
Graham, A. William 87
Greek philosophy 96, 116, 123, 124
Guantanamo Bay, Cuba 76, 184
Guillaume, Alfred 79, 80
Gulf War (1st) 16, 43, 54, 206, 231
Gulf War (2nd) 11, 43

Hadith 46, 86–7, 90, 92, 94, 97, 101, 138–42, 158, 161, 165
Isnad 95, 138

Matn 95, 138
Qudsi hadith 94
Hajj, the 36, 54
Halliday, Fred 2, 10
HAMAS 215, 217
Hamdi, Mohamed Elhachmi 41
Hanafa, Abu 21, 233
Hanafi school 42
Hanbal, Ibn 21, 54, 96, 123, 138
Hanbali school 49, 54, 138
Ul-Haq, Zia 52–3, 55, 147
Haram 52
Hardy, Roger 36
Harun al Rashid 154
Harvard University 7, 31, 248
Fundamentalism project 7
Hasina, Sheikh 137, 138, 253
Dedworth, Donald 212–3
Hijrah 180, 190, 191, 193, 207, 222, 228
Al-Hijrah Education Trust, Birmingham
Hinds, Martin 48
Hindus/Hindusim 6, 71, 108, 164, 173–5, 192, 251
Hisbah 69, 76, 77, 78
History, role of 25, 28, 37, 75–6, 136–7
Hizb-ut-tahrir-al-Islami xiv, xv, 14, 22, 40, 43, 44, 51, 53, 54, 64, 67–8, 159, 184, 189, 225, 227
on human rights 67–8
model constitution 53, 68
on the West as Islam's enemy 14, 4367
Homo islamicus 4, 61, 71, 112
Hudaybiya, Treaty of 157
Hudud 20, 50, 75, 137
Hunter, Sir William Wilson 20–1, 183
Huntington, Samuel P. 11–12, 15, 42, 197, 239, 246–7, 256
threat thesis xii, 11, 239, 246–7
test of democracy 42, 256
humanization of knowledge 107, 126
human rights xiii, 3, 64–84, 144, 147, 164, 173, 236, 255
Husayn, Taha 77
Hussain, Naseem A. 253–4
Hussein, Saddam 11, 152, 168, 189, 239
hijacking xii, 184, 209, 214, 227

Ijtihad 18–19, 21, 38, 47, 117, 122, 179, 219, 234
Ijmah 47, 119
Ijmali 119–120
Ikhtilaf 48, 125, 165
Ikhwan-ul-muslimin (Muslim Brotherhood) 19, 21, 22, 78, 109, 159, 201, 205
'ilm (knowledge) 34, 107, 114, 124
imagination, the 78, 83, 126, 154
India 3, 19, 22, 49, 108, 160, 180–4, 192, 204, 251, 255
1st war of independence 1857 20
1st non-Hindu PM 193
BJP 182, 192–3
British power in 180–183
Congress Party 57, 182,

Election 2004 192–3
Muslims in 174–5, 180–184, 255
Shah Bano Case 192
Indonesia 42, 109, 171, 255
International Convention on the Elimination of all forms of Discrimination Against Women 74
International Court of Justice 68, 234
International Institute for Islamic Thought 110, 225
International Monetary Fund 36, 68
Iqbal, Justice Javid 53
Iqbal, Sir Muhammad 19, 21, 22, 54, 56, 102, 104, 128
Iran 48, 111, 121–2, 147, 164, 188, 213, 215, 218, 239
call for regime change 218
Iraq 11, 44, 62, 198, 206, 207, 212, 213, 220, 225, 230
under British mandate 212
Irfan, Soroush 22
Irvine, Martin 26–8
Inayatullah, Sohail 36, 116
Islah/i (reform/ist) 8, 101
Islam, as complete system 6
as ideology xvii, 21, 67, 117, 163
liberal 22, 148, 203
as master signifier 5, 31
neo-traditional 18–19, 22, 23
modernist/s 18, 20–1, 23, 114, 124
political 18, 60, 70, 140
progressive 22, 23, 85, 86, 104, 121, 183
radical revisionist 19–20, 23
rationalist Islam 70, 72, 123, 126, 148
rethinking vii, 72, 101
as a threat 11
Islamic Council for Europe 68, 76
Islamic epistemology xiii, 107–128
Islamic feminism 130, 135–42
Islamic Foundation, Leicester 86, 191
Islamic fundamentalism 4, 8, 11, 20, 60, 72, 110, 113, 114, 124, 175, 249
Islamic science 111, 116, 117, 119, 120
Islamic State (concept of) 18, 23, 42, 45, 51, 53, 68, 159, 163, 168, 215, 231, 254
Nizam islami 58
Islamic terrorists/terrorism 12, 205, 229, 237, 249
Islamic traditionalists 18, 19
Islamization of knowledge 107, 108, 118, 127
Islamophobia 4, 55, 129, 177
Ismailis 47, 119, 123
Israel 45, 62, 172, 189, 198, 206, 209–15, 225, 226
1st and 2nd Aliyahs 212

Jahilia 52, 200
Jahili society 200, 201, 204
Jamaatt-i-islam 17, 18, 49, 52, 53, 159, 167, 191, 201, 245, 251, 253, 255
Jerusalem 5, 110, 207, 210, 211, 212, 218
Mufti of 5, 210
re-conquered by Saladin 211

Jesus 60, 88, 92, 110, 186
Jews 158, 161, 162, 163, 165, 166, 168, 169, 170, 171, 172, 173, 175, 186, 207, 211, 225
expulsion from the Hijaz 158
expelled from Spain 162
Jihad xvi, 1, 12, 19, 23, 56, 106, 157, 181, 184, 193, 195–235, 238, 239, 249
defined 232
lesser and greater 220
Jihadists promised paradise 227, 234
Jinnah, Muhammad 5, 31, 245
Jizya 159, 161, 162, 172, 175, 202
Johnson, Paul 208
Jordan 47, 62, 210, 214, 217
Prince Hasan of 173
peace treaty with Israel 216
Joseph 92
Judaism 108, 115

Ka'bah 46
Kabirm Humayun 182
Kabbani, Rana 9, 15–16, 79, 98, 99, 135, 183
Kahini (poets) 98
Kalam 96, 112
Kalima (Shahada) 1, 109
Kanem Cheikh Hamidou 10
Kant, Immanuel 197
Kashmir, Islamist movements in 181–2, 208
Al-Qaeda links 181, 208
Kepel, Giles 236–7
Khadduri, Majid 42, 157, 159, 161, 162, 177, 179, 230–4
Khadijah 90
Khalifate, the 47, 49
Kharijites, the 19, 23, 48, 93, 122, 205, 237
Neo-kharijites 55
Khaldun, ibn 21, 47
Concept of asabiyyah 47
Khan, Muqtedar 60, 159, 160, 167–8
Khan, M Salimullah 253–4
Khan, Sir Sayyid Ahmed 4, 19–20, 21, 26, 121, 158, 166, 182–3, 219
Khattami, Mohammad Ayotollah 121
Khomeini, Ruhullah Musavi (1902–1989) 47, 78, 79, 82
Al-Kindy 99, 204
Kufr/kafr (unbeliever) 14, 54, 67, 167, 172, 175, 191
Kureish, Hanif 30, 64, 65, 81–3, 194, 195, 196
Kurdi, Abdulrahman Abdulkadir 53, 58
Kurzman, Charles xiv, 16, 18, 22, 139
Kyoto Treaty 36

Laden, Osama bin 11, 13, 14–15, 45, 55, 181, 198, 199, 205–8, 226, 227, 229, 236, 237–9
fatwas 15, 206, 211, 227
Poole, Stanley Lane (1854–1931) 129
Lawrence, Thomas Edward 62
Lebanon 57, 172, 208, 211–12, 213–45
Civil war 214–5
Hezbollah/Hizbullah 208, 215
Lean, David 241

left–right categorization xvi–xvii, 23–4, 85–6, 255
Leiden University 77
Lennon, John 107
Lewis, Bernard 42, 48, 55, 79, 118, 162, 191, 208, 214, 227, 236
  on PLO-linked terrorism 214
liberalism 21, 37–8, 134
Lindholm, Charles 53
London University 31, 188
  City University, London 36
  Regents Park Mosque 189

Mabro, Judy 150
Macauley's Minutemen 240, 241
Al-Mahdi, al-Sadiq 18, 205
  Grandfather's jihad 205
Mahfouz, Naguib 10, 79, 130, 150–51
Madhhab/Madhahib (the 4 Sunni legal schools) 21, 58, 138
Madani, Abassi 246–9
Madonna 15, 37–8
Madrassas 112, 125
Mailer, Norman 43
Maimonides (1135–1204) 162
Malik ibn Anas 21, 163, 179, 233
Malaysia 42
Malcolm X 191
Makkah, Sharif of 62, 212, 234
  Sons Faisal and Abdullah 62, 212
Makruh 51
Mansur, Khalif (754–775) 162
Marcotte, Roxanne D. 131
Maqsood, Ruqaiyyah Waris 142
Mary 92
Marxism 25, 30, 66, 67
Maslaha 47
Matlab 51
Al-Mawardi 47, 48, 191
Mawdudi, Syed Abu'l A'la xiv–xvii, 1–2, 17, 18, 44, 49–53, 65–6, 68, 71, 74, 86, 93, 97–9, 105, 107, 109, 114–15, 130, 131–35, 145, 147, 149, 159–64, 168, 198, 199, 200, 205, 219, 223, 228, 245, 246
  on epistemology 114
  on gender 131–135
  on human rights 65–66
  on the Islamic state 49–53
  imprisonment, 49, 52, 205
  on jihad 1–2, 219
  on minorities 51, 159–164
  as mujaddid 51
  on Qu'ran 93, 97–99
McCartney, Paul 107
McGooihan, Patrick 107
media, role of 9–10, 33–5, 60, 67
Mernissi, Fatima xiv, 16, 17, 41, 44, 45, 54, 57, 59, 64, 75, 107, 121, 122–4, 126, 128, 129, 130, 136–42, 144, 148, 156, 160, 168, 230
  on democracy 41, 56
  on epistemology 122–23
  on gender 136–42
Mihnah 97

Mill, John Stuart 25
Minorities (non-Muslim) xiii, 23, 45, 156–76
Modernity xiii, xv, 24–7
Modood, Tariq 185, 186, 194, 197, 225
Moghissi, Haideh 7–8, 31, 37, 60, 130, 144, 147, 149
Mohamed, Matathir 209, 211
Morality 24, 25
  intercivilizational/international morality 69, 72, 169
Morocco 16, 47, 55, 109
Mortimer, Edward 32
Mostyn, Trevor 12, 78, 79
Mother of the book 89, 113–14
Mu'awiyyah 47
Muhajiroun 179, 180, 184, 227
Muhammad 44, 46, 57, 79, 80, 87–90, 139–42, 158, 166, 221
  seal of prophets 88
  unlettered 91–2
  Western view of 80, 91
  and women 139–42
  grandson 151
  and poetry 98, 154
Muhammad, Elijah 186, 191–2
  Sister Clara and Elijah Muhammad Schools 186
Muhammad, W. W. Deen 191–2
Muir, Sir William (1819–1905) 4, 20, 78, 79, 95, 99, 112
Mujibur Rahman, Sheikh 252, 254
  Awami League 252–53
multiculturalism 70, 193
mulk 137, 138
Mu'minin/un 156, 164
Murad, Khurram 167, 191
Murjites, the 19, 23, 48
Mutawakkil, Khalif 162
Mu'tazalites 21, 23, 77, 95, 96, 100, 102, 117, 120–4, 126
Muttaween 136
Musharraf, Pervez 16, 181
Muslim–Jewish dialogue 110
Muslim American Society 178, 192
Muslim, virtual 2
Muslimin/muslimun 56
Muslim Parliament of Great Britain 187–8
  Muslim Manifesto 188
Muslims as fifth columnists 12, 81
Muslimism-anti 2, 9, 10
Mustad'afun (oppressed) 104, 156

an-Nabhana, Taqiuddin 22, 51
an-Na'im, Abdullahi Ahmed 63, 64, 65, 66, 73–5, 117, 130, 143, 145, 156, 159, 160, 164, 167, 168
Naipaul, V. S. 108, 113, 251
naksh 56, 93–4, 167, 223, 228
Nasser, Gamal Abdel (1918–70) 205
Nasr, Seyyed Hossain 2, 6, 8, 92, 107, 111–15, 118–19, 121, 127, 128, 158, 176, 255
Nasrin, Tasrina 130, 148–9, 159, 160, 173–75

fatwa on 148
Nation of Islam 178, 186–7, 191–2
nation state xiv, 43, 255
NATO 59
Neuman, Lawrence W. xvi
new world order 11, 14, 35
Nielson, Jørgen xii, 187
Nine/Eleven (9/11) September 11 xii–xiii,
    11, 12–15, 43, 86, 98, 184, 207, 220, 224,
    226–7, 229, 236–9
    Muslims on 224, 226–7

Oklahoma City bombing 9
Organization of Islamic Conference
    (Munazanat Al-Mutamir Al-Islami) 42,
    209, 226
Orientalists/Orientalism 2, 3, 4, 6, 9, 61, 97,
    98, 109, 112, 129, 203, 204, 219, 228, 241
Oslo Peace Accord 216
Osman, Fathi 46, 55
Ottoman, Sultan/khalifs 5, 47, 54, 55, 59, 62,
    162, 205, 209, 211–12, 234
Oxford University 13, 14, 20
    Centre for Islamic Studies 43

Pakistan 16, 17, 31, 36, 52, 63, 86, 101, 136,
    137, 144, 147, 159, 163, 164, 175, 181, 182,
    183, 184, 188, 205, 207, 213, 245, 251–2, 254
Palestine 5, 62, 108, 164, 171, 198, 209–218
    British mandate 212–3
    PLN 216, 218
    PLO 214–18
Pan-arabism 57, 62, 108–9, 171–2
Parekh, Lord Bhikhu 9, 134, 196–7
Pasha, Syed 190
Perennial philosophy (religio perennis) 114, 110
Persia, Queens of 139–140
Peters, F. E. xiv, 47, 48, 56, 75
Peters, Rudolph 205, 219, 220, 232
Pfander, Karl G. 204
Phenomenology 3, 6
Pipes, Daniel 15, 41, 42, 79, 164, 184, 185,
    186, 190, 191, 192, 193, 197, 237–9, 247–8
    appointed to US Institute for Peace 238
    criticism of John L. Esposito 42, 237
Plato 116
Pluralism 33, 45, 67, 68, 70, 83, 104, 125, 165,
    168, 169, 175, 178, 193, 197, 230, 249
polygamy 56, 133, 134, 143
postmodernity/postmodernism xiii, xv, 17,
    27–39, 71, 118, 147, 148–9
    as hybrid, impure 28, 33, 36
Poston, Larry A. 191
Powell, Walter W. 131
Pulcini, Theodore 183, 186, 191
Press, Bill 44
Princeton University, NJ 31, 236
The Prisoner 107

Al-Qaeda xii, 11, 206–8, 209, 225, 226, 228, 238
    related groups 207–8
Al-Qaradawi, Yusuf 21, 199, 219, 220, 223–26

on Israel/Palestine 225
    rejects imported solutions 21, 224
    in UK 225
    as Islam's foremost ideologue 226
Qiblah 119, 141
Qiyas 47, 181
Qutb, Sayyid xvi, 19, 22, 40, 49, 52, 64, 66, 124,
    133, 172, 194, 198–206, 219, 225, 228, 237
    on the Jews 225
    on jihad 198–206, 219, 220, 223
    on justice 66,
    on decadent West 19, 133, 202
    on role of women 202
Quraishi 47, 80, 203
Qur'an 85–106
    clear/unclear verses 103
    created/uncreated 95–6, 102
    execution 198
    gradual revelation 89, 102
    inimitability 88
    language 97–8
    meaning 87
    textuality of 88, 100, 102
    recension 92–3
    untranslatability 98–9

Rahman, Fazlur 53, 86, 101–02, 105, 106, 107,
    121, 122, 126, 229
Rahman, Omar Abdel 185
Ramadan, month of 90, 164, 246
Ramadan, Tariq 39, 125, 194
Raspail, Jean 193, 195
Ra'y 123
Raza, Mohamed S 183, 184, 189, 190
al-Raziq, 'Ali 'Abd 19
rebellion 48–9, 123, 205
Republican Brothers 56–7
Religious Studies xvii–xviii, 3, 6, 30
Renan, Ernest Joseph 10
Rida, Rashid 20, 49, 61, 234
ridda (apostasy) 66, 80
Road Map for Peace in the Middle East 216–17
Rodinson, Maxime 91
Roosevelt, Theodore (1858–1919) 62
Rumsfeld, Donald 44
Ibn Rushd 10, 103, 124, 126, 157, 179, 223,
    233, 234
Rushdie affair 9, 65, 75, 78 –81, 188
Rushdie, Salman 9, 13, 27, 28, 29, 37, 69, 78–
    81, 84, 94, 112, 128, 182, 190, 241
    fatwa on 9, 66, 75, 78, 82
Russian Federation 216
Ruthven, Malise 41, 55, 205, 208, 234, 237, 238

El Saadawi Nawal 7, 77, 127, 128, 130, 151–4,
    246
    husband 151
    Women's Solidarity Association 151
Sadat, Mohjammed Anwar (1918–1981) 151, 206
    assassination 151, 198, 206, 237
Safi, Omid 22
Sarh, Allah ibn Abi 80, 90

Said, Edward   4, 8, 9, 12, 61, 112, 144, 236, 241, 243, 244
Saif, Walid   25–26
Sardar, Ziauddin   xv, 7, 8, 11, 16, 21, 22, 27, 29, 31, 36–9, 53, 75, 79, 96, 101, 107, 112, 113, 115, 116–22, 127, 128, 177, 183–4, 189, 194, 226–7, 240, 247–9, 251
   on Bucaile   115
   on al-Faruqi   116–118
   on minorities   183–4
   on Nasr   118–119
   on 9/11   226–7
Satan   80–81, 98, 103, 153, 184, 207
The Satanic Verses   28, 69, 77–81, 94
Satanic verses affair   80, 90, 153
Saud, King   54
Saudi Arabia   13, 15, 18, 44, 51, 53–6, 63, 64, 66, 183, 189, 205, 206, 207, 208, 211, 218, 224, 237, 238, 251
   US troops in   15, 54, 206, 229
Sayyid, Bobby   xv, 2, 5–6, 60
Schacht, Joseph   94–95
Secularism/secularisation   26, 45, 57–9, 121, 126, 169, 171, 182, 183, 251
Segal, Aaron   117–8
Shaf'i   21, 94–5, 158, 233
Shahin, Abd el-Sabour   77
Shaltut, Mahmud   199, 219, 220–3, 233, 235
Sharastani   123
Shari'ah   xii, 19, 22, 23, 40, 44, 48, 49, 51, 52, 53, 54, 57, 58, 63, 65, 66, 74, 75, 113, 114, 117, 123, 136, 143, 153, 163, 170, 177, 180, 187, 188, 200, 201, 205, 208, 223, 246, 251
Shariati, 'Ali   122
Sheba, Queen of   140
Shi'a   47, 93, 122, 180, 211, 215
   Imam Jafar al-Sadiq   191
Shura   46, 47, 51, 53, 55, 163
Siddiqi, Muhammad Zubayr   142
Siddiqi, Shamin A   184, 187
Siddiqui, Ghayasuddin   188, 226
Siddiqui, Iqbal   188
Siddiqui, Kalim   187–8
Sina, ibn   123, 126, 135
Sirah   90
Sivan, Emmanuel   18, 21, 48, 171
Slomp, Jan   xvi, 51
Smith, Jane I.   51
Smith, Wilfred Cantwell   2–6, 17, 30, 94, 105, 167
Sociology   xvii, 3, 16, 116
El-Sohl, Camillia Fawzi Soueif, 150
Sonn, Tamara   126, 172
Sorbonne, the   101, 165
Soueif, Ahdaf   9, 61–62
South Africa   63, 104, 144, 164, 172, 230
Soroush, Abdolkarim   xiv, 26, 44, 57, 59, 71, 100, 107, 120, 121–2, 126, 128, 156, 168
   on democracy   57
   expansion and contraction of religious knowledge   121–22
   on gender   143
   on human rights   71

Soviets   182, 184, 206, 207, 236, 239
Spain (Moorish)   70, 113, 160, 168, 171
Spinner-Halev, Jeff   25
Spinoza, Baruch   24   27
Sudan   56, 206, 207, 214, 237
Sufis/Sufism   18, 53, 56, 109, 114, 117, 119, 122, 174–5, 180, 183, 189, 251
   inner/outer meanings   56, 103
   Qutb (world pivot)   54
   and politics   53
Suicide bombers   225, 227–8,
Sukarnoputri, Megawati   137, 138
Sunnah, the   18, 46, 47, 53, 54, 92, 94, 95, 117, 142, 143, 159, 181, 255
Sunni   47, 48, 122, 191, 211
Syria   7, 9 , 210, 211–12, 213–15, 217, 218
   Golan Heights   214, 215, 217
   call for regime change   218

Tafsir   85, 103, 104
Tagore, Rabindranath (1861–1941)   252
Taha, Mahmoud Mohamed   xiv, 22, 56–7, 73, 74, 130, 143, 145, 149, 156, 159, 160, 164, 167, 168, 199, 228–9, 230
Al-Tahtawi, Rifa'a   40
tajdid (renewal)   xvii
takfir (charge of apostasy)   7, 126
Talbi, Mohamed   143, 145, 157, 161, 164–5, 199, 220, 222, 229
Taliban   76, 104, 180, 195, 206, 208
   Mullah Omar   208
Tamadonfar, Mehran   51, 55
Tamimi, Azzam S   41, 42, 57, 121
Taqlid (imitation)   21, 117
Taqwa   106, 229
Tawhid   46, 66, 96, 109
Ibn Taymiyya   19, 48, 49, 191, 205, 206, 237
The 9/11 Commission Report Executive Summary   xii–xiii, 12, 56, 238
Tibi, Bassam   xiv, 2, 4, 5, 7, 12, 14, 17, 22, 24, 42, 43, 44, 53–60, 64, 66, 67, 69–73, 75, 78, 100, 107, 109, 112, 113, 117, 124–27, 143, 156, 168–72, 178, 183, 187, 192–4, 196–7, 230, 238, 247, 255
   on civilization v. culture   13–14, 247
   on John L. Esposito   42
   on secularism   57–58
   on epistemology   124–126
   on human rights   69–73
   on jihad   230
   on minorities   168–172, 187, 192–4
Thatcher, Margaret   171
the War on Terrorism (also Operation Enduring Freedom; Infinite Justice) xii, 12, 14
   as a crusade   12, 228
   as a war on Islam   12–13, 228
Tours, Battle of   157, 231
Al-Turabi, Hasan   42, 51
Turath (authenticity)   18
Turkey   44, 59, 78, 137, 162, 185, 204, 212, 213, 234
   Jews in   162

Truman, Harry (1844–1972; 33rd president of the US) 213

Ulama 19, 45, 53, 54, 56, 77, 79, 104, 113, 148, 206, 229, 242
Ummah 17–18, 42, 47, 57, 110, 124, 167, 171, 194
'Umar 47, 139, 161, 211
'Umar 11 (682–720) 162
'Umayyads 47
United Nations 36, 45, 63, 67, 68, 164, 213, 216, 226, 230, 234
   Resolution 181 213
United States of America 12, 14, 15, 16, 19, 27, 28, 36, 43, 45, 50, 51, 55, 67, 76, 101, 108, 124, 178, 179, 180, 181, 182, 184, 185, 186, 190–2, 197, 201, 206, 207, 216, 218, 225, 227, 228, 236, 230–9, 246
   CIA 182, 206, 207, 209
   Constitutional Rights Foundation 84
   FBI 180, 185, 196
   Foreign policy 15–16, 239
   Islam/Muslims in 184, 186–7, 190–92, 227
   Prohibition law 50
   detains Muslims after 9/11 185, 225
United Kingdom 183, 184, 187–90, 192, 194, 197
   Cantle Report 194,
   Islam in 183, 187–190
   Commission for Racial Equality 225
   BNP 192, 195
   proposed law against inciting religious hatred 225
University, origin of 113
Universal Declaration of Human Rights 63, 64, 65, 66, 68, 69, 73, 76, 148
Universal Islamic Declaration of Human Rights 64, 68–69, 71, 73, 74, 76
'urf 54
Uris, Leon 209–210
Usul 47
Al-usul-al-fiqh 112
'Uthman 47, 135

veil *(hijab)* 56, 129, 134, 136, 137, 140, 143, 147
vilayat-I-faqih 48

Wahaj, Siraj 185

Al-Wahhab, Muhammad ibn 'Abd 18, 53, 237
Wahhabis, the 18, 44, 53, 54, 55, 110, 183, 189, 237
Wahi 87
Waliullah, Shah 180,
Walker, Mary 135
Wansborough, John 97, 105
Washington, DC 1
   Georgetown University 27
   American University 31
Waqf 59, 125
Warraq, ibn 105
Watt, William M. 4–5, 91
Weapons of Mass Destruction 218
Western epistemological imperialism 116
Western preoccupation with sex 19, 34, 35, 37, 133, 196, 202
Westphalia, Treaty of 43
White House, Washington, DC xii
Women, status of 23, 61, 66, 69, 129–55, 167
World Bank 68
World Trade Center, NY xii, 185, 196, 207, 223
World Trade Organization 36
World War 1 59, 62, 241
Wright, Robin 41

Yazid 47
Yemen 206, 207, 209, 213
   attack on USS Cole 207
Ye'or, Bat 159, 172

Al-Zawahiri, Ayman 206, 207
Zaid bin Thabit 92–93
Zakaria, Rafiq 44, 57–9, 62, 162, 168, 172, 182, 245, 247
Zakat 52, 75, 161
Zamakhshari, Khalif 162
Zarkashi, Badr al-Din 100, 141
Zia, Khaleda 137, 138, 253
Zia ur-Rahman (1936–1981) 252
   BNP 253
Zionism 31, 209, 212, 213, 217, 236, 238

Index of Qur'an Verses Cited

2 *(al-baqarah)*
2　　46
23–4　98
41　　46
62　　166, 170
106　94
109　166
111　170
143　42, 157
148　167
177　167
190　203, 222, 223,234, 235

190–4　222
191　　223
193　　203, 223
194　　222
215　　231
216　　235
223　　145, 147
228　　145
256　　66, 167, 204
282　　69, 145
285　　164

3   (Al Imran)
3   88
7   103
15   229
21–2   187
70–1   166
85   166
98   166
110   42, 124, 202
113   166
159   46
169   234
195   140, 145
199   170

4   (Al-Nisa)
1   146
2   143, 146
11   146
32   140, 146
34–5   74, 145
46   146
58   50
59   46
71   233
74–6   204
75   222
84   164, 222
90–1   219, 222
128   135
135   66

5   (Al Ma'idah)
5   179
8   66
88
19   221
32   65
38   18
43   167
44   87
47   167
48   164, 166, 170
51   170
66   166
68   166
82–3   163, 170
100   55

6   (Al-An'am)
116   55
165   50

7   (Al-A'raf)
157   91
158   166

8   (Al-Anfal)
38–40   204

39   222
41   231
60   223, 235

9   (Al-Tawbah)
5   203, 204, 208, 223, 233, 234, 235
6   158
7–16   222
13–14   222, 223
29   159, 162, 170, 222, 235
29–32   163, 204
31   170
36   222, 223
39   223
40   219
71   140, 145
122   233
123   222

10   (Yunus)
57   105
94   166
99   221

11   (Hud)
117   221

12   (Yusuf)
         93
3   98
20   55
76   50
103   55

16   (Al Nahl)
59   134
68   87
97   145
103   98
124   235

19   (Maryam)
8   219

22   (Al Hajj)
17   166
39–40   125, 222
52–3   80
77   219, 229

24   (Al-Furqan)
25–32   89

27   (Al Naml)
23–44   140

28   (Al Qasas)
4   104
7   87
49   98

29   (Al 'Ankabut)
5   219, 229
6   229
46   64, 170
50–2   221

30   (Al Rum)
21   145

31   (Luqman)
14   219

33   (Al Azhab)
22   46
35–6   74, 140
40   88
53   140,   148

41   (Fussilat)
34   235

42   (Al-Shura)
38   46
49   145
50   87

43   (Al-Zukhruf)
2–4   89
3   96
18   134
31   46

47   (Muhammad)
3–6   208
4   233

48   (Al-Fath)
29   88

48   (Al-Hujurat)
9–10   221
13   164
14   231

57   (Al-hadid)
26   166

58   (al-Mujadilah)
1   140
11   509
23   53

59   (Al Hashr)
21   89

60   (Al Mumtahinah)
9   223
10–12   140

61   (Al-Saff)
11   231

62   (Al Jumu'ah)
2   91

65   (Al-Talaq)
        135

66   (Al Mulk)
9   231

74   (Al Muddaththir)
1–5   91

80   ('Abasa)
1–4   94

81   (Al Takwir)
8–9   134
85   (Al Buruj)
21–22   89

87   (Al A'la)
6–7   94

88   (Al Ghashiyah)
21   235

90   (Iqra')
1–3   74

99   (Al Zalzalah)
7–8   167

Index of Hadith Cited

Mishkat-ul-Masabih V1: 45–6   47
MM V2: 1726   142
Bukhari V1, Bk 1 hadith 1 and 2   91
Bukhari V1, Bk 1 hadith 3   90
Bukhari V1, Bk 3 hadith 80–81   111
Bukhari V1 Bk 3, hadith 109   95
Bukhari V4 Bk 52 hadith 174   161
Bukhari V4 Bk 52 hadith 384   161
Bukhari V4 Bk 52 hadith 288   158
Bukhari V5 Bk 59 hadith 19   46
Bukhari V6 Bk 61 hadith 510   93

Bukhari V7 Bk 76 hadith 456   142
Bukhari V8 Bk 74 hadith 273   173
Bukhari V8 Bk 76 hadith 456   142
Bukhari, V9 Bk 87 hadith 113   103
Bukhari V8, Bk 88 hadith 119   136
Bukhari V9, Bk 88 hadith 183   111
Bukhari V9, Bk 88 hadith 187   111
Bukhari V9, Bk 88 hadith 219   139
Bukhari V9, Bk 89 hadith 254   47
Bukhari V9, Bk 89 hadith 258   48
Bukhari V9, Bk 89 hadith 261   51